FAMILY NAMES OF COUNTY CORK

FAMILY NAMES
OF
COUNTY CORK

Diarmuid Ó Murchadha

The Collins Press

Published by The Collins Press, Carey's Lane, The Huguenot Quarter, Cork, 1996

First published by Glendale Press, 1985
© Diarmuid Ó Murchadha

Printed in Ireland by Colour Books Ltd., Dublin.

Jacket Design by Upper Case Ltd., Cornmarket Street, Cork.

ISBN: 1-898256-13-6

To my wife, Marie

CONTENTS

LIST OF ILLUSTRATIONS

PREFACE

This book is designed to provide a reasonably detailed account of the origins and early history of the principal family names in Co. Cork. In choosing fifty such names, two main criteria were employed. The first test, a numerical one, was complicated by the fact that there is no census of surnames available for Co. Cork. Matheson's survey of 1909 does include some estimates based on the 1890 births' index, but only for the twenty-seven numerically strongest surnames in the county. Possibly the surest way to get a reasonably accurate estimate would be to scrutinize all the voters' lists for the county, but this Herculean task was by-passed in favour of a judicious use of directories which enumerate a fair cross-section of the population.

The second criterion was one of origin. I have included only such family names as originated in Co. Cork or at least were well-established there by the 16th century. (The only exception to this rule is Kingston which though a 17th century arrival can fairly be claimed as a Co. Cork surname.)

The numerical dimension ruled out many indigenous family names — for example, O Coffey, Coppinger, Hodnett — tempting though it may have been to include them on historical grounds. On the other hand, such widespread surnames as Kelly and Burke and Shea — not to mention O Brien — were excluded on the score of origin. In the case of a small number of family names, a third obstacle emerged, namely, the lack of sufficient historical material to justify an article of the type presented here. Notable omissions in this regard were Kelleher and Lucey.

The main reason for the exclusion of post-16th century arrivals is that the work as a whole deals with the history of cohesive family groups. It is generally accepted that the battle of Kinsale (1601-02) dealt a fatal blow to the sept or clan system as it existed in Ireland, although the seeds of destruction had been sown some decades previously. So it is that very little material from 1700 onwards is admitted, except for the purposes of rounding off some sparsely-documented account or of making a passing reference to a noted bearer of the name. (Only exceptionally are living persons referred to.)

Accordingly, this work will not greatly assist those wishing to trace their ancestors back to the 17th century since each account ends approximately where the modern genealogist begins. It may provide a starting-point for such a search but, generally speaking, is not concerned with the very personal — and nowadays highly specialized — discipline of genealogy. The even more rarified science of heraldry was not taken into consideration at all since it had so little impact on the life of the average Irishman from the 11th to the 17th century. Many 'family' coats-of-arms were issued to individual members of families long after the 'clan system' had broken up. Readers who are interested in coats-of-arms and crests will find these expertly treated in MacLysaght's *Irish Families*.

My main endeavour is to give the average Cork person some idea of the rock whence he was hewn — or she, as the case may be, though it must be acknowledged that the transmission of surnames from one generation to the next has, up to now, always been a predominantly male preserve. The rock, in this instance, comprises not only the family name itself but also the places associated with that name. In the writing of these place-names, particularly townland-names from the Fiants, I have normally (except in cases where they could not be identified) given them their modern standardized forms. This is in direct contrast to the surnames themselves which, again in almost all cases, I have spelt as they were written in the documents from which they were taken, in order that some idea may be formed as to the pronunciation of the name in different periods.

A problem arose here in relation to the apostrophe usually placed after the 'O' of a surname in English — e.g. O'Sullivan. This does not appear in Irish (Ó Súilleabháin) nor is it found in English documents prior to the 17th century. Accordingly, it proved more convenient and more consistent to omit it entirely, particularly as there is no logical basis for its existence. (This usage was followed in the *Shell Guide to Ireland* some years ago and should, in my opinion, become normal practice.)

Copious material on some of the better-known family names has already been published, but mainly in books long out of print or in learned journals accessible only in the larger libraries. Many people who take an interest in their family background have neither the time nor the inclination to spend long hours in research. But for the benefit of those who wish to delve further into the past, there is an appendix listing useful books and articles which may contain more extensive details than could be included in this work.

It will be noted that a large proportion of these articles are in the *Journals of the Cork Historical and Archaeological Society*. Cork and its county have been well served by the journals of this society where for almost a century successive generations of historians have been amassing a store of material relating to family and local history. In this context, particular mention must be made of the late John T. Collins whose studies of such west Cork families as the Mac Carthys, O Crowleys, O Heas and O Regans proved an invaluable aid in the preparation of this book. Surprisingly, however, some well-known families — O Leary is a typical example — never had a full-length account of their history compiled, so that in such cases this is the first attempt at doing so. Furthermore, many of the previously published works on family origins were compiled before the appearance in print of various collections of annals and genealogies relating to Munster, sources which would nowadays be regarded as indispensable. Accordingly I have re-examined all statements concerning origins in the light of these sources.

I have also sought the assistance of fellow-researchers and rarely in vain. My special thanks are due to those who read some or all of the text in manuscript. These comprised Mr. C.J.F. MacCarthy, whose work on behalf of the Cork Historical and Archaeological Society forms a history in itself, and whose advice and encouragement greatly assisted the publication of this book; Mr. R.I. Henchion who placed his library and his knowledge of local history — both extensive — continually at my disposal; the late Pádraig Uas. Ó Maidín, Cork Co. Librarian, whose articles on local history gained a national reputation; and Professor Pádraig Ó Riain, U.C.C., whose proficiency in Old Irish was at all times available to me. Professor Donnchadh Ó Corráin, also of U.C.C., a recognized expert in the early genealogical field, read and advised on the introduction. Others who supplied aid and information on request were: Dr. E. MacLysaght, Irish MSS Comm., Mr. Gerard J. Lyne, National Library of Ireland, Mr. Donal Begley, Genealogical Office, Máirín Ní Dhomhnalláin, R.I.A. Library, Dr. Richard Kingston, Ulster Polytechnic, Dr. Peter McClure, University of Hull, Mr. T. Desmond, New York, Rev. T.J. Walsh, P.P., Blackrock, Rev. J. Coombes, Adm., Skibbereen, Bro. Henry Allen, Letterkenny, Mr. Bernard O Regan, Aughadown, Colmán Uas. Ó Mathúna, Monkstown. A special word of thanks to Mr. Peter Tynan O Mahony who designed the accompanying map showing location of families. I also wish to acknowledge the courteous assistance of the staffs in the Cork libraries — County, City and University College, as well as the vital financial aid provided by the now-disbanded Cork Historical Guides Committee. In the absence of any other grants-in-aid, necessary finance was sought by way of pre-publication subscriptions. My sincere thanks to all those whose contributions rendered feasible the publication of this book.

Finally in recording my gratitude to all of these, I must stress that any shortcomings in the text are entirely my own responsibility. In a work of this scope, errors and omissions are bound to become evident, and corrections or additional information which readers may wish to convey will be most welcome.

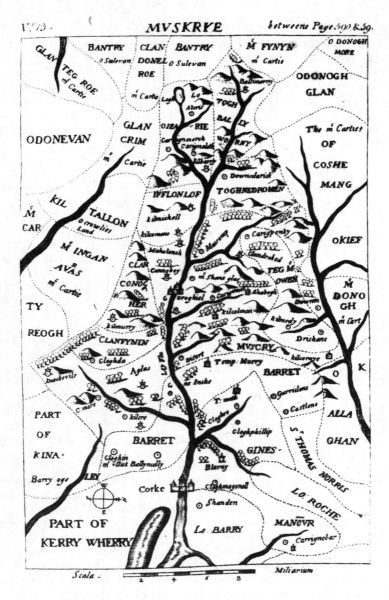

MAP OF MUSKERRY, *c.* 1600 *(Pacata Hibernia)*

INTRODUCTION

Even though most family names in Ireland did not evolve before the 11th century, their rudiments were established in an earlier era. The question of early Christian and pre-Christian settlement in the area now known as Co. Cork is still primarily a subject for learned disputation but the political situation from the 9th century onwards has a good deal of relevance and is reasonably documented in the annals.

The groupings then in Munster were by no means homogenous. Dominating or attempting to dominate the scene were the Eóganacht whose eponym was Eógan Mór from whom all the later great Gaelic families of the province claimed descent. Eóganacht Locha Léin ruled over west Munster, Eóganacht Raithlind over what is now south Cork and Eóganacht Glennamhain over the Fermoy region, while in the east Eóganacht Caisil, based on the rock of Cashel, claimed supremacy over all others. Their claim was a somewhat exaggerated one, according to Donnchadh Ó Corráin who describes 9th century Munster as '... more a confederation of dominant dynasties rather than a kingdom in which one dynasty is paramount.'

Before the penetration of the Eóganacht, Co. Cork seems to have been populated mainly by tribes of Érainn stock (popularly known as Fir Bolg). These were later represented by such groups as the Múscraige (M. Mittaine in mid-Cork, M. Trí Maige in north Cork, etc.), the Corcu Lóegde who were pushed into south-west Cork by the Eóganacht, and in east Cork Uí Liatháin and Uí Meic Caille.

This disposition, of course, never remained static, and boundaries tended to alter as septs increased and declined in power or as new ones burgeoned. By the 12th century Eóganacht Caisil, having been eased out of their Cashel stronghold by the Dál Cais (Brian Boru's people), had encroached extensively on south Munster. Their principal family, the Mac Carthys, took the title of kings of Desmumu and remained the most prominent family in Desmond for many centuries. A companion-group, the O Sullivans, were later concentrated in south Kerry and in the Béarra peninsula. Eóganacht Rathlind, better known as Uí Echach, lost ground, and their leading family, the O Mahonys, eventually occupied the extreme western peninsulas of Co. Cork. This concentration of O Sullivans, O Mahonys and Mac Carthys in west Cork tended to further compress the Corcu Lóegde into the area which later became the diocese

1

of Ross. We are fortunate in having an early genealogical tract which enumerates the family names deriving from this tribe. The foremost one was O Driscoll and the others included O Coffey, O Leary, O Hea, O Cronin, O Duggan, O Dineen, O Hennessy and O Flynn.

It is noticeable that Fir Maige Féne (in the Fermoy area), of whom we have a similar early account, produced several identical family names, O Duggan being their chief one with O Hennessy, O Leary and O Dineen among the others. This indicates a certain affinity between the two groupings although the genealogists do not connect Fir Maige with the Érainn. Unexpectedly we find that some of the Fir Maige family names – Ó Hiongardail (Harrington), O Coghlan and O Regan – are almost exclusively west Cork names in the 16th century. The Fir Maige suffered a diminution in power also when the chieftaincy of the territory was assumed by the dominant family of Eóganacht Glennamhain, the O Keeffes.

Regrettably, we have no such early accounts of the other non-Eóganacht tribes in Co. Cork. As indicated in the text, it is reasonable to assume that such family names as Ó Flainn and Ó Murchadha emanated from the Múscraige, Ó Conaill from the Uí Liatháin, Ó Colmáin from the Uí Meic Caille, and so on, but we cannot be certain of this in the absence of documentary evidence.

Abundant information regarding the origin and formation of Irish surnames is available in the works of John O Donovan, Fr. Woulfe, Edward MacLysaght and others, making such a survey unnecessary here. Briefly, family names generally took root in Ireland in the 11th century. Brian Boru (d. 1014) provides a good exemplar; his grandsons used the title *Ua Briain* ('grandson of Brian') and so did their descendants. Most family groups tended to do likewise around the same time, choosing the name of a famous ancestor and prefixing it with either *Ua* (later Ó), 'grandson,' or *Mac*, 'son'. The O Callaghans took as their eponymous ancestor Ceallachán of Cashel (d. 954), the O Donovans chose Donnubán (d. 980), and so on. The ruling family of Eóganacht Caisil did not feel the need for a distinctive surname until after the death of Carthach in 1045.

Hence it is obvious that there is little point in trying to 'explain' or translate into English a surname derived solely from a personal name – any more than there would be in trying to 'explain' Johnson or Peterson. It could even be misleading. *Mathghamhain* is an old Irish word for a bear, used as a personal name among the Dál Cais. But because of a marriage connection it occurred just once among the Uí Echach in the 10th century – the Mathghamhain who died in 976 – and happened to be adopted by their chief family, henceforth known as the Uí Mhathghamhna. It needs to be emphasized also that these had no connection with the Uí Mhathghamhna who were kings of the Ulaid (in Ulster). Likewise it cannot be assumed that the O Regans, Coughlans, O Flynns, Lynches, Murphys, etc., of Co. Cork are in any way cognate with those bearing similar family names which originated in other parts of Ireland.

A more extraneous ninth-century settlement was that of the Norse-men or Vikings who are generally credited with the founding of the island city of Cork. Some of the influential city families in medieval times are believed to have had Norse origins, for example, the Coppingers and the Skiddys, but these names are now rare and the Viking dimen-sion is represented in this work by a single family name, Mac Oitir or Cotter.

Far graver were the consequences of the 12th century Cambro-Norman invasion which brought warfare and widespread disruption to most parts of what then became the county of Cork. But as the con-quest was never completed, Gaelic families (especially the Mac Carthys) recovered a share of the conquered lands, so that by the 16th century the position which obtained was that if one drew a line roughly from Kinsale northwards through Mallow, almost all the lands to the west of that were occupied by families of Gaelic descent. Eastwards, lords of Norman origin ruled – principally the Barrys, Roches, Condons and Fitzgeralds, all of whom are dealt with here, along with the Barretts, Cogans, Nagles and Walshes.

One effect which the invasion had on the Limerick area was the displacement of its leading families who then moved southwards into Co. Cork – in particular the O Donovans and some of the Uí Choileáin (Collins). Another family to arrive in west Cork in the 13th century were the O Crowleys who seem to have moved there from Connacht. Two centuries later the Mac Carthys introduced an Ulster-Scottish family of gallowglass, the Mac Sweeneys, who increased and pros-pered in the southern climate. This was the last such arrival until the plantations of the 17th century produced an influx of new landowners and new family names. The only one of these latter to have proliferated in the county was Kingston which is also dealt with in this work.

The fifty families are set out in alphabetical order under the primary forms of the names (as used in the 16th century). The more common secondary forms, in both Irish and English, are also given. With the aim of providing a more readable (and less costly) text, source refer-ences have been kept to a minimum and footnotes entirely excluded. In any case, as the bulk of the sources drawn upon are printed ones, the discerning student should have little difficulty in identifying them, once the dating has been supplied.

The origins of most of the Gaelic families were derived from the com-pilations entitled *Corpus Genealogiarum Hiberniae I* (ed. M.A. O'Brien), *The O Clery Book of Genealogies* (ed. S. Pender), *An Leabhar Muimh-neach* (ed. T. Ó Donnchadha), *The Genealogy of Corca Laidhe* (ed. J. O Donovan) and *Críchad an Chaoilli* (ed. P. Power). Early history was supplied mainly by the Irish annals, in particular *The Annals of Inisfallen* (ed. S. Mac Airt) and 'Mac Carthaigh's Book' published in *Miscellaneous Irish Annals* (ed. S. Ó hInnse). The period from 1169 on is well-documented (from the point of view of Norman families) in the various official documents assembled in the *Calendars of Documents, Ireland, Calendars of Justiciary Rolls*, etc. The 14th and 15th centuries are somewhat neglected both by official sources and by the Munster annals, but the *Calendars of Papal Registers* supply some details though naturally in an ecclesiastical ambience.

The outstanding 16th century source for the quarrying of information on Irish families, especially those of minor importance, is, of course, the 'Fiants,' in particular those of Elizabeth's reign. *Fiant litterae patentes* 'let letters-patent be made,' is normally the initial phrase of these official warrants, signed by the Lord Deputy on behalf of the crown. Some relate to the redistribution of confiscated abbey-lands, etc., but most are pardons granted to individuals or groups who applied for them. The granting of a pardon does not necessarily indicate the commission of an offence. Quite often they were sought in order to provide the recipient with a clean sheet following some military or political upheaval in which he might or might not have been involved. In other cases pardons were issued in return for the recipient's agreement to overlook payment for cattle or horses 'supplied' to the Queen's army. The important thing about these Fiants is that they furnish names and surnames of practically every able-bodied man in the countryside, and oftentimes his place of residence and occupation as well. In the case of chiefs, heads of families, and their close relatives, this last was invariably given as 'gentleman.' One step below this rank came 'horseman,' followed by 'yeoman,' a title which indicated a semi-independent 'strong farmer' type, whereas a 'husbandman' was probably a less secure tenant-farmer. Terms such as 'labourer,' 'smith,' 'surgeon,' need no explanation, but at the bottom of the pile came 'kern' (Irish *ceithearnach*), a lightly-armed footsoldier, the material supplied by a chief to his overlord (or to the crown) in times of war and rebellion as (to use a modern term) cannon-fodder.

Frequently a pardon was granted to the head of a sept or family group and to all his relatives and followers who are specified in the list. This is of inestimable value when attempting to place a particular family name in its proper locality. I have in all cases endeavoured to pinpoint the actual parishes, townlands and castles occupied by members of the various families, since people in general like to be able to identify a particular *fons et origo* from which their ancestors came — and in which some of the name may still be flourishing today. For despite all the plantations and upheavals throughout the centuries and all the incentives to migration provided by modern travel facilities, name-distribution in Co. Cork today is not all that different to what it was in Elizabethan times. Plantations normally affected only those with the rank of gentleman or, perhaps, horseman. There is a tendency in family chronicles to concentrate on the chief members or main line at all times — understandably, since records of the rank and file occur much less frequently.

It must be borne in mind that an extremely rigid caste system obtained in medieval Ireland, with a small self-perpetuating aristocratic clique accorded the unquestioning service and respect of a large but obscure mass of commoners. Yet it was this silent majority of yeomen, husband-men, labourers and others who, because they were not disturbed to the same degree, kept the family name extant from generation to generation. So it is that even today we look for Barrys and Roches in the eastern half of Co. Cork while O Driscolls, O Mahonys and O Sullivans are still most numerous on the western peninsulas.

In the unlikely event of a reader perusing the whole of this work non-stop, a certain sameness — inevitability perhaps — would become apparent as one family history after another unfolded. However diverse their origins, by the 16th century most families had formed hierarchical landowning groups of varied size and power. As such they were sus-ceptible to the pressures of the centralizing Tudor establishment on the one hand and the acquisitive propensities of the younger sons of English landowners on the other. In the case of the families of Norman descent in east Cork the chief or lord was the feudal owner holding his lordship of the crown *in capite*. But the Gaelic chiefs held only part of the sept-lands as mensal lands for their own support, the remainder being allotted to various members of the sept. This system gradually disintegrated in the face of the temptation to submit to the 'Surrender and Regrant' policy which meant, in effect, that by surrendering all the septlands to the crown the reigning chief became the legal feudal owner of the entire lordship. He could then obtain a licence to alienate (i.e. sell) property which had been the patrimony of the sept for generations. More frequently, however, resort was had to mortgaging, the benefits of which had just been introduced to impecunious Irish chiefs who found therein a convenient and perennial source of ready money. Accommodating land-sharks, many of them merchants from Cork city, soon made their appearance in the remotest extremities of west Cork making the question of land-ownership even more complicated than before.

But the major drawback in the regrant policy was the inherent vul-nerability to forfeiture now created. If the legal owner were to be con-victed of treason or slain in rebellion, his attainder would deliver every-thing into the hands of the crown, for distribution among loyal subjects. A particularly blatant case of such confiscation occurred when Conoghor O Mahony was 'slain in rebellion' (by his own relatives) in 1580. Despite the fact that Kinalmeaky had never been subjected to surrender and re-grant and the even more pertinent fact that Conoghor had never been regarded as chief in either Irish or English law, the government seized the opportunity of declaring all the O Mahony lands of Kinalmeaky for-feit to the crown. How much more vulnerable, then, were those lord-ships whose legal ownership was vested in one man.

The period from 1603 to 1641 brought no official confiscations but saw a good deal of selling and buying, mortgaging and letting, reflecting the new role of the Irish lords as 17th century landed gentry. A few — notably Lord Barrymore — conformed to the established religion and by sailing close to the prevailing winds managed to avoid shipwreck during the cataclysms which marked the second part of the century. But the majority joined the Catholic Confederation at the outbreak of the 1641 rebellion, were outlawed two years later, espoused the cause of Charles I as against Cromwell in 1649 and lost everything in the ensuing confiscations and plantations. A few regained all or part of their lands after the restoration of Charles II in 1660. Prominent among these was the Earl of Clancarty (formerly Lord Muskerry) who had the whole of Muskerry restored to him only to lose it all again in the battle royal between James II and William of Orange. This conflict witnessed the final despairing effort by many landless cadets of historical families to recover their ancient patrimony. But it was not to be, and soon the wrack of once-illustrious names was strewn over every arena from Dunkirk to Belgrade.

At home the survivors, bereft of everything their family names had represented, subsided for the most part into an amorphous community of tenant-farmers, fishermen, innkeepers, servants, governed by a new aristocracy bearing alien names redolent of another culture. Here and there a native historian or poet, remnant of a long line of scholars, sat by a turf-fire and strove to pen the flickering memories of former glories, but for the mass of the people these melancholy memorials had little relevance any more.

Nevertheless, even today, the half-remembered tale can now and then stir a covert pride of race among latter-day descendants. The old septs, like their castles, have crumbled away, yet somehow the ruins still cast their ancestral shadows across the byways of our minds.

MAC AMHLAOIBH

MAC AULIFFE

Although the personal name Amlaíb or Amhlaoibh is undoubtedly Viking in origin (Anlaf or Olaf), the genealogies derive the Mac Auliffes of Co. Cork from the Gaelic royal stock of Munster. According to O Clery and others, the eponymous ancestor was Amhlaoibh Áluinn, great-grandson of Tadhg mac Muireadhaigh mhic Charthaigh, the Tadhg who was king of Eóganacht Caisil and whose brother, Cormac, was ancestor of the Mac Carthys. (See MAC CARTHAIGH.)

By the 14th century — perhaps earlier — Amhlaoibh's descendants had settled in Duhallow, as Ó Huidhrín tells us:

Fada ó Abhainn Ealla fhéil
siar tar Gleann Salcháin slaitréidh,
gealfhonn gan ceilt cnuasaigh caoimh,
fearonn Meic uasail Amhlaoibh.

(Reaching from the bountiful river of Ealla, westwards beyond Gleann Salcháin of the smooth rods; a bright land not concealing its goodly store, the territory of the noble Mac Amhlaoibh).

Early in the 15th century the annals record the killing of Amhlaoibh Bodhar Mac Amhlaoibh Ealla at Claonghlais, as he was going to the house of James, Earl of Desmond. Claonghlais or Clonlish is in the south-west of Co. Limerick and would have been on Amhlaoibh's route to either of the Desmond strongholds of Newcastlewest or Askeaton. This slaying may have sparked off a family feud; over a century later, in 1535, Mac Amhlaoibh, we are told, gained a great victory, killing the (Geraldine) lord of Clonlish as well as Fitzgibbon and a great number of Clann Síthigh. The Mac Sheehys were a gallowglass family. Mac Amhlaoibh had a gallowglass constable at this stage too, namely, the son of Maelmuire son of Brian Mac Suibhne, who was killed at the beginning of the fray.

The family territory, which became known as Clann Amhlaoibh or Clanawley, consisted of the north-east corner of Co. Cork, from the Allow river in the east and the Brogeen river in the south to the borders of Cos. Kerry and Limerick. It lay mainly in the parish of Clonfert (of which Donatus Macmycamlaybh or Donnchadh mac Mic Amhlaoibh was vicar in 1494). A head-rent was payable to Mac Carthy (known as Mac Donogh), lord of Duhallow. Two townlands in Clonfert parish bear the family name — Tooreenmacauliffe and Castlemacauliffe, the latter being the site of Mac Auliffe's principal castle, a mile to the south-west

7

of Newmarket, overlooking the river Dalua. No trace of this castle now remains but there are some ruins of a second Mac Auliffe castle, at Carraig an Chaisil or Carrigcastle. This stood two miles north-east of Newmarket, at the entrance to Priory Glen, formerly called Gleann an Áir (Glen of the slaughter) because, it was said, of a bloody encounter that took place there when the O Keeffes pursued the Mac Auliffes who had taken a *creach* of cattle from their neighbours.

After the first Desmond rebellion had ended in 1573 a pardon was issued to Malaghlin Mac Awly of Carrigcashel, gent. This was probably Maoilsheachlainn Mór, chief of his name. (Maoilsheachlainn was then replacing Amhlaoibh as the favourite personal name.) Also pardoned in the same year were Dermod óg Mac Auly of Ballynwallishig (?Walshestown, par. Churchtown) and his three sons, Owen, Donogh and Conogher, all described as gentlemen. In the following year the chief was again pardoned, along with Morighe, Owen and Donald Mac Awlie, gentlemen. In 1576 Owen Mac Auliffe of Castlemacauliffe was pardoned, and a year later Moroghe Mac Awley of Duhallow, gentleman, and Moriertagh mac Melaghlin Mac Awley, gentleman.

While pardons of themselves do not provide evidence of disloyalty, there is no doubt concerning Mac Auliffe's involvement in the second Desmond rebellion. On 29th November, 1579, Melaghlen mac Dermodie Mac Awliffe of Castlemacauliffe joined forces with the rebel Earl of Desmond and John Browne of Cnockmonihie, among others. But the rigours of the campaign proved too much for his aged frame and he died a month later, at Coggyrrykiery (?Curraghakerry, near Doneraile). He had at least six sons and was succeeded by Maoilsheachlainn óg, also known as Maoilsheachlainn riabhach, referred to in the genealogies as *An Fáidh* (the prophet). The prophecies ascribed to Mac Amhlaoibh na Fáistine were in great vogue among the poets and scribes of the 17th-18th centuries, particularly the one which begins:

> *Sin a haon, Loch Léin gan daingean ar bith;*
> *An tarna haon, gan tréine i nGearaltachaibh;*
> *An tríú haon, gan géille i nDúth-alla dom shliucht;*
> *An ceathrú haon, beig Éire ag Sasanachaibh.*

Also about this time there appears to have been a succession dispute or family row of some kind, as in 1583, according to the annals, 'the son of Mac Auliffe, Donnchadh Bán mac Maoileachlainn mic Diarmata, and his brother's son, Tadhg mac Conchobhair, mutually slew each other.' The 'Mac Auliffe' referred to was, apparently, the deceased Maoilsheachlainn Mór, so Donnchadh Bán must have been a brother of Maoilsheachlainn óg.

Early in 1580 the Lord Deputy and the Earl of Ormond ravaged Duhallow and other regions which gave support to the rebel Earl of Desmond. In July, 1583, as the rebellion dragged to its inevitable end, Mac Auliffe — along with Mac Donogh and O Callaghan — submitted to the Earl of Ormond in Cork. Two years later pardons were issued to Melaghlin Mac Awly (captain of his name), Ellaen Mac Awly, Ellynny Mac Awly, Teige na Skarty mac Conor mac Awly and Fynyn reaugh mac Conor Mac Awly. All was not forgiven, however. In 1587 Mac Auliffe was imprisoned by Lord Deputy Perrot while Clanawley was confiscated and later acquired by Patrick Graunt of Waterford. Patrick must have had second thoughts about moving to Clanawley, as in 1592 he sold it back to Mac Auliffe for £150 'to hold for ever as the premises were granted to the said Graunt.'

When Hugh O Neill came south to Inishcarra in 1600 he was attended by the sons of the chiefs of Duhallow. According to a list compiled by Carew, Mac Auliffe at this time had but 60 kern in his forces, but his 80 horsemen outnumbered those of any other chief in Desmond. After O Neill's departure, pressure from Carew compelled Mac Donogh, Mac Auliffe and O Keeffe to submit to the queen. Before the year was out, however, according to *Pacata Hibernia* '. . . Sir Francis Barkley, finding good cause and fitt opportunitie to plague Mac Awley (and his Tenants, who under protection, relieved the heart-broken Rebells) with the Garrison which he commanded at Askeiton, he harassed all the countrey of Clanowlie, and took from thence 1,000 cowes, 200 Garrans, besides sheepe and other spoyle, and had the killing of many Traitours, which harboured themselves in the bogs and woods thereof.'

Though Maoilsheachlainn óg submitted, his son, Dermod Mac Awly of Carrigcastle, continued to support O Neill and travelled to Ulster with him. Returning in May, 1601, and realizing his precarious position, Dermot, having first made contact through intermediaries, went voluntarily to Carew and supplied him with copious details — how authentic we cannot judge — of the rebels' plans. His conversion, if it was genuine at all, was of brief duration, since he remained a diehard rebel even after the battle of Kinsale. On St. Patrick's Day, 1602, Dermot was killed in action and Carew triumphantly wrote: 'The death of these two rebels, and also of a notorious rebel by name Dermot Mac Awley, who was an intimate man and a great practising instrument with Tyrone, will greatly quiet these parts, and your lordships can hardly think what a great change we find already by their so happy and timely cutting off'. An inquisition of 1609 found that Dermitius Mac Melaghlin Mac Awliffe had been unlawfully in possession of the castle and lands of Carrigg Cashell which he had seized from his father and that he had been slain in rebellion in 1602, his father being then alive and a faithful subject.

The Dermod Mac Auliffe of Carrigcashel, gentleman, who was pardoned in May, 1602, may have been Dermot óg, one of Dermot's four sons. A similar pardon was issued to Cormac of Castlemacauliffe, a son of Donnchadh Bán. In 1603 a pardon was granted to Teige Mac Morieg Mac Auliffe of Castlemacauliffe, gent. On 17th October, 1602, John Mac Auliffe gave recognizances and O Callaghan of Clonmeen with Mac Carthy of Cloghroe went bail for him 'as long as John Mac Auliffe shall continue of dutiful behaviour'. John ended up in Spain where in 1605 he was a gentleman pensioner of the Spanish army. In the same year, his brother Dermot was in receipt of four crowns monthly; later he served in the Spanish infantry in Flanders (having served in his own country in defence of the Catholic cause). A third brother, Conoghor, was also a pensioner, while William Mac Auliffe (of Muskerry) served as a sergeant to Teig mac Donal (ne County) Mac Carthy. The chief, Malachy Mac Auliffe, then a prisoner of Sir Thomas Roper at Castlemaine, was ordered, on 5th December 1602, to appear at Code's castle in Co. Cork within twenty days, and in default to give up Castlemacauliffe and Carrigcastle and all the lands thereunto belonging to be disposed of for her Majesty's services. Malachy died around 1606, and in 1609 the lands of Clanawley, including Castlemacauliffe and Carrigcastle, were granted to John Wakeman, an Englishman, and sold the following year to the Sir Thomas Roper who had kept Mac Auliffe prisoner at Castlemaine.

Two years later James fitz Nicholas Barry of Walshestown (near Buttevant) paid Roper £2,500 for much of Clanawley and then jointly with Melaughlin Mac Auliffe demised Castlemacauliffe to John Mayhew for 700 years at £81 per annum. (This Melaughlin was the eldest son of the slain Dermot, and grandson of Melaughlin óg; he resided at Carrigcastle.) In 1615 a government commission was set up to enquire into the complicated tenure of Clanawley and following this, Roper, Graunt, Barry and Mac Auliffe were all induced to surrender their rights to the king. If they expected a regrant, they were due for a disappointment as Sir Richard Aldworth, Provost-Marshal of Munster, gained possession of Carrigcastle and adjoining lands on which he undertook to settle English families.

Mac Auliffe still retained more than half of Clanawley (much of it mortgaged) including Castlemacauliffe. In 1634 a dispute arose between Mac Auliffe and O Keeffe concerning lands between the Araglin and the Blackwater. Both were married to daughters of O Callaghan of Clonmeen and the dispute was settled amicably with Mac Auliffe retaining the eastern portion and O Keeffe the western. By then Melaghlin was dead, his successor being his son, Dermot, who died in 1637 and was buried in Clonfert. Dermot's only son and heir (Melaghlin) was still a minor, so the chieftaincy was assumed by Dermot's uncle, Fínghin, who led the clan when they joined the rising of 1641.

A deposition by Edward Vauclier of Tralee claimed that eleven men and one woman coming from Co. Kerry were murdered in the mountains near Newmarket by the rebels of Cork and Mac Auliffe of Duhallow in January 1642. Vauclier also stated that he himself had been taken prisoner on Sliabh Luachra by Teigue Mac Auliffe of Castlemacauliffe, Bawne Mac Auliffe, Connogher Ceogh of near Liscarroll and Owen O Callaghan of near Newmarket with 560 men who brought him to the camp near Adare, where there were 7,000 men then prepared to fight against the English. He was later exchanged for Capt. James Brown. In Carbery, Donogh Mac Dermot Mac Auliffe was accused of rebellion by the Archdeacon of Ross. We do not know how the Mac Auliffes fared as the rebellion dragged on but a local tradition relates that in November 1647 they were on their way to Knocknanuss when news reached them of the crushing defeat of the Confederate army by Lord Inchiquin and that they were 'on the run' for several months subsequently.

Among those outlawed in 1643 were Fynnyne and Teige Mac Auliffe (alias Teige Ivegher) of Carrigcastle, gents., as well as Cornelius and Donough Mac Owen Mac Auliffe of Lismeelcunnin, gents. Owen was the sixth son of the Melaghlin who went into rebellion in 1579. Of these Fínghin was the only legally recognized landowner, holding about 2,000 acres in Drominarrigle, Coolavota and Knocknehorny (Barleyhill). These lands were confiscated and later granted to Baron Worth, Col. John Gifford and Lord Broghill (Earl of Orrery). The latter, a son of the ubiquitous Richard Boyle, was already involved in the Clanawley lands and now became a rival to Sir Richard Aldworth in that area. In 1662 Broghill's agent wrote to complain of the actions of a tenant, Loghlyn Mac Auliffe (perhaps son of Dermot who died in 1637) . . . 'Disputes are being kept afoot by those who sold the estate to your father . . . The man who was so successful in getting much of Carrig-cashell is now challenging more by a patent . . .'

Loghlin and Finn Mac Auliffe were still tenants in Clanawley in 1671 while Henry Hedges was tenant of Castlemacauliffe. But due to the complicated feoffments and leases the Boyles' legal position became extremely precarious and it was not improved by the emergence in 1683 of a new Mac Auliffe claimant to the inheritance of all Clanawley, one who was willing to sell his title to the highest bidder. Mainly through lack of finance the Mac Auliffes failed to press their claims in court, and appear to have made a settlement eventually with the Boyles.

The remnants of the landowning Mac Auliffes joined the last-ditch stand of the Catholic gentry in 1689. In that year, Major Dermot Mac Auliffe was third in command of Nicholas Browne's infantry in King James' army, and was stationed at Kinsale. Daniel Mac Auliffe was a lieutenant in the same regiment and Teige Mac Auliffe lieutenant in another, probably the Lieutenant Mac Auliffe who fought with Sarsfield at Limerick and lies buried at Abbeyfeale.

The chief of the name, John, son of Fínghin (outlawed in 1690 as 'John de Auliffe, Castlemacauliffe') sailed for France with his family in 1691. For this he again incurred outlawry (for foreign treason) along with his son, Dermot, and Denis Mac Auliffe of Lismeelcunnin. Dermot was probably the Don Demetrio Mac Auliffe who was appointed colonel of an Irish regiment in Spain in 1710. By 1715 Don Tadeo Mac Auliffe had taken over the command. This regiment later became known as *Regimente de Infanteria de Ultonia*. According to D'Alton, the last reputed chief of the family, Michael Mac Auliffe, died while colonel of a regiment in Spain in 1720 — probably the same 'Ulster Regiment.' A daughter of Melaghlin son of Dermot, namely Honora, married an O Donoghue of Glenflesk, and their son, Dubh, was the father of Máire Ní Dhuibh, the poetess, who was grandmother of Daniel O'Connell, the Liberator.

According to the poet, Edward Walsh, a well-known Newmarket character styled John Mac Auliffe 'the active', was in the early 19th century regarded by the local people as the last representative of his race, but according to John O Donovan, there was a weighmaster in Kenmare in 1840 'who had been born to a handsome estate' and who claimed to be the last chieftain of the Mac Auliffes.

In 1659, after the Cromwellian plantations, while Duhallow presumably remained the principal stronghold of the surname, there were eleven Mac Auliffe families in Orrery and Kilmore and eleven others in West Carbery. The name is well-distributed throughout Co. Cork today but is most numerous in north Cork and south Limerick.

BALLINCOLLIG CASTLE *(O'Callaghan Newenham, 1826)*

BARRETT

BARÓID

This is one of the family names associated with the advent of the Normans in Ireland, although it is not among the better-known ones found in the first wave of that invasion. By the time the Barretts appeared on the Irish scene at the beginning of the 13th century, most of the sword-land had already been appropriated so that they became sub-infeudatories rather than tenants-in-chief.

The earliest reference to the name in Ireland appears to be in Mac Carthaigh's Book which lists Norman castles in Desmond in 1214, including... *Cloch leisin mBaroideach annsa tsradbaile os cinn Cuain Dor* (A castle by Barrett in the village above Glandore). Carew, who is named in the same list (as the builder of the castle of Dunnamark) was probably Barrett's overlord here; in 1299 William Barrett held 'Clardor' of Maurice de Carreu.

At some period of the Barretts' stay in west Cork one of them gave name to the townland of Coomavarodig (*Cúm an Bharóidigh*) near Baltimore. Also, in Inchigeelagh parish in the 17th century there was a townland named Millinavarodig — perhaps the modern Milleen. The castle at Glandore (*Cloch an tsráidbhaile*) was apparently forsaken after the battle of Callann in 1261, when many Norman families were driven out of west Cork. In later centuries it was an O Donovan castle.

The *Annals of Connacht* record that Tomás Baróid was killed in 1260 at Kilbarran, Co. Clare, while aiding the Fitzgeralds in an attack on the O Briens.

The extension of the Barretts' activities into Connacht was probably due to the Carews. Around 1237 Richard de Burgh granted lands in Tirawley (Co. Mayo) to Robert de Carew whose son Richard enfeoffed William Barrett with the tuath of Bredagh. It seems, however, that the Petits had got an earlier grant and had sub-infeudated Adam Cusack in the same place. In or about 1247 William (Fionn) Barrett ejected Adam Cusack from Bredagh and, despite several legal decrees against him, refused to give up possession. The dispute continued into the next generation when William (Mór) Barrett met Adam Cusack (junior) in a pitched battle at Moyne in 1281, many being killed on both sides. Uilliam Mór na Maighne was imprisoned in Cusack's castle and died there, leaving a three-year-old son and heir, William (Óg). The Barretts later spread widely throughout Co. Mayo where their surname was Bairéid or sometimes Mac Bhaitín, after Batin Barrett who flourished in the late 13th century.

An inquisition into the Barrett lands in 1299 reveals that William (Mór) as well as holding lands in Connacht had several holdings in Co. Cork, namely: Grenagh of John de Cogan; Fresketh and Castelgeych (both near Ballyhea) of Maurice de Rocheford and John de Barry, respectively; Clardor of Maurice de Carreu and Dumbolgyn (? Dunworly) of the bishop of Ross. He held no lands directly of the king.

Regarding the lands held of the bishop, it is of interest that in the early 14th century the bishop of Ross recovered some of the see's possessions 'which had been unjustly usurped by Thomas Barrett', namely Killangal and Lissarankin in Castlehaven parish, with Clontaff and Listarkin in Myross. These may, perhaps, be some of the lands (in Desmond in the county of Cork) donated by William Barat (presumably William Fionn) to the Priory of Bath, and handed over by the Benedictine prior in Cork to the Justiciar of Ireland in 1260.

A list of 1301 shows that William Baret held land in Courcys' country, not far from the Old Head of Kinsale. This townland was known in 1299 as Barretstown and is probably the modern Ballinvredig; the form *Baile an Bhairéidigh* shows that even in Co. Cork Barrett was sometimes *Bairéid* rather than *Baróid*.

In 1306 a John Barrett of Glanworth brought an unsuccessful legal action against Robert and Fynwel (*Finnghuala*) Russell of Dourwagh (Drough near Mitchelstown) claiming that he had bought eight beams from the Russells for the making of his hall and that he was prevented from taking them away.

It was presumably the brothers of William Mór — the *Annals of Inisfallen* call them 'the sons of William Barrett' — who in 1283 slew Tomás son of Mael Dúin Ó Caoimh and carried off a prey from the O Keeffe country. Perhaps it was as a result of such forays that in 1295 'suit of peace' was pardoned to Mathew Barrett, Richard Barrett, Thomas Barrett, Philip Barrett, Richard son of William Barrett and their followers — who included O Donovans and other Irish — 'for all forfeitures etc. to 3rd August, for £40'. In 1311, Richard, Mathew and Thomas appear again, together with Robert Barrett and Robert son of Robert, as followers of the Roches to whom suit of peace was pardoned for their good services in fighting against the Condons.

Six years later, in consequence of the service of Robert Baret against the king's enemies in the marches, Edward II granted to William Barrett (Robert's son) the arrears of two parts of the lands of Gronagh (Grenagh), Co. Cork, which had come into the king's hands.

This was in East Muskerry where the Barretts were making a determined effort to establish themselves in the latter half of the 14th century when their chief representative was Richard óg Barrett. In 1359 Richard sought justice against the Barrys and Courcys who had destroyed his lands, but nine years later he and five other Barretts were charged with having unlawfully ejected Geoffrey de Cogan from certain lands in Muskerry. John Lumbard also complained that Richard óg

Barrett had ejected him from Manokyth, Glascortan, Cnocnemarw (Knocknamarriff) Oldecastell and Faigh near Mayoly (Faha). Richard claimed that in 1366 the king had granted him these lands between the Lee and the Blackwater for an annual rent of one red rose, as a reward for his services and seeing that the same lands were unoccupied due to Mac Carthy attacks. Though he failed to prove his case Richard does not seem to have been dispossessed, and the doubtful royal grant seems to have been the foundation-stone of the Barrett tenure in and around the parish of Inishcarra. When Peter de Cogan, the last of the direct Cogan line, died in 1371, his widow married William Barrett who thereby enhanced his claims to Cogan lands in Muskerry. An inquisition into Peter de Cogan's lands found that those at Ballyhay were worth but little on account of the destruction wrought by the Geraldines while those at Mora (Mourne Abbey) were worth nothing *causa destruccionis Barrettensium*!

Although Stephen fitz William Barret and John fitz Thomas Barret were appointed collectors in Muskerry in 1375, by 1377 the Barretts were officially regarded as 'rebels in the county Cork'. In 1381 a fine of 1,000 cows was imposed on Richard óg Barrett and William, his son. Apparently, the fine was not paid and a week later the mayor and bailiffs of Cork were commanded to provide horses to bring Richard óg Barrett and others of the Barretts who were in custody to Waterford as hostages. We are not told what their ultimate fate was. In 1382 they were again described as Irish enemies and rebels.

Nevertheless, the Barretts had by now so firmly entrenched themselves in the former Cogan lands that a new barony was eventually carved out of eastern Muskerry. Today the barony of Barretts embraces only a small area between Whitechurch and Mourne Abbey but in the 16th and 17th centuries it reached southwards to the Lee taking in the parishes of Carrigrohanebeg, Matehy and Inishcarra, and even south of the Lee where it embraced parts of the parishes of Aglish, Athnowen, Kilnaglory and Carrigrohane — including Ballincollig, where their principal castle stood.

But the Barretts had powerful rivals in the acquisition of the rich lands of east Muskerry, namely, the Mac Carthys who were at this time relentlessly pressing on eastwards. At first the two families were in alliance. An inquisition taken at Buttevant in 1345 found that Thomas Glas Barret, William, John and Richard sons of Richard Baret and Thomas son of Thomas Baret were in the following of Dermot Mac Carthy who attacked Curragh'Bothir (Curraghbower, par. Kilshannig) killing, among others, two knights, Robert Barry and Philip Prendergast. On the same day Dermot Mac Carthy's forces, this time including Simon Baret, Richard son of Thomas Barret and Thomas Pussagh Barret attacked several places around Ballyclogh, in support of the Earl of Desmond's bid to take over the kingdom.

By the close of the 14th century however, the alliance was at an end, and the Barretts, now established landowners in east Muskerry, were regarded by the Mac Carthys as legitimate targets for their attacks. In 1402, according to the *Annals of Connacht*:

'The sons of Cormac son of Donnchadh Mac Carthy made an attack on the Barretts and the Barretts defeated them. The son of Donnchadh Mac Carthy's son was captured with many of his followers, and Art O'Keeffe was killed as well.'

Two years later, perhaps in retribution, Andrew Barrett was killed by the Uí Mhurchadha, who were Mac Carthy followers. This may have been the Andrew Barrett 'felon and rebel' whom the king commanded Philip Barry and Patrick Galvy of Kinsale to keep in custody in 1392. Two years later the king accepted the submission of William Barrett and Magu Barrett Carraghe.

By this time the Barretts must have taken over and perhaps rebuilt the former Cogan castle at Carrigrohane. In 1420 Cormac and Domhnall of the Mac Carthy Mór family went to conquer the territory of the Barretts. This they did and held it for a year, defeating a rival group of Carbery Mac Carthys at the ford of Carrigrohane. Some of the defeated Carbery men took refuge in Carrigrohane castle. The Barretts eventually recovered their lands and castles but had to pay an annual rent of £11 to Mac Carthy Mór. A few years later, in 1426, they covenanted to be obedient to the Earl of Desmond and as a result had to pay an annual rent of 12 marks to that great lord.

Ballincollig, according to a legal document of the early 17th century, was purchased by the Barretts in 1468 from Robert Coll, a knight. (*Baile an Chollaigh* = Coll's town.) Here they erected their principal stronghold.

Later in the century they yielded possession of Cloghphilip castle, near Blarney. In 1488 John son of Richard son of Symon de Rede Bared, lord of Cloyth Phylyb, granted his will and lands to Eoghan Mac Carthy. Eoghan of Cloghroe, as he was called, was a brother of the lord of Muskerry and the Mac Carthy occupation of Cloghphilip, Cloghroe and Blarney effectively divided the barony of the Barretts into two sections.

The late 15th century tower-house of Castle Inch (now demolished as a result of the Inishcarra hydro-electric scheme) may also have been built by the Barretts but was for long a bone of contention between them and the Mac Carthys. Diarmaid Mac Carthy, lord of Muskerry, is stated to have died 'at his own house of Castle Inch' in 1570 but in 1593 Catherine Barrett sued the Mac Carthys for having besieged Castle Inch for two days, 'threatening to cut the heads off her servants if they would not yield up same'. Cormac Mac Carthy got a fine and a jail sentence as a result but gained possession of the castle which was held by the Mac Carthys until after the Jacobite wars. Incidentally, Cormac married (and later divorced) Ellen *liath* Barrett who was his own first cousin.

The Elizabethan Fiants contain many references to Barretts in and around Inishcarra. In 1573, after the first Desmond rebellion, a pardon was granted to Ullig (Ulick) Barrett of Currabeha (par. Inishcarra) but after the second rebellion he was attainted. Apparently he retained his lands since an inquisition taken after his death in 1602 declared James (who was pardoned in 1601) to be his son and heir in Currabeha. Nevertheless, 'Curribehie, late possession of Ullick Barrett, attainted' was still numbered among the crown lands in 1606-7. An old man told Bishop Downes in 1706 that his grandfather had paid Bishop Lyon (1583-1617) 13s per annum chiefry for the bishop's defence to secure his estate from Esqr. Barrett for Curribaghagh . . . 'this estate came to Friar Ulick Barret, who died 12 years ago; upon his death Pourdon, Coulthurst and others got possession of it'.

Ulick was not the only unusual personal name in use among the Barretts in Elizabethan times. One named Connleigh was pardoned in 1576 and this name recurs in later generations. It appears to be the old – and rare – Irish name, *Conlae*. An even more hibernicized 'Conleghe O Barret' of Balleaghleigh (Ballyleigh, par. Inishcarra) was pardoned in 1601. William Barrett fitz Conlogh of Cork forfeited lands in Barretts barony in Cromwellian times while 'Coomeleigh' Barrett of Ballyanley was outlawed in 1691. Other unusual Barrett personal names found in the Elizabethan Fiants and seemingly derived from old Irish romances were Beany or Beny (?*Béinne*), Eiver (? *Éibhear* or *Íomhar*) and Magu!

A bitter family dispute in this period split the Barretts into two opposing factions. In 1583 Margery, widow of James *riabhach* Barrett, chief of Barrett's country, petitioned the Queen that her daughter, Katherine, might be restored to her former inheritance, and so inquiries were instituted the following year. Margery was a sister of Lord Roche and claimed that five of her brother's children had been slain in Her Majesty's service. Apparently when her husband died, the sons of his uncle William had seized Ballincollig castle (which was stated to be in tail male) and lands appertaining to it. It is significant that when William Barrett's three sons, Edmond, Conleigh and James *riabhach*, were pardoned in 1576 they were described as of Inishcarra but in 1585 their pardons describe them as of Ballincollig. Edmond seems to have been the recognized chief of Barrett's country in September 1588 when the gentlemen and freeholders of that area protested that the only head-rent payable by them was one rose per annum.

However, two grants of livery (formal possession) in the same year clearly favoured Katherine. One was to Edmond fitz William Barrett, described as kinsman and heir of James fitz Richard Barrett of Rathneniell (now Rathcoola, par. Donaghmore) who held in socage by the payment of one rose yearly the manors and lands of Rathnenyell, etc., including Knocknamarriff and Ballymacoo in the parish of Inishcarra and Lackenshoneen in Carrigrohanebeg. There was also a chief rent out of

'Clane mc donnell', i.e. *Clann mhic Dhomhnaill*, a minor sept of the Mac Carthys long established in Barrett's territory.

But Katherine, described as daughter and heir of James Barrett, late of Ballincollig, gent., got the lion's share. Her list of lands begins with Cloghmcullig, a townland-name no longer extant, but the site of an old castle on the hills south of Ballincollig, as shown in *Pacata Hibernia*. (The Ulick whose son or sons gave name to this castle may well have been a Ulick Barrett.) Then follow most of the townlands in Inishcarra parish — Moneyflugh, Garravagh, Carryknaveen, Ardrum, Curraleigh, Ballyanley etc., as well as others in the parishes of Carrigrohane, Kilnaglory and Donaghmore, ending with . . . 'other hamlets adjoining Castlenyhinchy (Castleinch) and Castlemore'.

It is strange that neither livery mentions Ballincollig which was at the centre of the dispute and then occupied by Edmond. Katherine married one Andrew Barrett who was a lawyer in Cork with many useful contacts. But when legal methods failed to dislodge Edmond, in July 1591 Andrew, accompanied by his friends William Barrett, Manus O Sullivan and sixty others, riotously assaulted Ballincollig castle '. . . with swords, guns, great sledges or hammers, skenes, stones and staves, removed one bolie house then and there standing into to the gate of the said castle did remove and then and there broke the iron grate and partly the wall of the said castle by the said gate did riotously with a great hammer break, and into the said Castle town and lands did expulse the said Edmund Barrett, and did also levy a great cry, to the disturbance of her Majesty's subjects and to the grievous damage of the said Edmund'. (Cormac Mac Carthy's assault on Katherine's house at Castle Inch, already referred to, may have arisen from the same dispute.)

In 1594 Edmond got a writ to dispossess Andrew but Sir Fineen O Driscoll, sheriff of Co. Cork, refused to execute it. The following year Andrew and his associates were tried and fined for the 1591 assault. Edmond then regained possession — forcibly according to Andrew — and mortgaged the castle to Robert Coppinger for two years. After Edmond's death, his son, William, remained an implacable foe of Andrew, who complained in March 1600 that at the outbreak of the rebellion (? 1598) William burned the castle of Ballincollig with sixty houses and corn to the value of £200, murdered certain soldiers and entered into rebellion. Andrew further claimed that though his tenants and himself had been spoiled of all their goods and cattle he had repaired and re-garrisoned Ballincollig castle at his own expense. He begged the Privy Council to bestow on himself the title by which William was generally known — Barrett of Barrett's country.

Although William had submitted to the Lord President by May 1600 and received several pardons — including one as late as March 1603 — he scorned to desert the losing side and is next found as captain of a company in Spanish Flanders listed in the company of such well-known exiled rebels as Donal O Sullivan Bear and Connor O Driscoll.

This conduct of the lord of Barrett's country gives the lie to the oft-quoted story that Hugh O Neill '. . . anno 1600, in his progress to Munster, said when he understood him (Barrett) to be of English extraction, that he hated him as if he had come but yesterday'. The story appears to have originated with Sir Richard Cox and later writers associated the alleged remark with Barrett's castle near Mourne Abbey, overlooking the fact that in 1600 this was a Geraldine castle (mortgaged to a Mac Sweeney) and even though it bordered on the lands of the Barretts it was never occupied by them until purchased by Andrew Barrett in the second decade of the 17th century. The original builders of the castle were the de Cogans, from whom the Earl of Desmond acquired it in 1439.

If further evidence were needed to demonstrate the unlikelihood of Cox's story, there is the fact that O Neill chose Inishcarra in Barrett's country as his chief campsite on his visit to Munster in early 1600. An inquisition taken in 1633 recalled that Redmond fitz Andrew Barrett of Pluckanes '. . . not having the fear of God before his eyes and regardless of his duty to the late Queen Elizabeth, at Pluckanes on 3rd August 1598 went into open rebellion and was associated with rebels'. William mac Robert Barrett and James mac William Barrett of Pluckanes were pardoned in 1601. Other Barretts to be pardoned at the time were James fitz Ulick of Currabeha, William mac Ulick and Ulick oge of Inishcarra and James fitz William of Lackenshoneen.

Andrew was left in possession of the Barrett estates but despite his loyalty almost lost them to covetous officialdom. In 1611 Carew engineered an attempt to take over Barrett's country for the crown. He wrote to Sir Dominic Sarsfield, then living at Ballincollig and, it was rumoured, intending to get one of his daughters married to Andrew Barrett's eldest son. If, said Carew, it could be proved that Catherine Barrett's father (James Reagh) was illegitimate, the rightful heir would then be William who because of his traitorous activities in Flanders would forfeit all to the crown. But despite Carew's bait '. . . if the King's title be good, you may make timely provision for yourself and your friends', Sarsfield refused to join in the conspiracy and also denied that there was any match intended between his family and Andrew's. He did, however, send Carew an interesting pedigree and account of the Barrett family in Elizabethan times. According to this James *riabhach* (father of Katherine) was son of James *liath* son of James 'Bulleragh' Barrett. (This last-named may be the 'James Bollerye' who in 1488 granted Bwyfeston to John, son of the Earl of Desmond.) The other sons of James Bulleragh were Richard and William. William's son, Oliverus, got possession of Ballincollig castle, though with opposition from John fitz Richard (said to be illegitimate). To settle the dispute he handed over the castle to Sir John Perrot, Lord President of Munster, until the whole question should be resolved. But Perrot refused to hand back the castle, whereupon Oliverus went into rebellion with James Fitzmaurice and was slain in rebellion. His brother, Edmond, then agreed that John fitz Richard might be Barrett but a younger brother, Beany (or Beny), murdered both John and Edmond fitz Richard (for which murders he was executed; he may have been the 'Bároideach' put to death by Drury, President of Munster, in 1576, as related by *A.F.M.*). So Edmond fitz William became chieftain, succeeded by his son, William.

Whether this account and the pedigree were accurate or not, the takeover bid failed and in 1614 Andrew Barrett of Ballincollig, then M.P. for Co. Cork, got letters patent from James I for all his estates in Co. Cork. In the same year an Act of Attainder was being drawn up by which the crown could confiscate the property of Donal O Sullivan Bear, Connor O Driscoll, William Barrett of Ballincollig 'and all other the natives of Ireland now fugitives abroad'. Despite this William Barrett must have retained a legal claim to Ballincollig. He redeemed the original mortgage and in 1619 mortgaged it again to Edmond Coppinger (son of Robert) who later transferred his mortgage to Sir Walter Coppinger of Cloghane. In 1630 William and his son Edmond released all their claims to Sir Walter whose family held Ballincollig thereafter. Andrew made his residence at Castlemore near Mourne Abbey though his lands included Maglin, Corbally (beg) and Grenagh with rents from Inishcarra etc. His eldest son, James, was knighted in Dublin in 1622 and married the daughter of Sir Dominic Sarsfield (as Carew had predicted). Their son, Andrew Barrett of Castlemore, was also knighted and became M.P. for Cork city in 1639. It was said that Sir Andrew Barrett, his cousin Viscount Kilmallock and Sir Edmund Fitzgerald of Imokilly were '... the only persons of the Romish party who continued loyal to the Crown in the county Cork during the 1641 rebellion.' Accordingly Andrew's estates were not forfeited; in the Book of Survey and Distribution he was described as 'Protestant'.

There were, of course, several junior branches of the name. Inquisitions taken during the first thirty years of the 17th century show Barrett families all over Inishcarra parish – at Currabeha, Gurteen (James *riabhach*), Ballyshoneen (two families), and Courticullynane (this name is no longer there) as well as Ballinguilly in Kilnaglory parish. James óg Barrett, son and heir of James fitz Thomas fitz Richard Barrett was pardoned in 1621 for alienating without licence the lands of Curraheen (par. Inishkenny) to John Kent in 1605. In 1616 a general pardon was granted to William Barrett of Malaculocke – a townland near Ballincollig, perhaps the modern Greenfield. Unlike Andrew most of these were involved in the 1641 rebellion – like the Ensign Barrett who was taken prisoner after the battle of Knocknanuss in 1647 – and so the following were outlawed in 1643:

Edmond Barrett, Ballymacoo.
John fitz William Barrett, Ballinguilly.

James Barrett, Gurteen.
James Oge and Richard Barrett, Curraleigh.
John and William Barrett, Ballyanley.
John and Redmond Barrett, Ballyshoneen.
Richard Barrett, Faha.
William Barrett, Knockane (-tindarry).
John and William Barrett, Pluckanes.
Richard Barrett, Ballycraheen.
John (Esq.) and Thomas Barrett (Gent.), Dunmanus.

When the rebellion was over, all of these had their lands confiscated. The Book of Survey and Distribution shows that Andrew's son (William) of Castlemore was the only remaining Barrett landowner. According to the Census of 1659 John Barrett was still a 'titulado' or person of note in Faha, James in Pluckanes and Robert in Lyradane (par. Grenagh), but they were no longer landowners. (In 1702 John Barrett was a tenant in Placus and Richard Barrett in Monaparson.) Andrew and John Barrett were living in Co. Clare. Oddly enough, Barrett does not appear among the principal Irish names in the barony of Barrett's — or anywhere else except in Cork city and Liberties which had 19 families.

Nicholas Colthurst of Ballyanley purchased much of the former Barrett land around Inishcarra for £100. The Colthurst family built a court at Ballyanley and later a large mansion at Ardrum before removing to Blarney Castle. Some Barretts must have remained in the area as substantial tenants since wills of Thomas Barrett, Currabeha and Edmond Barrett, Curraleigh, both farmers, were registered in 1766 and 1783 respectively. Edmond and William Barrett of Inishcarra conformed to the Protestant religion in 1753. Even up to the present day Inishcarra and Donoughmore graveyards remain the principal burial-grounds of Barrett families.

After Sir Andrew Barrett died, his widow married Hayward St. Leger who resided at Castlemore and was M.P. for Mallow in 1661. Andrew's only son and heir, William, was made a baronet in 1665 and died, childless, seven years later. In his will Sir William Barrett left his entailed estates to his second cousin, John Barrett, and the remainder to his mother's brother-in-law, John St. Leger, who was also appointed John Barrett's guardian. St. Leger spotted a flaw in the will, namely that the estate had never been entailed and promptly seized the lot for himself. A complicated law suit followed in 1677-8 until eventually John Barrett recovered part of the family property and became M.P. for Mallow in King James II's parliament. As Colonel John Barrett he raised a regiment of foot for King James, and his estates, amounting to 11,570 acres, were confiscated as a result. After Marlborough's capture of Cork in 1690, Col. Barrett was taken prisoner and while awaiting deportation to France had a narrow escape from death following an explosion on the man-of-war *Breda* in Cork harbour. He was specially excluded from the benefits of the Treaty of Limerick, and his lands were sold in 1702 at Chichester House to Nicholas Colthurst, Sir John Meade and others. John Barrett later became Colonel of the *Gardes du Roi Jacques* and was, like Patrick Sarsfield, killed at the battle of Landen in 1693 while boldly leading his regiment who were first to breach the enemy lines.

Thus fell the last great Barrett landowner of the barony that bore his name. John's daughter, Elinor, married John Creagh of Killowen, ancestor of the Creaghs of Ballyandrew, Doneraile. The family residence of Castlemore soon became a picturesque ruin.

Others of the name outlawed for supporting King James were Andrew and Edmund mac Shane Barrett of Castlemore, Edmund, John, James and Richard, the Barretts 'Reagh' of Placus (Greenhill), James of Curraghanearla, Coomeleigh of Ballyanley, James of Gurteen, James of Carhue, William, Edmund, Andrew and Richard of Turlagh (? Curra-leigh). Most of these were outlawed for treason 'beyond the seas' — perhaps in Colonel John Barrett's regiment. (William Barrett, born in Cork city, was a captain in the Spanish service in 1712.) James of Curraghanearla (par. Aghinagh) claimed his lands in 1694 under the articles of Limerick but his claim was rejected. Successful claimants in 1699 were John of Placus, James of Carrigduff, Edmond of Corbally-more and Richard of Glanballycullen.

The quartermaster and one of the ensigns in Col. John Barrett's regiment were both named Edmund Barrett. It may have been one of these who became tenant of a large tract of land at Toames near Macroom in the early 18th century. His son was known as Edmond 'Leigh', showing a connection with the Barretts of Ballincollig. In the 19th century the then representative of the family, John Barrett, married a daughter of Richard O Donovan of O Donovan's Cove. Windele noted that the chief representative of the name in his day was Edward Barrett of Carrigboy (par. Kilmichael).

The use of hair-colour adjectives to distinguish Barrett families is noticeable from an early period — 'fionn', 'de rede', 'glas', 'leigh', etc. The Ballincollig family was sometimes called 'Mac William' in the 16th century due to the prevalence of the name William. 'Reagh' or *riabhach* (swarthy) was used in the 16th and 17th centuries, and even in the 18th, Seán Ó Tuama wrote a poem in praise of the Barróideacha Riabhacha — Éamonn, Séamus, Seághan, Risteárd and Rudhraighe, no doubt the same family (of Placus) who were outlawed Jacobites in 1690.

(DE) BARRY

DE BARRA

A small island off the coast of Glamorgan in south Wales was the site of an ancient church dedicated to St. Barruc, and it was obviously this saint's name, plus the Norse suffix -ey (island), that caused it to be named Barry. The island is now connected with the mainland where the modern seaport of Barry has grown up, seven miles south-west of Cardiff. It was this place, so Giraldus Cambrensis tells us, which gave name to the family of de Barry.

But the castle of William de Barri (father of Giraldus, born c. 1110) was not at Barry but further west, at Manorbier in Dyfed (Pembrokeshire). William married Angharad, daughter of Nesta and of Gerald of Windsor (see FITZGERALD). Accordingly his family was closely related to the Geraldines and aided them in the invasion of Ireland. William's son and successor was named Philip while a younger son was Gerald, Archdeacon of Brecon, better known as Giraldus Cambrensis, the historian, inter alia, of the Norman invasion of Ireland. Another son, Robert, was among the little band of Norman knights who effected the first landing at Bannow Bay in May 1169. He took a prominent part in the assault on Wexford shortly afterwards, and in the taking of Limerick in the following year.

About the year 1180 Philip de Barri received from his uncle Robert Fitzstephen (the grantee of the eastern portion of the 'Kingdom of Cork') a sub-infeudation of three cantreds — Olethan, Muskerry-Donegan and Killyde. Olethan, the former Uí Liatháin tribeland, is now known as Barrymore; Muskerry-Donegan approximates to Orrery and Kilmore while Killyde was in the south of the present Co. Limerick. (In 1282 John fitz Thomas held a cantred of John de Barry at 'Killyde Hy Connil'.) In 1183 Philip crossed to Ireland to relieve his uncle who, following the slaying of Milo de Cogan, was besieged in Cork. After a short stay in Ireland he returned to Manorbier where he died in 1200, leaving a son, William, to succeed him. Another son, Robert, had been killed near Lismore c. 1185. He must be the Roibeard Droma Fínghin placed (incorrectly) in the Barry pedigrees in An Leabhar Muimhneach. Next in line was David — Dáibhidh Mór in the genealogies. By this time the Barrys had established manors at Buttevant and at Carrigtwohill, as in 1234 King Henry III granted a fair and market at Buttevant and a market at Carrigtwohill to David de Barry. Another stronghold built in this century was Castlelyons, known as Castrum Olethan or Caisleán Ó Liatháin — the castle of Uí Liatháin. Yet another, one of the largest

LISCARROLL CASTLE *(O'Callaghan Newenham, 1826)*

castles in Ireland, was sited at Liscarroll.

It must have been in David Mór's era that the Barrys obtained lands in Connacht as a reward for their part in the conquest of that province. Although their period of tenure there was short they left their mark in the name *Caisleán an Bharraigh* (Castlebar). In 1235 David enlarged the revenues of Ballybeg Abbey, about the same time as he was knighted. David Mór must also have been the Barry who, according to the *Annals of the Four Masters*, founded a friary in Buttevant in 1251 and chose a burial place for his family in the choir, opposite the great altar.

Ten years later he was buried there, being succeeded by his son David Óg, who was Justiciar of Ireland in 1267. This David died about 1278 and was also buried in Buttevant friary. His son, David III (*Dáibhidh an bhuille mhóir* in the genealogies), was his heir but the lordship seems to have been taken by a relative, Sir John de Barry, who was knighted in 1283. Two legal actions resulted in the restoration by Sir John to David fitz David de Barry of the manor of the castle of Olethan (Castlelyons), and the manors of Buttevant, Liscarroll and 'Ardnogrothan.' (Yet, it was under the protection of this John, according to Archdall, that the Carmelite friary of Castlelyons was founded in 1307.) John had also alienated lands in Gortroe parish – Rathcobane to William de Barry and Killamurren to Nicholas de Barry of Ely. (This latter place was Ely O Carroll where the Barry's held lands for a time before being driven out by the O Carrolls.) All these dealings came to light in 1358 when a series of royal writs was issued to clear up the legal tangle. Apparently at that stage the lands in question had been taken into the king's hands due to alienations without licence. However, it was proved that at the time of the alienations the lands were not held of the king *in capite* but of Maurice de Carew (who was regarded as the heir to Fitzstephen's moiety of the Kingdom of Cork) and so did not require a licence to alienate. Accordingly the Barrys got their lands back, the then heir being yet another David (probably *Dáibhidh Loscanach*). It was made clear that the Barrys had become tenants *in capite* of the king in 1336, in which year they received a quitclaim from the Carews.

In 1359 Gerald de Barry was consecrated bishop of Cork and held the see until his death at the age of 90, in 1393. His many kinsmen were given to more warlike pursuits, and during the 14th and 15th centuries, no doubt because of the lack of strong government, they were involved in frequent minor wars with neighbours of both Gaelic and Norman extraction. In 1306 David O Keeffe was slain (treacherously, the annals say) by William *Súgach* de Barry and by Martel. Three years later, the Geraldines, Powers, Barrys etc., were all locked in conflict over the inheritance of Agnes de Valence, so that the king had to intervene. In 1317 war broke out between the Barrys and the Cogans, and the Barrys laid waste the Cogan lands as far as Barnahely. Later in the same year, at the instance of John de Barry, the king pardoned William fitz David de Barry, Thomas fitz Stephen de Barry, William fitz Thomas de Barry,

Robert fitz Thomas de Barry, and Robert fitz Stephen de Barry for their infraction of the peace. This shows that there were already many groups and sub-groups of Barrys in Co. Cork; we know that by 1300 they were established at such places as Caherduggan, Kilbrin and Mogeely.

In 1320 they joined in an internal feud involving the O Donegans (the former proprietors of Orrery and Kilmore) and slew Maigiu O Donegan. In an inter-Norman feud nine years later the Roches and Barrys slew about 140 of the Keatings, Hodnetts and Condons, while in 1331 the Mac Carthys and O Briens were plundering the Barrys, Cogans and Roches, with, it was said, the assent of the Earl of Desmond. The year 1344 saw a serious internal dispute sunder the Barrys when Adam de Barry of Rathcormack (ancestor of the Mac Adam Barrys of that place) refused to recognize David fitz David de Barry of Castlelyons as his lord. Severely harassed by David, Adam went into open rebellion and accompanied by John de Barry of Dungourney, William of Carryugynach (? Carrigogna), Odo of Conna and a large contingent of Condons, first attacked and burned Rathcormack, then attacked Castlelyons itself and burnt the hamlet of Lisnagar nearby. In this they were aided and abetted by Maurice, Earl of Desmond who, in the year following, brought a sizeable Norman-Irish army to attack the Barrys and Cogans, killing, among others, two knights, Robert de Barry and Philip Prendergast.

In 1374 the Barrys killed Cormac Mac Carthy, Lord of Muskerry, in Cork city. Three years later, the Condons imprisoned David de Barry, and the government held two of the Condons as hostages until he should be released. This David, who died in 1392, was father of John (*Seán Ciotach*) who married the Earl of Desmond's daughter. John is probably the Barrach Mór mentioned in the annals as having slain Domhnall Ó Briain, crown prince of Thomond – though it could also have been Philip who, in 1402, as Lord of Olethan and Muscrydonegan, agreed not to levy exactions on the bishop of Cloyne's manor of Kilmaclenine. Later lords did not descend from Philip, however.

John died in 1420. Next in line came William, then John (*Seán bacach*) who was slain by the Mac Carthys of Duhallow where he had gone on a predatory excursion on Christmas day, 1486. Seán was succeeded by his sons, Thomas and William, the second of whom was slain in 1500 by his brother David Barry, Archdeacon of Cork. In retaliation, David was killed by Thomas de Barry and the O Callaghans, and the Earl of Desmond caused his body to be disinterred and burnt to ashes. Perhaps it was as a result of this feud that Domhnall Ó Ceallacháin (see Ó CEALLACHÁIN) made the Barrys' lands the target for so many of his mid-16th century *creachs*. According to his eulogy, he raided Rathcobane, Castlelyons, Rathcormack, Kildinan, Ballyvodock, Rathbarry, Ballincurrig, Dunkettle, Kilcurfin, Leamlara, Ballyclogh, Bruhenny and Buttevant.

John, son of William, succeeded to the title, but after his death it reverted to (or was taken by) William's brother, Seán Riabhach. Yet John, son of William, may have had issue. The du Barry or Dubarry family of the south-west of France claim that they are descended from a son of John, 'Noble Jean du Barry', who emigrated to France and settled in the Gascogne where he married Dauphine de Bédat of an ancient noble family in 1514.

At home, Seán Riabhach's three sons, John, Edmond and James, all died without male issue. James, 16th Baron Barrymore, left an only daughter who married Richard, Lord Power. Before his death in 1558 James conveyed his manors of Carrigtwohill (Barryscourt), Castlelyons, Buttevant and Liscarroll to James fitz Richard Barry Roe, Lord of Ibane, a more distant cousin than many in Barrymore, but one who appeared strong and unscrupulous enough to thrust aside the Power interest. Edmond Mór Barry of Rathcobane, a great-grandson of Seán Ciotach and probably the closest male relative of James of Barrymore, was induced to assign his interest in the lordship to James Barry Roe. (A copy of this deed of indenture was produced in a Cork court in 1617 by William fitz Robert fitz Edmond Barry, harper.)

A suit commenced by Lord Power, in his wife's name, against David, son of James Barry Roe, was unsuccessful, and the Queen, to avoid further contention, arranged a marriage between David and Lord Power's daughter. James was now recognized by officialdom as Lord Barrymore, but he had taken on the lordship at a most turbulent time, the period of the two Desmond rebellions. As a precautionary measure against possible confiscation, he alienated all his lands in Barrymore, Orrery and Barryroe to Nicholas Walsh, John Bayer and Christopher Arthur, trustees who must have been considered politically secure while James himself was not. He was reprimanded for allowing the Earl of Desmond free passage through his country to sack the town of Youghal, even though the passage meant destruction for all the villages, farmhouses and cornfields in the invaders' path, but since the English had a similar 'scorched earth' policy he was reluctant to call on their assistance. In 1580 after Lord Justice Pelham had described him as 'the most obstinate and malicious' of the noblemen who were succouring the rebels, James was imprisoned in Dublin Castle where he died the following year.

His eldest son, Richard, being deaf and dumb, his second son, David, took the lordship of Barrymore, while his third son, William, got the Barryroe estates. When his father was imprisoned David burned Barryscourt castle, thus forestalling Sir Walter Raleigh who had a commission to seize Barryscourt. David then became one of the Earl of Desmond's chief lieutenants. Aided by Mac Sweeney, he put the garrison of Bantry to the sword and in 1582 defeated and killed many of the Roches. But after a quarrel with the seneschal of Imokilly he was surprised and defeated by General Zouch at his encampment at Dromfineen on the banks of the Blackwater (where one of the first Barrys, Roibeard Droma Fínghin, met his death in 1185). After this, David submitted and received a pardon. His brother, John, was one of the last to desert the Earl and seek a pardon. In all, fifteen of the Barrys were pardoned, including those of Barryroe, Rahanisky, Poulacurry, Bruhenny (Churchtown), Ballyclogh, Ballinacurra, Little Island and Dungourney. But John Moyle Barry of Ballygoran, whose son James was slain in the rebellion, was attainted in 1588, and his lands were granted to the Earl of Kildare in 1609. Edward Barry of Bregoge was also attainted.

By Elizabethan times, as the Fiants show, Barry families bearing various nicknames were to be found all over Barrymore — Dungourney (*maol*), Carrigtwohill (*fionn*), Ballyrichard near Carrigtwohill (Richard *riabhach*), Garrane (*doicheallach*), Poulacurry, Scartbarry, Ballyspillane, Ballymacsliney, Leamlara, Courtstown, etc. According to a manuscript source at Lambeth, Lord Barry's own estates *circa* 1600 amounted to 392 ploughlands centred around Barryscourt, Inchinabacky, Castlelyons, Buttevant, Liscarroll, Timoleague, Rathbarry and Lislee. In 1588 David Barry repaired his principal residence of Barryscourt, inscribing his initials — together with those of his wife, Ellen Roche — on the chimney-piece. He put an identical inscription on the chimney-piece of Timoleague castle.

Fearing to put his broad acres at risk, David refused to join Hugh O Neill's rebellion when it spread to Munster in 1598. Instead, he garrisoned the castles of Barrymore and Orrery — Buttevant, Annagh, Castlelyons, Robertstown, Dungourney and Barryscourt. When O Neill marched into Munster early in 1600 he spoiled the whole of Barrymore in an effort to force the Barrys into his camp. But his action had the opposite effect of putting Lord Barry and his brother John among the active supporters of the crown both before and after the battle of Kinsale.

David did remain a Catholic until his death in 1617; he and Lord Roche were, in 1611, regarded as the chief supporters of priests and Jesuits in Munster. But as his elder son (David) had predeceased him, his grandson and heir (another David) as a ward of chancery was brought up a Protestant. Having come under the control of the Earl of Cork, young David at the age of 16 was married to the Earl's daughter, Alice, and for his attachment to the Protestant religion was created Earl of Barrymore in 1627. So when the rebellion of 1641 broke out, far from supporting it he joined his brother-in-law, Lord Dungarvan, in attacking the castle of the rebel Condons at Ballymacpatrick (Careysville) where sixty men and a hundred women and children were slain, including Patrick Condon's wife who was David Barry's own grand-aunt. David also took Cloghleigh castle near Kilworth. At the battle of Liscarroll in 1642 he commanded his own troop of horse, but shortly after this he died unexpectedly at Castlelyons and was buried in the Earl of Cork's family tomb at Youghal.

As it happened, one of the leaders of the Irish army at the battle of Liscarroll was General Garrett Barry 'who had long served under the

King of Spain and was reputed to be a good old soldier.' To avoid a dispute among the great lords who went into rebellion in 1641 he was chosen as supreme commander of the army in Munster. When John Barry of Liscarroll received a commission from the King of Spain in 1636 as colonel of an Irish regiment to be newly recruited, this Capt. Gerald (Garrett) Barry of his Spanish Majesty's Council of War was commissioned as major of the regiment — a regiment which never came into existence. Later, Colonel Garrett Barry seems to have acted as informant to the Marquis of Ormond concerning the Confederation of Kilkenny. At that Confederation one of Rinuccini's strongest supporters was Robert Barry, bishop of Cork, son of David Barry of Britway. He was buried at Nantes in 1662.

Although few, if any, of the Barrys of Barrymore were outlawed in 1643 — an indication that they were following where Lord Barry led — in 1657 many were listed as 'forfeiting proprietors' perhaps solely on account of their religion. Over half of the fifty-two 'forfeiting proprietors' in Barrymore were Barrys. They included the Barrys of Dungourney, Leamlara, Garranekinnefeake and Great Island. Some did lose their lands and a few were transplanted to Co. Clare but many others retained and even increased their estates, particularly so, of course, the Earl of Barrymore himself.

The history of the Barrymores henceforth followed the usual pattern of the Irish landed gentry. They supported King William in the late 17th century, became army officers and M.P.s and spent much of their time in England. Their principal residence was the renovated mansion of Castlelyons until its accidental destruction by fire in 1771. Successive earls mortgaged and sold the greater part of the estates. In 1791, Richard, Earl of Barrymore, in order to clear debts amounting to £130,000, disposed of about a dozen townlands in his manor of Castlelyons and about fifty in Barryscourt, as well as his rights to fairs, markets, and advowsons in Shandon, Barryscourt, Buttevant, Timoleague and Rathbarry. Henry, the eighth and last earl, died in 1823 without issue and was buried in Paris. His estates had already been sold in 1807. There were several claimants for the viscounty of Buttevant but all were unsuccessful. The Smith-Barrys of Foaty were the nearest relatives of the deceased earl and the Lord Barrymore of this century was of that family, a new barony of Barrymore having been created in 1902. Foaty House and its lands were purchased by University College, Cork, in 1975.

Junior branches in Barrymore

Throughout east Cork various offshoots of the Barry family continued to flourish, mainly as tenant-farmers. Though differing in religion, language and outlook from the Earls of Barrymore, many of them could trace their ancestry to the main Barry line of the 16th century, or even earlier. The Barrys of Dungourney were descended from a younger son of a Lord Barry. His name was Robert and in 1315 he was seized of the castle of Dungourney. Garrett Barry of Dungourney forfeited most of Dungourney parish after 1641, but much of it went to John Barry of nearby Walshtown. The estate eventually came — by dubious methods, according to tradition — into the possession of the Brodericks of Bally-annan (later Lords Midleton). John Barry of Walshtownmore was out-lawed in 1690. The Barrys of Couragh (in the same parish) are believed to have been descendants of the Barrys of Dungourney castle. The oldest headstone in Dungourney (Edmond Barry, 1751) belongs to this family. Edmond was probably the Éamonn de Barra whose death was lamented by the poet Éamonn de Bhál.

The Standish Barrys of Leamlara were another ancient branch who in the 14th century had a moated castle there. Garrott mac Shane *láidir* Barry of Leamlara was a juror at an inquisition in 1604. His lands were confiscated in Cromwellian times and were given to John Barry and Dr. Richard Cogan. More fortunate in this respect were the Mac Adam Barrys of Lisnagar, Rathcormack, another branch of great antiquity. Redmond Barry of Rathcormack managed to retain his estates. Though outlawed in 1690, James Barry of Rathcormack, be-cause he was a Protestant and living in England at the time, had his outlawry reversed.

The FitzJames Barrys of Annagh (par. Churchtown) were descended from Nicholas Barry, a younger son of William *Maol*, first Lord of Ibawne. Their castle of Annagh figured prominently in the war of 1641. FitzJames Barry of Annagh was outlawed for high treason beyond the seas in 1691. Another Barry castle was Ballyclogh near Mallow. John Barry, known as Mac Robinson or Mac Robston, forfeited his estate after 1641. As compensation he was decreed extensive lands in Clare and Galway while Ballyclogh was acquired by Sir Nicholas Purdon. John Barry alias Mac Robitowne, gent., of Mallow, was outlawed in 1690.

A son of Seán Ciotach (David) was ancestor of the Barrys of Rath-barry (later Garranekinnefeake) while another son was ancestor of the Barrys of Ballinaltig (par. Ballyclogh). James Barry (gent.) of Ballinaltig conformed to the Protestant religion in 1763.

The Barrys of Dundullerick and Rahanisky were descended from David fitz David Barry Roe, who should have been Lord of Ibawne after the death of his two elder brothers, but was ousted by his cousin, James fitz Richard. As a 'peace-offering' James gave David Rahanisky castle with 10,000 acres. In 1614 Richard (son of David) died in possession of Robertstown or Ballyrobert castle (par. Castlelyons) and Rahanisky castle as well as Ballymore and other lands on the Great Island. All these estates were confiscated by the Cromwellians, the then owner, Richard Barry, being offered recompense in Connacht but choosing instead to follow the fortunes of the Royalist cause overseas. For this service, his estates were restored by King Charles II only to be con-fiscated once more in 1690. (Another to lose his estate at this time was Edmond Barry; his lands in the parishes of Ballydeloher and

Killaspugmullane were sold at Chichester House in 1702.) The second son of David of Barryroe, Redmond *Buidhe* Barry, was ancestor of the Barrys of Dundullerick. Redmond's grandson, Edmund, built Dundullerick House which remained the family residence down to modern times.

One gets the impression that the various branches of the Barrys in east Cork, more so than any other family in the county, maintained during the 18th and 19th century a semblance of the former 'clan system'. Even though the majority were tenant farmers they appear to have been more substantial and independent than most, possibly due to faintly traceable links with the still powerful Earls of Barrymore. Many poems were written by Seán na Ráithíneach Ó Murchadha and his fellow-poets of the 18th century eulogizing such people as Standish Barry of Leamlara, Col. Redmond (Mac Adam) Barry of Lisnagar and another branch of the Mac Adam Barrys at Ballynaglogh (Carraig na bhFear) where William Mac Redmond Barry had six or seven stalwart sons, several of whom took part in a celebrated hurling match between Cork and Tipperary at Gleann na nGall near Buttevant in 1741.

It is noticeable too that the Barrys left a deeper imprint on the place-names of Co. Cork than any other family, Gaelic or Norman. Great Island in Cork harbour was formerly *Inis Mór* and in the 14th century any Barrys there were merely tenants of the manor of Inchiquin. But spreading rapidly, they built the castle of Ballymacshaneroe, probably Walterstown as well, and held Belvelly too in the early 16th century. All these lands were forfeited after 1641 but not before the island's name had been changed to *Oileán Mór an Bharraigh*.

Two of the county's baronies are Barrymore and (Ibane and) Barryroe, each with a parish called Rathbarry (The Barrymore one is now Garranekinnefeake.) Another Rathbarry is a townland in the parish of Castlelyons. Ballinvarrig (*Baile an Bharraigh*) is the name of four townlands — in the parishes of Whitechurch, Gortroe, Clonpriest and Tracton — as well as of a former one in Tisaxon. Barryscourt is in Carrigtwohill parish; Barryshall and Killavarrig are in Timoleague. There are two townlands called Knockbarry in Buttevant and Liscarroll. Garraunawarrig (*Garrán an Bharraigh*) is in the parish of Clonfert (Duhallow) and Portavarrig in Templebodan. Crossbarry (*Crois an Bharraigh*) and Barry's Head are in the Barry Óg territory of Kinalea while farther west are Barry's Point, Barry's Cove and Mount Barry. The parish of Bregoge in north Cork has Dunbarry; there was in the 17th century a Dunebarry in Templenacarriga (Barrymore) and a Farranwarrig in the parish of Aglish in Muskerry. We have even a 20th century example in 'Barry's Path' (in Gougane Barra State Park) which commemorates the escape of Commdt.-Gen. Tom Barry's I.R.A. column from encirclement by British forces in 1921.

Barry Roe *(An Barrach Rua)*

Although physically separated by a large tract of Co. Cork, the Barrys Mór never lost their connection with the branch which settled in Uí Badhamhna. This settlement came about through Henry Butler, whose castle of Timoleague was captured by Domhnall Mac Carthy in 1219. Henry's daughter, Annabel, married David de Barry (i.e. Dáibhidh Mór, who died in 1261) and as a marriage-portion Henry granted to David the castle of Timoleague with the half-cantred of Obatheme (*Uí Badhamhna* or Ibane) and the half-cantred of Rosyletir (*Ros Ailithir* or Rosscarbery). He also conveyed to David the land which he (Henry) held of Geoffrey fitz Odo — seemingly the ancestor of the Hodnetts of Courtmacsherry (*Cúirt Mhic Shéafraidh*, 'court of the son of Geoffrey'). That land was probably Lislee. Witnesses to this agreement included Lord Odo de Barry, Philip son of Lord William de Barry and Robert de Barry.

Furthermore, in 1229 agreement was reached between the bishop of Ross and David de Barry in regard to the boundaries of their respective properties. The bishop granted David the *villae* of Timoleague, Rathynunchy (? Rathbarry), Munisege and Killude, 17 carucates for which an annual rent was payable to the bishop. When, in 1260, the bishop of Ross brought ejectment proceedings against some landholders in his diocese, he called David de Barry to give evidence on his behalf. Lands in Ibane (as well as in Barrymore and Muskerry) were held in 1301 by John de Barry — presumably the Sir John who for a time assumed the lordship.

As yet there had been no divergence from the main line but this occurred shortly afterwards in the time of David (II), lord of Barrymore. David's younger son, William *Maol* (the bald), married Margaret, eldest daughter of Lord Courcy of Ringrone, and settled in Ibane which then became a separate lordship. In 1355 the manors of Rath (i.e. Rathbarry), Timoleague and Lislee belonging to William fitz David de Barry, knight, which had been taken into the king's hand because of unlicensed alienations, were released when it was discovered that Rath and Timoleague were held of the bishop of Ross and Lislee of Robert fitz John of Rynnanylan (apparently a Hodnett of Courtmacsherry). In 1372 William and Margaret got one fourth part of the inheritance of Milo de Courcy (Margaret's brother) who had died without issue. Margaret herself died in the following year and was buried in the friary of Timoleague, 'founded' (probably renovated) by her husband. Timoleague, with its castle, friary and sheltered seaport, was for long the headquarters of the Barry Roes. William Maol was succeeded by William 'Roche' (i.e. *Ruadh* or Roe) whose tenants in Obahoun (Uí Badhamhna) and Drommanagh were 'for the greater part destroyed' in 1385. He must have died without issue as it is from Laurence (presumably his brother) that the lords of Ibane descend. Laurence may also have been red-haired and it must be from this generation that the soubriquet *an Barrach Rua* comes.

In the *Annals of the Four Masters*, A.D. 1507, we read that: 'Barry Roe, i.e. James son of James, went on a pilgrimage to Spain, attended by many chiefs of his people; and after having performed their pilgrimage they embarked on board a ship to return home, but no further account, as to whether they survived or perished, was ever received.'

Another unusual maritime incident occurred in 1537, when the citizens of Cork, incensed by the harassment of Mac Carthy Riabhach, declared war on that chieftain and set off in their galleys to invade his lands. Unfortunately, they oversailed their mark, and plundered in error the village of Carrigeen in Lislee parish. Lord Barry Roe spent several years vainly seeking compensation for the damage done.

The Barry Roes intermarried with the great Norman and Gaelic families of that era — the Mac Carthys, O Briens of Thomond, Earls of Kildare, O Driscoll of Corca Laoighdhe. In the early 16th century, James Barry Roe married Ellen daughter of Cormac Mac Carthy of Muskerry, by whom he had a son, Richard. Some years later, however, the marriage was declared null and void on the grounds that James had previously been betrothed to Ellen, daughter of Mac Carthy Riabhach, a cousin of the other Ellen. James then married Ellen Riabhach and by her had two sons, James who died without issue and David (*Donn*) who succeeded to the lordship but whose four sons met with opposition. The Richard who had been declared illegitimate because of the nullity of his father's first marriage had been granted the extensive manor of Rathbarry (now Castlefreke). He was known as Richard of the Rath and married a Kildare Geraldine. His son, James, married a daughter of Mac Carthy Riabhach, so strengthening his claim to the lordship of all Barryroe. It is said that after he had killed Redmond (eldest son of David Donn) and his brother, the remaining two sons fled to the protection of the Earl of Desmond, leaving the spoils to James fitz Richard. The spoils turned out to be greater than were expected, since James became not only lord of Barryroe but also of Barrymore, as above related.

James' son, David, succeeded him in Barrymore, while another son, William, became lord of Barryroe until his death in 1584. William had a son, James Barry of Lislee. (Rathbarry, Timoleague and Lislee were the three chief manors in Barryroe.) James died in 1640 and his son, William Barry of Lislee, had his estates confiscated for his part in the 1641 rebellion. John óg Barry was another prominent confederate, being one of the leaders of the assault on Rathbarry Castle (then held by Arthur Freke) in 1642. William's son, David, went to live with his uncle, Charles Mac Carthy of Castlemore, whom he succeeded in 1674. Capt. David Barry of Lislee was outlawed in 1691 'for high treason beyond the seas' as were also Colonel John Barry and his sons of Derryloane (Tullyneasky).

In 1825 before the House of Lords at Westminster, the Viscounty of Buttevant was claimed by James Redmond Barry of Donaghmore (near Lislee) on the grounds that he was descended from William who forfeited Lislee after 1641, but he failed to prove his descent. James, who was born at Mount Barry in 1789, was a noted philanthropist. He is especially remembered for his construction of a model village in Glandore and for his interest in Irish fisheries.

Barry Óg

For many centuries the name Barry Óg was associated with the barony of Kinalea (*Cineál Aodha*) between Cork Harbour and Kinsale. Philip de Barry (*Pilib an airgid*) was the founder of the line — according to the Irish genealogies which make him a younger son of William (Barry Mór) and so a brother of the first David. This was probably the Philip who in 1237 received a pardon for his part in the rebellion of Richard, Earl Marshal and in 1240 a grant of Innishannon with the right to hold a fair there.

But this grant cannot have been the basis of the Barry Óg tenure since we know that as early as 1222, two Cistercian abbots were inspecting the site where Odo de Barry wished to found a monastery and that in 1224 the monastery of Tracton was completed and staffed with monks from Alba Landa in Wales. Odo was probably a brother of Philip (and of David Mór) and was married to Hilary de Cogan. He does not appear to have had any children but his stepdaughter married Philip's son, another Odo de Barry. Odo's son, Philip, is mentioned as holding the lands of Kenaleth (Kinalea) from the heirs of John de Curcy in 1297, the de Courcys being heirs of Milo de Cogan. Philip was also involved in a lawsuit with the abbot of Albo Tractu (Tracton) in 1295. His chief residence at the time must have been in Innishannon as in the same year Philip was charged with pardoning Domhnall óg Mac Carthy who had committed many robberies in Kinalea and with publicly proclaiming the fact in his town of Innishannon after receiving a fine of twenty cows from Domhnall. He managed to get an acquittal.

After Philip, according to the genealogies, came Seán (John), and then William, described as *Uilliam Cnuic an Bhile* which probably indicates that he was killed at Knockavilla in the north-western marches of his territory. This borderland was the scene of conflict with the Mac Carthys and others and by the 15th century the Mac Carthys and their followers (e.g. the Murphys who gave their name to Ballymurphy) had taken over much — though not all — of Knockavilla parish. Crossbarry (*Crois an Bharraigh*) owes its name to the Barrys. 'William de Barry of Raweram, Esq.' was summoned to attend the Justiciar in his expedition to Scotland in 1335. Raweram is probably Ringcurran (now the site of Charles Fort) which from then became the chief castle of Barry Óg.

William's son was Philip whose *floreat* was in the late 14th century. He is the Philip son of William de Barry who in 1372 paid rent to Milo de Courcy of Ringrone not only for the cantred of Kinalea but for Kinalmeaky and Ifflanloe as well. After Philip came Odo fitz Philip de Barry of Ryncorran who was pardoned in 1415 for a breach of the peace, but a more serious breach must have followed as a result of which either Odo or his son Philip incurred attainder. In the mid-15th century the loyal inhabitants of Cork complained that although 'the King's majesty hath the lands of the late Young Barry by forfeiture, the yearly revenue whereof, besides two rivers and creeks, and all other casualties, is one thousand eight hundred pounds sterling,' yet Barry was there 'upon the King's portion, paying his Grace never a penny of rent.'

At this period also the Barrys were being hard-pressed by the Mac Carthys of Muskerry at the Knockavilla end and by Mac Carthy Riabhach who was directly across the river from Innishannon. In 1476 the Barrys built the castle of Dundanier ('Downdaniel') at the point where Kinalea met Carbery and Kinalmeaky. Its picturesque ruin still stands at the confluence of the Bandon and Brinny rivers but it obviously failed to stem the onrush of the Mac Carthys as in the early 16th century Barry Óg was described as a vassal of Mac Carthy Riabhach.

In June 1487 Sir Richard Edgcomb arrived at Kinsale with five ships and Lord Thomas Barry Óg did homage for his barony and took his oath of allegiance. In 1516 Philip Barry of Kinalea sold Ballymychell (Mitchelstown, par. Clontead) to Maurice Roche of Cork. William Barry was Lord of Kinalea in 1531 and Philip Barry Óg ten years later. In 1548 the Sovereign and Council of Kinsale complained to the Lord Deputy of the ravages of pirates, and that 'of late cometh one Richard Colle (pirate) with a pinnace and eighteen or twenty men and married with Barry Oge's aunt, and dwelleth in his castle (Ringcurran) and would suffer none to come to the town but taketh them and spoileth them.'

Sir Thomas (son of Philip) was the Barry Óg during the period of the Desmond wars. Although the very first outbreak occurred in Kinalea when in 1569 James Fitzmaurice and Mac Carthy Mór assaulted and captured Tracton Abbey from the undertakers, Barry Óg seems to have steered clear of the rebellion. Nevertheless, he must somehow have incurred the government's displeasure. In 1586 a commission was instructed to enquire into (1) the attainder of Barry Óg in Henry VI's time (2) whether the lands were not in remainder to Her Majesty since Sir Robert (? Thomas) Barry who had the estate in tail had no issue, and (3) whether he was the seneschal or inheritor of the barony of Kinalea. As a result Dundanier was apparently taken into the queen's land and conferred on Mac Carthy Riabhach whose castle it then became. At the same time the castle and lands of Innishannon (12,000 acres) were allotted to Hugh Worth of Somerton in Somerset. In the east of the barony the St. Legers and Daunts had moved into Tracton and Gortigrenane. A late tradition tells how Daunt's Rock near the mouth of Cork harbour took its name from one of the family who was left there to drown by Philip Barry Óg.

Tracton Abbey, though founded by the Barrys, does not seem to have been of any particular concern to them until the 15th century. It was dedicated to the Blessed Virgin but in a Papal mandate of 1483 the abbot is described as *S. Crucis de Albo Tractu*. An account by Sir Richard Cox (1685) provides a reason for this name '. . . they pretend to have a piece of the Crosse (which Barry Oge at a great price obtained and gave to that Abbey); and this is so firmly believed that on every Holy Thursday vast multitudes from far and near resort to pay their devotion to this relick.' It is noticeable that from 1483 up to the dissolution of the abbey in 1540, all the abbots were Barrys.

Despite the activities of the undertakers, Sir Thomas Barry Óg died in 1592 possessed of Ringcurran Castle, Preghane, Ballycoghlan, Lissanisky, Dunkereen, Garryhankard and Tuocusheen, as well as several other townlands mortgaged to various people, plus rents and services from many parts of Kinalea. His nephew Henry as next heir seized and entered Ringcurran castle. As Henry Barry Óg he received a pardon on 17 January 1601 and does not seem to have taken part in the battle of Kinsale, though his strategically placed castle of Ringcurran was occupied by the Spaniards and then captured by Carew, whose artillery reduced it to a heap of rubble. (Another of the family, David fitz Garrett Barry of Ringcurran, with his wife, children — Garrett, Nicholas, John and David Óg — and retainers, sailed from nearby Kinsale with de Aguila in March, 1602.) Attainted for having been 'slain in rebellion' were Egidius otherwise Eadye Barrie fitz Richard and John Barrie fitz Philip who jointly forfeited the castle, town and lands of Brinny, Tuocusheen, Currentwellshane and Tullymoghilly (part of Ballyhandle). These lands were leased to Francis Blundell in 1613 but the Barrys seem to have recovered them subsequently.

In 1611 Henry Barry Óg gave his brother, John Óg, who had served as a captain in the Spanish army, the castle and lands of Dunbogey. (On the clifftop at Barry's Head in this townland is the site of a castle but there are no remains now left.) John also demised the castle and lands of Ballinaclashet to David fitz James Roche. Henry died in 1617 and was succeeded by his son, William, who died in 1623 at Youghal. William's brother, Philip, was the next heir.

Philip Barry Óg was admitted a freeman of the city of Cork in 1639. Two years previously he had made an affidavit that he was the owner of Ringcurran, Rathmore, Preghane, Tuocusheen, Curra, Fahanalooscane, Knocknanav, Ballinaclashet, Ballinwillin, with chief rents out of many other townlands in Kinalea, including Innishannon. There were, naturally, junior branches of the family throughout the barony. Ballinvarrig in the parish of Tracton must have been an early settlement. Among those attainted for rebellion in 1643 were David, John and Philip Barry of Dunbogey, Philip of Curravohill (par. Nohoval), John and William of

Ballyfeard, David of Ballyginnane (par. Liscleary) and Philip Óg Barry of Ringcurran. All are described as 'gentlemen.'

Philip was among the first to take up arms in the rebellion and was one of the leaders in the Confederate camp at Belgooly until it broke up in 1642. Because of this his lands of Ringcurran, Preghane and Rathmore were confiscated and granted in 1648 to Capt. William Parsons by the Commonwealth authorities. They later came into the hands of Robert Southwell of Kinsale. Philip also forfeited Tuocusheen, Curra, Ballyfoyle and Ballindeasig. Another Philip Barry, son of James, lost Brinny; David Barry lost Dunbogey and Ballinreenlanig, and William Barry forfeited Ballyregan and Ballynamaul (par. Ringcurran). By 1659 there was only one 'titulado' of the name left in Kinalea — Richard Baroy, gent., of Piercetown. Barry was not even listed among the 'Principal Irish families' of the barony.

Philip Barry Óg, now a landless exile, served King Charles in Flanders until his death in 1656. His son, William, saw his king restored but not his lands, even though both Capt. William Barry of Ringcurran and Capt. Philip Barry of Dunbogey were named in the Declaration of Royal Gratitude (1660). John Barry Óg was adjudged an 'innocent Papist' in 1663. Ever faithful to the Stuart cause, Philip Barry Óg — presumably son of William — was a captain in Lord Mountcashel's infantry in 1689. Others of the family who backed the losing side in this final catastrophe were James of Brinny, John of Shanagraigue, Garrett of Robertstown and Garrett of Lissanisky.

Finally, in 1737 we hear the last dying echo of the ancient title when a Lieutenant-Colonel in the Spanish army proudly styled himself Dom Felipe Barry-Oge.

Ó BUACHALLA

BUCKLEY

This surname apparently originated from the use of *buachaill* (a boy or young man) as a personal name in pre-surname times, although this occurred but rarely and mainly in Ulster. (A group named Moccu Buachalla was to be found in east Ulster in the 8th century while an abbot named Cian Ua Buachalla died in the Derry region in 1089.) It is sometimes anglicized as Boughla or Buhilly but more frequently altered to Buckley, a name of English origin. In the 17th century the surname was prevalent mainly in the Tipperary-Offaly area but nowadays Cork and Kerry have the largest concentration.

As in so many cases, two distinct families may be involved here. Those in Co. Cork are probably descended from one of the family groups of Fir Maighe Féne, a tribe which inhabited the Blackwater valley in north-east Cork in early Christian times and from which the name Fermoy is derived. The 15th century tract *Crichad an Chaoilli* lists among the lands of a sub-sept named Hi Bece Abha:

Áth an Crainn thall s abhus is as atáit hÍ Buachalla

(Áth an Chrainn on both sides [*i.e.*, of the river]and from it are the Uí Bhuachalla.) The editor of the tract, Rev. P. Power, tells us that this place can only be Killavullen, so the lands of the Uí Bhuachalla included Ballymacmoy and Glannagear on the south side of the river and Ballygriffin on the north.

These lands were taken over by powerful Norman families in the 12th and 13th centuries and the Uí Bhuachalla, in common with many others, dispersed. They were, however, to be found in east rather than in west Cork in succeeding centuries, and not all settled down obediently under their new masters. In 1311 one Roger Oboyghil was a member of a band of outlaws (described as 'common robbers and incendiaries') who plundered many a wealthy holding in north Cork, including that of Reymund de Cauntetoun (Condon) and that of David le White of Ballysallagh (par. Rathgoggan).

We have, regrettably, no further records of the name until 1547, when William Boughill, a shoemaker of Cork, was pardoned for the death of Edmond Nownane of Cork, labourer. Several of the name were among those pardoned around the time of the battle of Kinsale (1601-2):

Morrice O Boughilie of Kielclugh (Killaclug, par. Clondrohid); Murtagh O Boghilie and Teige leagh O Boghilie, of Banduff (same parish); Donell O Bohillie of Birren (Berrings); John O Bwoeghele (Kanturk area); Moriertagh mac Shane O Bwoeghele; Gillpatrick mac Conoghor O Bwoeghele; Dermod mac Philip O Boghilly; Teig O Boghillie; John O Bahillye; Donell mac Shane O Bowghylly of Clonmeen, carpenter. These entries show that the surname Ó Buachalla was well scattered throughout Co. Cork by 1600. There were some in the town of Youghal in the 17th century — James Buckelie, a victualler, in 1623 and Teige Boghely in the Cromwellian period. Maurice Boghley had a house in St. Peter's parish, Cork, prior to 1616.

In King James' army list (1689) appears the name of Edmund Bohilly who was Quartermaster in the famed Clare's Dragoons, but he may have been from Co. Limerick. Martin Bucaile of Limerick and Darby Bohely of Camass, Co. Limerick, were among those who successfully claimed restoration of their lands in 1699, under the articles of Limerick. Teige Broghilly and Donogh Bohilly were living in Macroom in 1702.

Quite a few of the name were to be found among the clergy. Rev. Daniel Boughilly, who was ordained in Ireland in 1672 by Dr. Lynch, Archbishop of Tuam, was parish priest of Carrigaline in 1704, while Rev. John Boughilly was P.P. of Mallow in 1722.

One of the folk-heroes of 18th century Co. Cork was the outlaw and highwayman, Dermot Buckley, popularly known as 'The Brickaloch,' described by Joseph Ó Longáin, who wrote an account of his deeds, as 'one of the last of the Rapparees.' Born in the parish of Carraig na bhFear about 1690, he was forced to go 'on the run' early in life, and operated mainly from a sod hut a little to the east of Bottlehill, which commanded the old Mallow Road. His feats of agility when evading his pursuers were legendary, the most famous being his leap over the Blackwater near Ballymagooly. He was eventually captured while ill and died in captivity in Mallow. In Whitechurch graveyard, where he was buried, 18th century headstones of Buohilly and Buckley families may be seen. There were several Bohilly families in nearby Glashaboy in 1766.

Cappeen (East) in Kinneigh parish must have sheltered another celebrated Ó Buachalla. An ancient wedge-tomb there was known as 'O'Boughalla's Bed'; a similar monument nearby (now destroyed) was named 'O'Boughalla's Grave' on the 1841 Ordnance Survey map.

In the early 19th century, Conchubhar Ó Buachalla composed the well-known poem in praise of Carraig na bhFear, beginning:

Mo shlán chun Carraig na gCaolfhear.

Conchubhar is thought to have come originally from Ballygarvan but he may have been related to Labhrás Ó Buachalla, another poet and a companion of Mícheál óg Óg Longáin. Diarmaid Ó Buachalla of Baile Uí Shionnaigh (Rockgrove, Little Island) and Domhnall Ó Buachalla of Carker, Doneraile, were two other Irish scribes of that era.

In our own century, an eminent local historian of the east Cork area was the late Liam Ó Buachalla of Ballintubber, Carrigtwohill, who made outstanding contributions to the *Journal of the Cork Historical and Archaeological Society* up to the time of his death in 1966.

Ó CAOIMH

(O) KEEFFE   (O) KEEFE

After the adoption of surnames, the Uí Chaoimh were the leading family of the Eóganacht of Glennamhain, around the modern Glanworth. Both Eóganacht Glennamhnach and Eóganacht Caisil claimed descent from Óengus Mac Nad Froích, a king of Munster who was slain in 490. As their descent was traced from different sons of Óengus, however, the genealogies diverged at an early stage. Cathal mac Finguine, who appears in the Ó Caoimh genealogy, was king of Munster for twenty-nine years. He died in 742 and was buried at Emly. His son, Artrí, reigned after him for twenty years and Artrí's son, Tuathal, for another fourteen, but after that, their dynasty must have been superseded since they supplied no more kings of Munster. One of Artrí's descendants, about the beginning of the 11th century, was named Cáem and it is from him that the Uí Chaím took their name.

Finguine, who lived in the early 12th century, was the first to be surnamed Ua Caím in the annals. In 1121 Toirdhealbhach O Connor of Connacht raided Munster and burned Ó Caoimh's house on the banks of the Abhainn Mhór (Blackwater). Two years later Ó Caoimh and other Munster chieftains deposed the ailing Tadhg Mac Carthaigh from the kingship of Desmond, replacing him with his brother, Cormac, an active opponent of the Connachtmen. Four years later the fiery Cormac was in turn deposed and replaced by a third brother, Donnchadh. When O Connor invaded Munster soon afterwards, Donnchadh Mac Carthaigh, Ó Caoimh and other Munster nobles submitted to him. But then the O Briens, who had been supporting O Connor, changed their allegiance and brought Cormac Mac Carthy out of retirement. Cormac promptly banished Donnchadh and Ó Caoimh to Connacht. They returned with a great fleet in the following year (1128) intent on vengeance but the expedition proved a failure and they were banished once more. Ó Caoimh is named as Finguine in that year. He must have returned at a later stage, as in 1135 in a foray against the men of Thomond, Finguine Ó Caoimh (king of Glennamhain) and many other nobles of Munster were slain.

The next Ó Caoimh (Aedh according to the genealogies) was prominent in opposing an O Brien invasion in 1137. In the year 1151 the Uí Chaoimh saw more action in a great battle at Móin Mhór (near Mourne Abbey) involving Connachtmen (led by Toirdhealbhach O Connor) and Leinstermen as well as men from both parts of Munster. The men of Thomond suffered a crushing defeat there but ten years later Aodh Ó

40

Caoimh was slain by them. In 1189 Fínghin Ó Caoimh and his brother Muirchertach also died in battle. The annals in 1194 mention a Gilla Ailbi Ua Caím, an interesting name indicating a cult of St. Ailbe of Emly (where Cathal mac Finguine was buried in 742).

By now, however, the Uí Chaoimh had settled on the banks of the Blackwater (as mentioned in 1121) as the chief family of Eoghanacht Glennamhnach and of Caoille (Fermoy) generally, a position from which they had apparently displaced the O Duggans (see Ó DUBHAGÁIN). *Críchad an Chaoilli* extols the *tuath* of Eoghanacht Glennamhnach as the noblest in the region, being one of the free *tuatha* of Cashel. According to the *Book of Rights* Ó Caoimh as king of Eoghanacht Glennamhnach was entitled to seven shields and seven swords from the king of Cashel. Canon Power states that the *tuath* itself comprised the modern parishes of Glanworth, Kilgullane, Kilphelan, Dunmahon and Killeenemer. He also places the site of Ó Caoimh's *dún* where the Roche castle of Glanworth was later erected. *Críchad an Chaoilli* lists Glennamha (Glanworth), Ceapach ingine Ferchair (probably Cuppage) and Gleann Cainntin (probably Clontinty) as the seats of the Uí Chaoimh and Uí Dhigi. Immediately following them are the Uí Fhinghuine of Corr Thuaidhi (Curraghoo) who, judging by their name, were connected with the Uí Chaoimh.

The arrival of the Normans terminated the hegemony of the Uí Chaoimh, with Condons and Roches gradually appropriating the rich lands along the Blackwater. Gilla Ailbi Ó Caoimh and his kinsman were slain by the 'Galls' in 1194 ('through the connivance of Mac Carthaigh's son'). In 1201 Finguine Mór Ó Caoimh (described as king of Fir Muige) died and then ten years later his son, Maghnus, was slain by the 'grey foreigners' – grey because of their coats of mail. In 1259 Corc, son of Finguine Ó Caoimh, died. 'A blessing on his soul' say the annals. He must have been the 'Corc Ochenn de Fermuy', one of the Irish chieftains summoned to aid Henry III against the king of Scots in 1244. A group with Norman-type names were charged in 1260 with having disseised Donenoldus Okym (*Domhnall Ó Caoimh*) of 14 carucates in Rathclar (Rathclare, par. Buttevant).

It must have been after Corc's reign that the Uí Chaoimh forsook the land of Caoille and settled in the west of the adjoining barony of Duhallow in a district later known as Pobal Uí Chaoimh. But they never forgot where their rightful patrimony lay. As late as 1703 the poet Eoghan Ó Caoimh wrote:

Agus isiad an dá Fhear Muighe, .i. Críoch Róisteach agus Cunndúnach fa hoighreacht duthchasa ag an sliocht sin Chonchubhair mhic Eoghain Fhinn.

It is worth noting too that the well-nourished abbot of St. Mary's, Fermoy, in 1355 was one David *ramhar* O Kyff, while in 1484 Tadeus Ochaym was *de facto* abbot of the same house.

In 1283 Tomás, son of Mael Dúin Ó Caoimh, was 'wickedly slain' by the sons of William Barrett, the son of Jacques Rochefort having laid hands upon him. 'The O Kyfs, malefactors of Desmond' is how they are described in the Justiciary Rolls for 1295 when some men of Norman blood in Co. Waterford were charged with receiving them. In 1302 Conchobhar Ó Caoimh died — 'a famous and illustrious king's son who was the most renowned of the Munstermen of that time' — as did his son, Corc, six years later — 'a great loss to all his friends'. (The illustrious king must have been Eoghan Fionn, son of Maghnus, who was in the direct line of descent.) In 1306 David Ó Caoimh was treacherously slain by William *Súgach* de Barry and by Martel while ten years later Finguine, son of David Ó Caoimh, was killed.

Another David O Koif appeared in a law case of 1307, where he was described as a *hibernicus* of Maurice Archdeacon. In 1336 Richard Fitzmaurice was authorized to receive into the king's peace Donald son of Donald O Kyff and his retainers with permission for them to reside in a 'land of peace', they giving security for good behaviour. Nevertheless, in 1345 Dermicius Okyf, Fynyn Okyf, Tayg and Douenaldus sons of Douenaldus Okyff were among those who aided and abetted the rebellion of the Earl of Desmond. Dermicius was probably Diarmaid son of David (son of Tomás mac Mael Dúin, slain in 1283) whom at this period one genealogy makes chief representative of the O Keeffes. Later chieftains, however, appear to descend from a brother of Mael Dúin.

In 1402 Art Ó Caoimh was killed while assisting the Mac Carthys who were in conflict with the Barretts. After this we hear no more of the O Keeffes until Elizabethan times. They were undoubtedly well-established in Duhallow before 1400. Ó Huidhrín, whose poem dates from about that time, in his anachronistic manner places Ó Caoimh in Glennamhain in one verse, but elsewhere styles him *triath Urluachra as ur fochuinn*, Urluachair being on the borders of Cork and Kerry. A poem by Gofraidh Fionn Ó Dálaigh (who died in 1387) names Art and Domhnall Ó Caoimh as lords of the famed hill of Claragh in the parish of Drishane. In the 16th century, Pobal Uí Chaoimh comprised parts of Dromtarriff and Cullen parishes, the Duhallow portion of Drishane and Nohovaldaly and the west part of Kilmeen, about 41 ploughlands in all. For this they had to pay an annual rent to the overlord (Mac Donogh Mac Carthy of Duhallow) consisting of beef, mutton, butter, oatmeal, six young cows and the cessing of several English soldiers as often as occasion did require. When Sir John Perrot was president of Munster, he recorded that O Keeffe kept a force of 3 horse and 100 foot.

In the Elizabethan Fiants the O Keeffes are first mentioned in 1573 when Donill ryog (*riabhach*) O Kif and Donogh mac Conogher O Kif, yeomen, of Kanturk, were pardoned, as was, later in the same year, Donald O Kyfe, yeoman, of Killinane (par. Dromtarriff). Also pardoned were Owen óg O Kife of Ballintober (par. Castlemagner), Owen óg beg O Kyfe, of same, Arthur mac Owen O Kife, of same, and Fynyny mac Owen O Kyfe, of same – all described as gentlemen. (Fynyny could be for the ancestral 'Finghuine' or for 'Fínghin' which seems to have been replacing it about this time.) Owen's *alias* was 'Mc Ga' i.e., *mac Dháith*, son of David, apparently the title borne by this branch of the O Keeffes. Further pardons in 1573 included those of Manus O Kif mac Lawe of Dromore, yeoman, Teig mac Eig Y Kif, Kahall mac Eigh and Maonas mac Eigh of Ballybahallagh (par. Churchtown). These pardons were obviously granted because of the ending in 1573 of the first Desmond rebellion. The O Keeffes had initially supported James Fitzmaurice but later submitted to the government, and appear to have avoided the second outbreak.

In 1582, according to the *Annals of the Four Masters* the Earl of Desmond (then fighting his final rearguard action) made an incursion into Kerry. His footsoldiers went to collect spoil in Pobal Uí Chaoimh and the O Keeffes pursued them to the Earl's camp at Clanmaurice. Here the Earl counter-attacked and captured O Keeffe himself (Art son of Domhnall son of Art) with his son, Art óg. Another son, Aodh, was slain. This is probably the incident referred to in the State Papers for 1582 – a slaughter of eighty gentlemen of Duhallow in an ambuscade by the 'traitors'. But not all O Keeffes opposed the Earl. One of those attainted in 1588 for having adhered to him was Thady O Keif of Knockaregan (? Knockardrahan, par. Dromtarriff) – perhaps the Teige mac Coeve mac Donell O Quiefe who with Donell mac Teige O Quiefe was attainted and his castle, town and lands of Conyengally and Knockycappull granted to Sir Edmund Fitzgerald in 1609.

Shortly after the 1582 incident, Art, the chieftain, was slain. At the time of his death he owned the castle and lands of Dromagh, a quarter of Cullen, a quarter of Duarrigle and a quarter of Claragh in the parish of Drishane. (*Ceirt Uí Chaoimh ó Chlárach* is ridiculed by Aengus na nAor Ó Dálaigh in his notorious satire – but somewhat untypically because the O Dalys were hereditary poets to the O Keeffes of Duhallow. The famed Aengus Fionn Ó Dálaigh composed several poems in praise of O Keeffes. See Ó DÁLAIGH.) Here too, we have the first mention of Dromagh (*Druim Each*) in Dromtariff parish, the principal seat of the O Keeffes. No doubt it was around this time that the castle of Dromagh was erected.

In place of the deceased Art, his son, Art óg, was installed as chieftain. In 1585 a pardon was granted to Arthur O Kief, alias O Kief of Dromagh, gent., and to Donell mac Owen O Kiev of Rathcool (par. Dromtariff). Art óg's wife was Eleanor O Callaghan, of neighbouring Pobal Uí Cheallacháin, who for a time became sole heiress to the O Callaghan lands. Because of this her son, Manus O Keeffe, became involved in his neighbours' affairs but wisely decided not to pursue his claim. (See Ó CEALLACHÁIN.)

There was a Kahill O Kyffe of Co. Cork who in 1595 petitioned the queen for some relief whereby he might return to his native soil. His three sons, he said, were in the last company of soldiers that departed out of England.

The period of Art's chieftaincy saw the spread of Hugh O Neill's rebellion to Munster and the ejection therefrom of the undertakers. In April, 1600, just after O Neill's encampment in Inishcarra, Carew informed the Privy Council that most of the Irish chieftains in Co. Cork — O Keeffe included — were friends and followers of the disloyal Florence Mac Carthy. But by August the scene had changed, and Mac Carthy of Duhallow, together with Mac Auliffe and O Keeffe applied for suit of protection of Her Majesty. Hostages were given in return; two years later Art óg O Keeffe, who had been a pledge for his father's behaviour, was released to the custody of Lord Fermoy.

In 1611, Art, having first surrendered his estates to King James I, obtained a regrant of the various castles, lands etc. which thereupon were erected into the manor of Dromagh, with markets, fairs, courts and tolls. An inquisition (*post mortem*) held in 1638 found that Art had died possessed of the castle and lands of Dromagh and of the castle and lands of Drominagh (both in Dromtarriff parish). He also owned over twenty other townlands in Dromtarriff, Nohovaldaly, Cullen and Drishane, many of them mortgaged. As his four sons, Domhnall, Manus, Art and Aodh had predeceased him, the estates descended to his grandson, Domhnall or Daniel, son of Manus.

Domhnall O Keeffe of Dromagh played an active part in the rebellion. He was a member of the Catholic Convention and obtained the command of a company of foot in the Confederate army. In 1643 he was outlawed, along with Donogh mac Donnell O Keeffe and Donogh oge, also of Dromagh, gents., Cornelius oge of Cullen, Gent., and Keiffe (i.e. Caomh) O Keeffe of Kilcolman, gent. The Hugh or Aodh O Keeffe whom Prendergast terms 'the then owner of Dromagh castle', (*i.e.* during the Cromwellian wars), was a brother of Domhnall. We are told that Hugh, (known as 'Paschalis' or 'Cáiscí'), was a firm adherent of the Duke of Ormond (*i.e.* of the Royalists) and an opponent of the Papal Nuncio. Hugh was imprisoned for a time by the Confederates but escaped by a ruse. During Cromwell's campaign he was governor of Dromagh castle until forced to surrender on 24th May 1652, the garrison being allowed to march out fully armed to join Lord Muskerry. Even after Ross castle capitulated he continued to fight as a tory but eventually surrendered in 1654 and was sentenced to transportation. According to the census of 1659 a Hugh O Keeffe was a 'titulado' in Co. Clare in that year. (There was a second Hugh in the Dromagh garrison in 1652.)

Because of their involvement in the rebellion, the O Keeffes of Dromagh forfeited most of Dromtarriff parish, the lands being acquired by Lord Kingston, Sir Nicholas Purdon and others. They also forfeited lands in Cullen, Drishane and Nohovaldaly. However, following the

Restoration the Earl of Clancarty certified that 'Mr. Daniel O Keeffe of Dromagh' constantly supported the Royalist cause and that in 1650 he raised a force of 200 men to man the castle of Dromagh which he handed over to Clancarty (then Lord Muskerry) who made use of it 'until his Majesty's then enemies forced the said castle to yield by siege to their cannons about the 14th May 1652, and is the second last holt that stood for his Majesty in Ireland.'

When this appeal for the restoration of the O Keeffe lands was made in 1660 the elder Domhnall was dead so the appeal was, in fact, on behalf of his son, Captain Daniel O Keeffe, who crossed to France in 1653 to follow the fortunes of King Charles. The petition was successful and Captain Daniel was restored, but he found considerable obstacles in the way of his obtaining full and profitable ownership of his estate. He does not appear to have resided at Dromagh — which may well have been ruinous by then — but rather in Dromtarriff which is mentioned in his will. He died in 1669. (Seán na Ráithíneach in 1750 refers, in a poetic list of former chieftains, to *Ó Caoimh Dhrom Tairbh*.)

His son, Domhnall óg, was probably the Captain O Keeffe in Sir John Fitzgerald's infantry in King James' army, 1689. Domhnall óg married Anne, daughter of Dominic Sarsfield of Sarsfield's Court in 1684. He was killed, along with so many of the Irish nobility, at the battle of Aughrim in July 1691, leaving a six year old son, Domhnall, who died at an early age in France. O Keeffe genealogies of 1703-5 name Domhnall óg's cousins, Domhnall and Cathaoir (sons of Conchubhar), as the then chief representatives of the family. The latter was, perhaps, the Cahir O Keeffe, gent., who got a 31 year lease of Derry (?Derragh, par. Cullen) in 1723; three years later, Hugh O Keeffe, gent., mortgaged Garryveasoge (par. Dromtarriff) to the Rev. Thomas Ryder for £300, — perhaps the Hugh who died (near Kanturk) in 1782, aged 110.

The family estates had been confiscated once more after 1691. The O Keeffes of Ballymaquirk (par. Dromtarriff) and of Knocknageeha (par. Cullen) were also outlawed in 1690-1, though Manus O Keeffe of Cullen and Arthur Keeffe of Ballyolughan (Ballyhoolohan, par. Kilmeen) were restored to their estates in 1699.

The chieftain's estates were never restored but sold (all 8,488 acres) at Chichester House in 1703 to the Hollow Blades Company. An inquisition taken in 1698 found that Daniel O Keeffe had been in possession, ten years previously, of almost 6,000 acres of mountain pasture in Duhallow. The Hollow Blades Company later disclaimed having purchased this mountain pasture and it was leased to various parties until the crown resumed possession of 'the Crown lands of Pobble O'Keeffe' in 1828. Road and land improvements were undertaken there as well as the construction of a model village named Kingwilliamstown (now Ballydesmond). The lands were later sold by the Commissioners of Woods and Forests.

The landless Domhnall son of Conchubhar may be the man associated with the well-known story of 'the Outlaw's Cave'. This almost inaccessible cave of Gortmore (par. Clonmeen) in a cliff over the Blackwater was the reputed haunt of Daniel O Keeffe, the outlaw who for long terrorized the new landowners of the neighbourhood. Discovering one day that his mistress was plotting treachery against him he stabbed her fatally — an incident dramatized in Edward Walsh's romantic ballad 'Mauriade Ni Kallaghe'.

An interesting relic kept by one of the O Keeffes of Duhallow, according to Cronelly, was a small brass-bound wooden box containing a piece of wood said to be a relic of the true cross. The *cuimhne* it was called by the local people who used to swear oaths on it until in 1856 the local parish priest took possession of it.

Cronelly also stated that the then (1864) representative of the ancient chiefs of Dromagh was Manus O Keeffe, J.P., of Mount Keeffe, Newmarket.

Other Branches

Two junior branches of O Keeffes flourished outside Duhallow — in Gleann an Phréacháin (Glenville) and in Dún Bolg (Dunbulloge). Both were descended from younger sons of Conchubhar son of Eoghan Fionn. One of these sons was Domhnall Cróch, ancestor of the Glenville (and Rathcormack) branch, according to a pedigree compiled in 1703 by Eoghan Ó Caoimh (later P.P. of Doneraile) who traced the descent from Domhnall down through seven generations to Art Caoch, a third cousin of his (Eoghan's) father.

Art mac Donill mac Art (O Keeffe) of Glanphrican, Esq. (grandfather of Art Caoch) was attainted in 1588 for having taken part in the Earl of Desmond's rebellion but may have been pardoned subsequently. His son, Domhnall, mortgaged the Glenville lands to John Coppinger in 1622 and although, in Art Caoch's time, the lands were confiscated from Dominick Coppinger after the 1641 rebellion, Robert Coppinger succeeded in regaining possession later, probably after Capt. Arthur O Keeffe of Glanifriacan, Co. Cork received a declaration of Royal gratitude in 1660 for his services. Art Caoch died in London, and his two sons, Conchubhar and Finghuine, died in France. His daughter, Mairghréag, married a distant relative, Art mac Eoghain O Keeffe of Baile Uí Mhíchíl (Ballymichael, par. Kilmurry) who had leased a large estate from Lord Muskerry. Local tradition has it that nineteen O Keeffe horsemen rode from the Kilmurry-Ballymichael area to fight at Aughrim, never to return. Art O Keeffe seems to have retained his lease under the new owners who replaced the Mac Carthys, and in 1704 is recorded to have given surety for seven priests at £50 each. His tomb and that of his son, Keiffe O Keiffe (both renovated by their descendants in 1827) may still be seen in Kilmurry (south) graveyard.

The Dún Bolg O Keeffes were said to be descended from Lughaidh, a brother of Domhnall Cróch. Also Domhnall's great-granddaughter,

Síle, married Donnchadh Ó Caoimh of Dún Bolg. In 1585 Fynine mac Arte O Kiev of Ballybrack (par. Dunbulloge) was pardoned. Three years later he was attainted for supporting the Earl of Desmond, but seems to have been once more pardoned. In 1618 his son, Art, surrendered — and was then re-granted — the manor, castle and mill of Dunbulloge, with various townlands, and the right to hold courts leet and baron.

Art mac Fineen O Keeffe, with his son Cahir (Cathaoir) and one of the O Callaghans of Dromaneen formed a kind of triumvirate in Dunbulloge parish. In 1638 they mortgaged Ballyndownrae (now part of Ballynaglogh) to Maurice Roche of Cork. Because of their activities in 1641 they forfeited practically the whole parish, most of it eventually coming into the hands of the Duke of York.

In 1697 Arthur O Keeffe, styling himself 'late of Dunbollog, Co. Cork', bequeathed his manors, lands, etc. (all confiscated many years before) to his eldest son, Daniel, with remainders to his other sons, Charles and Arthur.

Arthur practised as a counsellor-at-law at Lincoln's Inn, London, and in 1738 had a pedigree compiled — corroborated by Mac Carthy Mór, O Sullivan Mór and O Donovan — showing his descent from the O Keeffe nobility. This was duly proved and recorded in the College of Arms, London. In 1743 Arthur devised all his estates in the parish of Heathfield, Sussex, to his wife, Isabella. He died in 1756 and was buried in Westminster Abbey. Arthur's roll of lineage was accompanied by a deed which founded bursarships in Paris, endowed by Rev. Cornelius O Keeffe, bishop of Limerick. Dated 1734, it declared that Denis O Keeffe, father of the bishop, had been turned out of his inheritance of Dun on the river Bride by the usurper, Cromwell, and that he finally settled at Dromkeen, Co. Limerick. ('Dun' may be Doonpeter which is near Glenville but in the parish of Dunbulloge.)

It is remarkable that around the same time (1740) Constans or Constantine O Keeffe applied to have his lineage and arms registered in France. Constans, who had been an ensign in Boisseleau's infantry in 1689, submitted evidence that he was an elder brother of Arthur O Keeffe, late Counsellor of the king in the Admiralty of France. It was certified that his father, Arthur O Keeffe, had had portion of his patrimony restored to him during the reign of James II and had rendered excellent service in the wars in Ireland as captain of a company which he had levied himself. (At least two Arthur O Keeffes were outlawed for supporting James II.) Five of his children had come to France where three of them died in service. Constantine was wounded and his brother killed at the battle of Ramillies (1706).

There were, of course, junior branches of the family in various parts of Duhallow. A pardon was granted to Teige mac Cnoghor O Keiffe of Ballymaquirk (par. Dromtarriff) in 1610. Cahir Keeffe of the same place was outlawed in 1691.

Then there was Luke (i.e. Lughaidh) O Keiffe of Prohus (Dromtarriff) who died in 1620 leaving Conoghor as son and heir, Art O Keeffe of Dysert (par. Dromtarriff) who was pardoned in 1618 and Manasses (i.e. Maghnus) O Keeffe of Castlehennig whose will was proved in 1684. Another branch settled at Kilcrea where a tombstone records 'the burial place of Thomas O Keeffe who died in 1796 and his descendants on whose property this abbey stands'. Dennis Keeffe of Kilcrea in 1770 sold lands at Meenagloghrane and in 1775 leased Knocknashannagh, both townlands being in Cullen parish in Duhallow. The family owned 69 acres (freehold) in Kilcrea in 1876.

According to the Census of 1659 there were twelve O Keeffe families in Cork city and forty-six in Barrymore, (which includes Glenville and Dunbulloge) while the rest of the county had too few to record. (It must be borne in mind that the returns for Duhallow are missing.) Also, there were thirty-two O Keeffe families in the adjoining Co. Limerick, and, more surprisingly, thirty in Co. Kilkenny.

MAC CARTHAIGH

MAC CARRTHAIGH   MAC CÁRTHAIGH
MAC CÁRRTHA   (MAC) CARTHY

Of all the descendants of the Eóganacht who once held sway over Munster from their rock-girt fortress of Cashel, the Mac Carthys were for centuries regarded as the most princely – *Na flatha fá raibh mo shean roimh éag do Chríost* as Aodhagán Ó Raithile styles them, 'the rulers under whom my ancestors served before the death of Christ'.

Eóganacht rule in Munster was not seriously challenged until the 10th century when the meteoric rise of Dál Cais culminated in the illustrious reign of Brian Boru. It was in the first half of the 11th century while Donnchadh, son of Brian, was king of Munster, that Carthach (from whom the Mac Carthys are named) ruled over Eóganacht Caisil. He was the son of Sáerbrethach, a personal name which the family monopolized in later centuries, translating it into English as Justin. Carthach was burned along with many others, the *Annals of Inisfallen* tell us, in 1045, but under what circumstances we are not told. Nine years later, two sons of his were slain but a third son, Muiredach, reigned over Eóganacht Caisil until 1092 leaving Tadhg, Donnchadh and Cormac, to succeed him. Tadhg made a determined effort to win back the kingship of Munster from the O Briens and although O Brien in 1118 brought an expedition which included the kings of Connacht and Meath as far south as Glanmire, his plan misfired when his allies made peace with Tadhg. The settlement then made was in effect a partition of Munster which left the O Briens as kings of Thomond while the Mac Carthys thenceforth reigned over Desmumu or Desmond (south Munster).

When Tadhg fell gravely ill in 1123 the chieftains of Desmond handed over the kingship to his brother, Cormac, known as Cormac Muighe Thamhnach from the place of his demise (and residence), namely, Mahoonagh or Castlemahon, Co. Limerick. An earlier residence of his (according to the inscription on the shrine of St. Laichtín's arm) was Rath Aine (Rathanny) near Knockainy, Co. Limerick. No sooner had his brother died than Cormac embarked on a warlike career. Having banished several of the Munster chiefs he led an expedition against O Connor of Connacht and in the following year, took the kingship of Limerick. Too fiery, perhaps, for his fellow-Munstermen, he was deposed by them in 1127 and retired to the monastery of Lismore, but a foray by O Connor which reached as far as Cork caused a change of heart and Cormac was brought out of his monastery to rule once again. He made many an onslaught on the O Connors before he was slain – at the instigation of the O Briens – in his own house at Maigh

Thamhnach in 1138. He was the founder of twelve churches at Lismore (according to Mac Carthaigh's Book), but is better remembered for the erection on the rock of Cashel of the graceful 'Cormac's chapel', consecrated in 1134. No doubt it was through Cormac's influence that Gilla Patraic Mac Carrthaigh became abbot of the monastery of Cork at this period. He died in 1157. About the same time (*c.* 1140) but further from home, Christian Mac Carthaigh was abbot of the monastery of St. Jakob in Regensburg (Ratisbon) in Bavaria.

The frequent expeditions and counter-attacks of Cormac's time were not mere local cattle-raids but rather a facet of the political power-struggle in which the leading families of Ireland had become embroiled. Donnchadh son of Tadhg, who succeeded Cormac, died in 1143 while a prisoner of the O Briens. Diarmaid son of Cormac, elected chief in 1151, rashly took on the combined forces of the O Briens, O Connor of Connacht and O Connor Kerry and suffered a disastrous defeat. As a result of this the Mac Carthys were banished out of the Golden Vale southwards into Desmond where their arrival caused a massive displacement of the various septs already settled there. Yet, before the year was out, the Connachtmen marched south again, this time to aid the Eóganacht families in inflicting a sanguinary defeat on the O Briens and their Kerry allies at Móin Mhór between Cork and Mallow. The end result of these wars was widespread famine in Munster in 1153.

Diarmaid Mac Carthaigh seems to have made his residence at Lismore. He encountered opposition among his own people and despatched several rivals. However, a new and more serious threat was the coming of the 'grey foreigners' in 1169. Dermot, the recognized king of Desmond at the time — his 'kingdom of Cork', as it was known to the Normans, reached from Lismore to Mount Brandon and from the Blackwater to the sea — has often been accused of tamely yielding to the Normans. But his first reaction was to assemble the men of Desmond and attack Strongbow at Waterford in 1170, inflicting, say the annals, a slaughter on the plunderers of Waterford with the loss of three of the nobility of Munster. The following year, however, Dermot Mac Carthy submitted to King Henry, probably under the mistaken impression that Henry would protect him from the rapacious Norman barons. What eventually happened, of course, was that Henry now regarded himself as feudal overlord of Dermot's lands and bestowed the 'kingdom of Cork' on two of his leading conquistadores, Milo de Cogan and Robert Fitzstephen. As always, the Normans were able to secure local assistance, this time from a disgruntled cousin of Dermot, Muirchertach Mac Carthaigh, who led them to Cork. The O Briens also seized the opportunity of renewing warfare with the Mac Carthys and so Dermot was driven out of the eastern half of his kingdom which was then divided between de Cogan and Fitzstephen. Another great resettlement movement took place among the Irish septs in west Munster. Dermot was slain in 1185 by the men of Cork and the followers of Theobald Walter on the occasion of a parley at Kilbane near Kilcrea. He was accordingly titled Diarmaid Cille Badhúna by native historians.

Domhnall, his son and successor — an elder son, Cormac Liathánach, had been slain some years previously after a dispute with his father — waged war against the Normans for over two decades and destroyed the castles of Imokilly and Lismore on at least one occasion. He also inflicted defeats on the foreigners at Kilmocomogue, at Innishannon and at the Pass of Redchair in the Ballyhoura Mts. 'During the twenty years he held the kingship', say the *Annals of Inisfallen*, 'he never submitted to a foreigner'. Domhnall Mór na Cuirre they named him because he died at Corr Tige Meic Urmainn in 1206.

His uncle Fínghin (Lice Lachtnáin) then took the kingship for a time, but with opposition, and he was killed by the O Sullivans in 1209. Diarmaid, son of Domhnall Mór, was next in line, though an attempt was made, with Norman backing, to have Diarmaid deposed and Cormac Liathánach II put in his place. Diarmaid, however, with the aid of the 'Galls of Cork' thwarted the attempt and remained *de facto* king of Desmond even though Norman officialdom continued to recognize Cormac. The carefully-fostered internal rivalries among the Mac Carthys gave the Normans an opportunity of building a ring of stone castles around the coast of Desmond, from Timoleague to Killorglin. The grant of custody of Decies and Desmond to Thomas fitz Anthony may also have been a factor, since several of the castle-builders appear to have been sons-in-law of Fitz Anthony with one in particular, John fitz Thomas, making a determined effort to become lord of all Desmond. But Diarmaid fought back and in 1219 captured the castle of Timoleague. Then the Cogans began to make inroads in Muskerry in consequence of a grant made to them by King John, and Diarmaid was killed at Dún Draighnein (later the site of the Cogan Castlemore, near Crookstown) in 1229.

Further dissensions among the Mac Carthys in 1232-3 during the reign of Cormac Fionn (brother of Diarmaid Dúna Draighnein) may have contributed to the rout of their forces at Tralee in 1234 when Diarmaid, son of Cormac Liathánach II, was slain. Two other sons of Cormac Liathánach were both named Domhnall; one was called Domhnall Ruadh and the other Domhnall Gall ('the foreigner') — appropriately, for on the death of his father, he handed over Domhnall Ruadh to John fitz Thomas, who promptly put him to death.

Cormac Fionn had a brother, Domhnall God, whom he imprisoned for a time in 1232. When released, Domhnall went into the O Mahony country in Carbery and slew three of O Mahony's sons. Because of this, he became known as Domhnall Cairbreach and his descendants retained possession of Carbery.

The fact that Cormac Fionn died in his own stronghold at Mashanaglass (east of Macroom) in 1247 indicates that the Cogans were unable to conquer all of Muskerry. In the following year, Fínghin (son of Diarmaid Dúna Draighnein) captured Geoffrey de Cogan and drowned him with a stone tied to his neck. Then he 'made war and wrought great havoc on the Galls of Desmond'. But the Cogans gained new allies in the Carbery Mac Carthys, represented by Domhnall God who slew his nephew, Fínghin. This Domhnall, in turn, was taken prisoner and put to death by John fitz Thomas, thus creating a rift between Geraldines and Cogans. The latter continued to support the Carbery Mac Carthys and when Fínghin, son of Domhnall, commenced an all-out war against the Normans in 1260, they gave no support to Fitz Thomas and his Norman allies. Fitz Thomas led a massive expedition into Desmond and encountered Fínghin's army at Callann near Kenmare on 24th July, 1261. Fínghin's lightly-clad fighting men inflicted a resounding defeat on the heavily-mailed Normans, killing John fitz Thomas, his son, and fifteen other knights. 'Eight good barons were also slain with many squires and soldiers innumerable'.

This was the turning-point in the struggle for supremacy in Desmond, and thereafter the Mac Carthys reigned unchallenged for three centuries. Fínghin followed up his victory by destroying Norman castles and lands throughout Desmond and Muskerry but met his death while attempting to capture Miles de Courcy's castle at Ringrone near Kinsale. His brother, Cormac, was slain in another battle against the Normans on Mangerton mountain in the following year but the Normans too suffered heavy losses and had to abandon the attempt to dislodge the Mac Carthys.

Ironically, it was Domhnall Ruadh, son of Cormac Fionn and representative of the main Mac Carthy line, who, although he had aided Fitz Thomas at Callann, benefited most from the weakening of Norman power. After the deaths of Fínghin and Cormac he held the kingship of Desmond for forty years until his death in 1302, though opposed by two other sons of Domhnall God who claimed the kingship for a time. In 1280 he made peace with the Carbery branch (then headed by Domhnall óg, nephew of Fínghin of Ringrone) and the two families apportioned Desmond between them, uniting to drive out the foreigners from the castles of Killorglin and Dunloe which were promptly burned. But within three years Domhnall Ruadh broke the truce and brought a large Norman force with him to attack and plunder Carbery. The Carbery Mac Carthys were now regarded as outlaws while 'Donald Rufus Mac Carthy, lord of the Irish of Desmond', was able to treat with King Edward as an independent prince and even visited England on one occasion to safeguard his position.

After Domhnall's death in 1302 the succession was as follows:

1.   His brother, Donnchadh, who died in 1315 and was buried *in antro de Corkagia*, i.e. Gill Abbey, Cork.
2.   Diarmaid of Tráigh Lí, son of Domhnall óg son of Domhnall Ruadh who was slain in 1325 and buried in Inisfallen.

3. Cormac, another son of Domhnall óg, d. 1359.
4. Domhnall, son of Cormac, d. 1391.
5. Tadhg (*na Mainistreach*) son of Domhnall, d. 1428, buried at Cork.

Tadhg made submission to King Richard II and from then on the term 'King of Desmond' is rarely used to describe the head of the family who is usually referred to as 'Mac Carthy Mór'. Furthermore, Mac Carthy Mór, though nominally head of all the Mac Carthys, at this time resided in and ruled over south Kerry — Tadhg na Mainistreach died in his castle of Ballycarbery — and was connected with Co. Cork only insofar as he was overlord of the O Sullivans and others in Bear and Bantry, though there were some small dues payable to him out of Muskerry and Duhallow. The Mac Carthys of Co. Cork had separated into three distinct groupings, whose fortunes we must now follow.

Mac Carthy of Carbery

The earliest offshoots of the main stock were the Carbery Mac Carthys whose story began, as already mentioned, when Domhnall God (brother of Cormac Fionn and fifth in descent from Carthach) in 1232 ousted the O Mahonys from East Carbery. To Fínghin, son of Domhnall God, was due the overthrow of the Geraldines at Callann. Relations with the main line were not always amicable; in 1306 Domhnall Maol (son of Domhnall God) imprisoned in his own house and beheaded Domhnall óg Mac Carthy who would have been eligible for the kingship of Desmond. The residence in question was at Ballymoney (near Enniskeane); the settlement of 1280 allotted 'Desmond south of the Lee' to the Carbery Mac Carthys.

At this period there was a remarkable succession of Domhnalls in the Carbery branch. Domhnall Glas Mac Carthy who succeeded in the early 15th century, was the son of Domhnall Riabhach son of Domhnall Glas son of Domhnall Cam son of Domhnall Maol son of Domhnall God son of Domhnall Mór. But the succession was broken when Domhnall Glas II left no descendants. His brother, Cormac na Coilleadh, was slain by the Mac Carthys of Desmond in a battle which was fought in the Barretts' country, in and around the castle of Carrigrohane in 1421. The sons of a third brother were then regarded by the genealogists as the Mac Carthys Cairbreach, but they were ousted by sons of the fifth brother who gave themselves a new title, Mac Carthy Riabhach or Reagh (striped or swarthy). It was in 1477 that this conflict took place and when the Muskerry Mac Carthys and others joined in, the *Annals of Connacht* reported that 'war spread throughout Munster and all the south was destroyed, Gall and Gael'.

This was also the era of the controversial Blessed Thaddeus Mac Carthy (1456-1492) believed to be of the Mac Carthys Riabhach. Thaddeus (Latin for Tadhg) was nominated to the see of Ross — where there was already an O Driscoll bishop — and to the see of Cork and Cloyne where he met with uncompromising opposition from the Geraldine faction which supported Bishop Gerald Fitzgerald. He died at Ivrea in Italy where he is still venerated.

It must have been early in the 15th century that the Mac Carthys ousted the de Courcys from their castle at Kilbrittain which from then on became the principal seat of Mac Carthy Riabhach. In 1430 a 'great contest' arose between Mac Carthy Riabhach and the Earl of Desmond. The Earl took the castle of Kilbrittain from Mac Carthy Riabhach and gave it to his brother, Donnchadh Mac Carthy, 'who was along with him demolishing the castle'. Nearby Coolmain also became a Mac Carthy castle; *Mac Carrtha Riabhach ó Chúl Méine* is referred to in Seán Ó Conaill's mid-17th century *Tuireamh na hÉireann*. Two other family strongholds were Kilgobbin and Carriganass on the west bank of the Bandon estuary, and Mac Carthy Riabhach later acquired Dundanier or Downdaniel castle near Innishannon from Barry Óg.

In 1505 Fínghin Mac Carthy Riabhach (son of Diarmaid an Dúna) died, as did in 1531 his son, Domhnall, 'a man of universal hospitality to scholars and the men of every art'. It was for Fínghin and for his wife, Catherine (daughter of Thomas, Earl of Desmond) that the famous manuscript 'The Book of Mac Carthy Riabhach' (now known as the 'Book of Lismore') was compiled. Catherine died in 1506, according to *A.F.M.*, who added that she was responsible for the erection of the castles of Beann Dubh (Benduff, par. Ross) and Dún na mBeann (? Dunmanway). Their son, Domhnall, was married to Eleanor, eldest daughter of Garrett Mór, Earl of Kildare. After the fall of the Kildare Geraldines, the surviving heir, eleven-year-old Gerald, was conveyed in secret to Kilbrittain castle to be cared for by his widowed aunt; Lady Eleanor then agreed to marry the northern chief, Manus O Donnell, as this enabled her to carry the young Gerald into the more secure fastnesses of the north.

Domhnall was succeeded by four sons in turn — Cormac na hEóine, Fínghin, Donnchadh and finally Eoghan. Next in line was Domhnall (*na píopaí*) son of Cormac, but his fame was eclipsed by that of his cousin and rival, Fínghin son of Donnchadh, who in 1588 married the daughter (and only legitimate child) of Domhnall Mac Carthy Mór, the newly-created Earl of Clancarty. This marriage caused consternation in government circles because of the fact that there was now a family connection not only between two of the chief Mac Carthy lords but also with the Mac Carthys of Muskerry, the remnants of the Fitzgeralds of Desmond, and Lord Roche. The government officials had hoped that the heiress would marry a son of Sir Valentine Browne, one of the English undertakers in Kerry, but were outwitted by Fínghin who secretly married his bride in the romantic setting of the ruined Muckross abbey on the shores of Killarney's Loch Léin. Fínghin paid for his contempt by being imprisoned in the Tower of London for several years; released for a time, he was again imprisoned in 1601 for alleged treasons. Two score years Fínghin (*anglice* Florence) spent in London, at least half of them as a prisoner in the Tower. He was buried in St. Martins-in-the-Fields on 18th December, 1640. Though he was never to revisit it, all Florence's letters and legal pleadings dealt with his homeland. As a patron of learning his interest in his country's past helped to while away many a weary hour in exile. It was also destined to benefit later generations, since he carefully preserved some old Irish annals (copied for him by Diarmaid Ó Súilleabháin in London in 1633), known to us as 'Mac Carthaigh's Book', which is an original and valuable source for the early history not only of the Mac Carthys but of Munster generally. The Mac Carthy Mór lands around Killarney were later restored to Fínghin's descendants, the last of whom to inherit (Charles) died in 1770 leaving his estates to his cousins, the Herberts. A fully-documented account of Fínghin's career is to be found in *The Life and Letters of Florence Mac Carthy Mór* by Daniel Mac Carthy (1867).

Florence had a brother named Dermot Maol who at the time of O Neill's rebellion proved the greatest threat to English security in Carbery. While Domhnall (*na píopaí*) was restrained by the responsibilities of the chieftaincy and Florence by incarceration in the Tower of London, Dermot Maol remained free of all shackles. He refused to give pledges to Carew and supported O Neill all through his campaign, even following him to Ulster and acting as guide to Tyrell's army on its way south to Kinsale. Two days before Christmas, 1601, Carew wrote to Cecil from the camp at Kinsale '. . . as yet no other septs of the Irishry in Munster are in rebellion but the Carties and their followers, and the chief among them is Florence's brother and cousin germains'. (The cousins were Fineen and Donogh Maol, of Phale castle, sons of Sir Owen, the previous chieftain.) During the siege, Don Dermucio Cartie, one of Florence's followers fighting on the side of the Spaniards, was captured and executed, while another, Don Carlos Cartie, received a fatal wound. After the defeat at Kinsale, Dermot Maol made peace overtures but shortly afterwards was slain in the course of a cattle-raid — mistakenly it would seem — by some of O Donovan's men commanded by his cousin, Fineen Mac Carthy. This 'principall Piller of the Catholique Cause', as *Pacata Hibernia* calls him, was buried with great solemnity in the friary of Timoleague. Dermot's lands at Murragh and Burrane were confiscated.

Mac Carthy Riabhach claimed the overlordship of the whole of Carbery, East and West, a huge area of over 500 square miles reaching from the Bandon estuary to Bantry Bay. He was the most powerful chieftain in Co. Cork in Elizabethan times having at his disposal an army of 1,000 foot and 30 horsemen. About half of Carbery was occupied by septs of O Driscolls, O Donovans, O Mahonys and others from whom a yearly rent was demanded. The other half was in the hands of the

Mac Carthys, either as demesne land of Mac Carthy Riabhach (mainly, though not exclusively, around Kilbrittain) or belonging to various offshoots and sub-septs among whom the following were numbered:

Sliocht Diarmada Reamhair and Clann Charthaigh Chlocháin, were both descended from Diarmaid Ruadh, a younger son of Domhnall God. In English documents they were known as 'Clan Dermod' and they occupied the castles of Kilcoe (near Ballydehob) and Cloghane (par. Caheragh).

Clann Taidhg Aighleann traced their descent from Tadhg Dall, another son of Domhnall God. Their agnomen was derived from the river Ilen, and the clan was based in the Skibbereen area – though not in the castle of Gortnaclogh which belonged to Mac Carthy Riabhach himself. A small sept called Clann (or Sliocht) Donnchadha held land in Templetrine parish (east of Coolmain) but they too could trace their ancestry to Donnchadh Mór son of Domhnall Maol, son of Domhnall God.

In the north of Desertserges parish (Maulbrack, Breaghna, Boulteen, Knockmacool) lay the lands of Clann tSeáin Rua, named from another son of Domhnall Maol.

To the south of these, in the parishes of Desertserges and Kilnagross, were the lands of Sliocht Inghine Uí Chruimín (anglice Clan Crimeen), descended from Diarmaid, great-grandson of Domhnall God. They had castles at Castlederry and at Ballinoroher. Dermot mac Daniel Mac Carthy, alias Mac-ni-Crimen, of Ballinoroher castle, was hanged in the 1650s for the alleged hanging of an Englishman, and his estates were confiscated.

Sliocht Cormaic Dhuinn (also Sliocht Fheidhlimidh) were the Mac Carthys of Gleann an Chroim, an area which included the castles of Dunmanway and Togher (par. Fanlobbus). Their ancestor was Felim, son of Cormac Donn, one-time lord of Carbery. Cormac gave these lands to Felim before being slain by his nephew in 1366. Togher Castle was built probably by Tadhg an Fhórsa Mac Carthy in Elizabethan times, after a 'Surrender and Regrant' made him owner of the clan territory. He was succeeded by his son, Tadhg an Dúna, who was noted for his extravagant hospitality and who forfeited his lands as a result of taking an active part in the rising of 1641. Although the lands of Dunmanway were restored to Tadhg an Dúna II under a Decree of Innocence, they were again confiscated in 1691 while his son, 'Jacques Mac Carthy Dooney Capitaine' fell with Sarsfield at Landen in 1693, leaving Tadhg in the condition described by a contemporary poet:

> *Ní Tadhg an Dúna t-ainm/Acht Tadhg gan dún gan daingean;*
> *Tadhg gan bó gan capall/I mbotháinín íseal deataigh.*

A direct descendant of Tadhg an Dúna (I) was Jerry an Dúna who died in the mid-19th century aged 84, in the house of his relative Timothy O Donovan of O Donovan's Cove. He was buried in the family tomb at Kilbarry.

Other descendants of Tadhg I included the 18th-century poet Eoghan an Mhéirín Mac Carthaigh and the 19th-century English-born historian Daniel Mac Carthy Glas, who compiled a history of the sept. (The castle of Kilgobbin in Ballinadee parish was in the *pobal* or territory of Sliocht Glas in the early 17th century.)

Phale castle (near Ballineen) which was taken down in the early 19th century, was the headquarters of Clann Diarmada an Fhiadhail descended from Diarmaid an Fhiadhail son of Domhnall Cam. Their castle was occupied in Elizabethan times by Dermot Maol Mac Carthy Riabhach, as already mentioned.

Sliocht Diarmada of nearby Enniskeane appear to have formed a separate group, claiming descent from Donnchadh son of Domhnall Riabhach. Their castle was on a rock in the townland called Castlelands. Fínghin mac Eoghain mac Diarmada Mac Carthy of Enniskeane was slain during O Neill's rebellion and his lands of Enniskeane, Tuath Bhaile na Daibhche (Ballinadee) and Tuath na Coillte (near Clonakilty) were confiscated.

Connected with this group were the Mac Carthys of Tuath Móintín who held most of the parish of Kilmaloda (near Timoleague) with the castle of Monteen, one of the castles burned by Captain Flower in Carbery in April 1600. In later centuries, this branch, under the title of 'Mac Carthy Rábach' produced many an eminent churchman – as for instance, Dr. Tadhg Mac Carthy, bishop of Cork, Cloyne and Ross, 1726-1747.

A portion of the parish of Kinneigh (Aghalinane, Derrigra, Lissicorrane, Cappeen, etc.) was occupied by Sliocht Cormaic na Coilleadh, descended from that Cormac who was killed at Carrigrohane in 1421. Similarly, part of Ballymoney parish (Kilcaskan, Buddrimeen, Edencurra, etc.) as well as Gortnamucklagh (par. Fanlobbus) belonged to a group known as 'Slught Corky' about whom nothing seems to be known.

At Skart, near Bantry, we find Clann Taidhg Rua na Sgairte, descended not from Domhnall God but from his uncle, Cormac Liathánach, while Clann Domhnaill Rua in Bantry (based at Dromnafinshin) and Clann Diarmada in Béarra were not connected with Mac Carthy Riabhach at all.

The Mac Carthys Riabhach and their sub-septs lost their lands in the Cromwellian confiscations, although a number of them appear as 'tituladoes' in the baronies of East and West Carbery and Kilbrittain in 1659. The chief, Cormac Mac Carthy Riabhach, was an officer in the Confederate army and had a price of £200 (dead or alive) on his head in May, 1652. Later he served as a colonel in the Duke of York's regiment in Flanders, and was included in the royal declaration of grace and favour by Charles II at the restoration in 1660. One branch of the family managed to maintain a social eminence near Bansha in Co. Tipperary until the mid-18th century when Denis Mac Carthy Reagh of Spring House, disgusted by the persecution of Catholic landowners, emigrated to France where his son was enrolled as Count Mac Carthy Reagh, of the city of Toulouse.

Mac Carthy of Muskerry

The cantred of Múscraighe Mittaine had been granted by King John to Richard de Cogan in 1207, but extensive inroads were later made there by the Mac Carthys. During the reign of Cormac Mac Carthy (1325-1359) the rebellious Diarmaid mac Diarmada (nephew of Cormac) was the 'king's enemy' in those parts. When Cormac assisted the Justiciar, Sir Thomas Rokeby, in driving out Diarmaid's followers, he was rewarded with a grant of Macroom and other lands in Muskerry at a rent of 20s. or one hawk per annum. Cormac forthwith set up his second son, Diarmaid Mór, as lord of Muskerry. (Hence the family is often referred to as Mac Diarmada or Mac Dermot.) As the Cogan lands had extended south of the river Lee, outside the original Muskerry, the Mac Carthys followed suit and their Muskerry is the Muskerry barony (East and West) of today.

Diarmaid Mór was slain by the O Mahonys at Inchirahilly in 1367 and was buried at Gill Abbey in Cork. He was succeeded by his sons Tadhg and Cormac, both of whom were also interred at Gill Abbey. A third son, Feidhlime then became lord by slaying his nephew, but was himself slain, probably in retribution, by the Uí Mhurchadha in 1382. The next to succeed were Cormac's two sons, Domhnall (for three years) and Tadhg (31 years). Tadhg too was buried in Gill Abbey in 1448, the last of the Mac Carthy lords to be brought there. His son and successor, Cormac, although he died in Cork city (after having been wounded by his own relatives at Carraig na Muc), was buried in the friary of Kilcrea which he had himself erected. Kilcrea subsequently became the chosen resting-place of the lords of Muskerry. This Cormac was aptly known as Cormac Láidir, since in the course of his forty years reign (1455-1495) he brought the Mac Carthy dominance to the walls of Cork city with the erection of Kilcrea castle and friary, Ballymacadane Abbey (six miles from Cork), and of course, the world-renowned Blarney castle which henceforth became the principal residence of the Muskerry Mac Carthys. In 1488 his brother, Eoghan, acquired Cloghphilip castle and lands (near Tower) from the Barretts. The Mac Carthys also came into possession of most of Currykippane within the city liberties; in fact for a time Cormac was in receipt of an annual 'Black Rent' of £40 from the citizens of Cork. For a period also he held the overlordship of the barony of Kerrycurrihy on the western shores of Cork harbour; this was recovered by the Earls of Desmond in the 16th century but not before the Mac Carthys had built there the castle of Ballea.

Cormac Láidir in 1488 obtained a patent of 'denization' granting him and his descendants all the rights of Englishmen, and later lords of Muskerry claimed that they held their lands by a grant from Henry VIII.

Because of this they became for a considerable period loyal adherents of the crown at a time when their ancient enemies, the Desmond Geraldines, were coming increasingly into conflict with the government. Cormac Óg (son of Cormac Láidir) gained a notable victory over the Earl of Desmond in a pitched battle at Mourne Abbey in 1520. He died in 1536 and was buried at Kilcrea. 'A greater calamity than any other suffered in this age' is the way the *Annals of Connacht* record the death of 'the very best prince among Galls and Gaels in Leth Mogha'.

Cormac Óg was succeeded by his sons and then by his grandson, Diarmaid mac Taidhg, who died at his own house at Castleinch in 1570. Diarmaid had two sons, Cormac and Tadhg, but after his death the lordship was (under the Irish *tánaiste* system) taken by his brother, Cormac mac Taidhg. This Cormac was made sheriff of Co. Cork and, reverting to the English legal system he surrendered all the lands of Muskerry to the crown in order to receive a regrant which made the lands his personal possessions instead of being, under the Irish system, the lands of the sept or clan to which he belonged. For his loyalty he was knighted and described by Lord Deputy Sidney as '. . . the rarest man that ever was born of the Irish'. Yet in his will in 1583 Sir Cormac mac Taidhg, despite the clause in his regrant agreement that he would hold 'in tail male', tried to preserve the Irish system of succession by willing to his brother and *tánaiste*, Callaghan mac Teige, the castles of Carrigadrohid, Castlemore, Macroom and the bulk of the lands and castles (Blarney excepted) throughout Muskerry, with remainder to his nephews Cormac and Teige mac Dermot. To his son and heir, Cormac Óg, he left lands at Cloghroe, Carraig na bhFear etc. with the reversion of Blarney castle which was to be his widow's for her lifetime. His youngest son, Tadhg, got Ballea castle with lands adjoining. He left the castle of Dooneens in Drishane parish to his brother, Donnchadh.

However, Callaghan mac Teige proved unable to retain the chieftaincy for more than a year and in 1584 his nephew, Cormac mac Dermod ousted him from the lordship of Muskerry. Callaghan retired to Carraig na Muc (Dripsey castle) and Cormac mac Teige's widow (Joan Butler) to Carrigadrohid leaving Cormac mac Dermod as lord of Muskerry in Blarney castle. Cormac then negotiated another 'surrender and regrant' to consolidate his position. Long drawn out legal proceedings failed to dislodge him but a bitter enmity ensued between himself and his cousin Cormac Óg until the latter died at Kilcrea in 1600.

By then Hugh O Neill's rebellion was in full swing but Cormac mac Dermod refused to take part in it and in fact, assisted the English forces at the siege of Kinsale in October, 1601, though not, it would seem, with any great enthusiasm. In fact, on 7 December 1601 Ormond wrote to Cecil that Tyrone (O Neill) had arrived in Muskerry, Cormac mac Dermod's country, and that Cormac's kinsmen and followers had joined him. In May of the previous year Carew had written that the two most cankered subjects were Lord Roche and Cormac mac Dermod, adding:

'Roche is a brain-sick fool but the other is a subtle fox.' After Kinsale Cormac was accused of treasonable traffic with the Spaniards and was imprisoned in Cork while his castles were taken over. He escaped, however, and joined Donal O Sullivan Bear who was still in rebellion. Together they captured Carraig an Phúca castle but after the death of Red Hugh O Donnell Cormac made his submission and in 1603 received a full pardon.

Meanwhile, the family of Sir Cormac mac Teige were still pressing their claims to Muskerry and finally in 1604 got a grant of eighteen ploughlands. But Cormac mac Dermod compensated for this by purchasing the confiscated lands of some of the O Mahonys. His son and heir, Cormac Óg, married a daughter of the Earl of Thomond and resided at Kilcrea castle. Another son, Domhnall, was settled on the Carraig na bhFear estate. On 22 February 1616 Cormac mac Dermod of Blarney died and was buried at Kilcrea.

Tadhg mac Cormaic, who had been willed the castle of Ballea near Carrigaline, managed to acquire a legal title to his lands after the Desmond confiscations. Always ready to take the opposite course to his sworn enemy, Cormac mac Dermod, he joined O Neill (by whom he was created 'Lord of Muskerry') and fought against the English at Kinsale. Later he regained Carew's favour, by laying information against Cormac and by fighting against him when he escaped from prison. Tadhg died in 1637 and was buried at Knockavilla. He was succeeded by his sons Charles (d. 1640) and Dermot who was killed while leading his troop of horse against Cromwell at Drogheda in 1649. Dermot's lands of Ballea were confiscated and passed to the Hodders who held them until the present century, though the Mac Carthys renewed their claim to them during the Jacobite wars and Denis Mac Carthy who died in 1739 was generally styled *Donnchadh Bhaile Aodha*.

Cormac Óg, son of Cormac mac Dermod, who succeeded his father as lord, was created Viscount Muskerry and Lord of Blarney. He died in 1640, so that his son Donogh was lord for but a year when the rebellion of 1641 broke out. Donogh became one of the principal leaders of the Confederate cause in Munster and a member of the Council of the Confederation of Kilkenny. His castle at Blarney was captured in 1646 and the other castles in Muskerry in 1650. Finally, Lord Muskerry himself surrendered at Ross castle, Killarney, in 1652. On his release he went to France where Charles II created him Earl of Clancarty in 1658 and three years later restored to him the confiscated lands of Muskerry. Donogh was succeeded by his son Callaghan and grandson, Donogh. Donogh II was a firm adherent of King James while his uncle, Justin Mac Carthy, Lord Mountcashel, was one of the most illustrious of the 'Wild Geese'. After the defeat of King James by William, Donogh was imprisoned in the Tower of London. Eventually he was granted a royal pardon on condition that he removed overseas, his lands having been confiscated. This time the confiscation was final and the vast estates

(139,372 acres) were sold at Chichester House in 1702. However, Colonel Charles Mac Carthy ('of Ballea') made good his claim to lands around Cloghroe and Knockavilla which the Mac Carthys continued to hold until through marriage and litigation they passed to the Mac Carthys of Carraig na bhFear.

This latter branch, distinguished by the agnomen *Spáinneach*, had managed to retain their property, conforming to the established religion and spelling their name 'Mac Cartie'. They remained in Carraig na bhFear as the last landed representatives of the Muskerry Mac Carthys until the estate was sold in 1924. It is now the property of the Sacred Heart Missionaries.

Apart from the Earl of Clancarty, many minor branches in Muskerry incurred outlawry for their support of King James — the Mac Carthys of Cloghroe and Ballea, Castleinch, Aglish, Dunisky, Tuath na Dromann (Dundareirke) and Carraig na Muc (Dripsey). Among those whose claims for restoration were allowed in 1699 were Lieut. Teige Mac Carthy of Aglish, Teage of Fergus, Donagh of Drishane, Finn of Augeris (par. Inchigeelagh) and Capt. Charles of Courtbrack. The last-named belonged to a branch known as *Máistir na Móna* (i.e. of Mourne Abbey) descended from Donnchadh, a son of Cormac Mac Teige, the lord of Muskerry who died in 1583. Cormac mac Donogh of Courtbrack was outlawed in 1643 but — although Donogh mac Cormac of Courtbrack was decreed 350 acres of limestone rock in the Burren of Co. Clare — the family seem to have retained their old seat since the last *Máistir na Móna*, Owen Mac Carthy, died at his residence in Courtbrack (par. Matehy) in 1790 and was buried at Kilcrea. Another ancient tomb in Kilcrea is that of the Mac Carthys of Ballineadig and Lyradane.

It is worth noticing that in Inishcarra parish (paying rent to the Barretts) dwelt the remnants of an early offshoot of the main line, namely, Clann Mhic Dhomhnaill (Mac Donnell) descended from Donnchadh Carrthainn son of Cormac Fionn.

An inscription on a tomb in Drishane old graveyard is worthy of being quoted in full, not only for its condensed history of the Mac Carthys of Drishane and Dooneens, remarkable though their longevity may have been, but also for the almost tangible pride of ancestry which illumines this sombre memorial:

'Sacred to the memory of Donough Mac Carthy of Drishane Castle Esq. whose great-grandfather Dermot Mac Carthy, second son of Teige, Lord Muskerry, built the castle of Drishane, A.D. 1450. Donough was born 1517 and died the 3rd of March 1639, aged 122 yrs. His son Dermot Mac Carthy of Drishane Castle, and his grandson Donough Mac Carthy of Dunine, Esq., who forfeited the family estate of Drishane in 1641 and died the 1st October 1725 aged 106 yrs. Donough Mac Carthy oge of Dunine, Esq. who died A.D. 1763 aged 96 yrs and his three sons, Justin, Denis of Glyn and Alex Mac Carthy of Knocknagree, Esq. who died March 1802 aged 84 yrs. Denis Mac Carthy of Coomlegane, Esq. who died A.D. 1825 aged 80 yrs. Alex Mac Carthy of Cork, Esq. who died the 12th July 1843 aged 72 yrs. His family having re-built the tomb A.D. 1844 Erected this tablet as a pious memorial of their ancestors.'

Mac Carthy of Duhallow

Ealla, later known as Dúthaigh Ealla (Duhallow), had come under Mac Carthy overlordship by the 13th century. The *Annals of Inisfallen* record the death in 1297 of Tadhg Mac Carthaigh son of Domhnall Ruadh and a royal heir 'in his own stronghold at Druim Comair', which is Dromcummer in the parish of Clonmeen.

In the hierarchy of Desmond the Mac Donogh Mac Carthys were recognized as overlords of all Duhallow, receiving certain dues from the O Callaghans, O Keeffes and Mac Auliffes. A smaller amount was pay-able to Mac Carthy Mór who was at the apex of the pyramid. Accord-ing to the *Leabhar Muimhneach* the Mac Donoghs were descended from Diarmaid Ruadh son of Cormac Fionn, king of Desmond. (Cormac died in 1247.) Diarmaid's grandson was named Donnchadh na Sgoile but it may not be from him that the Mac Carthys of Duhallow took their *alias* 'Mac Donogh'.

Cormac óg, son of Donnchadh na Sgoile, died in 1380 according to the *Annals of the Four Masters*. Nothing further is recorded for over a century until 1486 when, the *Annals of Ulster* inform us, Barry Mór was killed in the course of a Christmas Day raid on the lands of Donn-chadh óg Mac Carthy, lord of Ealla. This Donnchadh, who died in 1501, was twice married (to daughters of the White Knight and of Mac Carthy Mór) and descendants of his sons of the two marriages were in contention for many generations as to who was the lawful lord of Duhallow. It may well be that the descent of both parties from Donn-chadh óg caused them to be known as 'Mac Donogh'.

Perrott's 1585 parliament included among its members (according to *A.F.M.*) '. . . the two who were in contention with each other about the lordship of Dúithche Ealla — namely Dermod son of Eoghan son of Donnchadh an Bhóthair son of Eoghan Mac Donogh, and Donnchadh son of Cormac óg son of Cormac Mac Donogh'. It was Cormac óg who in 1524 defeated the invading O Connors of Kerry but in 1561 the lord and captain of Dowally pardoned was 'Dermot m'Donoghue O'Cary alias Mc Donoghowe of Keantoirke' — probably a son of Donncadh an Bhóthair. In 1569, after the lord of Duhallow, accompanied by Mac Auliffe and O Keeffe, had joined the rebellion of James Fitzmaurice, Lord Deputy Sidney marched into his country pulling down castles, burning villages and spoiling his fields until he (Mac Donogh) and his followers were forced into submission.

But the contention for the lordship continued. Donogh Mac Cormac when he prosecuted some of the Mac Carthys of Drishane for taking over Dromsicane and two other townlands in 1592 was described as 'alias Mac Donogh'. Florence Mac Carthy too in 1589 called him 'Chefe Lorde of the countrie of Dowalla' but five years later gave Dermot mac Owen the title of 'the young Mac Donogh'. While Florence was imprisoned one of his fears was that Dermot Mac Owen would be put in his place as 'Mac Carthy Mór'. Florence and Dermot, Hugh O Neill and James fitz Thomas of Desmond were the four who wrote to the Pope asking him to depose Elizabeth from the throne of England.

The chieftaincy dispute did not go unnoticed in government circles. In 1598 Cecil wrote to Norreys in a cold-blooded fashion '. . . It shall be convenient you do promise Donogh Mc Cormack the other part of the Dually, if he will do service upon (i.e. dispose of) his competitor Derby Mc Owen'. Hugh O Neill removed the threat by making a prisoner of Donogh in 1600. Carew, in turn, secured the submission of Dermot Mac Owen, – 'a man for wit and courage nothing inferior to any of the Munster Rebels' according to *Pacata Hibernia*. Carew regarded this as one of the highlights of the year 1600, and to make doubly sure had Dermot imprisoned the following year before the arrival of the Spaniards at Kinsale. Donogh mac Cormac was then released by O Neill 'to set a fire in Munster' but he was killed in O Shaughnessy's country in March, 1601.

In 1604, when the hostilities had ended, Dermot mac Owen was released, and a royal letter authorized acceptance of his 'surrender and regrant' although this does not seem to have happened until 1615. Dermot's next project was the erection of a new residence. The previous castles of the Mac Donoghs were at Curragh, Lohort, Dromsicane and Kanturk. Curragh is in the parish of Kilbrin and no trace of its castle now remains, but Dromsicane castle in Cullen parish and Lohort castle in Castlemagner parish are still in a good state of preservation.

The original castle of Kanturk which was their chief residence, the one taken and plundered by the Earl of Kildare during a raid on Duhallow in 1510, must have been in or near the town of Kanturk (par. Clonfert). Dermot mac Owen's massive ornate structure, the present 'Kanturk Castle', was erected about a mile to the south of Kanturk in the town-land of Paal East and parish of Kilmeen. The building was not completed, however, as the roof and parapets were never put on. Because of its non-completion many legends grew up around it, the best-known being that the castle was never finished because of complaints made to Queen Elizabeth who objected to 'this strong and regular fortress' within her realm of Ireland and ordered work on it to be stopped. But one wonders how a Jacobean castellated mansion with large windows could prove any greater threat to the security of the state than the many similar buildings of the period elsewhere. There is a more likely if more prosaic explanation, namely, lack of money. It was later claimed that Sir Philip Percival had lent more money by way of mortgages to the Mac Carthys, prior to 1641, than the whole manor of Kanturk and lands of Duhallow were worth.

KANTURK CASTLE *(Smith's Cork, 1750)*

Dermot Mac Owen died about 1620 leaving Dermot óg as his heir, though once more a claim was laid to the estates by Donogh mac Cormac's son, Cormac, then living at Curragh. Soon Dermot and Cormac were to be united in misfortune since both, along with many of their relatives in Duhallow, were swept along on the tide of rebellion in 1641 to inevitable destruction. Dromsicane had its moment of glory in 1645 when Dermot welcomed there the Papal Nuncio, Rinuccini, who was on his way from Kenmare to Kilkenny. Lohort castle was taken in 1650 by Sir Hardress Waller after being severely battered by cannon and Dermot himself is said to have been slain as he charged at the head of his squadron of horse during the battle of Knockniclashy in 1652. His estates were duly confiscated and at the Court of Claims in 1666 Sir Philip Percival's mortgages were certified and since Dermot had lost his equity of redemption by engaging in rebellion Percival got possession.

The estates were never restored but we find Mac Carthys described as 'of Kanturk' and 'of Lohort' outlawed for siding with King James in 1690. The landless Colonel Charles Mac Carthy, alias Mac Donogh, was still looked upon as lord of Duhallow, and although he submitted to King William before the final defeat at Aughrim he was nevertheless attainted. A Lieut. Dennis Mac Carthy, alias Mac Donogh, of Church-town, was successful in his claim for restoration, under the articles of Limerick in 1699. After this the Mac Donogh Mac Carthys fade into oblivion, recalled only by a few ruined castles and a handful of place-names such as Glantaunmacarthy in Kilmeen parish and the four 'Tooreens' — Tooreenfineen, Tooreencormack, Tooreendermot and Tooreendonnell in the parishes of Kilmeen and Clonfert.

The numerical and political strength of the Mac Carthys generally is demonstrated by the fact that no less than 115 landowners of the name were outlawed in Co. Cork in 1643. The Cromwellian confiscations and plantations had a more devastating effect on them than on any other clan in the county. There were over one hundred Mac Carthy proprietors in Carbery in 1641 and forty-three in Muskerry, apart from those in other areas. Very few retained any of their ancestral estates in the 18th century. Yet a large number remained as lessees or tenants on their former lands, and down to the present day there are those who can trace their ancestry back to one of the branches of a sept which dominated the history of Desmond for many centuries, even though its princes are no more.

To quote Ó Raithile once again (in Stephens' translation):

> *They are all gone. Mac Caura Mór is dead,*
> *Mac Caura of the Lee is finishèd,*
> *Mac Caura of Kanturk joined clay to clay*
> *And gat him gone, and bides as deep as they.*

Ó CEALLACHÁIN

(O) CALLAGHAN   CALLAHAN

The O Callaghans were another family directly descended from the kings of Eóganacht Caisil, one of the most renowned of whom was Ceallachán who died in 954. His son, Donnchadh mac Ceallacháin, also king of Cashel, died in 963. One of Ceallachán's grandsons was Sáerbrethach – the father of Carthach from whom were named the Mac Carthys – and another was Murchadh from whom the Uí Cheallacháin descend. Murchadh may have been the father of Donnchadh Ua Ceallacháin, *ríoghdhamhna Caisil*, slain by the Osraighe in 1053. However, the descent continued through another son, Domhnall, the father of Ceallachán – presumably the Cellachán Ua Cellacháin who in 1092 slew the reigning king of Eóganacht Caisil, Donnchadh son of Carthach. Twenty years later Ceallachán's grandson, Aodh, slew another noble of the Eóganacht, one connected to him by marriage. In 1115, no doubt in retaliation, Cellachán Ua Cellacháin ('of Cashel') was himself slain.

These killings and counter-killings indicate a succession dispute which seems to have ended with the death in Cork in 1121 of Mael Sechnaill Ua Cellacháin (described as 'King of the south of Ireland') after which the Mac Carthy line remained in the ascendant. The early 12th century shrine of St. Laichtín's hand (formerly preserved in Donaghmore and now in the National Museum) bears an inscription asking for prayers for (a) Tadhg son of Mac Carthaigh, king (of Desmond) (b) Cormac, his brother, then *righdhamhna* (crown prince) and (c) Mael Sechnaill U Cellachain, described as *ard rig na feinni* ('chief king of the warrior band'), the man who fashioned the decoration of the shrine.

A son of Aodh Ó Ceallacháin was killed, again in an internecine battle, in 1158. This was probably Murchadh from whom the later chieftains of the family were descended. After this they are not mentioned in the annals until 1283 when the Uí Cheallacháin were aiding the O Mahonys and Mac Carthy of Carbery in a revolt against Mac Carthy, king of Desmond. By then the Norman invasion had had its disruptive effect on the O Callaghans, who appear now and again in English official documents. Two of the O Fyns (one was vicar of Kinsale) were, in 1295, charged with receiving Griffin Ocallochan, apparently a 'felon'. Half a century later we find two O Callaghans together with Mac Carthys, O Mahonys and others charged with having been part of the army assembled by the Earl of Desmond to subvert the king and destroy his lands. Their names are given as Mc Craygh O Kaillaghan and Donghwyth Ocaillaghan; a Donnchadh is to be found in the O Callaghan genealogy (in the *Leabhar Muimhneach*) who would have lived about this period, and Mac Craith (a name which occurs more than once) may have been his brother.

By this time the O Callaghans must have been settled in what came to be known in the 16th century as *Pobal Uí Cheallacháin* (O Callaghan's country) west of Mallow, on both sides of the Blackwater. Ó Huidhrín, whose topographical poem was compiled around 1400, mentions Ó Ceallacháin twice, first as lord of Cineál Aodha (Kinalea) — an obvious mistake — and later, more correctly, as lord of some unnamed territory in Duhallow:

> *Ó Ceallacháin an chnis ghil*
> *do shíol Ceallacháin Chaisil.*

(O Callaghan the fair-skinned, of the seed of Ceallachán of Cashel).

Pobal Uí Cheallacháin formed the south-eastern angle of Duhallow barony, namely, the parishes of Kilshannig and Clonmeen south of the Blackwater together with Roskeen and parts of Ballyclogh, Castlemagner and Dromtarriff to the north. Their principal castles were at Clonmeen (*Cluain Mhín*) and Dromaneen (*Druiminín*) with a lesser one at Dromore. The Mac Donogh Mac Carthys were overlords of this territory. In the 16th century they claimed out of Pobal Uí Cheallacháin, meat, drink and wages for twenty-seven gallowglass or soldiers with their boys, and meat, drink and lodging for one third of all strangers which Owen Mac Donogh might please to entertain as often as occasion did require. Also twenty-one cows out of every felon's goods in the barony, and liberty to hunt, kill, fowl and fish.

At the start of the 16th century Conchubhar *Laighneach* Ó Ceallacháin was chief, perhaps as early as 1500 when Muintir Cheallacháin were aiding Thomas Barry in the killing of David Barry, archdeacon of Cloyne and Cork, in retribution for David's slaying of his own kinsman, Barry Mór. Conchubhar was succeeded by his son, Tadhg Ruadh, who died in 1537, and Tadhg by his son, Donnchadh.

This Donnchadh was celebrated in an anonymous poem (of between 400 and 500 lines) which detailed all the places in Munster from which he had taken a *creach* or cattle-spoil. *Deacair comhaireamh a chreach* (difficult it is to enumerate his spoilings) the poet begins, and thereupon proceeds to list approximately two hundred places in the counties of Cork, Kerry and Limerick — some even in Tipperary and Waterford — which had been visited by the marauding Donnchadh. The account is patently exaggerated but even if only half of it were true it would indicate that Donnchadh, throughout his more than forty-year reign, gloried in medieval-type *creachs*, apparently regarding them as a facet of normal living. There is some confirmation of the custom from official sources. Early in his reign, in 1539, there is a record of 'peace made with Donough O Callaghan'. Much later a 'presentment' at the 1575 sessions held at Cork says '. . . we present that Teigg Ettarremon mac Owen and Donyll Keigh mac Thomas mac Teigg, of Pobble Ycally-ghan, not only to be notoriuse theeffes but also wrongfully came in August with force and armes, viz., in the night tyme, to Barnehelly (Barnahely near Ringaskiddy) and then and their thre caples . . . there found, felloniously toke and lead awaye contrarie to her Majesties peace'. (Tadhg a'tearmainn and Domhnall Caoch were obviously O Callaghans; in 1576 amongst those pardoned in Duhallow were Donald mac Thomas I Kallaghan of Roskeen and Thady mac Owen mac Donogh of Gortmore (par. Clonmeen.)

Despite his many forays, Donnchadh died of extreme old age in 1578, his son, Conchubhar, having pre-deceased him. Four years before he died, Donnchadh, disregarding the old Irish custom of tanistry, enfeoffed, in the English fashion, his grandson Ceallachán with his inheritance for life, with a remainder to Donnchadh (nephew of Ceal-lachán) and remainders to the heirs male of both.

As it happened, Ceallachán was drowned in the Blackwater just four months after his grandfather's death, at which time his nephew, Donnchadh, was but twelve years of age. (He died at the age of eighteen, leaving no heirs.) So the chieftaincy was assumed by Conchubhar na Carraige whose father, Dermot, one of old Donnchad's six brothers, was known as 'prior' of the suppressed abbey of Ballybeg. At his in-auguration Conchubhar 'of the rock' was presented with the white rod of chieftaincy by Domhnall Mac Carthy Mór, according to the ancient Irish custom. But though Conchubhar was obviously taking advantage of the Irish law of tanistry, once he had attained power he used the English 'Surrender and Regrant' system in order to obtain legal possession from the crown. Before he got permission to do so, an inquisition was held, in October, 1594, before Sir Thomas Norris, the findings being that while O Callaghan was lord of his 'country', the tanist (then Tadhg O Callaghan) was entitled to the lands of Gortroe (par. Kilshannig), Pallas (par. Roskeen) and 'the Fandems', while every kinsman of O Callaghan was to have a certain parcel of land to live upon. The lands allotted to each were named and the group as a whole was confined to sons and grandsons of former chiefs. A brother of Conchubhar's named Irrelaugh (*Írgalach*) had Kilcolman (par. Kilshannig) as his portion. The jurors verdict, however, indicated that the chief alone was the true legal owner of the lands, a verdict which did not exactly reflect Irish custom. So Conchubhar was enabled to make his surrender on 2nd December, 1594, and five days later received his regrant. The lands comprised all the townlands of Pobal Uí Cheal-lacháin (the boundaries of which are stated) including the castle and lands of Clonmeen, the castle and lands of Dromaneen and the castle and lands of Dromore.

There is now no trace of the last-named castle but it is said to have been situated on the west bank of the Clyda, between Dromore Lodge and Old Dromore House, a short distance to the north of Barrett's Castle near Mourne Abbey. (The townlands of Dromore, Dromore North, Dromore South and Newberry between them contain over 2,300 acres.) The castle of Dromore in 'O Kalehann's land' is mentioned in a document relating to the Earl of Desmond's lands forfeited in 1584. (The only O Callaghan to be attainted in 1588 for taking part in this Earl's rebellion was Patrick Callaghan of Clonmeen though in the reign of James I mention is made of 'Rathmore ¼ ploughland, parcel of the estate of Tady mac Morrogho O Callaghane and Morrice mac Teige O Callaghane, attainted'.) In 1573 pardons were issued to Conoghor mac Teig O Kallaghan of Dromore and to Dermot mac Owen O Callaghan alias Baron of Dromore. This title was not an English creation and must have been assumed by the family who lived there. Dromore later passed to the Newman family — although John and Timothy Callaghan, 'gents.', were at Dromore in 1735.

Returning now to old Donnchadh's enfeoffment of 1574 we find that both Callaghan and his nephew died without legitimate offspring, leaving Callaghan's sister, Eleanor, as his heiress. Eleanor was married to Art O Keeffe of neighbouring Pobal Uí Chaoimh and when she died, her son, Manus O Keeffe, inherited her interest. But realizing the inadvisability of pursuing his interest in the lands of another clan, Manus transferred his claim to his cousin Cahir O Callaghan (Cathaoir Modartha of the pedigrees), illegitimate son of Callaghan. Cahir occupied Dromaneen and Dromore around 1600. (In 1599 he obtained muskets and gunpowder from the Earl of Essex on the pretext of defending his castle for the queen, 'but within two dayes after he turned traytor'.) In the meatime Conchubhar 'of the rock' had enfeoffed one Fagan with the castle of Dromaneen and Fagan in turn had enfeoffed Brian mac Owen Mac Swiney, whose daughter was married to Conchubhar's son. (Conchubhar himself was married to a daughter of Turlogh *bacach* Mac Swiney.)

Cahir was ejected from his castle and in 1605 brought an action against John Barry, sheriff of Co. Cork, Brian mac Owen (Mac Swiney) of Castlemore and Conogher O Callaghane of Clonmeen for having with the aid of 200 persons taken forcible possession of his castle of Dromaneen. He won his case and Conogher, as 'one of the principal setters on' of the riot, was fined £100. A second law-case followed and although the court's findings cut across the law of tanistry, a compromise solution was reached and in 1610 both parties surrendered their lands once more so as to receive letters patent for them. Cahir continued to hold Dromaneen castle — which appears to have been completely rebuilt about this time — as well as Dromore, while Conchubhar 'of the rock' remained at Clonmeen where he died in 1612. Callaghan, son of Conchubhar, who married Joan Butler, daughter of Lord Dunboyne, was drowned while swimming, 28th May 1631, and his only daughter and heiress, Elena, then married Cahir's son and heir, Donnchadh, thus uniting the two factions once more.

The chiefs of Duhallow all came out in support of the 1641 rebellion and foremost among them was Donnchadh O Callaghan of Clonmeen. He was a member of the Supreme Council of the Irish Confederation of Kilkenny and a colonel in the Confederate army at the battle of Manning ford where Vavasour was defeated in 1642. In the same year Rev. Urbanus Vigors wrote that 'great O Callahane's castle' had been captured by the forces of Parliament, but if Clonmeen is the castle in question it must have been recaptured or restored by 1645 in which year the Papal Nuncio, Rinuccini, on his route from Ardkilly to Kilkenny stayed at Clonmeen where he was munificently entertained by O Callaghan, as were the nobles and gentry of the surrounding countryside who came to do homage to the Nuncio.

Naturally, Donnchadh and others incurred the enmity of the English interest. Thomas Bettesworth deposed, after the rebellion, that part of his goods was driven away by soldiers of Dermot Carty, alias Mac Donogh and by Donogh Mac Cahir O Callaghan. Cnoghor Keogh O Callaghan was accused of having basely deserted Sir Philip Percival's interest and of endeavouring to betray Liscarroll into the rebels' hands. In 1643 a total of seventeen O Callaghan 'gentlemen' were declared outlaws – Donnchadh and Tirleagh of Clonmeen; Cahir, Callaghan, Cornelius and Teige Roe of Dromaneen; Cahir, Donogh and Teige of Kilpadder; Cahir of Dromelegagh, Cahir of Trrorowe; Cornelius Reigh of Coolageela (par. Kilbrin); Dermott of Gortroe (par. Kilshannig); Dermod and Owen mac Donagh of Kilbranty; John of Coolemoty and Teige of Ruanes (par. Ballyclogh). Callaghan O Callaghan was a colonel in the Confederate forces and one of the signatories of the final surrender at Ross castle, 28 June 1652.

In the ensuing confiscations the O Callaghans forfeited estates amounting to about 24,000 plantation acres. Donnchadh, the chieftain, was the registered owner of about 20,000 acres; others who forfeited were Callaghan and Owen of Clonmeen, Cahir of Kilpadder, Dermod of Gortroe, Teige Roe of Roskeen, and Cnogher who lost over 1,200 acres in Dunbulloge parish (held by Cahir O Callaghan of Dromaneen in 1638). The lands were allotted to such people as Sir Nicholas Purdon, Dame Elizabeth Fenton, Lord Kingston, John Hodder, Richard Newman and Sir Richard Kyrle. Despite a royal declaration of gratitude and favour in 1660, Donnchadh was refused a Decree of Innocence in 1663 – though one was granted to Teige Callaghan, son and heir of Knogher, who had 233 acres restored in Dromalour (par. Dromtarriff). Eventually, however, Donnchadh regained about 2,000 acres in Co. Cork. By then he had removed into Co. Clare where, as a transplantee, he had received 2,500 acres. The census of 1659 lists as 'tituladoes' in the townland of Montallone (Mountallon), parish of Clonelea: 'Donnogh O Callaghane, Esq., Teige, Donogh and Cahir his sons, gent.'. In Ballyquin (par. Killogenedy) was Connor O Callaghane, Esq., (who had been allotted 400 Irish acres). There were 19 O Callaghans among the principal Irish families in the barony of Tulla. In the same year an order was issued for the apprehension of Callaghan O Callaghan and Charles O Callaghan in Co. Clare. Colonel Callaghan O Callaghan accompanied Lord Muskerry on his return from the continent to face imprisonment in 1654.

Donnchadh óg succeeded his father at Mountallon and was, in turn, succeeded by Domhnall who died in 1724 in the parish of Whitechurch (Co. Cork) where he had gone to take up the executorship of the property of his kinsman, Melchior Lavallin. He was buried in Kilcrea. In the same year his brother Conchubhar also died and was buried at Quin abbey, Co. Clare. Both brothers were the subjects of elegies by the poet Seán na Raithíneach Ó Murchadha while Domhnall was also lamented by the celebrated Aodhagán Ó Raithile, who painted a vivid word-picture of life in the good old days in the castle of Cluain Mhín:

> *Puirt ar chruitibh dá seinm go ceolmhar*
> *Startha dá léigheadh ag lucht léighinn is eoluis,*
> *Mar a mbíodh trácht gan cháim ar órdaibh,*
> *Is ar gach sloinneadh dar geineadh san Eoraip.*

A man's genealogy was all-important in those days and in his poem Ó Raithile traced Domhnall's back to Adam! Domhnall's son and heir was Donogh, of Kilgory castle, Co. Clare. Donogh was succeeded by his son Edmund, a barrister, who had five daughters, but no son. In 1944 official recognition as 'The O Callaghan' was granted by the Genealogical Office to Don Juan O Callaghan of Tortosa, Spain, a descendant of Cornelius O Callaghan of Lahardane, Co. Clare (grandson of Col. Donogh), who entered the Spanish army in 1717. The O Callaghans are still represented in Co. Clare where they gave their name to the village of O Callaghan's Mills in the barony of Tulla Lower.

Meantime, back in Duhallow, where the majority of the O Callaghans still remained, most of their confiscated estates were acquired, from fellow-grantees, by Sir Richard Kyrle who later sold them to Richard Newman. In 1678 Kyrle passed patent for Clonmeen, Dromaneen and other lands in Duhallow 'saving to Donogh O Callaghan and his heirs all such right, title and interest as the Commissioners shall adjudge to him, as one of the 54 persons appointed to be restored in the Explanatory Act'. (Callaghan O Callaghan, son of Donogh, wrote (from Blarney) to Lord Orrery in August of that year telling him that he could not put bread into his own mouth but for the generosity of Sir Richard Kyrle.) In that year also there was a Cahir O Callaghan at Curragh (par. Kilbrin), gent., the same Cahir, perhaps, who assisted James Wall in an attempt to recover Wallstown in 1689.

Their position in Duhallow was further weakened by their support of the losing side in the Jacobite wars. In October 1690 Lord Barrymore wrote to the Duke of Wirtemberg: 'I have within these two days received a very humble petition on behalf of Colonel Mac Donogh,

Chief of the Country called Duhallow and of another chieftain of a country called O Callaghan in order to obtain the protection of their Majesties (i.e. William and Mary). It is of very great consequence to draw over people of their quality and interest, who will bring with them a thousand men and at least seven or eight thousand cows.' Among those outlawed in 1690 for supporting King James were Donogh O Callaghan alias O Callaghan of Clonmeen and Donogh O Callaghan of Mountallon. These were, apparently, father and son; Donogh óg was Lieutenant-Colonel in Barrett's Infantry in King James' army. Also outlawed were Thady Callaghane of Drumalour and Cornelius Callaghan of Carrigoon. Others of the name were outlawed in the following year for 'foreign treason' — Callaghan and Charles, two other sons of Donogh of Clonmeen; Major Dermot of Curragh; Cornelius, John and Owen of Laghnane; Morgan and Patrick of Mountallon. (A Major O Callaghan was wounded at Villaviciosa in Spain while fighting for King Philip in 1710.)

After the hostilities had ended, however, several of these were successful in their claims for restoration under the articles of Limerick. They included Colonel Donogh, now of Kilgory, Co. Clare, Teige of Mountallon, Darby of Killurane (Co. Clare), Charles of Roskeen, Dennis of Subulter and Teige Reagh Callaghan of Rossline (par. Clonfert). The last-named was adjudged 'eligible' having been in the garrison of Ballyclogh on 3 Oct. 1691 and having submitted to the government and taken the oath of fidelity.

Clonmeen itself remained an O Callaghan seat in the 18th century, though whether as part of the lands restored or as land on lease from Kyrle or Newman is not clear. In 1718 Cornelius Callaghan presented an inscribed chalice to the Protestant church of Clonmeen and was buried in a newly-erected vault there in 1736. When Smith wrote (c. 1750), Clonmeen was 'a good house of Cornelius O Callaghan, Esq., near it is the parish church, and more east are the remains of the castle of Clonmene, ruined in the wars of 1641.' This Cornelius was the second son of the elder Cornelius. His nephew Robert (son of Robert who died c. 1727) was the actual heir and his name is to be found in deeds relating to Clonmeen c. 1750. Eventually he sold or let the lands and went to live in Cork city. The *Hibernian Chronicle* records the death on 6th March 1778 of Robert O Callaghan, the last of the ancient family of O Callaghan of Clonmeen, at Bachelor's Quay, Cork.

A more socially successful branch of the family settled in Shanbally near Clogheen, Co. Tipperary. The first of them was Cornelius O Callaghan, son of Timothy O Callaghan of Banteer. Cornelius was a distinguished chancery lawyer and M.P. for Fethard, 1713-14. His son, Robert, and great-grandson, Cornelius, were also M.P.s for Fethard. The last-named was created Baron of Lismore in 1785. A century later Lord Viscount Lismore possessed estates of 42,206 acres in Cos. Tipperary, Limerick and Cork — including some of the ancestral lands in Duhallow.

Many O Callaghans of lesser note had moved out of Duhallow by 1659 when, according to the census of that year (which has no returns for Duhallow) there were three families of the name in Mallow, ten in the north Liberties of Cork and ten in the barony of Connello, Co. Limerick.

Mac Ceallacháin

There are no census returns for Muskerry, either, but in the barony of Barretts (which once formed part of Muskerry) seventeen families of *Mc Callaghanes* were recorded. These were the Callaghans of Muskerry who had a slightly different origin to the O Callaghans of Duhallow, though basically of the same stock. According to the *Leabhar Muimhneach*, 'Clann Cheallacháin i Músgraighe' are, like the Mac Auliffes, descended from Tadhg Mac Carthy, brother of Cormac Muighe Thamhnach who was killed in 1138. From the 15th century on the name occurs in ecclesiastical contexts. Cornelius Mackeallachayn was vicar of Clonfert (Duhallow) up to the time of his death in 1401. Donald Mackeallacayn was abbot of Gill Abbey prior to 1469. Donatus Mickellachayn was appointed to the parish of Knockavilla in 1492 while Donald Veckcallaghan was vicar of Garrycloyne in the 16th century.

A document dated 1600 names the 'Clancallaghans' as followers of the Mac Carthys in Muskerry, holding three ploughlands from them. Amongst the Mac Carthy followers to get pardons in 1573 and 1576 were Owen mac Moriertagh O Keallaghane of Castleinch, yeoman, Keallaghan mac Wohny (*Uaithne*) I Keallaghain and Kallaghan mac Donogh mac Kallaghan of Carrigadrohid, yeomen, Shane mac Dermot O Caellaghain alias Mac ny flahe of Blarney, Donald, Conoghor and Owen mac Teige mac Donogho I Kallaghan of Pluckanes and Teige mac Owen Brycke (*mac Eoghain bhric*) I Challaghan of Gort Donoughmore. Again, in 1601-2 many Mac Callaghans and O Callaghans, obviously Mac Carthy followers, were pardoned in Muskerry. They included Owen mac Moriertagh Mac Callaghan of Curraghbeg (par. Athnowen), gent. and his son Donnell, of Blarney, gent. Others were to be found in Cloghroe, Carrigadrohid and Donoughmore. In Ardamadane (par. Garrycloyne) and Loughane (par. Matehy) the same people were listed as Mac Callaghans in one fiant and as O Callaghans in another.

The most celebrated member of this family was John Mac Callaghan of Carrigadrohid (*Rupes pontis*). Ordained priest in France, he obtained a doctorate in Paris and returned to Ireland in 1645. In the following year the Supreme Council of the Confederation of Kilkenny (prompted by Lord Muskerry) nominated him for the vacant bishopric of Cork, but this was vetoed by the Papal Nuncio, who had Robert Barry appointed instead. John died in 1654.

The form Mac Callaghan seems to have died out in Muskerry soon afterwards. When a son of Eugene son of Cornelius of Carrigadrohid became a knight of Spain in 1722 he was named as Matthew O Callaghan.

Ó COCHLÁIN

COUGHLAN   COGHLAN   COHALAN

More than one family group of this name appear to have originated within the confines of the present Co. Cork. A Cochlán, son of Fiachna, is to be found in the genealogies of the Uí Liatháin though it is not stated if any descendants were named after him. In the Fir Maighe Féne territory, *Críchad an Chaoilli* names Hí Cochláin, along with Hí Diarmada as the inhabitants of Daire Hí Diarmada in the tuath of Magh Finne, a district between the Awbeg and the Nagles Mts. both north and south of the Blackwater. Daire Hí Diarmada would be roughly equivalent to the modern Ballymague (par. Caherduggan). The Hí Cochláin were also hereditary clerics of the church of Kilcummer.

An Leabhar Muimhneach names Tuath Chochláin as one of the *tuatha* of Clann Sealbhaigh, a tribal area in Uí Eachach territory centred on Kinneigh which gave its name to one of the old deaneries of Cork diocese. Ua Cochláin was chieftain of this *tuath*. John Windele, who visited Kinneigh in 1840, recorded an oral tradition there that Cian O Mahony endowed his daughter with a hundred ploughlands on her marriage to Sealbhach O Coghlan. The daughter of O Coghlan in turn married Dermot O Crowley and the lands then passed to the O Crowleys.

A tradition such as this is hardly to be taken literally, but it may reflect an actual change of occupiers in 1283 when, as a result of the defeat of the Carbery Mac Carthys by Mac Carthy Mór, Clann Sealbhaigh fled from their own territory into An Fonn Iartharach (the western peninsulas) and were replaced with immigrants brought in by Mac Carthy Mór — including, perhaps, the O Crowleys from Connacht.

This would explain why, in later centuries, the Uí Chochláin were continuously associated with the parishes of Kilmoe and Skull in An Fonn Iartharach. As early as 1290 when Maurice de Carew took legal proceedings against his tenants in 'Catherach Cro and Inysfade' (?Colla, Croagh and Long Island, par. Skull) one of those tenants was Walter Ocothelan, the others being mainly O Mahonys. Ten years later, Maurice Ocoghlan is mentioned in connection with the king's land.

Before the dispersal the Uí Shealbhaigh were a noted ecclesiastical family who supplied several bishops to the see of Cork between the eighth and twelfth centuries. It is interesting that Clérech Ua Sealbhaigh, *ard-chomharba Bairre*, who died in 1085, was succeeded by a learned bishop, Ua Cochláin who died in 1096, according to the *Annals of the Four Masters*. (There was another Ó Cochláin occupant of the see of Cork in the present century.)

Several clerics of the name appear also in the 15th century. Donnchadh Ocochlayn was perpetual vicar of Kilmoe (Goleen) in 1458, in succession to John O Coughlan. (He was charged with having neglected the cure of his parishioners on account of his ignorance of letters.) The O Coughlans seem to have taken the term 'perpetual' literally, for in 1472 Donaldus Ochoclayn was perpetual vicar of Kilmoe and twenty years later Johannes Ochoclayn filled the same position. Even after the reformation Dermot O Coughlan was Church of Ireland vicar of Kilmoe from 1619 until the 1641 rebellion forced him to cross to England where he died. The Thadeus Coghlan who was a landowner in the parish in 1700 was perhaps a descendant or relative of his. Strangely enough, in 1700 also, the parish priest of Kilmoe and of the western part of Schull was a Tadhg Ó Cochláin. There were many Church of Ireland clergymen with the surname Coghlan in the dioceses of Cork and Cloyne in the 19th century.

Turning to the lay members of the name, it is again obvious from the Elizabethan Fiants that the Kilmoe-Schull area was their principal stronghold. The following were among those pardoned:

1576: Maurice Mac Donagh O Cughlane of Kilmoe.
1584: Teig Mac Dermod mac Teig I Coughlain of Ardintenant.
1585: Conoghor roe O Coghlane, horseman.
1586: Philip bwy mac Donogh mac Conoghor O Coughlane of Kilbrittain, horseboy.
1594: Philip bwy O Coghlane of Kinalea.
1601: Donell O Coghlaine of Whiddy.
Teige riogh (*riabhach*) O Coghelane of Dunbeacon, husbandman.
Donell oge O Coghlane of Ballytrasna.
Dermod, Teig and Shane mac Donogh Coghlane of Enaghoughter (par. Kilmoe).
1603: Dermod mac Shane O Coghlane of Ardintenant.

In the 16th century also, More ny Coghlane of Ivaghe married Seán Mac Carthy of Sliocht Seáin.

At least one family — perhaps that of Teig of Ardintenant — rose in the world. In 1627 Donal O Mahony Fionn of Ballydevlin leased to Dermot mac Teige Coghlane of Carrigmanus, gent., the castle of Dunlogh (Three Castle Head) with the ploughlands of Dunlogh, Kildunlogh and three others. A later document indicates that Richard Boyle, Earl of Cork, gained an interest in these lands. From the Book of Survey and Distribution we learn that after the Cromwellian wars Dunlogh and other lands of Dermod Coghline — 1,868 acres in all — went to the Earl of Cork. Dermod may well be the 'Dermond O Coghlan, Rebell, of Scull' named by Sir William Hull in his deposition (1642) as one who owed him money 'before the troubles'. Dermod Mac Teige O Coghlan and Donogh mac Teige O Coghlan, gentlemen, both of Long Island (par. Skull) were outlawed in 1643 for taking part in that rebellion.

Among the wills registered in the 18th century were those of Donell O Coghlan of Crookhaven (1620) and John Coghlan of Crookhaven (1678). The list of those outlawed for supporting King James II in 1690 includes the names of John and Richard Coghlan of Crookhaven, also Dermot Coghlan of Ardintenant.

That some of the name and their descendants may have remained in the Kinneigh area up to the mid-17th century is indicated first by the fact that Thateus Ocochlayn was perpetual vicar of Kinneigh in 1484 and later by the outlawry in 1643 of Philip O Coghlane of Enniskeane, gent., and Donogh O Coghlane of Buddrimeen (par. Ballymoney), yeoman. There was also a Philip Coghlane who became a freeman of Cork in 1633.

Capt. John Coughlan of Bandonbridge whose will was registered in 1709 was married to Dorothy Gookin and had five English tenants on his lands which comprised Kilmeen and Lissivoanig als. Adesses land in Kinalmeaky, Ratharoon (par. Ballinadee) Lisbealad (par. Drinagh) Drombofinny and Aghyohill (par. Desertserges). John Coghlan, Esq., had a seat at Rossmore (par. Kilmeen) in 1741. William Coughlan of Ballea, gent., had a will registered in 1731. In the 19th century there was an Irish scholar in Bandon named Domhnall Ó Cochláin, for whom Finghin O Halloran of Garranes (Templemartin) copied a manuscript of *Cath Fionntrágha*.

The only townland in Co. Cork embodying the family name is Ballycoughlan (Baile Uí Chochláin) in Innishannon parish, a name which perhaps originated in the 15th century. In Dromkeen in the same parish we find 'Dermod Coughlane and John his sonn' listed as 'tituladoes' in the 1659 census – probably the 'Darby Coghlane of Drumkeen' whose will was registered in 1676. Dromkeen, at the time of the 1659 census, was in the cantred of Kilbrittain, which had 18 families of Coghlanes. There were also 12 families in the barony of Barrymore, possibly descendants of the Fir Maighe family of that name. The bulk of the Coghlanes or Coughlans were still in west Cork however, with 18 families in East Carbery and 37 in West Carbery, and it is there that the majority of them may be found today. There is an interesting divergence between the two sides of the county in that in east Cork the surname is usually pronounced 'Caul-en' while in west Cork it is always 'Cock-len'.

(DE) COGAN

DE COGÁN   GOGÁN   GOGGIN

The small parish of Cogan, near Cardiff in South Wales, gave its name to this Cambro-Norman family which rose to great eminence in Ireland in the 13th century. A certain Milo held the manor of Cogan from the Earl of Gloucester in 1166, and the redoubtable Milo de Cogan who accompanied Strongbow to Ireland in 1170 was probably a son of his — a younger son, since neither he nor his descendants inherited the family property in Wales. Aided by his brother, Richard, Milo distinguished himself in the capture and subsequent defence of Dublin, of which he was made constable. He also served King Henry overseas and was rewarded (in 1177) with a grant of half Dermot Mac Carthy's 'Kingdom of Cork' reaching from Lismore to the tip of the Dingle peninsula. (The other half went to Robert Fitzstephen.) This was in the nature of a speculative grant as their inadequate Norman forces could not hope to conquer such a large area. The grantees 'allowed' Mac Carthy to retain 24 cantreds (for which they hoped to collect rent) and assigned seven to themselves, three to the east of Cork harbour being Fitzstephen's and four to the west de Cogan's.

Milo enjoyed his grant for a mere five years, as he was slain by the Uí Meic Thíre in 1182. Any settlements he made on his lands seem to have been near Cork city and Kinsale. He left no son to succeed him so his only daughter, Margaret, became a wealthy heiress much sought after in marriage. She appears to have had three husbands in succession: firstly, Ralph Fitzstephen (illegitimate son of Robert); secondly, a de Courcy (probably an illegitimate son of John de Courcy); and thirdly one Simon le Poer. Her son, Patrick de Courcy, was progenitor of the de Courcy family of Kinsale and the de Courcys later claimed the inheritance of Milo's half of the Kingdom of Cork. The original grant was, however, disregarded by King John who parcelled out large sections of it to new grantees. One of these was Richard de Cogan who, in 1207, was given the cantred of Múscraighe Mittaine, roughly equivalent to the modern baronies of East and West Muskerry (north of the Lee) and Barretts. This Richard was probably son of the elder Richard, Milo's brother. As well as acquiring lands in Co. Cork he also inherited the Welsh estate (which remained in the family until the 14th century). The Cogans were prominent in the struggle against the Irish in Desmond and appear to have been responsible for the death of Diarmaid Mac Carthy, king of Desmond, in 1229. Diarmaid's father, Domhnall Mór (d. 1206) was credited with the slaying (and flaying) of Geoffrey de Cogan

(probably another brother of Milo) together with his 'speckled kerne
. . . the most hated kerne who ever came into Ireland'.

Richard (II) married Basilia de Ridelesford and spent some years
on lands in Leinster given to him by his father-in-law. A strong Norman
thrust into Munster and the building of a string of castles around the
south-west coast *circa* 1215 A.D. induced him to settle in his Muskerry
lordship. Richard, and his successors, built several castles there, the
principal one being Castlemore (*Caisleán Mór Gógánach*) now Barrett's
Castle near Mourne Abbey. Furthermore, they came into possession of
lands south of the Lee, in what was formerly the western part of
Kinalmeaky. Here they built another big castle at Dundrinan (Castlemore near Crookstown). Other Cogan castles were at Magh Oiligh
(Moyola, now Aglish), Maglin (near Ballincollig), Carrigrohane and
possibly Macroom and Dún Uisce (Dunisky).

When Richard died (*c.* 1240) he was succeeded by his son John who
had married Maria, grand-daughter of Philip de Prendergast. Philip was
another of the original Norman conquistadores and had been rewarded
with a grant of the barony of Kerrycurrihy west of Cork Harbour,
where he built the castle of Carrigaline. John de Cogan died in 1278,
his son and heir (John II) having pre-deceased him (in 1272) leaving a
twelve-year-old boy (John III) to succeed him. When John III came of
age in 1281 he inherited all his grandfather's land in Muskerry along
with some in Connacht (where John I had founded the friary of Clare-
galway). Because of the lack of male heirs in the Prendergast family, he
also inherited the bulk of their estates – Carrigaline castle in Kerrycurrihy, lands to the east of Cork city and further holdings around
Ballyhea in north Cork.

Young John de Cogan, accordingly, was now one of the great Norman lords of Ireland – not least because his mother was Juliana,
daughter of Gerald fitz Maurice Fitzgerald. On the death of her brother
and nephew, Juliana became heiress to the vast Geraldine estates in
Leinster and Munster. A widow with a young son, however, was no
match for the manoeuvres of her influential relatives, particularly her
cousin John fitz Thomas. By one means or another Fitz Thomas
induced Juliana to hand over her estates to him, and though young
John when he came of age made several efforts to recover them – even
going so far on one occasion as to eject by force Fitz Thomas' men
from the manor of Athlacca (Co. Limerick) – he failed to dislodge the
powerful Geraldines, and John fitz Thomas went on to become the
first Earl of Kildare.

John de Cogan resigned himself to the inevitable and made his
principal residence at Mora (Mourne Abbey) although his manor of
Ballyhea appears to have been a more important one, for it was there
he held his manorial court. He later gave Ballyhea and neighbouring
Rathgoggan to his brother Henry in exchange for Connacht lands which
his father had given to him (Henry). Rathgoggan or Ráth Gogán where

the town of Charleville was later built took its name from the family. It will be noted that the form Gogán (rather than Cogán) was in use in Ireland in the 13th century and indeed was probably the pronunciation brought over by the Cambro-Normans themselves. This explains why the form Goggin is frequently — though not exclusively — used for this surname.

Meantime, life was not easy in the marches of Desmond particularly since the defeat of the Normans at Callann in 1261. Although the Cogans had not taken part in this battle — indeed they tended to ally themselves with the Carbery Mac Carthys against the Geraldines — they were, nevertheless, subjected to the attacks on castles, burnings of villages, etc. that ensued after Callann. Three castles on Cogan lands were burnt by Fínghin Mac Carthy — Macroom, Dunisky and Magh Oiligh. The Cogans never seem to have repossessed Macroom or Dunisky, though one branch remained in Magh Oiligh (Aglish). Less than a century later the Mac Carthys had taken (or retaken) so much of the barony that a new Mac Carthy lordship of Muskerry was created.

Dissension among the lords of Norman descent helped to create this situation. The Barretts, originally Cogan tenants, became so powerful that eventually a new barony (Barretts) was carved out of East Muskerry. The Barrys, Roches and Fitzgeralds also felt free to raid the lands of the Cogans, of whom there was now a number of minor branches. Apart from Milo, Richard and John, the Cogans favoured such Christian names as Geoffrey, Eustace, Henry, Walter, William, Michael, Thomas and David.

When John (III) de Cogan died in 1311 he left two sons, Milo and Peter. Both were minors, a factor which did not help their declining fortunes. Milo was still but a youth when, in 1316, he was killed in Connacht while attempting to quell a rebellion that followed the arrival of Edward Bruce. The *Annals of Ulster* describe him as *in Gogánach, in t-aen barún ba saire do bi in Erinn* (Cogan, the noblest baron in Ireland).

Peter was then only twelve years old, much too young to aid his people when in the following year the Barrys and Roches devastated David Cogan's lands from Cloghmacow (par. Kilmurry) to Barnahely on the shores of Cork harbour and burned the Cogan castle at Aglish. When Peter came of age in 1325 the king released to him an inheritance comprising 'one broken castle at Carrigaline, worth nothing per annum'. Six years later Peter was dead, again leaving an heir (Walter) who was a minor. Lord Barrymore got the wardship of this heir and also married Peter's widow, so that when Walter came of age, *circa* 1347, the Barrys had a firm foothold in the Cogan estates. Walter died unmarried and his brother, Peter, succeeded him. Peter seems to have lived at Ballyhea and died in 1371, leaving no heir, thus bringing to an end the premier line of de Cogan. The inquisition taken after his death refers to the destruction of the estates around Ballyhea by the Geraldines, and of

Mora (Mourne Abbey) by the Barretts. (William Barrett married Peter's widow!) Lands in West Muskerry were not even mentioned; they were long since under Mac Carthy domination.

A distant cousin, Geoffrey de Cogan, probably Geoffrey of Aglish, was eventually declared heir to what remained. At this period there were also Cogans in Carrigrohane, Maglin, Liskillea and Currykippane. Geoffrey strove to regain what had been lost to the Barretts and others, and when he died in 1388 he was succeeded by his son, Robert, who was sheriff of Cork in 1400. In 1405 Robert was described as *dominus de Kerycorthe*, i.e. Kerrycurrihy, which was now their chief stronghold. According to Smith, the barony was at one time known as *Long an Ghógánaigh*.

As a last resort, Robert Cogan in 1439 granted the ancient title to all lands in Co. Cork (and in Wales) to James Fitzgerald, Earl of Desmond, in order to gain the protection of that powerful lord. Carrigaline then became a Geraldine castle, while the Cogans resided at Barnahely castle (near Ringaskiddy) which along with nearby Coolmore castle they continued to hold for a further two centuries. There was a Lord Cogane in attendance on the Earl of Desmond when he went to greet Richard, Duke of York, in 1449, and after that we lose sight of the family for over a century.

William Cogan of Barnahely, who was born about 1540, is frequently mentioned in Elizabethan documents. He was one of the three M.P.s for Co. Cork in Perrot's Parliament of 1585-6. Many other Cogans received pardons in the Elizabethan Fiants. Among them was Donnell Chogan of Tracton Abbey, the first Cogan recorded as having a Gaelic first name. It is interesting that in Kinalea the Cogans were then known as Ogegoyaines (Ó Gogáin).

In 1600, during O'Neill's rebellion, John Meade, mayor of Cork, wrote to Cecil:

> One William mc miles Goggan, who was reported to have been a great malefactor and hath hanged one of Mc Teig's two sons, was lately apprehended near the franchises, and executed by martial law.

This was not, of course, William (M.P.) of Barnahely who, as far as we know, took no part in rebellious activities, but it may have been a relative of his. Another kinsman, Richard Gogaine fitz Philip of Barnahely, fought at Kinsale and afterwards accompanied de Aguila on his return to Spain.

The Cogans still held lands in the western portion of Kerrycurrihy, around Ballinhassig. They appear to have had a small castle at Ballinaboy, while Gogginshill townland (*Cnoc an Ghogánaigh*) nearby was named from the family.

William's great-grandson, another William, was fated to be the last Cogan owner of Barnahely. It was in the year 1642 when the Earl of

Cork wrote as follows to Dublin Castle:

> Goggan's Castle of Barnahely, which stands upon the sea in the barony of Kerry-Wherry, was the magazine of store for the rebels in that barony. On Friday last Sir Charles Vavasor boated from Cork two pieces of ordnance with a party of musqueteers, sailed thither, and landed one of his pieces of ordnance; the Lord Inchiquin, with his horse, went by land, and met him there, and upon discharging the first piece the ward desired quarter, which was given, to depart with their swords and skeins only. In the castle was above 1,000 barrels of wheat, wherein they placed a ward of 40 men and returned to Cork.

So the Cogans left their last stronghold. Apart from William and Edmond of Barnahely, other Cogans (Gogganes) outlawed at this time were Edmond of Ringcurran, James of Ballinaboy, James and Philip of Knockanevarody (Barretshill) and Peter of Ballynacourty (par. Cullen). James Cogane of Coolmore castle also forfeited all his lands. It may have been the same James Cogan (of Coolemore, Esq.) or his son who, along with James Gogan of Carrigoline, Esq. was outlawed in 1690 for supporting King James II, in a last bid to recover ancestral property. (There was a Capt. Cogan in Boisseleau's regiment in 1689.)

None of these Cogans regained any of his lands, but a Dr. Richard Cogan got most of the parish of Lisgoold in Barrymore (previously held by Garrett Barry of Leamlara) after the 17th century confiscations. There were obviously a few of the name in east Cork; there is a townland named Gogganstown not far from Lisgoold, while near Ballymaloe in Imokilly there was formerly a townland called Ballingogannigg.

According to the 1659 census, however, Kerrycurrihy and Kinalea were the only baronies where the name was plentiful. In the former 'Cogane' was the most numerous Irish surname, with 22 families, while in Kinalea there were 14 families of 'Gogan'. It is clear that many of these remained on as tenants on lands once owned by them. Headstones in the graveyards of Barnahely, Carrigaline and Ballinaboy record many of the name who were buried there in the 18th and 19th centuries, while at the present day Cogans are still prominent in the farming and business community of the Carrigaline area.

Philip Cogan (1748-1833), the noted Dublin-based organist and composer, was a native of Cork and received his early musical training in the choir of St. Fin Barre's cathedral.

Ó COILEÁIN

COLLINS

Although Collins is a well-known English surname, in Co. Cork it is nearly always used in substitution for an original Ó Coileáin. But there is more than one possible origin for this family name.

In east Cork the Uí Chuiléin of Fir Maige Féne occupied a place called Tulach Finnleithid near Mallow. This family could have given name to Ballycullane (*Baile Uí Choileáin*) in the parish of Mogeely. We also find mention – in 1180 and in 1300 – of a Carran (or Garran) Okyllan in the Corkbeg-Aghada area of Imokilly. There may have been a family of the name among the Uí Meic Caille; according to their genealogy one of the sons of Mac Caille was Cailléne Dubh. In the parish of Modeligo, Co. Waterford, a Drechlachan (or Creglehan) Oculan held the townland of Ballykerin in 1253 – perhaps the three carucates of wood and mountain which Sir William de la Rochelle, onetime sheriff of Waterford, claimed in 1275. Sir William stated that it had belonged to Oculan, an Irishman in Desmond, and that he had taken it to farm after the death of Oculan.

According to the Pipe Roll of Cloyne, in the mid-14th century Magister Dionysius Oculan held land at Balynegygouth (? Ballynageehy, par. Monanimy). Odo Ocuylleayn, a canon of Cork diocese, was prebendary of Dunbulloge in 1484. In Youghal, Collen/Collins became one of the prominent family names in the 16th-17th centuries. John Collins was mayor of Youghal in 1575 and James Collen M.P. for the town ten years later. The name Gasparius Collen in Youghal in 1596 appears as Jasper Collins in 1642. The Jasper of that year whose ten thatched cottages in Youghal had been pulled down, requested (and was granted) permission from Lord Inchiquin to go into Imokilly, there to reside and make benefit of what estate was left to him. Melchor Collins was another resident of Youghal in 1611. (Jasper, Melchor and Balthazar, the reputed names of the Magi, were all in use in Youghal at this period.) To this family also belonged Brother Dominic O Colan, the last survivor of the siege of Dunboy castle, who was barbarously executed in Youghal in 1602.

The surname Collins is, however, much more frequent in west Cork than in east Cork at the present day, and a different source must be sought for its prevalence there. A linking of the name with the Uí Echach, as found in *Duan Catháin*, can be disregarded. Of more significance is the name Ó Cuilin or Ó Cuilein in the Genealogy of the Corca Laoighdhe. It was one of the family names in Tuath Ó nAenghusa (see Ó HAONGHUSA for boundaries). It is reasonable to assume that some of the west Cork Collinses are derived from this source.

It has been frequently stated that the Uí Choileáin of west Cork originated in Co. Limerick, and there is in fact some evidence that the more influential branches did. The Uí Fidgente who ruled over most of Co. Limerick in early Christian times were divided into Uí Chairbre in the east and Uí Chonaill Gabhra in the west. In 1053 Aed Ó Cuiléin was slain by Domhnall Ruadh Ó Briain. A century later, Cuilén Ó Cuiléin, king of Uí Chonaill Gabhra, attacked and burned Ardfert in 1152 and was killed four years later by Ó Cinn Fhaoladh (of a rival dynasty). In 1177 another Cuilén Ó Cuiléin, perhaps a son of the first, was raiding east Munster. In 1189 he razed the castle of Lismore but was killed in battle later in the same year. The Uí Chuiléin continued to rule over Uí Chonaill Gabhra during the 13th century. In 1266 Mathghamhain Ó Cuiléin – who was fatally stabbed in bed by his wife (a daughter of Mac Carthy) through jealousy – was described as king of Claenglais (Clonlish), no doubt his place of residence. It was afterwards the seat of a branch of the Geraldines. It is clear that pressure from the Normans – as well as from the O Briens – drove many families from Co. Limerick southwards into Desmond. Principal among these were the O Donovans of Uí Chairbre who migrated around 1200, and it seems that some of the Uí Chuiléin did likewise. Not all, however, since the annals record exploits of the Uí Chuiléin in Thomond in the years 1295, 1296, 1305 and 1312. At the time of the 1659 census O Cullane was still among the principal Irish names in Connello barony, the former Uí Chonaill Gabhra territory.

There is in the *Leabhar Muimhneach* a genealogy headed *Geinealach I Choileáin Chairbrigh* which traces the descent from before the time of Fiacha Fidhgheinte down to one Diarmaid son of Raghnall son of Raghnall. It is not easy to fix either the time or place of this Diarmaid. The adjective *Cairbreach* would lead one to associate the name with Carbery, Co. Cork, but then the Uí Chairbre were originally in Co. Limerick and the name was actually brought into Co. Cork by the O Donovans. Admittedly the Uí Choileáin were not of the Uí Chairbre but of Uí Chonaill Gabhra. Still, the occurrence in the pedigree of such names as Tadhg Mháighe (of the Maigue) and Coileán Caonrígheach (of Kerry) indicates that its origin lay in Co. Limerick rather than in Co. Cork.

So we must assume that those who migrated southwards were junior branches of the family. They must have passed through Duhallow and seem to have been connected with that area for a time. In 1400 Maurice Ocuyllan, clerk, held the vicarages of Clonmeen and Roskeen and in the following year Donald Ycullayn, priest, obtained the vicarage of Eanachtrayn or Clonfert. There is also the townland-name Glencollins in Nohovaldaly parish, corresponding to Mountcollins (*Cnoc Uí Choileáin*) in the adjoining part of Co. Limerick.

References to the family in west Cork are few from the 13th to the 15th centuries. Among the perpetrators of a raid on Norman lands in Co. Cork in 1260 led by Fínghin Mac Carthy, we find the names of Mathenian Olulair and Tathyth Oculan — probably Mathghamhain and Tadhg Ó Coileáin. A Cristyn Oculan was among the followers of the de Cogans in 1311. In 1492 Thateus Yculeayn (*Tadhg Ó Coileáin*) became vicar of Drinagh. It is with the neighbouring parish of Fanlobbus (Dun-manway) that the Uí Choileáin were chiefly associated and it is there we find the townland-name Coorycullane (*Cuar Uí Choileáin*). (The Down Survey map of the parish of Fanlobbus shows 'O Cullane' and 'O Cullane mount' on the western side; a royal grant of the lands to Jeremy Cartie in 1684 refers to Oculane alias Carnocullane.) The area was formerly called Gleann an Chroim, the glen being that of the infant Bandon river, and An Crom the name of an O Donovan slain *circa* 1258. It became the patrimony of a branch of the Carbery Mac Carthys known as Sliocht Fheidhlimidh whose principal seat was the castle of Dunmanway. In 1601 a pardon was granted to the then chief, Teige mac Dermodie Cartie of Glanycroyenie, gent. (known as *Tadhg an Fhórsa*). His followers were likewise pardoned, including Teige O Collane, alias O Collaine — obviously the chief of his name. O Collaine's wife was named as Ellen ny Ranell Marhelly, apparently a daughter of Randal Hurley of nearby Ballynacarriga castle. (Randall, in turn, married Catherine O Cullane of Ballincourcey.) In the same pardon we find Conoghor mac Teige oge O Collaine, Teige mac Donell beg O Collaine, Dermod O Collane alias Dermod Cronagh, Dermod mac Conoghor O Collane, Donogh mac Teige O Collaine, Teige mac Dermodie owre O Collane, all of Gleann an Chroim, as well as Donogh oge O Collaine of Dunmanway and several others of the name in various parts of Carbery.

Some years earlier when Cormac Donn Mac Carthy was chief and received a pardon in 1573, his followers included Conogher óg O Cullan, Donald mac Conogher O Cullan and Conogher mac Donill I Cullan, all yeomen of Dunmanway, while Teig O Cullan was a tailor. Other followers were Teig and Dermod O Cullan of Malyghanys, and in the 1601 pardon these were named as Teige O Collaine of Mauley ganife, Shilly ny Donell, his wife, Dermod oge O Collaine and Donogh mac Dermody O Collaine. (This townland is no longer extant; it appears to have been absorbed into Lettergorman in Drinagh parish. After the Cromwellian wars, Cormack Cullan's 174 acres in Maule Iganniffe were confiscated and granted to Lord Kingston and Thomas Woogan.) Cappagh — probably Kippagh, also in Drinagh parish — had Teige O Cullaine, gent., and Dermot and Donall O Cullayne, kerns.

In Elizabethan times the Mac Carthys of Gleann an Chroim built a second castle at Togher. In company with Phillimie Mac Carthy of Togher in 1601 there were pardoned twelve of the O Collaines, including Shane Mac Donell ny bowly (? *na babhlaí*), Shane mac Conoghor ny grokyn (*na gcroiceann*), Morris mac Shane O Cullaine of Togher and Deirmod mac Shane O Collaine, of same. This last pair are mentioned again in January 1603 when Tadhg óg mac Dermod Mac Carthy of Dunmanway was granted recognizances on condition that Morris mac Shane O Cullane, Dermod mac Shane O Cullane and others 'shall be forthcoming and answerable for all offences by them committed since 6 December last, and shall continue of good behaviour'.

In 1584 a pardon was granted to Diermod mac Donnoghe oge O Cullaine, Donell bege O Cullayne of Glannycruim and Donoge oge Lodiragh O Cullayne, described as 'Florence Carthie's men'. This was the Florence Mac Carthy Riabhach so greatly feared by the English. A list of his 'followers cosens and kinsmens' (in Carbery) sent by the Lord Deputy to Lord Burghley in 1594 included Hurleys, Mac Sweeneys, O Regans and Crowleys; the first two named were Donell Mc Carthy als Mc Carthy Reogh and Donogh oge O Collen.

The personal names used by the O Cullaines, as given in the Fiants, were the standard west Cork ones — Tadhg, Donnchadh, Diarmaid, Conchobhar, Domhnall — from which they rarely deviated. There was one Ranell and one Whony (*Uaithne*) as well as a small sprinkling of Norman names of which John was the most popular. Nicknames included the common ones — óg, beag, ciotach, crom, bán, rua, — as well as some more unusual ones, e.g., 'owre' (*odhar*, 'dun'), 'cronagh' and 'lodiragh' (? *leadarthach*, 'of the smiting').

Another unusual nickname is to be found among a further group of the name also pardoned in 1601. This group comprised John mac Donogh O Collane, Teige mac Donogh O Collane alias Teige Itolane, Teige mac Dermod rowe O Collaine, Teige mac Whony O Collaine, and Donogh oge row O Collaine, all of Killmoledy, Dermod mac Donogh oge O Collaine of Cowrsiestowne, Teige mac Donogh oge O Collaine of Kaherowe and Shilie ny Donogh O Learie, his wife. Killmoledy is the parish of Kilmaloda near Timoleague; Carhoo is in Timoleague parish and Ballincourcey in nearby Templequinlan parish. Several of those named could have been sons of Donogh oge mac Donogh mac Mahone I Cullayne, of Timoleague, gentleman, who was pardoned in 1576. (Shane mac Dermody vic Donnough oge I Cullaine who went to Spain with Conor O Driscoll in July 1602, was probably a grandson.) The second-named, Teige Itolane, appears again in a 1603 pardon as Teige O Collane, alias Teige ytotane — more correctly, as the nickname is obviously *Tadhg a' tóiteáin* ('of the burning').

In spite of — or possibly because of — his incendiary activities, Tadhg prospered for many years and when he died his sons erected one of the most prestigious tombs in Timoleague friary over his last resting-place. It bore the inscription *Hic jacet bonus vir dominus Thade O Culleane al Totan cum suis filiis eorum et successoribus. A.D. 1635.* The sons were not as fortunate, however, as six years later they were embroiled in rebellion. Sir William Hull who made depositions concerning his losses in west Cork in 1641 listed among the rebels: 'John mac Teig O Toton of Killmalodye, Daniel mac Teig O Toton of same, gents., Mahowne mac Teig O Toton of same, gent'. It was a modern descendant of the Uí Choileáin, the late John T. Collins, for so long the doyen of local historians in Co. Cork, who pointed out that 'O Toton' was not a surname at all but a nickname for the O Cullanes of Kilmaloda. Hull's depositions probably ensured the inclusion of the brothers among the Co. Cork landed gentry who were outlawed in 1643. On this list Dermot takes the place of John and the family name is again given simply as 'Itotane' which seems to have been used to the exclusion of their original surname. After the rebellion there followed the inevitable confiscations, though their lands do not seem to have been extensive. (Their Kilmaloda lands appear to have been mortgaged to the Coppingers before 1641.) Teige O Cullane als. Tortane held 81 acres of Knock-I-garnaiffe in Templequinlan parish and this went to Major John Allen while Dermund Cullane's 106 acres in Darrary (par. Templeomalus) fell to the Earl of Barrymore. The former, no doubt, was the Lieutenant Tiege O Cullaine alias Totane specially mentioned as being in favour with Charles II in the royal declaration in 1660. (Also restored at the same time was Donee O Culan of Ballincourcey in Templequinlan parish; he was descended from Donat oge O Cullan of Ballincourcey who died in 1598.)

Sir Richard Cox (*c.* 1690) remarked with regard to Carbery: 'Besides the Carthys, the Tolanes were of some account hereabout, but that is a nickname, for the Tolanes are Cullanes and the Cullanes are Donovans originally.' Though the latter part of his statement is obviously incorrect, it does indicate a recollection that both the Uí Dhonnabháin and the Uí Choileáin came originally from Co. Limerick. Cox's use of the past tense reminds us that the 'Totans' were now landless and heading for obscurity. Denham Franklin, who wrote about their Timoleague tomb in 1892, mentioned that a small farmer named Collins, the last of this family, was interred there 'about three or four years ago'. Rev. J. Coombes gives 'Tóiteán' as one of the nicknames of Ó Coileáin families in Carbery, the others being 'Carraige', 'Baany', 'Scuabaire', and 'Cronach' (Gurranes); this last name is also to be found in the Fiants.

There were O Cullanes further west too. In 1633 Dermod mac Owen Mac Carthy of Baravilla in Caheragh parish married Shile, daughter of Teige mac Dermod mac Donogh oge O Cullane of Cashelfane (par. Skull). In return for a dowry of thirty cows and some horses he enfeoffed Dermod mac Teige O Cullane of Cloghanecullen (par. Kilmoe), gent., and Donogh mac Daniel O Cullane with lands in Caheragh parish, to hold for the use of Shile for her natural life.

Eastwards, we find a branch settled in Ringrone parish in Courcey's country. An inquisition into the lands of Lord Courcey, taken in 1620, found that Coolyrahilly and Dromdough had been mortgaged to him by Teige mac Donogh O Cullane, and that he would be entitled to possession of Currahoo and Ballyhander after the extinguishment of the male heir of Donogh oge O Cullane, the ploughlands being then in the possession of Donell mac Dermody O Cullane. Donogh's heir seems to have been extinguished after the Cromwellian confiscations, when Dermod O Cullane's 96 acres of Ballyhander were granted to Lord Kingston.

Quite close to Cork city, near the present-day Wilton, a pardon was granted in 1577 to John O Kyllayn of Garrenedaragh in the parish of St. Finbarr's. In 1607 Thomas Cullane of Garranedaragh was one of the freeholders brought within the 'County of the City of Cork' by the new boundary line then drawn, but we have no later references to this branch of the family.

For the O Cullanes, as for so many landowners of native stock in Co. Cork, the year 1641 marked the beginning of the end. A letter from Lord Broghill's chaplain in 1642 describes how 'O Sullivane Beere, Teige O Douna, fflorence mc Cartee of the castle of Banduffe, Black O Cullane and other ffree holders near Rosse ioyne their forces together and have taken great store of pillage and robbed the English'. Then came the outlawries — Cnogher O Cullane, Coolkellure (par. Fanlobbus), gent., Donnell O Cullane, Coolkellure, gent., Dermod O Cullane, Castle-lyons, gent., — and finally the confiscations.

Yet, though landless, the O Cullanes remained numerous in Co. Cork, particularly in Carbery where, according to the 1659 census, there were 92 families in East Carbery and 42 in West Carbery. They were also to be found in Kinalea (9), Kinalmeaky (13), Ibane and Barryroe (12), Courceys (6), Kilbrittain (24) and Barrymore (28). But their chief members were scattered.

A Don Juan Ocullane served in the French army in the Spanish Netherlands in the 1660s. Only three are recorded as having been outlawed in 1690 for their support of King James — Darby Collins, Buttevant, esq., John and Daniel Cullane of Bauravilla, gents. John and Daniel were probably descended from the O Cullanes of the 1633 settlement in Caheragh parish.

During the 18th century the O Cullanes, now rapidly becoming Collinses, formed part of the 'Hidden Ireland' of west Cork. One of them is, in fact, to be found in Daniel Corkery's great work, namely, Seán Ó Coileáin (1754-1816), a well-known poet of his day. He is said to have been born — and was later buried — at Kilmeen, a few miles to the north of Clonakilty. (A Fiant of 1577 pardoned Thady O Cullane of Lisnabrinny in that parish.) In the early 19th century, Dr. Michael Collins (d. 1831) was Catholic bishop of Cloyne and Ross.

In Clonmel graveyard on the Great Island in Cork harbour stands a tombstone with the inscription: 'In this Tomb are deposited the remains of John Collins, Esq., descended from the once powerful and opulent family of O Culleans, who died at Cove on the 2nd of September, 1794. Requiescat in pace.' There is also a Collins tomb, dated 1736, at Templerobin, on the same island.

The best-known bearer of the surname, Michael Collins, was one of the outstanding soldier-politicians who fought for Irish independence in the early part of this century. He was born at Sam's Cross, near Clonakilty, in 1890 and was killed in an ambush at Béal na Bláth near Crookstown during the civil war in 1922.

TIMOLEAGUE FRIARY *(O'Callaghan Newenham, 1826)*

Ó COLMÁIN

COLEMAN   COLMAN

This family name is found in many parts of Ireland and it is clear that there were several distinct family groups of the name. There is also a similar surname of English origin which may explain why Colemans were plentiful on the east coast between Swords and Drogheda in the 17th century. Colleman or Coleman is a name frequently mentioned in the Justiciary Rolls of the early 14th century in relation to the Dublin area.

It is quite likely, however, that there was a separate group long associated with the eastern half of Co. Cork, particularly with Imokilly. There are no Uí Cholmáin now traceable in the southern genealogies but in regard to some, at least, the name may originally have been Mac Giolla Cholmáin. As Colman was patron saint of Cloyne, Giolla Cholmáin (servant of Colman) is a name one would expect to find there, and a descendant of such a one could have taken the name Mac (or Ó) Giolla Cholmáin, just as the surnames Mac Giolla Phádraig, Mac Giolla Bhrighde etc. originated in other parts of the country. (There was an Uí Ghiolla Colmáin family, as well as Uí Cholmáin Chuidchi, among the Dál Cais.) And just as Mac Giolla Cheallaigh (Kilkelly) sometimes became Kelly, so could Mac Giolla Cholmáin have become Colman.

The small one-townland parish of Aghacross lies near Kildorrery in the barony of Condons and Clangibbons. In 1260 Thomas le Blund and Domhnall Ogeveny were charged with disseising David O Killecolman of 32 acres in Athcros and Rennath. Later in the year the bishop of Cloyne took proceedings against the tenants of Adcros, including David Hogilleoolman who held half a carucate there. In the Pipe Roll of Cloyne there is a reference to a settlement of 1270 when the bishop handed over to John Caunton (Condon) all the land which Dermitius Macgyllecolman held in the tenement of Acros.

But the more usual form of the family name was also in east Cork at that period. In another disseisin case of 1260 Robert Ocolenan was charged with taking five acres from William fitz Benedict at Lastnehusky (prob. Lissanisky in the parish of Carrigleamleary). According to a taxation of the diocese of Cloyne, *circa* 1306, Philip O Colman was vicar of the church of Kilmayne and co-rector of Balygorum (probably Kilmahon and Ballintemple parishes in Imokilly). Philip was a canon of Cloyne by 1322, in which year he was unlawfully imprisoned by the archbishop of Cashel who was attempting to usurp the see of Cloyne.

Also in Imokilly, in the parish of Ardagh, north of Killeagh, is the townland of Ballycolman (*Baile Uí Cholmáin*) but we do not know at what period this place was connected with a Colman family. In Youghal there was a Daniel Collman, juror, in 1615 and William Coleman, bailiff, in 1732.

The Elizabethan Fiants contain only sparse references to the name in Co. Cork. In 1576 a pardon was granted to David mac Donoghe I Colman of Kylmoreumlam, yeoman, apparently a follower of Cormac Mac Carthy of Blarney. Pardons were granted in 1601 to John and Dermod mac Teig O Collmaine of Enniskeane and to Dermod mac Shane I Collman of Kilmoney. Kilmurryomullane is now Marmullane, the parish in which Passage West is situated, while Kilmoney is near Carrigaline. At the present day, Coleman is a well-known surname in the area between Cork harbour and Kinsale.

A will made by William Collman of Kinsale was proved in 1638. John Coleman was constable of Ringrone in 1683 while Joseph Coleman was Sovereign of Kinsale in 1746, perhaps the Joseph Coalman, gent., whose will was proved in 1791. John Coleman, gent., in 1659 was a 'titulado' in the townland of Ballyduhig between Ballygarvan and Cork (the owner of which in 1641 was Robert Haly). In Killingley graveyard near Ballygarvan there are several early 18th century Coleman headstones.

The John mentioned above was probably the John Coleman of Cork who was listed among the forfeiting proprietors in the barony of Imokilly where he must have held lands before 1641. In Elizabethan times (1584) Denis Colmaine of Cork (whose wife was named Anstace Mac Donell) was buried in Christ Church. Quite a number of the name are referred to in the *Council Book of the Corporation of Cork* between 1617 and 1630. John Colman fitz Philip, John Colman fitz David fitz John and David Colmane fitz David were admitted as freemen of the city during that period. Richard Collman had a house adjoining the highway to Knockrea – perhaps the Mr. Collman who was a wine importer. In 1641 John Coleman had a house in Goold's Lane while Philip and David Coleman had houses in Fort St., in the south suburbs. In 1653 Pastor Coleman, one of the first Baptist ministers in Cork, had a meeting-house in Coleman's Lane, which lay between Nos. 92 and 93, North Main Street. (It is difficult to say how many of these were originally Uí Cholmáin and how many were of English derivation.)

The 1659 census does not record the name Coleman as having been prevalent in any of the baronies of Co. Cork, but in the barony of Coshmore and Coshbride (Co. Waterford) which adjoins Imokilly, there were fifteen Coleman families, while John Coleman of Lismore ('Irish Papist') held the small townland of Farran O Norragh prior to 1641. (The will of James Collman of Cappoquin, farmer, was proved in 1714.)

There are some scattered references to Colemans in various parts of Co. Cork. Donnell O Colmane paid a levy on property in Drishane parish in the early 17th century. Daniel Coleman with two others took a lease of Ballynoe from John St. Leger of Doneraile in 1685. In 1700 James

Coleman entered a claim at Chichester House concerning a mortgage (dated 1676) for £350 which he held on the lands in Mourneabbey parish, the late estate of John Barrett. Catherine Coleman lived in Macroom in 1702.

At the end of the 17th century a Dr. Domhnall Ó Colmáin was parish priest of Glounthaune and later of Knockraha. He was also tutor to James Cotter the younger, who was hanged in 1720 (see MAC OITIR). In or about 1697 he wrote, and dedicated to the young James (who would then have been about eight years old) a treatise known as *Párliament na mBan*, an early exposition of the equal rights for women theme.

One of the founder-members of the Cork Historical and Archaeological Society and one of the foremost contributors to its journal for many years was the late James Coleman of Cobh who died in 1938.

Ó CONAILL

(O) CONNELL

Mention of the surname O Connell invariably recalls the O Connells of Derrynane, Co. Kerry, one of the few Catholic families to retain their lands and position during the Penal times, and the family which gave us the legendary Daniel O Connell, the 'Liberator'. But since Conall was an extremely popular personal name in ancient Ireland there were undoubtedly several other families of Uí Chonaill. Fr. Woulfe refers to one in Derry and to another in Galway.

In Co. Cork, while many of the name may have originated in neighbouring Co. Kerry, there are indications of families of local stock. A reference in *Duan Catháin* to Uí Chonaill supposedly derived from Conall son of Donnghail of the Uí Eachach shows that there was a family of the name in west Cork in the 14th century. Originally these may have been of the Corca Laoighdhe whose genealogy mentions Uí Chonaill descended from Duach son of Maicniadh (as well as Ua Conaill of Cathair Durlais, descended from Eochaidh Ceannreithe). A townland which could have derived its name from the family is Derryconnell (*Doire Uí Chonaill*) in the parish of Skull.

Still, O Connells in the early Norman period appear more frequently in east Cork, and as Conall was a favourite name among the Uí Liatháin of that area — one of the sons of Eochaidh Liatháin being named Conall — there could have also been a family of Uí Chonaill of that stock.

In 1295 at Cork, suit of peace for his trespasses (saving only for the death of Englishmen) was granted to Gillebrenyn Oconyll (*Gilla Brénainn Ó Conaill*). In 1311 Comdyn Oconyll, from the Norman area of Co. Cork, was charged with burglary and found not guilty. John Oconyld was a juror at an inquisition at Britway, *circa* 1366. In 1395 Nicholas Oconyll, an S.C.L. at Oxford, obtained the vicarage of Castlemagner and five years later the canonry and prebend of Inishcarra. In 1402, among the burgesses of Cloyne, were Thomas Oconyl and Johannes Oconoyl.

In Elizabethan times the O Connells were well scattered throughout the county, but the Fiants show that quite a number of these were in the eastern half. Thomas O Coinill, a follower of the Barrys, was pardoned in 1579; so were Thomas O Connell of Castletown (roche) and Teige O Conell of Korrah in the Caherduggan area (? Curraghakerry) in 1584. Morishe O Conell was one of Lord Barry's garrison in Annagh castle in 1598. Several of the name were pardoned at Kilcredan in 1601, namely: Teige O Conell, Donell mac Teige O Conell, Morris mac

Donell O Connell, Conoghor mac Donogh O Connell, Donell mac Shane Y Connell and Donell mac Mortagh O Connell. The following year, Teige boy O Connell of Monanimy (in Nagle's country) was pardoned. One of the above may be the Donell O Connell in whose house an anonymous English official held a conference with the Seneschal of Imokilly in 1580.

Others seem to have taken service under the Mac Carthys in whose territory they are found. In Muskerry Teige mac Y Conell of Killumney, husbandman, was pardoned in 1585, as were Dermod Y Kwneg mac Y Connell and Shane ny Hensy mac Y Conell of Berynyclehy (Berrings). In his will of 1583 Cormac mac Teige of Blarney referred to '. . . the coming in and out of Donocke Rwo mac Shaine I Conill and Richard fitz Davy Oge, as the men chiefly to be trusted in the behalf of my said heir, Cormac Oge'.

The largest concentration of O Connells in Muskerry was at Dundirig or Dromderricke (presumably Dundareirke) where in 1601 more than a dozen received pardons. Others were to be found at Carrigrohane, Gortmore, Mashanaglass and Killaclug (par. Clondrohid). They used quite a variety of personal names, both Gaelic and Norman — John, Donnchadh, Maurice, Conchobhar etc. — but easily the most popular were Domhnall and Tadhg. There was formerly a townland named Cloghyneogonell (? *Cloichín Ó gConaill*) in Muskerry.

A still greater number, however, were followers of the Mac Donogh Mac Carthys and other families in Duhallow. Amongst these were:

1573: Shane O Konill of Castlecor; Conchor mac Donil O Kuonill of Corbally, yeoman; Philip mac Donill O Konill of Ballybahallagh, yeoman; Conoghor riogh O Conyll of Meelaherragh; Mahowne og O Konill of Rossline; Donald, John, Donogh and Shiary O Conill of same; Donald, Dermot and Teig O Conill of Clonrobin; Shane ny henoye O Konill of same; Donagh ro Konnall of Dromore, yeoman.

1576: Conoghor oge O Conell of Gortmore (par. Clonmeen; he was a follower of the O'Callaghans).

1577: John mac Conor Y Conell, Philip mac Shane Y Conell, John oge O Conill (followers of Mac Carthy of Lohort).

1578: Dermot mac Donogho mac Connell, Dermot oge O Connell (followers of the Mac Auliffes).

1601: Gillenenewe O Conell, Shiarhige O Conell (Kanturk area).

1621: Cormack O Connell of Rossline.

It is worth noting also that there is a townland named Cummeryconnell (*Comar Uí Chonaill*) in Clonfert parish in Duhallow. O Connells appear to have been still prominent in the barony at the time of the Williamite confiscations. Successful claimants for restoration of their lands in 1699 were Connell O Connell of Dromanarrigle and Daniell Connell of Cloongeal, both in Kilmeen parish. Daniel Connell of Rossnanarney (par. Liscarroll) was another successful applicant.

There were also some of the name in and around Cork city in the early 17th century when John Connell paid a levy on lands in the county of the city of Cork while Richard Connell, Clerk of the Crown of the city and county, was admitted as a freeman of Cork city in 1617. (It is unlikely, though not impossible, that this was the Riccard O Connell who, according to English intelligence in 1610, was agent in Ireland for Domhnall (Cam) O Sullivan, then in Spain.) At the end of the century, James, Peter and John Connell of Cork city were outlawed for treason as supporters of King James II; so also was Daniel O Connell of Corbally.

Prior to this, two of the name were among the Catholic proprietors outlawed as a result of the 1641 rebellion. They were Charles oge O Connell and Philip O Connell, gentlemen, of Knockrobbin — presumably Knockrobin near Kinsale. (There was a Thomas Conyll residing in Kinsale in 1513.) Another who forfeited lands after the rebellion was Cnogher O Connell of Garryantornora in Inchigeelagh parish where he was surrounded on all sides by O Learys. But John Connell, who had lands in Barrymore — Labaun (Carrigtwohill par.) and Ballyedmond (Templenacarriga par.) — was described as an 'Irish Protestant' and so held on to his estates; in fact he gained some in Dungourney parish. The census of 1659 shows that O Connell was at that time predominantly an east and north Cork family name. Families of O Connells were to be found in Cork city and Liberties (9), Kerrycurrihy (7), Barrymore (21), Orrery and Kilmore (45). (Figures for Muskerry and Duhallow are not available.)

In Penal times, Peter Connell and Connell O Connell of Clonherke (now part of Matehy parish) were named in the 'Robbery Warrants' of 1713. The prior of the Carmelite friars in Kinsale in the mid-18th century was Tadhg Ó Conaill, known in religion as Raymond St. Patrick. He assisted the secular clergy in several of the parishes around Kinsale, and translated into Irish a well-known French religious work under the title *Trompa na bhFlaitheas*. He died in 1779 and was buried at Passage West. Another Tadhg Ó Conaill was a well-known Irish scribe in Sunday's Well, Cork, *c.* 1820 (as was Seághan Ó Conaill in the Kilworth-Mitchelstown area half a century earlier). In the late 18th century one of the Gaelic poets of west Cork was Seán 'Máistir' Ó Conaill of Tuath na Dromann (Kilnamartery).

(DE) CONDON

CANTON   DE CANNTÚN   CUNNDÚN   CÚNDÚN

This family name first appeared in Ireland as 'de Caunteton', 'de Caunton' etc., that is, of Caunteton or Canton, a parish in Glamorgan where Jordan de Caunteton was a tenant of the Fitzgeralds. Nicholas de Caunteton, probably his younger brother, married Mabilia, sister of Raymond le Gros, and it seems likely that the Cauntetons came to Ireland as followers of Raymond.

One of Nicholas' sons, *Reimundus Kantitunensis*, a youth favourably mentioned by Giraldus Cambrensis, was killed in Osraige *circa* 1185. Other sons were Robert and William — and probably Roger, Jordan and Adam as well. Because Raymond le Gros left no children to succeed him, his many nephews — including the Cauntetons — benefited accordingly. They acquired lands in south Leinster and also in the eastern half of Co. Cork where Raymond le Gros succeeded to the inheritance of his uncle, Robert Fitzstephen.

Glanworth and Kilworth were among their earliest family seats in Co. Cork. A deed of *circa* 1230 mentions that Thomas de Cantiton was rector of Glanworth, and it was witnessed by William son of Adam de Cantiton and Ithiel, his brother. (About the same time, Jordan de Cantiton witnessed a charter concerning lands at Rosscarbery.)

Nicholas de Kantinton was lord of Glascarrig (Co. Wexford) in 1247 and also held lands in the Glanworth-Kilworth area. His daughter and heiress, Amicia, married David de Rupe or Roche, who thereby became tenant of Glanworth and other lands. But David de Caunteton was overlord of Nicholas, and so after Nicholas' death became overlord of David de Rupe. He also acquired the inheritance of his uncle Roger at Corkbeg. A tenant there, Richard de Barry of Finure, in 1260 claimed that Nicholas had handed over to David de Caunteton the manor of Glascarrig (Co. Wexford) and Baliederthawel (Co. Cork) in exchange for all rights in the Corkbeg-Finure area, but David denied that. (*Baile idir dhá abhainn* is now Ballyderown in the parish of Kilcrumper, where the Araglin river joins the Blackwater.)

Others of the name were to be found in north-east Cork at that time. Philip de Cantuncon was a tenant of Gerald de Prendergast. In 1260 Adam de Cautinincton was in dispute with Cathel Ohanegus (O Hennessy) and others over ten acres in Mathuehenan. In 1283 the Condons, together with Barrys, Roches and other Norman families, were assisting Domhnall (Cairbreach) Mac Carthy in his rebellion against Mac Carthy, king of Desmond. In 1295 Robert, Gregory and Thomas de Canteton were in contention with Milo le Waleis over a site at Athlyskymeleth. This place appears in *Crichad an Chaoilli* as *Echlasca Molaga*, now Ballynahalisk, south of Kildorrery.

Meanwhile, the death of David de Kantatun occurred in 1261 according to the *Annals of Inisfallen*. David seems to have been succeeded by William and William by his son and heir, Maurice, who in 1289 commenced legal proceedings to establish his overlordship over David de Rupe (husband of Amicia) in respect of Glanworth, Gurteenaboul (Brigown par.) and other townlands in Kilcrumper and Clondullane. In 1302 (by which time David de Rupe, senior, had been succeeded by his grandson, another David) the whole issue of the lordship was brought once more before the courts. The legal overlord of the cantred of Fermoy was Maurice de Carreu who, as heir of Robert Fitzstephen, held it of the king *in capite*. Carew admitted that there was great discord between the Cauntetons and Roches over the lordship and that knowing Maurice de Caunteton to have the right to be mesne lord between himself (Carew) and David de Rupe, he had granted him (Maurice) the said lordship – for a fee of 100 marks. This was held to have been illegal alienation without licence, and the upshot of the matter was that the whole cantred was taken into the king's hands. This meant that David Roche now held two thirds of the cantred directly from the king, without interference from the Condons. It also followed that the Condons henceforth were mainly confined to the north-east corner which became a separate cantred (now Condons and Clangibbons).

In the same year (1302) mention is made of lands at Corkbeg belonging to Jordan de Caunteton. Four years later Jordan failed in his attempt to recover the advowson of the church of Corkbeg from the prior of St. Nicholas, Exeter. (It had been granted to Exeter by Roger de Caunteton about the year 1185.) In 1303 William de Caunteton was in favour for having rendered good service in Scotland, and in 1305 for having led an expedition against the felons in the mountains of Leinster, as a reward for which he was given the post of sheriff of Cork between 1306 and 1310.

But the majority of the Condons were at continual variance with the law, both in Leinster and Munster. In 1291 David de Cauntinton paid a fine of 10 marks 'for having peace of the death of Eustace de la Roche'. In 1302 Maurice de Cauntetone was fined five marks because he would not become a knight (although Robert de Caunton and David son of John de Caunteton were knights in Co. Cork at this period).

In 1308 Gilbert de Cauntetoun and four others of the name were summoned by Richard Taloun for taking oats and other goods to the value of £200 from Rathnagearagh, Co. Carlow and were committed to gaol as a result. This instigated a family feud and Maurice de Cauntetoun and his friends slew Richard Taloun, after which they were sheltered by David de Caunteton, knight. Maurice and David were accused of having openly put themselves at war with the king, with standards displayed, and of having combined with Donlyng Obryn (*Dúnlang Ó Broin*) and other Irishmen from the mountains of Leinster, doing many murders, robberies and other evils. The Roches, on the other hand, for their good services against the rebels, were pardoned for all trespasses and felonies committed by them. It was the Roches who slew Maurice Condon in 1309 while David Condon was hanged in Dublin.

All the lands and property of the Condon rebels were ordered to be taken into the king's hand. David's lands were in Co. Wexford, and Maurice too, held Glascarrig and other lands in that county, lands which, immediately after he had committed the felony, were despoiled by the Mac Murroughs, Irish enemies of his. In Co. Cork Maurice had land at Corkbeg with rents from Finure and other townlands in the parishes of Corkbeg and Aghada. In the Fermoy area he held Bally-derown (par. Kilcrumper), Shanacloon and Carrigatoortane (par. Clondulane), Monadrishane (par. Kilworth), Laynoght (Ballynoe), Macroney, four other townlands, and a mill at Kilworth. He also had some land in Co. Limerick. This shows that the Condon lands at the beginning of the 14th century were more or less those held by them up to the 17th century.

For the year 1309 the *Annals of Inisfallen* report: 'Great warfare in Leinster between the foreigners themselves, in which were slain Talon on the one side, and Maurice Condon on the other by the Justiciar of Ireland and by William Roche and by Pátraicín, his brother, who laid violent hands upon him (Condon). And on that account great strife arose between the Condons and Roches.'

Two years later the same annals record: 'War between the Condons and Roches, with burnings, raidings and killings between them on both sides. David, son of Elisrant (Roche) Lord of Fermoy, was taken prisoner by the Condons therein, but they released him to the Justiciar on the consideration that all who were outlawed on their side would obtain the king's peace and their own lands (back again).'

There is no record in the Justiciary Rolls of this suit of peace being granted, but there may have been a tacit agreement which enabled the Condons to hold on to their lands. Matthew and William de Caunteton were among the great lords who received writs to attend parliament in Kilkenny in 1310. William was also in the royal army which engaged Bruce's forces at Skerries in January 1316. This did not end the feud, however. There is a reference in the Latin annals under the date 1323 to the killing of Philip Talon, his son, and about 26 of his followers by Edmund Butler and the Condons. About this time Bartholomew Apilgarth was fined £3.10s. when Redmond son of Roger de Caunteton escaped from his gaol in Co. Cork.

The 1320s and 1330s witnessed the rebellion of Maurice Fitzgerald, first Earl of Desmond, in which one of his chief lieutenants was Robert de Caunton, son of the knight Matthew de Caunteton. The rebel forces ravaged many parts of Munster. In 1344 the brothers David, Nicholas and Robert de Caunton with George son of Robert were declared outlaws for the killing of David de Caunton, knight, the king's sheriff in Co. Cork. But on 29th July of that same year the outlawed Condons, together with Condon of Cregg, the Earl of Desmond and many others assembled at Glanworth and swore a mutual oath to keep up the fight against the king until they would have won the lordship for themselves. Eleven days later an inquisition found that David, Nicholas and Robert (the outlaws), Gerald son of William of Clondullane, David son of Raymond, John son of Gerald of Cregg, Gregory son of Robert, Raymond Legh, Friar John, abbot of Fermoy and William son of Peter (all Cauntons) with their followers, attacked and burned Barry's lands of Castlelyons without interference from the Earl of Desmond.

Eventually the Earl himself was outlawed but the outlawry was annulled in 1351. Yet in 1377 the Condons were still embroiled with the authorities when Redmund son of Peter de Caunton and his men imprisoned David son of Sir David de Barry and Miles Caunton. In retaliation the Justiciar imprisoned John *Buidhe* son of Redmund and Edmund son of Gerald Caunton until the others should be released. Five years later Robert de Condon was paid £100 for keeping the person of Guydo de Condon, a felon and a rebel lately taken near Cork, and for conveying him from Cork to Dublin.

Yet despite their rebellious acts and outlawries, when the smoke cleared the Condons still held a firm grip of their lands in north and east Cork. The Pipe Roll of Cloyne mentions William son of Jordan Caunton as holding Corkbeg around 1364; it had been inherited from John son of Nicholas Caunton, deceased. Nicholas Goule held a place called Cauntonstrete in Clenor from Matthew Cauneton. (There are in Barrymore three townlands called Condonstown and one called Curraghcondon.) The see of Cloyne from 1394 to 1409 was occupied by Bishop Gerald Canton, an Augustin Hermit and Vicar-General of that order in Ireland.

The turbulent nature of the Condons' activities may have been due to their location in the marchlands between Gael and Gall, the Gaeil being the O Briens of Thomond while the Gaill comprised the powerful houses of Fitzgerald and Butler locked in a perpetual struggle for supremacy, not to mention the often aggressive Roches and Barrys to the south. This encirclement by potential aggressors also explains why Condons' country became so thickly encastellated. Cregg castle was probably built by the Condons but by the 16th century it was a Roche castle while the chief Condon residence was the castle of Cloghleigh near Kilworth, still in a good state of preservation. (*An Chloch Liath*; a mid-17th century poem by Seán Ó Conaill has a reference to *Cúndúnach na Cloiche Léithe.*) Other Condon castles were at Carrigabrick and Ballymacpatrick (now Careysville) near Fermoy, and Dún Galláin (now Castle Cooke) a mile and a half east of Ballymacpatrick. North of the

Blackwater stood the castles of Ballyderown and Licklash. Further north were Kilgullane, Turbeagh, Ballybeg, and Caherdrinny, the ruin of the last-named castle being a well-known landmark to the south of Mitchelstown. The most northerly castle was Carriganoura in the townland of Drough (par. Marshalstown), said to have been the residence of a Mitchel Condon from whom, according to tradition, Mitchelstown got its name. (It is noticeable, however, that the name Mitchel, or Michael, was very rarely used by the Condons.)

Corkbeg castle is also said to have been built, in the late 14th century, by the Condons whose family tomb was in the adjoining cemetery. In 1591 William Condon of Corkbeg sold the castle and lands to John fitz Edmond of Cloyne.

By the 16th century the Condons were a closely-knit family group bearing a curious mixture of Norman-Irish personal names. A fiant of 1552 names David Condon of Cloghleigh, gent., as chief of his name; his followers were known by their first names — Hugh boy mac Donnoghe; Richard duffe mac William; Donnogh Farshynne, Thady moyll and Maurice Leigh (three sons of David oge); Richard boy mac Padrycken, and so on. A pardon of 1573 provides similar evidence and also gives locations for various Condons: Patrick Condon of Cloghleigh, gent., John mac David Condon of same, gent., Richard mac Jordan Condon of Manning, Donald in Glanney (*Domhnall an Ghleanna*) of Cloghleigh, Peter mac Richard mac Padrykyn of Carrigatoortane, Patrick Morice of Carrigabrick (Richard Condon of Carrigabrick, gent., sheriff of Co. Cork, was pardoned in 1567), Peter and John mac Richard mac Shane of Garrynagoul, Edmond boy mac David og of Ballymachadrigyn (*Baile mhic Phádraigín* or Ballymacpatrick), Richard mac Morice of Clondullane, Redmond rowe Condon of Cloghleigh.

Another pardon of the same year was granted to Richard mac John Condon alias Mac Maug of Carrickynoury, gent., on payment of five fat cows. This is probably the Carriganoura (castle) near Mitchelstown, already referred to. (It may also be the *Carrac in Furnaidi* mentioned in *Críchad an Chaoilli* as being in the Brigown area.) But most of Mac Maug's lands appear to have been in the parish of Leitrim, which straddles the Cork-Waterford border. This branch derived their alias from Máigheóg or Máigh, apparently a form of Matthew or Maheu. (The surname Mawe is a modern rendering of Mac Máigh; the townland of Ballymacmague in Dungarvan parish may also have been named after one of the family.) Although Richard (Mac Maug) surrendered to Carew in May 1600, his lands at Leitrim had already been confiscated and granted in 1598 to George Sherlock. In 1628 Richard Condon otherwise Mac Mawge was pardoned for having alienated Carriganowrie to Richard Roe Condon. The title appears as late as 1691 when John Condon alias Magher was attained for supporting King James.

The 1573 pardons obviously resulted from the Condons' involvement in the first Desmond rebellion. In January 1576 Sir Henry Sidney who had spent Christmas at Cork, tried and executed many 'notable malefactors'. 'Condon or Canton of Armoy was attainted and judged to die, and yet stayed from execution, but his lands, which are great, are escheated to Her Majesty.' This must have been Patrick Condon of Cloghleigh who, as soon as he was released, became once more a doughty supporter of the Earl of Desmond. When the conflict flared up again in 1579 Edmond Condon of Marshalstown, John Condon fitz Daniel, gent., and William fitz Edmond Condon, yeoman, received pardons.

In 1581 Warham St. Leger wrote to Burghley that the Earl of Desmond, David Barry, the seneschal of Imokilly and Patrick Condon had burned 36 towns in the Decies and carried off 7,000 kine. In January 1583 Patrick entered the town of Youghal at the head of 700 fighting men with the war-cry 'Condon Abú!' and hoisted the Pope's banner with his own guidon on the highest place in the town. For five days Youghal was ransacked from end to end. Shortly afterwards Condon and the seneschal carried out a daring ambuscade at the very gates of Cork, having a force of 600 men which included two colourfully-named characters – *Donnchadh an tsneachtaidh* (Mac Grath) and *Tóin Buí Riabhach* (Gerald mac Thomas). By July, however, the rebellion was all but over, and Patrick Condon in company with many others 'came in' and gave pledges for his loyalty. This did not save him from attainder, and in 1586 Arthur Hyde got a certificate for 12,000 acres of Condon lands, including Aghacross, Derryvillane, Manning, Carrigabrick and Carriganeady. In the following year Patrick Condon, the seneschal of Imokilly, the White Knight, Patrick Fitzmaurice and Donogh Mac Carthy, were all imprisoned in Dublin Castle. An inquisition taken in 1588 found that Patrick Condon of Cloghleigh and John fitz David Condon of Kilbree were concerned in the Earl of Desmond's rebellion, for which they were attainted. Evidence against Patrick was provided by his hereditary enemy, Lord Roche, who said that in Kilcrumper parish there were two castles, a Roche one at Ballyhendon and a Condon one at Ballyderown, and that Condon had burned the castle of Ballyhendon. (Condon later maintained that he did so only because there were malefactors in it.) It is no surprise to find the Condons and the Roches on opposite sides. The *Annals of the Four Masters* tell us that four sons of Lord Roche were slain in two separate raids by 'traitors' – the Seneschal of Imokilly and Giolla Pádraig (or Pádraigín) Condún. On 7th December 1588 Sir Warham St. Leger wrote to Lord Burghley that it would be a great relief if Patrick Condon and the other state captives were executed since otherwise they would certainly escape and cause grievous trouble to the Queen (as did their fellow-prisoner, Red Hugh O Donnell).

Condon was released, however, in 1590 when he succeeded in persuading the Queen that his attainder was unjustified, and he got a letter of Council for the restoration of his lands. These had been allotted to undertakers; Hyde had got the lion's share but Marmaduke Redman got 2,400 acres while Sir Thomas Fleetwood acquired Cloghleigh castle. Condon at once petitioned to have Hyde's grant revoked but the ensuing proceedings had not concluded by 1598 when, angry and frustrated, he once more joined the ranks of the rebels. Though Queen Elizabeth wrote to Norreys desiring him to assure Condon that if he should leave the rebels she would take order to relieve him in the suit against Hyde, Patrick did not submit until May 1600, after which he took action against the rebels and lost his life in so doing.

'He was cruelly bound and had his thigh broken in an expedition against the rebels of which he afterwards died', according to the plea of his son, David, who renewed his father's claims to the ancestral lands. In 1610 David finally got a regrant and four years later Arthur Hyde (the younger) acknowledged Condon's rights. But Hyde retained Carriganeady (which became Castle Hyde) and Fleetwood kept Cloghleigh castle, which left Ballyderown as the principal Condon manor.

David seems to have been as rebellious as his forbears. In 1628 the Lord Deputy wrote of a conspiracy among the O Byrnes of Leinster; the Munster malcontents were represented by one David Condon. Three years later an informer conveyed to Lord Dorchester information he had received in a town called Burbrook in Flanders from an Irishman named Condon who told him that certain Irish planned to wipe out a whole new planted town of English, and that his own chief and kinsman, Mr. David Condon, was one of the main plotters. Whether or not this story was believed, we know that David Condon was a prisoner in Dublin in 1642, the year after the outbreak of the great rebellion, while his sons, Richard and John (of either Ballydorgan or Ballymacpatrick), led the rebel clansmen in a campaign which produced even bloodier engagements than those in other parts of the country.

Richard Condon captured the castle of Cloghleigh in which all the English inhabitants of Kilworth and the surrounding areas were sheltering. These were stripped of all their possessions but were not killed. Richard also took Turbeagh castle from Mr. Osborne's servants, but it was recaptured at the beginning of March by Lord Broghill who burned all the houses in Condon's country south of the Blackwater. On 10th May 1642 Lords Barrymore and Dungarvan led their troops in pursuit of the Condons, a party of whom took shelter in the castle of Ballymacpatrick (Careysville). Other Condons tried to relieve the castle by fording the Blackwater but were driven off. The English kept up an artillery barrage until they had made a breach in the castle walls wide enough for a carriage to drive through. The Condons then sent a party to burn Fermoy and Carrigabrick, hoping thus to divert the besiegers. But the siege continued until the garrison surrendered whereupon over fifty men and one hundred women and children (including Lord Barrymore's great-aunt) were all slaughtered. This apparently was in reprisal for the wiping out by the Condons of a party of Lord Barrymore's troops, twenty-three in all, as they rode to fetch corn from Coole near

Castlelyons. Rev. Urban Vigors, on 16th July 1642, wrote that '. . . Cloghleagh castle and Dungallane castle the enemy still mayntaynes and keepes; they are two very strong castles, but they want water both of them. Daniell mac Shane O Bryan is captayne of Dungullane castle, he hath a company of desperate naughty fellows about him. . . . The souldiers which doe belong unto Mr. Cundane of Kilgullane castle . . . commit many outrages and stealthes.'

Another slaughter of Condons took place when Sir Charles Vavasour retook Cloghleigh castle on 3rd June 1643, with twenty men, eleven women and seven children being put to the sword. This time, however, the killings did not go unavenged, since the besiegers were overtaken on the following day by the Confederate army under the Earl of Castlehaven who had been endeavouring to relieve Cloghleigh. The English troops tried to escape towards Fermoy but were forced to stand and fight at Manning ford where they suffered a crushing defeat, with Vavasour and his officers being made prisoners.

No less than 21 gentlemen of the Condons were outlawed in 1643. They comprised Richard and John of Ballydorgan; Richard, John and John mac Edmond gauragh of Ballymacpatrick; David, John and Maurice of Kilbarry (par. Clondullane); Edmond of Ballybeg, Edmond of Carrigane, Edmond of Turbeagh and James of Kildrum, all in Brigown parish; Maurice of Ballyarthur (par. Marshalstown); Maurice and Redmond of Ballybridock (? Ballybride, par. Knockmourne); James and Thomas of Aghelinske (?) in Brigown parish; John of Billeragh (par. Macroney); John of Curraheen (par. Kilgullane); John and Patrick of Carriganowry.

As the war drew to its close, in May 1652 rewards were offered for a number of Irish officers, including £200 for Colonel John Condon (dead or alive). After the war a clean sweep was made of all the Condons and up to 10,000 plantation acres of theirs were confiscated. The only 'titulado' left in 1659, after the Cromwellian plantations, was David Condon of Kilbarry, and he was no longer a landowner. The Fleetwoods and Nortons were in Cloghleigh. (It was later sold to the Moore family — whence Moore Park.) George Prater was in Ballyderown, the Carys in Ballymacpatrick (soon to become Careysville), and the Hydes in Carriganeady and Caherdrinny. The Fennels, the Fentons, Lord Kingston and others divided up the rest. The 'principal Irish families' in Condons and Clangibbons in 1659 are not listed, but there were thirteen Condon families in Barrymore, with others in the adjoining counties of Limerick, Tipperary and Waterford.

In 1660, Rev. Devereux Spratt was sent as preacher to Mitchelstown where he met one Ensign White who sold him the townlands of Turbeagh and Ballyboy for 6s. 8d. an acre. Three years later he was summoned to the Court of Claims by Richard Condon. Richard, who had been transplanted to Co. Galway where he got 300 acres, failed to make good his claim. But Patrick Condon (with Ellen, his wife, who was daughter and heiress of Edmund Roche) got a decree of innocence in 1663 and was to be restored to 193 acres 'with encumbrances'. In 1671, the Rev. Spratt tells us, 'Patrick Condon, who rented my retrenchments from the Lord Kingston at Ballybeg, began his pranks, disturbing my tenants and impounding their cattle'. In the following year 'he (Condon) gave alarms of war and many threats' but he was accidentally killed later in the year.

The war between William and James witnessed the last military effort of the Condons to regain their former glory. Attainted for rebellion in 1691 were John Condon of Carriganonta (?) — perhaps the Lieut. John Condon of King James' army — David of Ballymacpatrick and John his son, John Condon alias Magher, John of Ballynalacken, gent., Garrett of Kilcor and Redmond of Ballywilliam. (In most cases, the locations given denote family descent rather than actual ownership; a grandson of John Condon of Dungullane castle became a knight of Spain in 1686.) After the war, in 1699, Edmond Condon of Marshalstown was successful in his claim for restoration. John Condon (gent.) was at Marshalstown in 1729 when he conformed to the established religion. In 1700 Julianne, widow of Richard Condon who had been a captain in Lord Mountcashel's infantry, failed to obtain a life estate in his Co. Cork lands.

The Condons were now bereft of lands and property. It is not surprising to find the names of Edmond and Maurice Condon among the 'Robbery Warrants' of 1712. Nor is it to be wondered at that the poet of the family, Dáibhidh Cúndún (described as *na Biolairídhe*, i.e. of Billeragh, par. Macroney), composed an essay of over 300 lines lamenting the condition of Ireland in the post-Cromwellian era:

> *Bíodh gur cailleadh sgata san Léith-chloich*
> *An chlú an uair cailleadh, chuaidh ainm i n-éaga.*

Seághan Cúndún was a well-known 18th century Gaelic poet, but a better-known one in the following century was Pádraig Phiarais Cúndún (1777-1857) who was born at Shanakill, Ballymacoda, emigrated to America in 1826, and sent home many a poem and song in his native tongue, including the celebrated *Tórramh an Bharaille*. He lies buried in St. Agnes' cemetery, Utica, in the state of New York.

Ó CRÓINÍN

CRONIN

This family name has long been associated with west Cork. The Genealogy of Corca Laoighdhe names Ó Cróinín as one of the hereditary proprietors of Tuath Ó bhFithcheallaigh, which was a stretch of territory west of Clonakilty, reaching to the coast between Inchydoney and Galley Head. The 14th century *Duan Catháin* claims the Uí Chróinín as an offshoot of the Uí Eachach but there is no real evidence of such a connection. The claim indicates, however, that the Uí Chróinín may have moved into Uí Eachach territory by the 14th century. It so happens that in west Cork there are two townlands embodying the name, one in the Corca Laoighdhe area – Cooscroneen (*Cuas Chróinín*) par. Myross – and one in the Uí Eachach sphere of influence, namely, Lissacroneen (*Lios Chróinín*) par. Kinneigh. There is no evidence to show when these townland names originated. (Ballycroneen in Imokilly does not appear to be connected with the family; it was written Ballymachronyn in 1301.)

The sparse early records we have of the O Cronins relate mainly to ecclesiastical affairs. In 1447 John Ocronyn, a student in canon law and rector of Templetrine, sought and was eventually appointed to the prebend of Kilbrittain. He was a canon of Cork between 1466 and 1484. In 1481 it was stated that the vicarage of Nohovaldaly had been occupied by David O Cronyn without authority and in 1500 David and William Ucroinyn were clerics in the diocese of Cork.

Quite a large number of O Cronins are named in the Fiants of Elizabeth. The first two pardoned – in 1573 – were Donald O Cronyne of Ballybahallagh (par. Churchtown, Duhallow) and Teig óg Cronyn of Cooldorragha (par. Kilmichael, Muskerry), both yeomen. The bulk of the O Cronins seem to have been followers of the Mac Carthys of Muskerry, in such places as Knockavilla, Kilbarry and Macroom. Where occupations are given, most are described as yeomen or husbandmen, i.e., farmers. They used a limited number of Christian names, over a quarter being named Tadhg, while the majority of the remainder were either Donnchadh, Diarmaid, Seán or Domhnall.

A sizeable group was to be found at Carrignacurra (par. Inchigeelagh) where they were almost certainly followers of the O Learys. Pardons were granted there in 1584 to Teige oge O Cronine, husbandman, and in 1586 (and in 1601) to his son, Domhnall. In 1601 also Dermod Mac Teige, Donell Mac Teige and Donell mac Shane I Cronyn were pardoned there, as well as Donnell mac Donogh Gankagh, a piper, probably another Cronin. Another 1601 pardon was granted to Teig mac Shane I Cronyne of Maninn (which was also an O Leary stronghold). At the

104

other side of the county, Dermod Cronyne of Ballymacphilip (par. Killathy, bar. Fermoy), husbandman, together with Teig, Philip, Matthew and Patrick O Cronyne all of Ballymacphilip, yeomen, were pardoned in the same year. A later pardon (1618) was granted to Donell mac Mahowne O Cronin of Dysert (par. Dromtarriffe).

One who did not receive a pardon was Fr. Donnchadh Ó Cróinín (teacher of Philip O Sullivan Bear) who was hanged at Cork in 1601.

It is remarkable that there was a Cronin family who were merchants in Cork city at this period when few of the old Gaelic stock were tolerated within the city walls. John Cronyne of Cork, merchant, was pardoned in 1577 and again in 1601. In 1618 there was a Patrick Cronyng, merchant, who served on juries in 1622 and 1625. William fitz Patrick Cronynge, gent., was lessee of premises in St. Peter's parish, Cork. A generation later, as a result of the 1641 rebellion, Andrew O Cronyne of Cork, merchant, was outlawed. At the same time Cnoghor Cronyne had a house in Fort St. The Cromwellian takeover in Cork meant that the Cronins, in company with many others, were banished from the confines of the city. (A Patrick Croneen of Cork became a Protestant in 1724.)

Another who was outlawed in 1643 was Cornelius Cronyne of Blarney, gentleman, – in all likelihood a supporter of Mac Carthy, Lord Muskerry. There was a Captain Cornelius Cronyn who in 1633 wrote to Secretary Windebank warning against seditious Irish in Spain. Later he petitioned the king for the right to levy a regiment in Ireland for service in France and hoped that a friend of his would be granted Kinsale and Courcies so that he (Cronin) could become tenant of same. The only one of the name suspected of rebellion (by the Archdeacon of Ross) in Carbery in 1641 was William O Cronin, yeoman. There are no records for Muskerry barony in the census taken in 1659, after the Cromwellian confiscations; the only barony in which there was a good number of Cronin families was Barrymore, which had twelve.

References to Cronins in Co. Cork show that they were well scattered throughout the county in the late 17th century. In 1678 Matthew Cronine of Noghavall and John and George Cronine of Ballynaginshe were involved in a debt case which, four years later, was in the course of settlement by Tymothy Troneene (i.e. Cronin) of Nohoval, gentleman. In 1686 John Cronine took a lease of Dromahoe (par. Dromtarriff) for five years from John Longfield. In 1691 Timothy Cronine took a lease of Nohoval(daly) and Knocklevane from Sir Mathew Deane of Dromore. In 1706 Cronin, 'of Killarney in the Co. of Kerry, gent.,' sued Deane in respect of this lease and other matters. He died about 1720 leaving Philip Cronin as son and heir. (Philip was at Curryglass in 1730, in which year he conformed to the established church.) This was the Tadhg Dubh Ó Cróinín who – being a kind of middleman of native stock – was bitterly lampooned by the poet Aodhagán Ó Raithile. (One of Ó Raithile's laments was occasioned by the drowning of three children of a Tadhg (or Pádraig) Ó Cróinín of the Rathmore district.) It is a coincidence that another noted Munster poet, Eoghan Rua Ó Súilleabháin, in 1784 presented a complimentary poem (in English) to Colonel Daniel Cronin of Park near Killarney. When this was rejected Eoghan composed a fierce satire which led to a violent altercation with Cronin's servants in a Killarney ale-house. Eoghan received a blow on the head and died of fever shortly afterwards. Daniel Cronin died two years later. His collateral descendants included the Cronin-Coltsmanns of Flesk Castle.

In 1691, Thady Crooneen of Collycassaigne (? Coolycasey), Co. Clare, gent., was outlawed for treason 'beyond the seas'. Perhaps he belonged to a family transplanted to Clare in Cromwellian times. After the war, in 1694, Teige Croneene was one of the band of outlaws in Annahala Bog for whose capture large rewards were offered by the lords justices. There was also, in 1731, a Timothy Croneen in Cork gaol charged with having barbarously murdered Andrew St. Leger of Bally-volane and his wife, Jane. William Turner and John Keeffe received £20 for having prevented his escape.

Perhaps the Cronins expelled from Cork city in the 17th century settled close by. In Kilcully graveyard, north-east of the city, there is a headstone to James Croneen (d. 1756) and his brother Edmund (d. 1761). In Carrigaline to the south there are headstones to Maurish Cronine (d. 1723), Patrick Cronyn (d. 1740) and one erected by John Cronin in 1717. John Cronin of Carrigaline had his will proved in 1729. In Cork city itself there was an Irish scribe named Tadhg Ó Cróinín in the early 18th century.

Ó CRUADHLAOICH

Ó CRUALAÍ   (O) CROWLEY

As far as is known, the only family of Connacht extraction to gain an early foothold in Co. Cork were the Uí Chruadhlaoich who came of the same royal stock as the O Connors and Mac Dermots. The *Leabhar Muimhneach* tells us that from Conchubhar son of Diarmaid son of Mael Ruanaidh came Mac Dermot Roe and Clann Donnchadha of Tirerill and the two O Crowleys in Munster with their various branches. A pedigree in the same book derives the family name from Conchubhar's son, Diarmaid, who acquired the soubriquet *An Cruadhlaoch* ('the hard warrior') and who flourished in the mid-11th century.

In Co. Cork the Uí Chruadhlaoich were for centuries associated with the area named after Clann Sealbhaigh. This lay to the north of the Bandon river between Newcestown and Dunmanway and now forms part of the barony of East Carbery. It was the scene of a bloody conflict in 1283 during the rebellion of the Carbery Mac Carthys and their allies against Domhnall Mac Carthy, king of Desmond. With the aid of several Norman families Domhnall defeated and scattered the Carbery men. 'Immediately after that', say the *Annals of Inisfallen*, 'the King caused great migrations into the borders of Clann Sealbhaigh on every side, so that famine well nigh killed all the Uí Chairpri.'

It may well be that among these migrants came some of the Uí Chruadhlaoich from Connacht, since later in that year (1283) according to the same annals, Raghnall Ua Cruadhlaích was slain by Eógan Mac Carthaigh. This is the earliest reference to one of the name in Munster. A Raghnall (son of Lochlann Mór) appears in the O Crowley pedigree, seventh in descent from Diarmaid 'An Cruadhlaoch'. The attribution to the O Crowleys of a descent from Mac Dermot of Moylurg (Co. Roscommon) was referred to by Sir Richard Cox who wrote in 1687. John Windele in 1840 recorded a tradition in Kinneigh to the effect that the first O Crowley married the daughter of a local chieftain, Sealbhach Ó Cochláin, and that the lands then passed to the O Crowleys. While this cannot be verified, it is clear that the O Crowleys increased in numbers and influence in Carbery while decreasing in Connacht.

A laconic entry in the Justiciary Rolls for 1295 records the fate of two in Co. Cork: 'Dermod and Conechor Ocroylly charged with homicides and other misdeeds, put themselves on the country. Guilty. Hung. No chattels.'

The townland of Curraghcrowley in the parish of Ballymoney — written Curry-I-Cruwolley (*Currach Uí Chruadhlaoich*) in 1576 — was

obviously an early seat of the family. So too was Caher in the parish of
Kinneigh, a townland formerly known as *Cathair Uí Chruadhlaoich*.
But in Elizabethan times the head of the family resided in the castle
of Ahakeera in Fanlobbus parish. At that time, Coill tSealbhaigh or
Kiltallow comprised the eastern part of Fanlobbus (Dunmanway)
parish and the western part of Kinneigh, 32 ploughlands in all, for
which O Crowley paid a head-rent of £9 4s. 4d. to Mac Carthy Reagh.
Around 1540 O Crowley maintained an armed force of eight horsemen and sixty kerne. In 1597 the freeholders in Carbery (described
as lords under Mac Carthy Reagh) consisted − apart from subsepts of
the Mac Carthys − of O Mahony Fionn, O Mahony Carbery, O Donovan,
O Driscoll and O Crowley.

Warlike by name and by nature, the O Crowleys frequently gave
cause for pardoning in Elizabethan times, as we see from the Fiants. In
1573 David and Conogher O Cruoly of Killtallwgh and Fynyne O
Crowley of Dromgarriff, gentlemen, received pardons. Four years
later pardons were granted to David O Crowley of Dromidiclogh (par.
Kinneigh) and Thady mac Dermot O Crowley (both of these being men
of O Mahony Carbery), Teige mac Dermot I Croly of Phale (par. Ballymodan), Conor mac Teige mac Awloey O Croley and Dermod ro of
Towneyne (? Tooreen, par. Caheragh) and Florence O Crowley, called
(the) O Crowley. Florence's place of residence is not given but the
castle of Ahakeera must have been in ruins after the Elizabethan wars.
Although Ahakeera townland was held by the O Crowleys until the
Cromwellian confiscations, the chief of the name appears to have
resided in Kinneigh parish. But the family connection with their former
residence was commemorated in the local traditional name *Cabhlach
Uí Chruadhlaoich* (O Crowley's ruin).

In 1584 in company with Randal O Hurley of Ballynacarriga, two
sons of Cormac Ó Cruadhlaoich were pardoned − Donnchadh gránna
('ugly') and Diarmaid na mbroc ('of the badgers'!). An inquisition of
1633 relates that Diarmaid na mbroc held lands in Dromfeagh, Shanagh,
etc. Cormac may have been the 'Cormack O Crulie of Carberry' whose
daughter, Maud, married John Lord Courcy (d. 1628).

In the same year was pardoned Conoghor mac Teige O Cruoly, one
of Florence Mac Carthy's men. This was the famous Fínghin or Florence
who took to himself the title of Mac Carthy Mór. When Florence was
imprisoned in the Tower of London in 1594, among his 'followers,
cosens and kinsmen' in Carbery who were scheduled to be 'examined'
was Teig mac Donell Icrooly, als. Brannagh, and in a letter which he
wrote in the same year Florence referred to 'som of mine owne men,
namlie Molrony O Croly and Edward Slabagh' whom he sent to keep
the castle of Timoleague for him. The name Maolruanaidh is of particular interest, due to its associations with the early pedigree of O
Crowley and of Mac Dermot of Connacht. (Another unusual name was
that of Tumultach, son of Tadhg Ó Cruadhlighe, whose death in 1569

was recorded in an Irish manuscript.)

When, in February 1600, Hugh O Neill arrived in Co. Cork, Florence Mac Carthy incurred suspicion by negotiating with him. In April of that year, Sir George Carew noted that the O Crowleys were amongst those of Florence's followers most likely to revolt if the Spaniards came. But under pressure the O Crowleys and the O Mahonys submitted and applied for protection. Florence Mac Carthy himself 'came in' in October. When Mac Carthy Riabhach of Kilbrittain and Domhnall O Donovan of Castle Donovan submitted in early May 1601, the pardons included the names of Teig mac Dermot O Crowley alias (the) O Crowley, of Kiltallagh, his son Dermot mac Teig, and Donal and Teig mac Randal O Crowley (Reagh) also of Kilshallagh. Other pardons were issued to the O Crowleys of Gillane (Gallanes par. Kilnagross), Dermod mac Conoghor O Crowley alias Mac y Vallirty of Monteen (par. Kilmaloda), Honora ny Teige O Crowley and her husband Teige O Regan of Burren, John mac Teige O Crowley of Kilshinahan (par. Kilbrittain), Teige oge mac Teige O Crowley and his wife Ellen ny Donnell Murhelly (Hurley) of Lislevane and Dermod mac Conoghor riough O Crowley of Ballynacarriga.

A pardon dated 29 May 1601, was granted to Dermod Moyle Mac Carthy (brother of Florence) and included the O Crowleys of Murragh, Kilshinahan, Burrane (par. Kilmaloda), Ballinaclogh (par. Ross) and Grange (par. Abbeymahon) — as well as David O Crowley alias David ny Madirie (*na madraí*) of Aghalinane (par. Kinneigh). A pardon was also granted to Donell mac Donoghye buye and to other O Crowleys buye of Dromfeagh (par. Kinneigh). On 30 August 1601, many of the O Crowleys of Killtallow were again pardoned.

Nevertheless, when the Spaniards finally landed, they were quickly joined by Donogh and Dermot Maol Mac Carthy and their followers. 'Therefore,' wrote Carew in November of 1601, 'the lord Deputy is to take heed of these and of the Mahownes and Crowlies'. After the debacle of Kinsale, in March 1602 the Earl of Thomond was sent into Carbery with orders to despoil the lands of those still in rebellion. 'Dermod Moyle Mac Carthy is most assisted by the O Crowleys; have a special care to prosecute him and his assistants', wrote Carew, while in November he informed Cecil that Sir Richard Percy was burning O Crowley's country. After this, pardons were sought by, and granted to several O Crowleys, including David mac Teige of Dromidiclogh and his son, Teige mac David.

The chieftain at this time was Teige mac Dermot O Crowley who succeeded to the title when his uncle, Fínghin or Florence, died without heir male. In 1592 Teige O Crowley, alias O Crowley and David O Crowley were among the Carbery gentlemen who agreed to pay £80 rather than have soldiers quartered on them. Now, late in 1602 Tadhg refused to surrender and joined the force organized by Owen Mac Egan, bishop-elect of Ross and led by the Mac Carthys of Phale (near

Ballineen). The insurgents were attacked in January 1603 by government troops led by Captain Taaffe and the White Knight. The latter lost two fingers, his signet ring, an ear and a horse in a fierce hand-to-hand encounter with Tadhg O Crowley (called Thaddeus Furiosus by Philip O Sullivan Bear). But Owen Mac Egan was slain and the resistance in Carbery was ended.

Two months later pardons were issued to those who took part in that last battle, including Teige mac Dermod O Crowley, alias Crowlie of Keiletallo, Dermod, Cormac, Donogh and Conoghor mac Teige and many other Crowleys, all of Kiltallowe. In the reign of James I a commission was appointed to dispose of lands whose owners had been slain in the rebellion. These included Dromfeagh, Gortaleen and Knockaduff (par. Kinneigh and Fanlobbus), the property of the slain Finnen and Maelrowney mac Cormock O Crowley. Teige, the chieftain, seems to have held his lands; he was one of the gentlemen and freeholders of Carbery who petitioned in 1610 for relief from the old tax known as 'the Earl's beeves' (then being collected by Sir John Jephson). Nevertheless the way had been opened for the speculators and mortgagors. In 1615 Randal Óg Hurley of Ballynacarriga and Florence mac Donell Mac Carthy of Benduff got a grant of extensive lands in Carbery which included their own lands plus those of several O Crowleys of Kiltallowe. (It was later discovered that many of these O Crowleys had alienated their lands to Hurley and Mac Carthy without licence and the two had to pay fines to obtain pardon for same.)

In the same year Richard Boyle (Earl of Cork) moved in and purchased a lease of lands in Kiltallowe from William mac Randal Hurley and from Dermod and Auliffe O Crowley. He also redeemed several townlands mortgaged by the O Crowleys and had others mortgaged to himself. In the following year Walter Coppinger's regrant included Curraghcrowley, Cahir I Crowley (Caher) and other townlands in Kiltallowe.

Bennett in his *History of Bandon* recorded a tradition that Capt. William Newce (described by Boyle as 'my honest servant') proposed building a town on the site since called Newcestown, but was diverted from his purpose by one Tadhg Ó Cruadhlaoich who drove a *sgian* into Newce's foot as he was surveying the site.

Yet the O Crowleys continued to flourish in their native habitat in the early 17th century, as inquisitions (post mortem) of that period show. These relate to:

David Bwy O Crowlye of Dromidiclogh, died *c.* 1617. Teige his son and heir.

Cormacke O Crowley of Dromerk, died 1602. Awliffe his son and heir.

Flynin O Crowley of Knockaghaduff, died *c.* 1612. Teige his son and heir.

Fynin Brannlaghe O Crowlie of Kinneigh beg, died *c*. 1622. David his son and heir.

David mac Fynine O Crowley of Kinneigh beg, died 1638. Teig his son and heir. Shile nee Swiney his widow.

Dermod mac Cormucke O Crowley als. na mrocke, of Shanagh, died before 1633.

Melroanie O Crowley of Dromfeagh, died 1613. Brien his son and heir.

Thadeus mac David O Crowlig of Kinneigh, died before 1640, aged 80 and unmarried. Fynyn was his brother and heir.

The rebellion of 1641 once more threw Carbery and the O Crowleys into a state of war. Sir William Hull, a colleague of Boyle's, deposed in 1641 that his land at Desert (near Clonakilty) was spoiled and kept from him by, among others, Daniel O Crowley of Burrane, while both Daniel and himself had suffered losses in Burrane, Baurleigh and Knockbrown which was being kept from them by Mac Carthy Reagh, Teig Óg O Crowley and divers others. In January 1642 Boyle was informed that all the country where the English dwelt was robbed and spoiled and their cattle driven into O Crowley's country. In 1643 a total of 25 O Crowley gentlemen were outlawed for their part in the rebellion, most of them from the ancestral lands of Coill tSealbhaigh — Auliffe of Dromerk, Cormack mac Cnogher of Lisheenleigh, Dermott 'Bacach' of Behagullane, David of Shanagh, Cormack mac Teige and Teige mac Fynin of (Knock-)aghaduff, Cnogher, David and Teige óg of Dromfeagh, David mac Teige of Buckree, Donnell mac Teige of Anaharlick, Fynyn mac David of Kinneigh beg, Teige mac David of Dromidiclogh, and Humphry óg of Enniskeane. Others came from Skeaf, Burrane, Maulmacredmond and Caheragh.

Once the rebellion was ended, any lands of which the O Crowleys were freeholders were promptly confiscated. Apart from some small parcels in the parishes of Kilmaloda (Skeaf East), Kilmichael (Curradrinagh) and Kilnagross, the O Crowley patrimony still lay in Kinneigh and Fanlobbus. In Kinneigh parish they lost through confiscation the townlands of Mallow, Dromfeagh, Buckree, Teenah, Kinneigh beg, Connagh, Aghfiard (?), Caher and Dromidiclogh West (Teige O Crowley als. O Crawly) and Dromidiclogh East (Teige O Crowly als. Maddery). In Fanlobbus parish they suffered the loss of Toom, Knockaghaduff, Dromerk, Behagullane, Shanagh, Glan and Ahakeera, the last-named being the site of their ancient castle. In all, 6,240 plantation acres were confiscated and divided up among the victors — the Earl of Cork, the Earl of Anglesey, Capt. John Jacock, Samuel Woodruff, etc.

Not an acre was ever restored to the O Crowleys. At the time of the census of 1659 a Teige O Crowley, gent., with his sons David and Fineene, resided in Co. Clare. This may have been the same Teige who was the recognized chieftain in 1641. The earlier Teige (mac Dermod), last mentioned in 1610, does not seem to have been succeeded by any of his sons. His place was taken by Fineen Bramulaghe (or Brannlaghe) of Kinneighbeg (d. 1622) who was succeeded by his son David (d. 1638 and buried at Kinneigh) and David by his eldest son, Teige. Teige had four brothers — Fineen, Cormac, Conoghor and David.

In Carbery the census of 1659 classed several of the names as 'tituladoes', even if landless ones — Teige mac Shane of Maulmacredmond, Teige of Teenah, Teige and Dermod of Glanbrack (par. Ross), Teige of Cashel (Kilmacabea), Cnohor og and David of Kilgarriff parish, John Oge O Crowley and his daughter in Lislee parish. (In the aftermath of the Cromwellian plantations a government supporter compiled a list of 'those in Ireland, England, Scotland now plotting for troubles.' In Carbery, he tells us, there were '5 other speciall perilous Instruments, the first Conor hoge begg O Cruoly 2. his cosen John Oge 3. the brother of that John oge.' (The fourth and fifth were Mac Carthys.)

In 1659 the distribution of the O Crowley families in Co. Cork — their sole habitat — was as follows: East Carbery (Crowley oge and O Crowley), 70; West Carbery, 19; Kinalmeaky, 9; Ibane and Barryroe, 18; Kilbrittain, 29. At this stage the only distinction made was between O Crowley and O Crowley óg, the latter apparently a junior branch. There were however, several nicknames — Brannlaghe, Buidhe, Na madraí ('Maddery'), Na mbroc, Bacach, Riabhach, Ciotach — some of which may have been the origin of different branches later on.

In 1662 John Read, a member of the Irish parliament, complained to the House of a forcible entry and distress made upon his lands of Castleventry, etc. by Shane oge O Crowley, and he prayed an order on the sheriff of Cork to restore and quiet his possession therein. Notwithstanding appeals made to the king, the O Crowleys apparently failed to get restoration orders — despite the fact that it was one Myles Crowley who fired the shot that killed the regicide, Col. John Lisle, in Lausanne, Switzerland. John Windele, the Cork antiquarian, related how in August 1837, a Mrs. Tuohy who owned a public-house at Evergreen in Cork showed him a royal patent in respect of lands in west Cork (Gortroe, par. Kilmichael and other lands) which had been confiscated after 1641 and later restored. She also had two wills, one being that of her ancestor, Miles O Crowley, who had failed to gain possession of the said lands, and the other of his son, Mowny O Crowley, made in 1720, which also stated that the lands had not yet been recovered. (Miles and Mowny are both anglicized forms of Maolruanaidh.) Windele records that Mrs. Tuohy, addressing her customers, asked them if they had any idea of the lineage of the woman who served them. She wept for the downfall of her people and cursed those who had robbed them of their lands.

Some O Crowleys took leases from the new grantees. The will of Donogh O Crowley of Behagullane, made in 1683, indicates that he still retained portion of the family lands; two years later, a Captain Crowley paid a nominal rent to the Earl of Cork for Behagullane. At the same time Dermod Crowley held Aghyohill and a Widow Crowley held Buckree.

The Williamite wars — in which the O Crowleys not unexpectedly took the Jacobite side — scattered the sept still further. Outlawries in 1690 included Thady Crowley of Templeboy, gent. (there was a Lieut. Thady Crowley in Lord Bellew's regiment and a Thady Croly who was a chaplain in King James' retinue in 1690), Humphry Crowley of Rossley (Ensign Crowley of Ross, also in King James' army, was son of Funhyr (? Humphrey) Crowley, gent.), Thady Crowly, Behy (? Behagh), gent., John, James and David Crowley of Aghafore (par. Abbeymahon) and others. After the war, in 1697, we find Cornelius Crowley alias Maddery, of Skibbereen, among the 'Irish Papists who have taught school and continue to do so'. Others found refuge on the continent. A Dermot O Crowley of Limerick (his family tree traces his descent from Cormac O Crowley who was born in Carbery *c*. 1559) settled in Cadiz where his son, Pedro Alonzo O Crowley was a noted writer and antiquary and had a street named in his honour.

Others, as became their name and tradition, took to the hills. One of the proclaimed outlaws for whom large rewards were offered in 1694 included Teige Crowley alias Mague, probably the same outlaw regarding whom many stories were told around Castletown Kinneigh. One such relates how he avenged the mutilation of a local child by hanging four English soldiers. His favourite refuge was a cave in a rock named Carrig Mague near Manch.

In 1798 in the only military engagement to take place in Co. Cork, that at the Big Cross near Shannonvale, one Donnchadh Ó Cruadhlaoich was among the handful killed there. Again, in Fenian days, one of the few killed in action in 1867 was Peter O Neill Crowley, of Kilclooney wood fame. He was a native of Ballymacoda. During the war of independence in this century many O Crowleys were again to the fore, men such as Diarmuid Crowley of Kilbrittain, a republican judge under the first Dáil Éireann, and Tadhg Crowley who was shot by the Auxiliaries in December 1920 and whose father, Florence Crowley, J.P., of Behagullane, was looked upon as chief of his clan.

Ó DÁLAIGH

(O) DALY

'There is certainly no family to which the bardic literature of Ireland is more deeply indebted than that of O Daly' is John O Donovan's tribute to this widely-known family. Originally the O Dalys appear to have been of the Corcu Adaim in Co. Westmeath and were probably of Érainn stock although the genealogists later derived them from the same stock as the O Neills and the O Donnells — one of the O Donnells' ancestors being Dálach, whence they were called Clann Dálaigh.

The one from whom the Uí Dhálaigh took their surname may have been Dálach of Dísert Tola (Co. Westmeath), a distinguished scribe who died in 1011. In 1139 Cúchonnacht na scoile Ó Dálaigh died at Clonard. He was described as 'chief ollamh of poetry', an *ollamh* being a poet and man of learning.

From his grandson, Aenghas, the genealogists derive the various branches of the family who, in later centuries, became poets or ollamhs to leading families all over Ireland — the O Neills and O Donnells of Ulster, the O Connors of Connaught, the O Byrnes of Leinster, the O Loughlins of Clare, etc.

As early as 1161 the death is recorded of Raghnall Ua Dálaigh, ollamh of Desmond in poetry, while four years later, Gilla na Trínóite Ua Dálaigh, also ollamh of Desmond, was slain. 'Of Desmond' at this period must mean that they were hereditary ollamhs to the Mac Carthys.

The peninsula of Muintir Bháire (Muntervary or Sheep's Head) in west Cork is the area particularly associated with the O Dalys of Desmond from an early period. They acquired the peninsula — as appears from a poem addressed by Tadhg Ó Dálaigh to Sir George Carew in 1618 — not from the Mac Carthys but from one of the Carews, probably Robert Carew, whose mother was a Mac Carthy and who built the castle of Dunnamark near Bantry. (*Muinntear Bháire na dtrácht dte/ód shinnser fuair ár bhfine*. Muinntear Bháire of the sheltered harbours/our family got from your ancestors.)

A plea roll of 1299-1300 records that Maurice Carew sued O Dalys and other Irish families in Muinntear Bháire in respect of land which they held from him.

The various branches of the Uí Dhálaigh were distinguished by colour names such as *Rua, Buidhe*, etc., *Fionn* (fair) being the soubriquet applied to the Munster branch. In 1387 the death occurred of Gofraidh (Geoffrey) Fionn Ó Dálaigh, 'the best ollamh of Ireland in poetry', author of several poems in praise of the Mac Carthy chiefs as well as a poem on the descent of the Uí Dhálaigh. 'I am Gofraidh, grand-son of Tadhg, from smooth lofty Mumha in the south', he tells us in one poem. Another Gofraidh Fionn Ó Dálaigh (son of Donnchadh) who died in 1507 was the author of a poem requesting the protection of the son of the Earl of Desmond; from then on O Dalys are found in the service of the Desmond Fitzgeralds. (In 1541 John Fitzmaurice of Co. Limerick and a certain poet called 'Odale the rymor' held between them 480 acres of former monastic land at Tullylease, Co. Cork.) At the end of the 16th century Aonghas Fionn Ó Dálaigh was known as *na Diadhachta* (the Divine) because of the great number of religious poems composed by him. His non-religious poems were mainly in praise of the O Keeffes of Duhallow, another family who sponsored the O Dalys. The Munster genealogists, in fact, derived the O Dalys from the same stock as the O Keeffes. Giolla Íosa Ó Dálaigh, *c*. 1575, wrote at the end of a poem addressed to Theobald Butler: 'To Ó Caoimh is due beyond all others the tribute which my race has always paid to his forbears, since this scion of the Uí Chaoimh must have from us a quatrain in every lay.'

In this area the O Daly lands – apparently given to them by Mac Carthy Mór – lay on the borders of Cos. Cork and Kerry, but mainly on the Kerry side. The parish of Nohaval Daly (*Nuachongbháil Uí Dhálaigh*) was (and is) divided between the two counties, with the O Dalys holding the Kerry portion. Later, we find 'the Crown lands of Pobble O'Keeffe' in the Cork portion. In the parish of Drishane the O Dalys held Curracahill, Kippagh, Coomacheo and Ballydaly (*Baile Uí Dhálaigh*), now in Co. Cork but formerly in Co. Kerry.

In 1600 there was slain 'Malone O Dolye alias dictus O Dalye Ffynne nuper de Noughevaill J. Dalye' while in 1601 a pardon was granted to Donell O Daly alias Vicker of Bally Daly, gent. In 1606 King James granted to John King of Dublin '. . . Noughavayll-Idally, 1 ar. and Kill-mcIllnie, ½ qr. lately the lands of Malone O Daly otherwise called O Daly Finn, of the former place, gent., dead in rebellion'. In 1612 a grant was made to Francis Blundell consisting of Killmackeloyne otherwise Ballydaly, parcel of the estate of Ennis O Daly, attainted. However, Eneas and Cormock Daly held Ballydaly and Coolecarragh in 1641. Perhaps the former was the Eneas O Daly of Nughvally (Nohaval), gent., who was outlawed in 1643, and/or the Aonghus Ó Dálaigh Fionn who wrote a poem in praise of Geoffrey O Donoghue of Glenflesk around the same time. A Lieut. Eneas O Daly was one of the Irish officers taken prisoner after the battle of Knocknanuss in 1647. The O Dalys suffered the usual confiscation and dispossession after the rebellion – although there was a will recorded in 1721 of John Daly gent., of Ballydaly (then in Co. Kerry). His brothers were named Owen and Bryan.

The O Dalys by no means confined their praise-poems to a single family. Several of them wrote laments for the O Sullivans of Béarra

– Domhnall son of Eoghan *c*. 1420, Eoghan son of Donnchadh who lamented the departure of Dermot O Sullivan for Spain in 1602, and Tadhg son of Diarmaid óg, who lamented the death of Eoghan and Diarmaid O Sullivan.

They may also have written in praise of the O Mahonys of Ivagha. Sir Richard Cox in his *Regnum Corcagiense* (1687) mentions '. . . Myntervary, a barbarous country. . . . This Territory was, according to Irish custome, given to O Daly who was successively Bard to O Mahown and Carew'.

Still, the Mac Carthys remained the chief patrons of the O Dalys in Desmond. Mahon mac Donall mac Eoghan O Daly was hereditary poet to the Mac Carthys Riabhach in the late 15th century. A letter to the Privy Council, dated 1569, lists O Dale among the followers of the Earl of Clancarty; five years later, they were among the important Co. Cork families who parleyed with Sir Peter Carew regarding his claim to their lands. In 1597 Odaly 'fun' (i.e. *fionn*) was among the chieftains described as 'Friendes to Mac Carthy More'. A document of 1600 detailing the lands of the followers of the Mac Carthys of Muskerry includes:

O dallies 2 ploughlands they are Rimors'.

(It is doubtful if these two ploughlands could have been Ballydaly etc., which, though now part of Drishane parish in Muskerry, then belonged to Co. Kerry.)

In lieu of monetary payments for their poetic output, the O Dalys were granted certain 'rights' by their Mac Carthy patrons, the most unusual being the right to the wedding garments of every girl married in Desmond or Duhallow. These were actually taken on the day of the wedding, as appears from the petition to a Cork jury in 1576 of an outraged Margeret ny Scally whose clothes were taken from her by force by Dermond Odayly on behalf of Odaly Fynyne (*Fionn*), 'their cheef Rymor otherwise called Olowe Dane' (*Ollamh dána*).

Co. Kerry appears to have been the birthplace of Cornelius O Daly who loyally supported the Earl of Desmond from beginning to end of the Desmond rebellions. He it was whom the Earl dispatched in a last vain effort to rally the support of those nobles who remained cautiously sitting on the fence while he struggled desperately against the Queen's superior forces. And when the inevitable ending came and the Earl was surprised by a party of the O Moriartys, O Daly was there, guarding some cattle nearby but returning too late to prevent his lord's death. His son, Domhnall, who was born at Kilsarkan near Castleisland, was better known as Fr. Dominic O Daly, O.P., a scholar of repute who compiled a history of his beloved Geraldines and who died bishop-elect of Coimbra (Portugal) in 1662. Another notable European scholar of the seventeenth century, a champion of the counter-reformation in Austria and Bohemia, was Donagh (Friar Cherubim) O Daly who was born in Co. Cork *c*. 1600 and died at Luggau in 1664.

We must now return to the O Dalys of Muintir Bháire who were sometimes distinguished by the adjective *Cairbreach* (of Carbery) as was, for instance, Aengus son of Aengus Caech Ó Dálaigh Cairpreach who died in 1507. A survey by Sir George Carew in 1599 showed that the O Dalys held 36 ploughlands in Carbery, most, if not all, in Muintir Bháire. The delimitation imposed by their peninsular patrimony formed these O Dalys into a more cohesive group than those of Duhallow. John O Donovan in his introduction to *The Tribes of Ireland* relates some traditions regarding them:

> The head of this family had his residence at Druim-Naoi or Drum-nea, in the parish of Kilcrohane, where a portion of his house, commonly called 'The Old College House', still remains, and forms the residence of a farmer, Mr. George Nicolas. According to tradition, two sons of a king of Spain who were at school here under the tuition of O Daly, died and were buried in Drumnea.
>
> The last professional poet of this house was Conchobhar Cam Ó Dálaigh Cairbreach, who wrote an elegy on the death of Donnell O Donovan, chief of Clann-Cathail, who died in 1660.

Besides the senior line of Drumnea, a junior branch dwelt at Caher where they had a bardic school. Eneas Keaghe (*Aonghas caoch*) O Daly of Moyntervarye was pardoned in 1590 and Eneas O Daly, otherwise O Daly, of Caher, in 1604.

Even after the battle of Kinsale, the O Dalys continued to support the old order, as represented by Domhnall Cam O Sullivan Bear. On 4th May 1602 Carew wrote that O Daly had been taken prisoner after coming from the rebel camp in an effort to induce Owen O Sullivan (son of Sir Owen) to join the rebels. But Owen informed on him and O Daly was committed to trial. He must have got an acquittal for on 20th June (after Dunboy) Tyrell sent 'his trustee servant, Dalie' offering to ransom the lives of the prisoners with money. When Domhnall Cam died in Spain in 1618, Domhnall mac Eoghain O Daly composed a lament of 51 quatrains commencing:

San Sbáinn do toirneadh Teamhair

Others, however, chose the Carew connection, in particular Aonghus rua Ó Dálaigh of Ballyroon (near Caher) known to Irish literature as *Aonghus na n-aor* (of the satires). He it was who, probably at Carew's instigation, vindictively satirized all the prominent Irish families of the south and for his pains was fatally stabbed by a servant of O Meagher in Co. Tipperary. This happened in 1617 according to an inquisition taken into his lands six years later. We are also told that Eneas junior, then aged 25, was his son and heir and that some months before he was killed, O Daly had mortgaged the western part of Ballyroon to Carolus (Cearbhall) O Daly. Aonghas óg does not seem to have been as loyal as his father; his name, 'Eneas O Daly, Ballyrowne, Gent.,' is to be found among those outlawed in 1643. One reason for this may have been the enmity of Sir William Hull (of Leamcon) who complained in October 1642 that he held a long lease from the bishop of Cork of two ploughlands of Kilcrohane but that all the land was taken from him by Enys O Daly of Kilcrohane, gent., Care O Daly of Caher, gent., Daniel O Daly of Raferigeen, gent., Margrett nyn Dermond O Daly, widow, of the same parish, gentlewoman, Teig O Daly of Rossnacaheragh, John O Daly, gent., and others.

John O Donovan states that a rock near the tower at Sheep's Head was called Bró Aenghuis after Aenghus na n-aor, and that several of the O Daly families of Muintir Bháire claimed descent from him.

Details of early 17th century families of O Dalys are to be found in the Inquisitions of the time. Donell O Daly of Letter and Ardahill died in 1597 leaving Donnoghe as son and heir; he paid annual rents to the O Sullivans (Mac Teige and Mac Gullacuddi).

Dermod O Daly of Oughererhiv (? Oughtihery, par. Aghabulloge) died c. 1609; Donoghe was his son and heir.

Dermod mac Donoghe oge O Daley of Cloghcarre and Derricluvane (par. Kilcrohane) died in 1624; his son and heir, Donoghe, died shortly afterwards, leaving Donoghe oge as his son and heir.

Donnell O Daley of Rossnacaheragh, Reenacappul and Foilakilly (par. Kilcrohane) died in 1625, leaving Teige as son and heir. Teige O Daley of Maulnaskehy (par. Kilcrohane) died in 1625; Dermot, his son and heir, married Margaret nyn O Sullivan and died before 1637, leaving Teige as son and heir.

Even these remote and rocky lands of Muintir Bháire did not escape the net of the Cromwellians but formed part of the spoils divided among the victors. In Kilcrohane parish the lands of Inis (*Aenghas*) O Daly (Rosreagh and Glanlough) and the lands of Donogh Daly (Fahane, Gearhies, Killovenoge) fell to John Eyres while Sir Richard Hull got his revenge on the O Dalys by acquiring Donogh O Daly's lands of Gurteen, Killeen and Maulnaskehy, Cormack Daly's lands of Dunbevour and Teige O Daly's of Reenacappul. In Durrus parish Owen O Dale's part of Killtowne went to Sir Theophilus Jones while in Abbeystrowry parish (Skibbereen) part of a townland known as Lahertidaly (*Láthair Tí Uí Dhálaigh*) was taken from Owen Daly and bestowed on Col. Richard Townshend.

It is hardly a matter for surprise that in the mid-19th century John O Donovan found the O Dalys of Muintir Bháire 'now reduced to the condition of cottiers or struggling farmers, the principal proprietors being four members of the O Donovan clan'. He also referred to the descendants of Cornelius Cam ('the last professional bard of the family') at Carrigtwohill, one of whom founded Daly's Distillery in Cork. (It is interesting that in the mid-17th century, Morrish O Daly lost 384 acres at Cloyne (Garrancloyne or Killacloyne) in Carrigtwohill parish.) This family claimed the O Daly tomb at Kilcrohane as their burial-place.

By the 16th century the O Dalys had spread to many other parts of Co. Cork. Their connection with the Earl of Desmond seems to have brought them into the barony of Kerrycurrihy, south of Cork city. In the late 15th century, Eneas (Aonghas), Tatheus (Tadhg) and Matthew O Daly were connected with the ecclesiastical prebend of Killanully near Ballygarvan. In 1573 pardons were granted to Brian mac Shane O Daly of Carrigaline, gent., Owen mac John O Daly of Kilnagleary, Donald mac Dermod, Shane mac Eany and Donald mac Donogh O Daly, all of Knocknamanagh (Minane Bridge). The first-named, together with Owen oge O Daly of Douglas, gent., received a grant of English liberty, the reason being that he had changed his allegiance (to support of the Government), his religion (to that of the Huguenots) and even his name (to Barnaby Daly). This earned him the bitter enmity of James Fitzmaurice Fitzgerald who, when he entered into rebellion in 1569 called on the citizens of Cork to 'abooliesh oute of that cittie that old heresy newly raised and invented, and namely Barnaby Daaly and all them that be Hugnettes, boothe men and women'. But to add insult to injury, when Lord Deputy Sidney recaptured Carrigaline castle from Fitzmaurice, he placed Barnaby Daly as warden there. Barnaby held his post for several years and gained the personal friendship of Nicholas Pett, Provost-Marshal of Munster.

Owen óg O Daly, 'one time schoolmaster', had as one of his scholars Garrett óg Rochford, and as a reward for his labours had half the plough-land of Rochfordstown settled upon him.

In the Cromwellian confiscations, William Dawly lost 280 acres in Killanully parish; these went to William Hodder. In 1690 among the Jacobite supporters outlawed were Owen Daly, merchant, of Cork city, and John Dawly, Cork, gent. A part of Leighmoneymore townland (near Dunderrow) is still known as Ballydawley. (There was a Donaldus O Daly in Kinalea in 1375.)

The Elizabethan Fiants record further O Dalys in Caherduggan, Carker and Burren, as well as in various parts of east Cork. Many of them bore the traditional family names, Aonghas, Geoffrey, Giolla Íosa — and in one case, Cúchonnachta. A typical example is Carrowell mac Goerie mac Enis O Daly (*Cearbhall mac Gothraidh mhic Aonghais Uí Dhálaigh*) of Ballinlogha (apparently in Muskerry).

Near Mitchelstown in the 18th century there farmed an Ó Dálaigh family, three generations of whom (all named Conchubhar) were custodians of the famed *Leabhar Breac*, compiled by another scholarly family, the Mac Egans. In 1789 when times were hard, it was sold to the Royal Irish Academy for three guineas.

According to the 1659 census, O Dalys were most numerous in West Carbery where there were 44 families. But there was a strong concentration too in Barrymore, also in Orrery and Kilmore, and the surname was well-represented in East Carbery, Kilbrittain, Kinalea, Kerrycurrihy and in Cork city and Liberties.

A census taken in 1834 showed that out of a population of 4,448 in Kilcrohane parish, 345 (or one in thirteen) were surnamed Daly, while after the famine, in 1849, the population was reduced to 2,820 and the Dalys to 217. Griffith's Valuation Survey of 1850-52 recorded around 500 Daly families in Co. Cork as a whole. At that time, the name Owen was still commonly used and there were several named Aeneas as well as a Godfrey and two Carrolls.

The late Cearbhall Ó Dálaigh, President of Ireland 1974-76, came of a Co. Cork family; his grandfather lived at Little Island, between Cork and Carrigtwohill.

Ó DEASMHUMHNAIGH

Ó DEASMHUMHNA   Ó DEASÚNA   DESMOND

Despite its anglicized form, there is no connection between this family name and the Earls of Desmond (Fitzgeralds), except in rare cases. There was, for example, a Desmond family in Co. Tipperary in the 1540s, with Christian names such as Maurice and John — an indication of Norman descent. A similar name is that of Maurice fitz James Dessemond who was appointed Archdeacon of Cloyne in 1550.

Generally speaking, however, the Desmonds of Co. Cork were originally Uí Dheasmhumhnaigh, a family of whose origin and history very little is known. We do know that they were in west Cork in the fourteenth century, since — as in the case of many other families — *Duan Catháin* claims them as part of the Uí Eachach hegemony, though it may be of some significance that the ancestor provided — Maonach son of Airtniadh — is not derived from the Uí Eachach themselves but said to have come 'from the north'.

> *I gcrích Fhloinn agus Luighdech*
> *Do goireadh de Deasmhuimhneach*
> *buan a mheasumhla re a mheas*
> *uadh Í Dheasmhumhna is díleas.*

(In the territory of Flann and Luighdech (i.e. south Munster) he was called 'Deasmhuimhneach'; long has he been esteemed; from him are sprung the Uí Dheasmhumhna.)

By the 16th century the name was to be found in several parts of the county, both east and west, as we learn from the Elizabethan Fiants, our only source for this period. Pardons were issued to the following:

1573: Donogh O Deason of Knocknamanagh (par. Tracton), tailor.

1574: Thomas mac Conoghor Iyassony (*Uí Dheasmhumhnaigh*) of Macroom, kern.

1585: Donogh mac Shane y Dashowne of Killnyhomyny (Killumney), smith.
Donogh mac Awliffe O Dasshowne of Tullevohelie (now part of Ballyhandle, par. Knockavilla).

1601: Dermod O Dassuny (apparently in Muskerry); Awliffe O Dassunughe (apparently in Carbery); Teige mac Conoghor I Yeasome of Ballionamlogh (?), baker; Donogh and Donell mac Awliffe O Dassanie of Knockavilla, yeomen; Dermod mac Awlie O Dassunie of same, yeoman; Dermod O Dassuny

121

of Killnehemny, tailor, Donell oge O Dassuny of same. (These last two were twice pardoned; in the other pardon the place name is spelt Killnyhone, which could be Kilnahone near Ballygarvan, but Killumney, as in the 1585 fiant, appears likelier.)

From this brief list the indications are that in Elizabethan times most of the Desmonds were engaged in trades (smith, baker, tailor etc.) though there was at least one family of yeomen farmers, in Knockavilla parish. They also seem to have been concentrated principally in the baronies of Muskerry and Kinalea. This is confirmed by the census of 1659 which has no returns for Muskerry but which lists Desmond as a 'Principal Irish family' in Kinalea only. Ten families were recorded there under an unusual form of the name – Mc Desmond. There was a John Desmond in Kinsale in 1724 and another of the same name in 1782. In 1792 Dan Desmond of Kinsale wrote to the Rev. John Cliffe of New Ross, giving particulars of landlords and tenants in the parish of Ballyfeard, most of whom were giving trouble. A will of Laurence Desmond of Tracton was proved in 1789, and the surname has remained prevalent in that area down to the present time. In Tisaxon graveyard near Kinsale are some old Desmond headstones, including one which commemorates two brothers of the name (said to have been involved in the smuggling trade) who were drowned at Ringabella in 1833 at a spot still known as Desmond's Rock.

Reverting to Muskerry, a well-known Franciscan was Fr. Cornelius Desmond, Guardian of Kilcrea, who was captured in 1606 between Kilcrea and Cork and after spending some time in prison was deported. In Spanish Flanders he became preacher to the regiment of Irish infantry of Colonel Henry O Neill. (In the same regiment, in the company of Capt. William Barrett, was one Dermot Dasman, who obtained a licence to travel to Ireland in July, 1609.)

Two other friars of the name, Thadeus (Tadhg) Desmond and Daniel Desmond, as well as an Augustinian, Fr. Thadeus Desmond, all from Cork diocese, were ordained at the College of Bordeaux in 1619.

A Dr. Desmond, according to Bennett's *History of Bandon*, was one of three Catholic 'rebels' who lived in the suburbs of Bandon prior to 1641 but who fled almost before the rebellion began and could not be caught. There was an Ensign Desmond in Nicholas Browne's regiment in King James' army, 1689. In the early 19th century, Seághan Ó Deasmhúmhna was a schoolmaster-poet to whose school in Innishannon Mícheál óg Ó Longáin sent his son, Pádraig, in 1818. In more recent times Daniel Desmond of Crosshaven was T.D. for his constituency from 1948 to 1964 and for a period led the parliamentary Labour party in Dáil Éireann.

In 1852 there were 103 Desmond families in Muskerry (east and west), 60 in Kinalmeaky, 46 in Kinalea and Kinsale and 61 in Cork city and district. Few of them lived in the east or in the far west of the county. While the family name does not seem to be embodied in any Co. Cork place-names — Ballydesmond in Duhallow being a modern name for the former Kingwilliamstown — there is a townland in Co. Waterford (a few miles north of Youghal) named Ballydassoon, which Canon Power renders as *Baile an Deasmhúnaigh*.

Ó DONNABHÁIN

O DONOVAN

While there was a family of Uí Dhonnabháin in Tuath Ó bhFithch-eallaigh — an area around Clonakilty and part of the long-established Corca Laoighdhe territory — their descendants, if any, became indistinguishable from the O Donovans who originated in what is now Co. Limerick. In early Christian times, this was the territory of Uí Fidgente who were divided into two branches — Uí Chonaill Gabhra in the west and Uí Chairpri in the east.

Donnubán (son of Cathal) from whom the family name originated, was king of Uí Chairpri and of the whole of Uí Fidgente in the late 10th century. This was the period of the meteoric rise of Dál Cais in north Munster. In 967 Mathghamhain (brother of Brian Boru) defeated the Norsemen of Limerick in a decisive battle at Sulchóid (Sologhod near Tipperary) and promptly assumed the kingship of Munster, taking hostages from Mael Muad of Uí Eachach and from Donnubán. Nine years later Mathghamhain was taken prisoner — treacherously according to the annals — by Donnubán who handed him over to Mael Muad for execution. This only cleared the way for Mathghamhain's brother, Brian, who proved an even more ambitious rival. Firstly, Brian slew Ivor, king of the Limerick Norsemen, and in 978 sacked the Uí Fidgente territory killing many Norsemen there. Finally he killed Mael Muad at the battle of Bealach Leachta and thereafter reigned without opposition in Munster.

Donnubán died in 980 and his son, Cathal, succeeded him. Cathal's mother and wife are said to have been of the Norse race which would explain why his son was named Amhlaoibh (Olaf). This Amhlaoibh was succeeded by Murchadh whose successor was named Aineislis. The name Donnubán does not occur again in the family genealogy although a Donnubán is mentioned in the *Annals of Inisfallen* as having slain Donnchadh, grandson of Eochu, in 1058.

In 1177, as the result of great warfare between O Briens and Mac Carthys, the O Donovans fled into Eóganacht Locha Léin and to the country around Mangerton. From there they appear to have moved into Co. Cork, where in 1201 Amhlaoibh O Donovan was slain when a mighty hosting, headed by the Norman William de Burgo and including many O Briens and Mac Carthys, devastated Muskerry and the country around Kinneigh. Amhlaoibh was described as king of Uí Chairpri, obviously a sept-name rather than a place-name but one which was soon to give its name to the whole barony of Carbery in west Cork. Four years after this, Cellachán Mac Carthy was slain by rival Mac Carthys who were aided by O Donovan of Uí Chairpri.

In the mid-13th century the chief of the Uí Dhonnabháin bore the unusual personal name of 'An Crom' (the stooped one). In or before 1259 he was slain, as the result of a cowherds' brawl, by the Uí Eachach (O Mahonys) at Inis Béil Átha Dos. This may have been at Inch in the parish of Fanlobbus (Dunmanway) in the valley of the infant river Bandon, known to later generations as Gleann an Chroim. The Uí Dhonnabháin in retribution slew the chief of the O Mahonys with the aid of Fínghin Mac Carthy of Carbery.

This was the Fínghin who so decisively defeated the Normans at Callann in 1261. In the previous year three 'O Dunevans' (Crorenav, Conyn and Padin) were noted by officialdom as having raided Norman lands in Fínghin's company and no doubt they were also at his side on the fateful day of Callann. This might explain how the O Donovans gained such prominence in Carbery where Fínghin's descendants ruled as lords.

In 1283 the sons of Gilla Riabhach and of Echthigern O Donovan were slain by the O Sullivans. Around the same time some of the name fell foul of the Anglo-Norman establishment. In 1295 Donkud (*Donnchadh*) O Donovan was hanged at Cork for the killing of John Clochan and for receiving his brother, Kennedy, who robbed the corn of William de Rupe. In the same year suit of peace for their trespass was pardoned to Cathel O Donovan, to Lothlyn O Donovan Machecrom (*Lochlainn mac an Chroim*) and to Molise O Donovan M'chekyr (*Maol Íosa mac Íomhair*).

This Ivor, father of Maol Íosa, may be the one referred to in a tradition recorded by Seán Ó Coileáin, the poet-historian of Myross, to the effect that in 1251 Ivor O Donovan built Castle Ivor (in Listarkin, parish of Myross) of which only a fragment now remains. In the folk-memory he was a celebrated navigator and necromancer, and it was firmly believed that his enchanted ship could be seen with all her courses set and colours flying on Loch Cluhir near the castle, once every seven years.

According to Mac Firbis, the three sons of An Crom, namely Cathal, Aineislis and Lochlainn, were the progenitors of Clann Chathail, Sliocht Aineislis and Clann Lochlainn respectively, the first and third being the main divisions of the O Donovans. Though there are few historical references to the sept for several centuries, we know that the O Donovans settled on a substantial wedge of Carbery, reaching from the coastline (between Castlehaven and the Roury river near Ross) inland as far as the Mealagh river which forms the boundary with Bantry barony.

Their territory comprised over 130 ploughlands. The northern section, Clancahill, was slightly the larger, but described in 1607 as 'a barren unfertile soyle, full of Bogges, rockes and Woodd'. It included most of Drimoleague and Drinagh parishes but also stretched into

Myross where it overlapped the Clanloughlin territory which was spread over the parishes of Myross, Kilfaughnabeg, Kilmacabea, Rosscarbery, Kilnagross and Caheragh. The lord of Clann Chathail had dues from all the havens west of Glandore; those to the east belonged to Clann Lochlainn. Both divisions paid a small head-rent to Mac Carthy Riabhach.

The principal castle of the senior Clann Chathail branch was at Castle Donovan (formerly the townland of Sowagh or Suagh) strategically placed on a rock in the centre of Drimoleague parish. To protect their maritime interests they erected the castle of Raheen in Myross parish. The chief seat of the lord of Clann Lochlainn was Glandore castle. *Cloch an tsráidbhaile*, as this castle was called, was originally built by one of the Barretts.

Several sub-septs of the O Donovans flourished in the 16th and 17th centuries. In Clancahill in 1607 were Sliocht Raghnaill (Gortnascreeny), Sliocht Diarmada Rua (Loughcrot), Sliocht Taidhg Mhic Niocaill (Aghagard) and Clann Chonghalaigh (Garranes, Minanes, Lahanaght, etc.). Other minor septs were Sliocht Íomhair and Sliocht Tiobóid. Sliocht Aineislis mhic an Chroim were scattered over both divisions — in Moyny and Derryclough lower in Clancahill as well as in the parishes of Kilmacabea, Kilfaughnabeg and Ross in Clanloughlin.

A family group of such prominence in the diocese of Ross was bound to be represented in its church hierarchy so it is not surprising to find a Domhnall Ó Donnabháin bishop of Ross in the late 15th century. It was his resignation and death in 1483 which provoked the succession dispute between Odo O Driscoll and (Blessed) Thaddeus Mac Carthy. Donatus (Donnchadh) O Donovan was archdeacon of Ross in 1470.

In the 16th century the first of the name to be mentioned in the Fiants was Donald mac Melaghlin Y Dunevan who, in company with some O Driscolls, was killed in 1551 by the chiefs of the O Driscolls for alleged piracy. In 1577 pardons were issued to Mac Carthy Riabhach and to the other Carbery chieftains including Donald O Donovan (of Castle Donovan; he was commonly known as Domhnall na gCraiceann) and Donald Juvenis O Donovan (of Cloch an tsráidbhaile; he was known as Domhnall óg na Cartan).

During the second Desmond rebellion Domhnall na gCraiceann seems to have supported the government. The *Annals of the Four Masters* record that in 1581 Captain Zouch sent some of the Mac Sweeneys with the son of O Donovan (Dermot) and some others of Carbery to plunder the son of O Sullivan (Bear), but in a counter-attack, Donal Cam O Sullivan slew nearly 300 of the Carbery men though his own forces scarcely exceeded 50. Dermot O Donovan was slain at Lathach na nDamh in the territory of Clanlaurence by Donal Cam who (according to John O Donovan) buried the body under an oak tree, since called Daróg (or Dairithín) Diarmada, in the townland of Rossmackowen. Domhnall na gCraiceann himself died in 1584. According to Seán Ó Coileáin of Myross, it was Domhnall who built

Castle Donovan. His wife was Ellen, daughter of O Leary of Carrignacurra.

His son and heir, another Domhnall, was much less amenable to the decrees of the government. He was only two years in office when he burned to the ground the bishop's house at Ross, a house which had been repaired three years before by the Protestant bishop, William Lyon. Although Domhnall had had the rod of office presented to him in 1584 by Mac Carthy Riabhach, his legitimacy was questioned by his brother, Tadhg. However, a decree from Chancellor Loftus in 1593 confirmed that he was the lawful son and successor of Domhnall mac Taidhg O Donovan.

Domhnall was one of the few southern chieftains to support the rebellious Hugh O Neill. In March 1599 Sir Thomas Norreys wrote to the Privy Council from Carbery relating how he had taken the pledges of all the chieftains of that area, saving O Donovan and some of the Mac Carthys '. . . whereupon I caused their castles and howses to be taken and razed, and their people and lands to be spoiled'. Despite this, a year later O Donovan was at O Neill's camp at Inishcarra, endeavouring to recruit support for the rebellion. This brought further 'pacification' on his people, as related by Capt. Flower, following an expedition into Carbery:

'From Ross we marched over the Leape, into O Donovan's country, where we burned all those parts, and had the killing of many of their churls and poor people, leaving not thereon any one grain of corn within ten miles of our way, wherever we marched, and took a prey of 500 cows which I caused to be drowned and killed, for that we could not trouble ourselves to drive them in that journey. Beyond the Leape we stayed three days in which time we burned and spoiled all the septs of the Clandermonds then in action'.

Since O'Neill had returned to Ulster, O Donovan had no option but to sue for pardon which was granted in May 1601 − to Domhnall O Donovan of Castledonovan, his wife Joan ny Cartie and many of his followers. Hope sprang up once more with the arrival of the Spaniards. A few days before the battle of Kinsale Carew wrote to Cecil listing those in the pay of the king of Spain; they included O Donovan who had 100 footsoldiers. After Kinsale, however, O Donovan and others submitted. 'Since their coming in, they are grown very odious to the rebels of those parts' wrote the Lord Deputy, so the Earl of Thomond was instructed to afford them 'all kind and mild usage'. It was a party of O Donovan's men who slew the rebellious Dermod Maol Mac Carthy.

Yet, when Bishop Eoghan Mac Egan landed at Kilmackillogue in June 1602 with financial aid for those still in rebellion, £200 was allotted to O Donovan. The fall of Dunboy soon afterwards, however, presaged the end of the rebellion. O Donovan managed to avoid attainder and loss of his lands. In 1604 Walter Coppinger and James Grant entered into bonds of £200 each for the good behaviour of Daniel O

Donovan of Castle Donovan. A condition was that Daniel's pledge, Donnough mac Hugh mac Donnell, should remain a prisoner in Cork. At least two of the name – Mortagh and John O Donovaine – were 'gentlemen pensioners' in the service of the king of Spain in 1605.

In the early 17th century the 'surrender and regrant' policy as utilized by the great chieftains in Elizabethan times was extended to lesser lords such as the O Donovans. In 1615 Domhnall of Castle Donovan surrendered and got regrant of his extensive personal estates in Clancahill together with chief rents from the rest of the clan territory plus the customs and harbour dues of Castlehaven, Squince, Conkeogh (*Cuan Caoch* or Blind Harbour) and the western part of Glandore. He was allowed two manors, to be styled, respectively, Castle Donovan and Raheen, with the right to hold fairs at Raheen, Bawnlahan and Drimoleague. Domhnall died in or about 1639 and was buried in Timoleague friary. He had been twice married (to Helena Barry of Lislee and to Joan Mac Carthy Riabhach) and left at least seven sons – Domhnall, Tadhg, Muircheartach, Donnchadh, Diarmaid, Riocard and Céadach.

Similarly, and also in 1615, Domhnall óg na Cartan got a regrant of his lands in Clanloughlin, with power to empark the manor of Cloghetradbally, plus the customs and royalties of the port of Glandore. At this time, his son and heir, Muircheartach, resided at Ardagh in the parish of Myross but after Domhnall óg's death in 1629, Muircheartach's son and heir, Daniel, lived at Cappanabohy (par. Kilmacabea).

Sliocht Aineislis retained a certain distinctiveness. Even as late as 1673 we find the name of Teige mac Cnoghor Kennislish – obviously a Mac Aineislis O Donovan. In 1584, a pardon was granted to Aulive gangkagh mac Donoghe Mac Eneslis, one of Florence Mac Carthy's men. In Ringrone parish near Kinsale, Donnell mac Cnoghor buy Mac Eneslis O Donovan who died in 1602 held Kilcolman from the de Courcys. His son, Cnoghor buoy, died in 1620 and was succeeded by Donnell who took part in the 1641 rebellion and then went to Spain. For this he forfeited his lands, and though they were restored by Charles as a reward for faithful service overseas they were again forfeited after the Williamite takeover. Teige mac Loghlen Mac Enestlis of Kell Mc Enestlis was one of the last group to be pardoned in March 1603. There was also a Teige Mac Anelis who forfeited Skahanagh in Myross parish after 1641.

Donogh mac Rickard Mac Eneslis who died in 1614 held Letter in the parish of Kilmeen. He was succeeded by Teige and Teige by Rickard who, together with Randal, owned Letter in 1641. After the confiscations it went to Captain Sam Foley and Francis Burnham. In the same parish is Lisnabrinny (west) where Dermod mac Teige Mac Enestlis died in 1631, Teige being his son and heir. Teige was also in rebellion in 1641 and his lands were acquired by Robert Childe and Lord Kingston. Diarmaid O Donovan Rossa, the noted Fenian, claimed descent from this Teige, his agnomen 'Rossa' being derived from the townland of Rossmore, also in Kilmeen parish. In 1639 an inquisition was held into the lands of Thaddeus mac Donogh O Donovan of Rossmore. Donagh mac Teige was his son and heir, and he, too, forfeited after 1641.

Another group of O Donovans, described as yeomen (farmers) — Donogh mac Dermody O Donovan, alias 'in lavig', Cnoghor mac Donogh Mac Dermody and Teige mac Dermody, alias Teige Leigh, of Ballygornagh ny Geannynigh — in 1613 mortgaged Ballygornagh and Creggane-I-Donovan to John Young (apparently an agent for Walter Coppinger) for £24. The places mentioned appear to be Barleyhill and Creggane in the parish of Ross.

It need hardly be said that the O Donovans played an active part in the 1641 rebellion. At the very outset five brothers of O Donovan (Mór) were named as supporters of Lord Muskerry, together with Daniel mac Owny O Donovan of the Freugt (? Froe, par. Ross), Morartagh O Donovan and his sons and Rickard O Donovan of Kilfinan. Arthur Freke, writing of the siege of Rathbarry castle in 1642 tells how Teige oge Mc Cartan O Donevane ambushed and captured some of the English, conveying to prisoners to '. . . Mc Morgan O Donevane about the Leape. Meantime the said Teige Mc Cartan O Donevane and Florence Mac Carty of Benduffe, O Donevant of the Flur, Rebells of Carbery, tooke away all my corne stacked by Rosse, on my land called Downings, and every night stole some of the cattle and sheepe from Rathbarry'.

Rev. Urban Vigors wrote in similar vein in July 1642: '. . . Great O Donovane as the Irish call him (i.e. Domhnall III) whose father was a most notorious Rebel, doth much spoyle about the Leape, Castlehevane, Bantry, Rosscarbery and divers other places; his father burnt the Towne of Rosse the last warrs. . .'

In 1643 eight gentlemen of the name were declared outlaws — Donnell and Donnell oge of Castledonovan, Donnell and Donnell oge of Derryvilline (Derryvreen, par. Kilmeen), Murtagh mac Donell of Cloghitradbally (Glandore), Hugh oge of Dellygmorr, Richard of Ballynegornagh and Morrogh of Carhoogarriff. 'Donnell Mac Ensils, Glearhy' was probably one of the Sliocht Aineislis. Two of the seven sons of Domhnall (II) of Castledonovan died serving the Royalist cause. Both were captains of companies of foot raised by Domhnall II. One (Murtogh) was cut down with his whole company at the battle of Rathmines; the other (Rickard) was slain in His Majesty's service beyond seas.

The Cromwellians then fell upon O Donovan's lands, killing his people and burning his crops. Castle Donovan itself was partly blown up with gunpowder and left a roofless ruin. According to an old tradition, Daniel O Donovan and Tadhg an Dúna Mac Carthy in 1641 hanged a Protestant woman named Dorothy Ford in the castle. Her family then, it was said, cursed O Donovan and caused a *braon sinsir* or corroding drop to trickle from the stone arch of the castle, never to cease until the last of his race would be extinct. But the tradition appears ill-founded in view of the fact that several Protestant gentlemen of Carbery were present at Domhnall's death-bed in 1660 and indeed composed a testimonial to his character, in the course of which mention was made of O Donovan's own account of his visit to Cork in 1648 to accept the king's offer of peace from the Earl of Ormond:

> '. . . and upon his entering into his Highnes' lodging ther, his quarter-master generall (who was formerly acquainted with O Donovane) said, with a loud voice, *Lá éigin dar éirigh Ó Donnabháin suas*, and upon that his Highness desired O Donovane to tell him how those Rimes first begun, which he tould him, as he heard from part of his ancestors, and there in the Lord of Inchiquin's presence, O Donovane voluntarily accepted and joyfully applauded his said Majestie's peace. . .'

Domhall's death was lamented in the traditional manner by Conor Cam O Daly. In the following year his only son, Domhnall (IV), after appealing to the king, was ordered to be restored to all his castles and lands. However, in 1666 Charles II confirmed Castle Donovan, Seehanes etc., (1,465 acres in all) to a Cromwellian officer, Lieutenant Nathaniel Evanson, and only a portion of the manor of Raheen (over 3,000 statute acres) was restored to Domhnall. In 1688 Colonel Daniel O Donovan (late of Castledonovan) raised a regiment of infantry in west Cork for King James, with many of his own sept among the officers. Col. O Donovan was an upright and humane officer, regarded with respect and even affection by many Williamite officers. In October 1690 he was Deputy-Governor of Charles Fort, Kinsale, which he defended with vigour. Eventually, having first made honourable terms, he surrendered the keys of the fort to the Earl of Marlborough. Also in 1690 he was outlawed but after he surrendered voluntarily in January 1692 he obtained the benefit of the articles of Limerick within two years. He established a new family seat at Bawnlahan in the parishes of Myross and Castlehaven and there he died in 1705.

Ten years later his son and heir, Richard, conformed to the Protestant religion. Richard's grandson, General Richard O Donovan died without issue in 1829. After this the title of 'The O Donovan' was assumed by the O Donovans of Montpelier, Cork. These were descended from a daughter of Colonel Daniel (of 1690) who married her cousin Captain Cornelius O Donovan who obtained a general pardon in 1700. This family is now represented by the O Donovans of Hollybrook, Skibbereen.

The chief of Clann Lochlainn (Muircheartach, son of Domhnall óg na Cartan) was outlawed in 1643. His son, Daniel, was also involved in the rebellion. Their lands were confiscated and the castle of Cloch an tsráidbhaile fell into disuse. However, portion of the septlands was restored to Jeremy Donovan (son of Dermot) who was a Protestant though also a Jacobite. In 1684 he obtained letters patent of his lands from Charles II; those in Co. Cork were erected into the manor of O Donovan's Leap. (Leap, in Irish *Léim Uí Dhonnabháin*, was so called from a wonderful jump made by one of the O Donovans across the deep ravine near the village.) In 1689 he became M.P. for Baltimore in James II's parliament, and was also appointed registrar of the Admiralty. He is not listed among those attainted in 1690 although several of Clann Lochlainn were – Daniel O Donovan and his son Daniel, Daniel mac Richard, William, and Murtagh mac Teige. Jeremy died in 1709 and was succeeded by his son, Jeremy junior, who in 1737 disposed of all the manor of O Donovan's Leap to Richard Tonson for £5,400. He died in 1743, unmarried, and his heirs-at-law tried without success to recover the family property.

The Cromwellian confiscations severely affected many O Donovans in the parishes of Drinagh, Caheragh and Castlehaven, amongst other places. Among those in Co. Cork who received transplanters' certificates in Co. Cork were Kedagh O Donovan and Dermond mac Cnogher O Donovan, both of the Garry. (*An Garraí* appears to have been an alternative name for Myross.)

Some O Donovans were also to be found in the Bantry area. Daniel O Donovan of Dunnamark was appointed portreeve of Baltimore by James II in 1687. Other O Donovan Jacobite burgesses of Baltimore were Cornelius of Ballincolla (par. Myross) and Daniel of Forenaght (par. Castlehaven). The last-named was a captain in Colonel O Donovan's regiment in 1689, and in March of that year, in a surprise attack he captured Bryan Townshend's fort at Castletownshend. His descendants lived at Cooldurragha (par. Myross) in the 19th century. In a similar attack on Castletown House in November 1690, Capt. Teige O Donovan of Drishane was one of the Jacobite officers killed.

Hugh Donovan of Letterlicky near Bantry was one of the fifteen O Donovans outlawed in 1689-90. It was probably this Hugh who was taken prisoner, along with six of O Donovan's regiment, by the Bandon militia in May 1691. Some years later William Donovan of Letterlicky was decreed to be entitled to the articles of Limerick – as was also Dr. Richard Donovan of Bantry. Still further west, O Donovan's Cove in Muintir Bháire took its name from a branch of the family descended from Teige O Donovan of Gurteeniher in Drimoleague parish. A local tradition there recalled a feud among the O Donovans, in the course of which, it is said, Gurteeniher village was burned to the ground. Following this, the O Donovans fled and divided into three families one of which, O Donovan Bán, settled at O Donovan's Cove.

The census of 1659 shows that O Donovans were then fairly widespread in Co. Cork – along with some ten families of the name in their ancestral east Limerick homeland (Coonagh barony). There were 49 families in East Carbery, 29 in West Carbery, 18 in Ibane and Barryroe, 17 in Kilbrittain, 12 in Kinalmeaky and 10 in Barrymore.

In the year 1798, the United Irish leader at the 'battle of the Big

Cross' near Clonakilty was Tadhg an Astna O Donovan, who is said to have lived at Lackanalooha in the parish of Kilnagross.

In the 19th century one of Ireland's outstanding scholars was John O Donovan. Although his ancestors had been resident in Co. Kilkenny for almost two centuries, he could trace his descent back to the chiefs of Clann Chathail. His laborious researches shed new light not only on the history and genealogy of the O Donovans but on numerous other families throughout Ireland.

Ó DUBHAGÁIN

Ó DÚGÁIN DUGGAN

The genealogical analogy between the Corca Laoighdhe of south-west Cork and the Fir Maighe Féne of the north-east is underlined by the fact that each produced a family of Uí Dhubhagáin. In the case of the former, we are told that one of the hereditary leaders of Dúthaigh Uí Ghillamichíl (around Castlehaven) was Ó Dubhagáin. We know nothing of the subsequent history of this family except that it may have been connected with the townland of Cloonties in the parish of Fanlobbus (Dunmanway) which in the 18th century was known as Cluanydugane — *Cluain Uí Dhubhagáin*, O Duggan's meadow.

Of more significance, politically, were the Uí Dhubhagáin of the Fir Maighe, who claimed descent from Mug Ruith, the magician of the Fir Bolg. An early legend tells how Mug Ruith assisted Fiachu Muillethan, king of Munster, in defeating the king of Tara at Knocklong (Co. Limerick) and as a reward was granted the fertile territory of Mag Féne in the Blackwater valley for himself and his descendants. The O Duggans were the original ruling family of Fir Maighe Féne, and, according to *Críchad an Chaoilli*, had their chief stronghold at Cathair Dubhagáin (Caherduggan) which must have taken its name from their eponymous ancestor, Dubhagán. The genealogy of the Fir Maighe begins: *Domnall mac Aeda mac Conchobuir mac Mael-Décláin mac Diarmata mac Aeda mac Dubacáin* and is traced back to Mug Ruith and Fergus mac Róigh. Caherduggan is now a parish and townland in the barony of Fermoy, but there is another Caherduggan in the parishes of Gortroe and Templebodan as well as a Lisduggan in Castlemagner.

According to the *Annals of Loch Cé*, Géibheannach Ua Dubhagáin, king of Fir Maighe, was slain at the battle of Clontarf where he was aiding Brian Boru. If this be so, it would explain the appearance of a new ruling family in the area, namely the Uí Chaoimh (O Keeffes) of Eóganacht Glennamhnach, the O Duggans being relegated to second place in the local political structure and possibly moving to a new stronghold as well. The topographical poem of Ó Huidhrín while bracketing O Duggan and O Keeffe in a single quatrain still gives O Duggan pride of place but in a new location:

> *Triath Fear Moighe na múr ccorr*
> *Ó Dubhagáin Dúin Manann*

(The Lord of Fermoy of the smooth ramparts; O Duggan of Dún Manann.)

133

Dún Manann is probably the same place as 'Manann' of *Crichad an Chaoilli*, now Manning in the parish of Glanworth.

The question as to which family group should take precedence among the Fir Maighe Féne was soon to become an academic one when in the 12th-13th centuries the whole area was conquered by warlike Cambro-Normans. Caherduggan later became the site of a Roche castle. The O Keeffes moved to pastures new in Duhallow; the O Duggans appear to have remained on to suffer dispersal and downgrading. In an Elizabethan Fiant of 1577 a pardon was granted to 'Maurice Roche of Cahirdowgane, esq.,' followed a little further on by 'Matthew O Dowgane, kern'!

As a sept, the O Duggans were now without a base of their own, and many took service under various lords. About 1366 Comedyn Odogyn had a cottage at Britway while Donaldus Odogyn held a 'messuage' from the Roches in Donoughmore parish. In 1455 reference is made to John Ydubagan, deceased, who had held the vicarage of Enachrocayn or Clonfert in Duhallow. Domhnall (Donnell or Daniel) became the most popular first name among the O Duggans, particularly in Elizabethan times when they appear mainly in association with the Mac Sweeney gallowglass who supported the Mac Carthys in Muskerry. Donald mac Donogho O Dowgan who was pardoned twice in 1577 as a Mac Carthy follower is described first as of Coultober and later of Coomlogane (par. Drishane). Donald O Dowgan of Downyn, a gallowglass and a Mac Sweeney follower, was also pardoned twice in the same year. This is probably Dooneens in Drishane parish. In 1584 pardons were issued to Mollaghlen O Dowgan, Edmond oge mac Swyny and Donogho enloghort (i.e. of Lohort) O Dowgane, all of Macroom and all gallowglass. The following year three Domhnalls were pardoned – Donill mac Moriertagh y Dowgan of Downyne, Donell O Dowgan mac Donogho of Gwortenruo and Donell mac Conoghor I Dogane of Marshalstown (in Condon's country). In 1586 Philip O Dowgaine of Mashanaglass (another Mac Sweeney stronghold) was pardoned as were William O Dowgan and Meilerie mac William of the same place in 1601. Others pardoned in 1601 included Connoghor O Dowgane of Kinalmeaky, Dermod O Dowgan of Innishannon, John and Melaghlin oge O Dowgane of Kilbolane, Donell O Dowgan of Killmidie (Ballymartle) and Teig O Dowgan of Donoughmore.

One whose name does not appear among the pardoned was Dermod O Duggan, a harper from Garryduff (probably Garryduff in Clonmult parish) and a follower of James fitz Thomas Fitzgerald of Conna castle. James was designated Earl of Desmond by Hugh O Neill (whom he actively supported) but nicknamed 'The Súgán Earl' by the English. Dermod's single-minded loyalty to his lord shines like a beacon light out of the murky labyrinth of double-dealing and treachery that enveloped Elizabethan Ireland. His heroic act is related as follows in *Pacata Hibernia*, an account of Carew's activities in no way sympathetic to the native Irish: 'The Lord Barry ... about the 14th of May (1601) knowing that one Dermond O Dogan, a harper dwelling at Garryduff, used to harbour this arch-rebel (James fitz Thomas), or else upon occasion of some stealth that had been made in his country, the thieves making towards this fastness, his soldiers pursued them into this wood, where by good fortune, this supposed Earl and two of his Baldons and this Dermod were gathered together, being almost ready to go to supper, but having discovered these soldiers, they left their meat and made haste to shift for themselves. They were no sooner gone out of the cabin but the soldiers were come in, and finding this provision and a mantle which they knew belonged to James fitz Thomas, they followed the chase of the stag now roused; by this time the harper had conveyed the Sugan Earl into the thickest part of the fastness, and himself and his two companions of purpose discovered themselves to the soldiers, and left the wood with the lapwing's policy, that they being busied in pursuit of them the other might remain secure within that fastness, and so indeed it fell out; for the soldiers, supposing that James fitz Thomas had been of that company, made after them till evening, by which time they had recovered the White Knight's country, whence, being past hope of any further service, they returned to Barry's Court and informed the Lord Barry of these incidents.'

Sad to relate, the White Knight with whom they sought refuge, later changed his allegiance, and for £1,000 reward betrayed Fitz Thomas who was in hiding in one of the Mitchelstown caves. The authorities promptly had the Súgán Earl incarcerated in the Tower of London where he died.

In the early 17th century a Donell O Dowgan paid a levy on lands in the parishes of Kilbrin and Kilmeen in Duhallow — perhaps the Daniel Dowgane who was witness to an O Keeffe bond in 1638. It was probably also the same Donnell O Dowgane, gent., of Castlecurry (Castlecor is in Kilbrin parish) who was outlawed in 1643 as a result of the rebellion. The only other one of the name outlawed then was William O Doogane of Mashanaglass, yeoman; as mentioned earlier, Mashanaglass was a former Mac Sweeney stronghold. After the confiscations a Thomas Duggan, in company with Theophilus Carey and Mary Mac Carthy, got a lease of the castle and lands of Derryleamlarie (now Castle Derry near Enniskeane), the confiscated property of Fineen Mac Carthy.

In the 18th century the Duggans of Knockininane (Mountinfant, par. Nohovaldaly) along with the Cronins (of Rathmore and Killarney) were agents to Lord Kenmare and became prosperous middlemen. At the beginning of the century a Duggan married a sister of Daniel Cronin. Later in the century Denis Duggan of Mountinfant married Frances Galwey, niece and heiress of Daniel Cronin of Park, Killarney, and their son, Daniel, in 1786 adopted the surname Cronin on inheriting his granduncle's estate. He was ancestor of the Cronin-Colts-manns of Flesk castle.

The name Thomas recurred more than once. Thomas Duggan, a schoolmaster at Ballincollig, was one of the Fenian convicts of 1865. He was transported to Australia and never returned to Ireland. His grandson, Archdeacon Thomas Duggan, one of the best-known clerics of the Cork diocese in this century, died at Lima in Peru, in 1961.

Ó DUINNÍN

DINNEEN   DINEEN   DOWNING

This family name originated in the same two areas of Co. Cork as did O Duggan. Firstly, one of the subdivisions of Caoille (the territory of Fir Maighe Féne) was Tuath Ó nDuinnín, which was situated in north Cork, on the borders of Co. Limerick, between the Bregoge and Funcheon rivers. In the same territory – and presumably named from the same source – is the townland of Ballydineen (*Baile Uí Dhuinnín*) divided between the parishes of Doneraile and Caherduggan. (In Co. Limerick Ó Duinnín was one of the chiefs of Eóganacht Áine.)

The second family group were of the Corca Laoighde, among whom we find Ua Duinnín as one of the chief family names in Tuath Ó nAenghusa (see Ó HAONGHUSA). Their fame for many centuries rested on their reputation as historiographers or family chroniclers. As early as 1098 the *Annals of Inisfallen* record the death of Mael Brénainn Ua Duinnín, lector and vice-erenagh of Ardfert. In the introduction to his great Book of Genealogies (1650), Dubhaltach Mac Fir Bhisigh listed the hereditary historian families who preserved the records of their chiefs, and for south Munster named only 'Muintir Dhuinnín (who) were mostly in Mumha, that is with Síol Eoghain Mhóir, that is Clann Charrthaigh, Síol Súilleabháin, and so forth'.

Cathán, son of Niall Ua Duinnín, in the 14th century composed a long poem which traces – somewhat erratically – the genealogies of the families of Uí Eachach Mumhan. These included not only the O Mahonys and O Donoghues but many lesser-known families of west Cork hardly mentioned anywhere else. *Duan Catháin* was later embodied in a work called *An Leabhar Muimhneach* which extended to the whole of Munster and which was partly compiled by another member of the family, Domhnall Ó Duinnín, in the early 17th century. It is, accordingly, to the Uí Dhuinnín that the credit must be given for preserving the records and chronicles of the great families of Munster. Regrettably they did not see fit to keep some account of members of their own family, details of whom are rather sparse. (A Leinster genealogy in *An Leabhar Muimhneach* makes Ó Duinnín a derivation of O Duinn – a not very inspired guess.) One name recorded is that of Donnchad mac Gillananaem hi Duinnin who transcribed a section of a manuscript for Fínghin O Mahony of Rossbrin castle in 1465.

In 1600 the families occupying Mac Carthy lands in Muskerry included: Hegans (Egans) who were brehons, 3 ploughlands; Aulyves

(Aulynes), surgeons, 3 ploughlands;   O dallies (O Dalys), rimors, 2 ploughlands, and:·

'Odonins ½ ploughland, they are chroniclers'.

Half a ploughland appears rather a poor return for performing this important function, nor do we know where the land was. Judging by the Fiants, it may have been at Aherla. There is a townland called Cappadineen (*Ceapach Uí Dhuinnín*) in the parish of Fanlobbus (Dunmanway) but this is in the barony of Carbery. It is noticeable that a distinction was made between 'rimors' (rhymers, i.e. poets) and 'chroniclers' which the O Dineens were. This distinction was overlooked by the Protestant Bishop Lyon of Cork and Ross, who wrote to Cecil in 1600, as follows: 'Charles McCarthie, now in England, and Owen O Sullivan told unto me the 4th of the last moneth, that O Downin a Rimer of Muskrie being in the north with O Neyll, O Neyll shewed him divers letters sent to him from Florence Mc Carthie; some, three yeares ago, some later.'

Only a few of the name are mentioned in the Elizabethan Fiants. In a pardon granted to followers of Cormac Mac Carthy of Blarney in 1573 appears the name of Gullyriough O Dunnyne (*Giolla Riabhach Ó Duinnín*) of Aherla Beg. In 1601 pardons were granted to Donogh, Cnoghor oge and Donell O Downyne of Aherla, Donell O Dowinen alias Mac Igallagh duff O Downine (followers of the Mac Carthys of Carrignamuck), Cormock O Donyne, labourer (an O Mahony follower) and Margaret ny Donnyne, wife of Owen mac Teige Cartie of Kilcoe. In 1602 William O Dunnyn of Ballymagooly, husbandman, was pardoned.

Also in the Elizabethan period, one Moenus mac Thomas y Duneayne was marshal of the county of Imokilly (for the seneschal of Imokilly). He purchased some lands from the Condons of Corkbeg and bestowed them on his foster-son James fitz Edmond fitz Morris Gerald, from whom Sir John (fitz Edmond) bought them. First on the list of those lands was Ballymoenus.

According to the census of 1659, there were then thirteen families named Dinane in East Carbery; Dineen was probably the name intended here. One of the 'tituladoes' in Innishannon parish was Cnohor O Dyeyneene. At the end of the century, Thomas Dynneen was a quartermaster in Carroll's (formerly Sir James Cotter's) Dragoons, according to King James' Irish Army list. Donogh Deeneen (alias Bariky) late of Clondrohid parish, was one of the outlaws in Annahala Bog for whose capture rewards were offered in 1694.

At Chichester House, in 1700, Timothy Dyneene, gent., claimed the residue of a 31-year lease (from the Earl of Clancarty, 1675) of the lands of Knocknagoul in the parish of Aglish in Muskerry. The claim was allowed. By then, of course, the O Dineens were merging in the mass of tenant-farmers with but little time for the learned sciences — though, no doubt, some still lovingly treasured manuscripts laboriously compiled by their ancestors. There is an interesting reference to one such in a pedigree of Dominick Sarsfield, Lord Kilmallock, in the Genealogical Office, Dublin. Beside the pedigree, which is written in French, an anonymous annotator wrote, apparently in 1710: 'I am to inquier for old Charles O Dinin livving near Killcreane (Kilcrea) in Muskerie, County of Cork, an antiquarist'.

Another learned one was Fr. Daniel Dineen, superior of the Irish college at Toulouse prior to 1751. He came from east Cork and was a friend of the poet Liam Ruadh Mac Coitir.

It was to poetry that many of the name turned according as the demand for family chronicles decreased. In 1649 An Giolla Dubh mac Conchubhair Uí Dhuinnín (a name which resembles 'Giolla Riabhach' of 1573) composed a poem in honour of Fínghin Mac Carthy. Belonging to a later period is a poem addressed to Donnchadh Ó Coileáin by Uilliam Ó Duinnín. The poet Tadhg Ó Duinnín was considered by Daniel Corkery to be the last official poet of the Mac Carthys of Blarney. His verses are melancholy ones, like those in which he lamented the defeat and dispersal of the native Irish nobility after the war of 1689-91. Realizing that his style of composition was now outmoded, he ended with the couplet:

> *Mo cheárd ó mheath le malairt dlíghe i nÉirinn,*
> *Mo chrádh go rachad gan stad le bríbhéireacht.*

(My craft being withered with change of law in Ireland, O grief that I must henceforth take to brewing.)

In actual fact, he retired to his farm, and so ended *Dámhscoil na Blárnan*. His retiral also seems to have silenced the literary output of the Uí Dhuinnín, though in the early 19th century Liam Ó Duinnín compiled Irish manuscripts at Cnoc an Phréacháin in Knockavilla parish.

In this present century, the age-old reputation for scholarship was once more revived in the person of An t-Athair Pádraig Ó Duinnín (1860-1934) who was born near Rathmore in Co. Kerry and who is best remembered for his massive contribution to Irish lexicography. Another giant of the early Gaelic League days, An tAthair Peadar Ó Laoghaire, also claimed descent from one of the name in that his ancestor, Conchubhar Ó Laoghaire of Carrignacurra castle, married one of a Dineen family from Ullanes in the parish of Ballyvourney.

FITZGERALD

MAC GEARAILT

The Geraldines who dominated the history of Ireland for several centuries were of Cambro-Norman origin. In the 15th century they claimed kinship with the Gherardini of Florence but it is clear that the Irish Fitzgeralds derived their family name from Gerald of Windsor, so called because his father, Walter fitz Otho, was constable of Windsor castle. (The Norman 'fitz' is a derivation of the Latin *filius*, a son). Gerald was appointed constable of the castle of Pembroke by Arnulf de Montgomery and married Nesta, daughter of Rhys ap Tewdr (the former king of south Wales). One of their sons was named Maurice. As Nesta bore several other sons (by King Henry I and by Stephen, constable of Cardigan, as well as by Gerald) Maurice fitz Gerald was related to quite a number of the first band of Norman invaders in Ireland — Carews, Barrys, Robert fitz Stephen, Meiler fitz Henry etc. It can be said, in fact, that this group spearheaded the whole invasion.

Gerald of Windsor had paid a visit to Ireland long before the invasion, namely in 1102 when he was sent there by Arnulf who wished to marry the daughter of Muircheartach O Brien.

When Maurice fitz Gerald landed at Wexford in 1169 he brought a small force of knights and archers as support for his half-brother, Robert Fitzstephen, who was already in Ireland. Strongbow rewarded his efforts by granting him lands in Kildare and Wicklow. Maurice died in 1176 leaving several sons, among whom were: William, Baron of Naas; Gerald who married Eva de Bermingham and became 1st Baron of Offaly and ancestor of the Earls of Kildare; Thomas, ancestor of the Earls of Desmond, whose castle of Shanid is still an outstanding landmark in west Limerick; and Alexander. The last-named appears to have been given lands in Imokilly by his relative, Robert Fitzstephen, and these, together with the lands of William (which included Maynooth) accrued to Gerald.

The Imokilly lands centred around the castle of Inchiquin and included the site of the town of Youghal, a town which developed rapidly under the Geraldines and received a royal charter in 1202. The foundation of the Franciscan friary (South Abbey) in Youghal is ascribed to Maurice (son of Gerald) in 1224, and several of the later Earls of Desmond were buried there. In 1244 an agreement was drawn up whereby Alan, bishop of Cloyne, renounced to Maurice, son of Gerald, all rights and claims to Inchiquin, Clonpriest, Killeagh, Kilcredan and other lands in Oglassyn (Imokilly) while Maurice in turn granted to the bishop Ballykinealy, Kilgrellane, Ballyglassane, Bally-makeagh, Barnabrow and other townlands around Cloyne. In 1251 Maurice was granted free warren (hunting rights) in his lands in Co. Limerick and Imokilly. Also he acquired Ballydonegyn and Lochne-horn (*Loch na hEorna*, now Deerpark par. Mogeely) from John fitz Eynon. After Maurice's death the lands were inherited by his grand-son, another Maurice, whose son (Gerald) died in 1287 leaving no heir so that the Geraldine lands became the inheritance of Juliana, aunt of Gerald and wife of John de Cogan of Muskerry. As described under DE COGAN her cousin John fitz Thomas by one means or another gained possession of her inheritance (and of that of another cousin, Amabilia) and was created 1st Earl of Kildare in 1316.

As well as that, the manor of Inchiquin which had been occupied by Maurice (2nd son of the Maurice of 1251) went, after his death in 1286, to his widow, Emeline de Longespee and afterwards to their daughter who married Thomas de Clare. In this way the manor passed out of the possession of the Kildare Geraldines but later it came into the ownership of the Desmond branch.

Because of a marriage connection the Kildare Geraldines involved themselves in the Rochford portion of the Prendergast estates (see DE COGAN) and in 1381 Gerald de Rochford surrendered his interests in these lands to Gerald fitz Maurice, son of the Earl of Kildare. The lands mentioned included Carrigaline, Curraghbinny, Uí Cuirb Liatháin (on the north side of Cork harbour) and Shandon. Up to the mid-17th century, if not later, a head-rent was payable to the Earls of Kildare out of the lands of Curraghbinny, while their descendants, the Dukes of Leinster, presented incumbents (alternately with the Earls of Barry-more) to St. Mary's Shandon as late as the 19th century.

The Earls of Desmond

The descendants of Thomas of Shanid had a still stronger influence in Co. Cork. As early as 1212, Thomas, apparently because of his kinship to Raymond le Gros, was claiming Fitzstephen's moiety of the kingdom of Cork. This claim was challenged — and finally set aside in 1331 — but another door was opened. In 1215 King John granted to Thomas fitz Anthony the custody of Decies and Desmond, as well as the custody of the lands and heir of Thomas of Shanid, namely, John fitz Thomas whom we later find, not surprisingly, married to one of Fitz Anthony's daughters. Fitz Thomas and the other sons-in-law of Fitz Anthony then built a ring of castles around the coast of Des-mond, Fitz Thomas being credited with the erection of one at Mola-hiff near Castlemaine. It seems as if Fitz Anthony and his sons-in-law were treating the custody as an ownership grant and were attempting to take over the whole of Demond. But it was Fitz Thomas who, because he remained loyal to the king during the rebellion of Richard,

Earl Marshal, in 1234 (while the other sons-in-law sided against the king) succeeded in obtaining in 1259 a grant from King Edward of the whole of Decies and Desmond.

By then, however, the native Irish of Desmond led by Fínghin Mac Carthy (see MAC CARTHAIGH) were engaged in a determined bid to recover their patrimony and John fitz Thomas' army was routed in 1261 at Callann near Kenmare where John himself and his son Maurice were numbered among the slain. Maurice left a baby son, Thomas, who (according to tradition), during the tumult occasioned by the news of the Callann disaster, was snatched from his cradle by a pet ape, carried to the castle battlements and down again, unharmed. Hence he was known as *Tomás an Ápa*! When Thomas came of age in 1282 the value of his inheritance had greatly depreciated. Ten years later he got a confirmatory grant of his grandfather's lands in Desmond, most of which had by then been overrun by the Mac Carthys. 'There was not in Munster a baron more modest, more hospitable or of greater prowess than he', the *Annals of Inisfallen* said of Thomas when he died in 1298 possessed of manors in Counties Kerry, Limerick and Waterford. In Co. Cork he claimed only 'land in Corkely (*Corca Laoighdhe*) which cannot be extended (*i.e.* enumerated) on account of the Irish.'

His son, Maurice fitz Thomas, was a notable 14th century Norman-Irish lord at a time when increasing Gaelicization was creating a desire for more independence from the crown. Though ennobled as Earl of Desmond in 1329 Maurice remained a thorn in the side of the government, even going so far as to summon parliaments of his own in opposition to the Justiciar's. By 1330 he was able to muster an army of 10,000 men including the forces of Brian (Bán) O Brien. Imprisoned several times, he was eventually outlawed and his earldom forfeited. In 1345 his partisans ravaged much of Munster but the Earl's castles of Askeaton and Castleisland were taken and he had to sue for pardon which was granted some years later. His earldom was restored and he even became Justiciar of Ireland before he died in 1356.

Maurice was succeeded by two sons in turn, first Maurice who survived him only three years and then Gerald who ruled from 1359 to 1399. This was the era of the Kilkenny statutes which attempted to reverse the Gaelicization of the lords of Norman descent. Gerald disregarded the spirit of these statutes to such an extent that he is known in Irish literature and tradition as Gearóid Iarla, a leading poet of his time and one of those who introduced the French style of courtly love-poetry into Irish. Even when defeated in battle and imprisoned by Brian O'Brien he spent his time composing love-poems in Irish. Furthermore his son James was fostered with the O'Briens. Because he was also credited with magical powers, an old tradition held that Gearóid Iarla never died but lay sleeping beneath the waters of Lough Gur, ready to ride forth on his enchanted steed when the appropriate time came.

His eldest son, John, was Earl for one year only, as he was drowned at the ford of Ardfinnan on the river Suir while raiding Butler territory. John was succeeded by his son Thomas who, like his grandfather, followed Irish customs and composed Irish verses. But when he married Catherine Mac Cormac, the beautiful daughter of one of his tenants, his ambitious uncle James seized upon this excuse to depose him. A state of warfare ensued and Thomas was imprisoned by James. After his release he found himself powerless to regain his estates and died in exile at Rouen in 1420. His funeral in Paris was attended by King Henry V.

James, the usurper, then reigned as virtual king of Munster for over 40 years. This was a period when a lack of strong central government led to amalgamation and consolidation under powerful overlords. One of Earl James' greatest coups was the acquisition of title-deeds to the extensive lands in Co. Cork formerly held by the Cogans, a family much weakened by a dearth of male heirs in the direct line and by attacks from their neighbours, both Gaelic and Norman. Indeed the Geraldines had themselves been responsible for the destruction of Cogan lands around Rathgoggan (later Charleville) and Ballyhea. Accordingly, in 1439 Robert fitz Geoffrey Cogan handed over to James, Earl of Desmond, the title to his ancient patrimony — Muskerry, Kerrycurrihy, Rathgoggan, etc. Other families followed suit and the Earl forced the Mac Carthys, O Sullivans and others to pay services to him. He was now lord of a great part of the counties of Cork, Kerry and Limerick, as well as half of Co. Waterford where he made his younger son, Gerald, first lord of the Decies. The chief harbours of the south — Limerick, Tralee, Youghal, and, to an extent, Cork — were under his control. He was also a great builder of castles and renovated the ancestral strongholds of Askeaton and Newcastle (West) as well as erecting friaries, both Franciscan and Dominican.

After James' death in 1462, his son Thomas rose to being the foremost potentate of his time in the country. He sided with the Yorkist party in the Wars of the Roses, smashed the Butler-Lancaster alliance in Ireland and was rewarded by being made Deputy for four years. One of his achievements was the founding and endowment of St. Mary's Collegiate church at Youghal in 1464. The end came, however, when his successor as Deputy, Sir John ('the Butcher') Tiptoft, Earl of Worcester, had both the Earls and Desmond and Kildare attainted in 1468 for 'horrible treasons and felonies'. Before Thomas could attempt to escape or appeal he was beheaded at Drogheda, a judicial murder which appalled the whole of Ireland, both Gaelic and Anglo-Irish. 'Injury and great outrage was done in Ireland this year' say the *Annals of Connacht*. 'Tomás Iarla ... was beheaded, though he was guiltless of any offence ... the hearts of the men of Ireland and of their wives were broken by these tidings.'

This barbarous act enkindled in the hearts of the Munster Geraldines a burning resentment which a century later erupted in rebellion and brought about their final downfall. Two of Thomas' sons and a grandson successively held the earldom, displaying a latent hostility to the government. In 1520 the Lord Lieutenant and Council exultantly notified Henry VIII that the Earl of Desmond and many of his kinsmen and supporters had been slain in a sanguinary battle against the Mac Carthys near Mourneabbey. A third son of Thomas, namely Tomás Maol, became Earl until his death in 1534. His grandson and heir, James, was brought up at the English court in an endeavour to loyalize the earldom. However, a fourth son of Thomas, old Sir John, refused to recognise the 'Court Page' and held the lands as *de facto* earl for two years, being succeeded by his son, James fitz John. In 1540 the 'Court Page' landed at Youghal and set off northwards to recover his inheritance. He had travelled only as far as Áth na Circe in Co. Limerick when he was ambushed and killed by his cousin Maurice Dubh (or *Muiris a' tóiteáin*), brother to James fitz John, James then becoming uncontested earl.

In order that he might rid himself of his murderous brother, the new Earl placed him in occupation of Carrigaline castle (newly-recovered from the Mac Carthys by the Lord Deputy) where Maurice was fully occupied in warring against the Mac Carthys who were supposed to pay an annual levy of cattle to the Earl. Maurice was finally killed in 1564 at the age of eighty by the sons of Tadhg Mac Carthy of Muskerry — one of whom, Dermot, was Maurice's son-in-law!

Maurice's son, James Fitzmaurice, was destined to become the outstanding leader of the Desmond Geraldines. It was, in fact, the mortgaging and takeover of Carrigaline castle by Sir Warham St. Leger that sparked off the first Desmond rebellion. In 1569, aligned for the first time with Mac Carthy Mór, Fitzmaurice attacked and captured Tracton Abbey (by then a fortified residence) as well as Carrigaline castle. The castle was recaptured by the Lord Deputy later in the same year but Fitzmaurice continued in rebellion for the next four years. (His cousin, Earl Gerald, as a result of the battle of Affane in 1565, was confined in London.) The rebellion turned into a kind of guerilla warfare until James finally sued for pardon in 1573. This was granted and the Earl of Desmond was permitted to return to Munster. Two years later, Fitzmaurice, accompanied by the White Knight and the seneschal of Imokilly, left for the continent to seek aid for a renewed struggle. Returning in 1579 with the small force of Spaniards and Italians who were fated to be massacred at Smerwick, James was killed in a skirmish by the Burkes of Castleconnell. The Earl, who had entered the conflict rather unwillingly, then led the rebellion for four years, gradually losing his supporters until finally he was hunted down and slain in Co. Kerry in 1583. It is believed that his headless body was interred in the old graveyard of Kilnamanagh, east of Castleisland. His vast estates were duly confiscated and utilized for the plantation of Munster.

Fitzgeralds of Imokilly

The Fitzgeralds who in the 16th century held Castlemartyr, Cloyne, Ballycrenane etc. were not Kildare Geraldines. Their pedigrees, which are somewhat confusing, indicate that they were descended from the branch known as the Knights of Kerry (of Rahinnane near Ventry) who claimed descent from John of Callann. This Kerry connection with Imokilly is referred to in a 17th century lament by Piaras Feiritéir for Maurice, son of the Knight of Kerry:

> *D'admhuigh bean do cheart ar Eochaill*
> *Bean sidhe ag Moigíle do chomhgas*
> *Íbh mac Caille is Cathrach Móna*
> *Is Cineál mBéice ag dréim re deoraibh.*

A pedigree compiled by Sir George Carew commences with the four sons of Maurice, a 15th century Knight of Kerry. The eldest, Edmund, was driven from his lands in Kerry by his brother, Nicholas, while the third brother, John, settled at Caermona in Imokilly and the fourth, Richard, became the first seneschal of Imokilly.

Caermona is Cahermone near Midleton. Its castle was in existence in 1535 when Lord James Butler camped there on his journey from Youghal to Cork. Around 1600 it belonged to the Fitzgeralds of Cloyne and in 1640 it was bequeathed by Sir John Fitzgerald of Ballymaloe to William Fitzgerald of Lisquinlan. Later it was acquired by the Broderick family.

Carew names the sons of Richard (seneschal of Imokilly) as Maurice of Ballintier (? Ballymartyr or Castlemartyr), Edmond of Curueveigh (Cornaveigh, par. Clonpriest), Gerald, bishop of Cloyne, Garrett of Ballymctample (? Ballintemple), James of Ballynmullyn (Ballinwillin) and William of Incheneycrenagh (Castlerichard). He also stated that these lands came to the Fitzgeralds through the mother of Maurice (Knight of Kerry) who was a daughter of Lord de Courcy. It is true that there were some de Courcy properties in Imokilly in the 14th century (e.g. Rathcoursey and Ballykinealy) but they were few. It seems more likely that the lands came through the Earls of Desmond who appear to have become overlords of the area. The manor of Inchiquin and lordship of Imokilly had been acquired by the Earls of Ormond and in 1422 James Butler constituted James, Earl of Desmond, as his seneschal over the baronies of Imokilly and Inchiquin, including the town of Youghal. This alliance was cemented by a Butler-Geraldine marriage settlement. James then appointed Richard Fitzgerald as his seneschal (i.e. steward or deputy) while retaining the overlordship – as well as the castle of Inchiquin. Katherine, widow of Thomas, Earl of Desmond (known as 'the old Countess of Desmond'), is reputed to have lived to a great age at Inchiquin. (Afterwards it came into the possession of Raleigh and Boyle.) From a list of lands and services formerly in the registry of Cloyne it would appear that the Fitzgeralds claimed rents from practically the whole of Imokilly — from Supples, Powers, Carews, Condons, Cotters, Magners, etc.

Castlemartyr

The seneschals of Imokilly resided at Baile na Martra (Castlemartyr). In Elizabethan times the seneschal was John fitz Edmond who was 6th in descent from Richard. His mother and the Earl of Desmond's mother were both daughters of O Carroll, Lord of Éile, while his wife was Honora, daughter of James Fitzmaurice. Accordingly, John is frequently mentioned as a firm supporter of the Earl from the very first outbreak of the Desmond rebellions. He aided Fitzmaurice in the capture of Carrigaline and Tracton in 1569. Later in the same year, however, Lord Deputy Sidney recaptured Carrigaline and after Christmas besieged and took Castlemartyr where he placed a garrison, making one Jasper Horsey the queen's seneschal of Imokilly. After the conflict ceased (for a time) in 1573 Fitz Edmond and Fitzmaurice sued for and received pardon. John repossessed Castlemartyr and then accompanied Fitzmaurice to the continent. In 1579 he took an active part in the renewed rebellion, being prominent in the capture of Youghal. He remained the Earl's chief supporter in the area even after Imokilly had been ravaged by the Earl of Ormond, his brother (Maurice of Rathcoursey) slain and his aged mother executed. He was responsible for the Earl's last victory in 1583 when they defeated the Butler faction at Knockgraffon near Cahir. Shortly afterwards, however, he yielded to the inevitable and sued for pardon. Though his life was thus spared, he was attainted by Act of Parliament in 1583 along with more than a score of other Geraldines from places in east Cork — Currabeha, Dromadda, Rathcoursey, Poulacurry, Rahanisky, Ballynaclashy, Ballintemple, Ballycrenane, Ballymacoda, Garranejames, Lisquinlan. John fitz Edmond was confined in Dublin Castle and died there in February 1589, possessed of Castlemartyr, Caherultan and Ballintotis (castle) — which do not seem to have been confiscated as his son in 1608 obtained livery of the lands. Another son, William mac Shane, was among those who sailed to Spain with De Aguila after the battle of Kinsale.

During the wars of 1641-1653 the Fitzgeralds of Castlemartyr, led by Edmund Fitzgerald, took the Confederate side and their strategically placed castle was several times attacked and plundered by the opposing factions. It was taken by Lord Inchiquin in 1645 and after the confiscations came into the possession of the Earl of Orrery, later becoming the seat of the Earl of Shannon, another of the Boyle family. Although Colonel Richard Fitzgerald of Balenamartery was included in the declaration of royal gratitude by Charles II in 1660, he never recovered Castlemartyr. The burial place of the Castlemartyr Fitzgeralds was in the old graveyard of Ballyoughtera.

Cloyne

This branch was descended from the youngest son of Richard, the first seneschal, namely William of Inchaneycrenaghe (*Inse na cruithneachta* now Castlerichard). William's son, James, and James' son, Edmond, were both nicknamed *An Déagánach*, being nominated Deans of Cloyne, though laymen. (It will be recalled that William's brother, Gerald, was bishop of Cloyne in the late 15th century and he was succeeded in the see by his cousin, John. Both bishops seem to have donated church lands and benefices to their relatives.) Edmond's son, John, unlike his relative and namesake at Castlemartyr, refused to join in the Geraldine rebellion and was rewarded by being made High Sheriff of Co. Cork in 1570 as well as by grants of confiscated lands. He was also granted a pension of 100 marks per annum in 1582 for having taken and hanged his rebel brother, James. By virtue of his being 'Dean of Cloyne' (like his father and grandfather) he managed to purchase the bishop's castle (or palace) of Cloyne, with its demesne, for £40. He represented Co. Cork as a member of Perrott's parliament in 1585-86. Once again, in 1599-1600, he refused to join the forces of the Súgán Earl of Desmond or those of Hugh O Neill. In March 1602, Lord Mountjoy, who was returning to Dublin after the battle of Kinsale, spent the night at Cloyne and was so impressed with the loyalty and hospitality of John fitz Edmond that he knighted him before he departed. To commemorate this event, Sir John set up at Ballymaloe castle (one of his properties which he had greatly enlarged at that time) a stone bearing his initials and the date 1602. In 1608 he surrendered all his property and received a royal regrant from James I 'in recompense of his faithful services.' After his death on 15th January, 1613, an inquisition (which takes up 36 MS pages) into his lands showed that he died possessed of the manor, castle, town and lands of Cloyne, Cross castle in Cloyne, Chore Abbey (Midleton), the castles of Ballymaloe, Cahermone, Corkbeg, Castleredmond and Cowlegorry (Mountuniacke) — along with scores of townlands throughout Imokilly, and indeed outside it, for he also held the castles and lands of Kilmaclenine and Castleishen in north Cork as well as lands in Kinalea and Barryroe, houses in Youghal and a tower on the walls of Cork city, near the King's castle. His son Edmond, heir to all this wealth, died ten months prior to his father's death. An elaborately inscribed tomb to father and son may be seen in the north transept of Cloyne cathedral.

The next heir was Edmond's son, John, who was aged only eighteen when his grandfather died, so the guardianship of the estate was assumed by his uncle, Thomas (fitz John) of Rostellan who had to withstand a determined effort then being made to recover the ecclesiastical property appropriated by his father, old Sir John. We know that in 1621 young John (son of Edmond) was living at Cloyne because in that year a beautifully carved harp was made for *Seaan m. Emaind gearalt a gCluain* according to the inscription thereon. John's wife was Ellen Barry, daughter of Viscount Buttevant, and the arms of both families appear on the harp. Eventually, in 1639, through the efforts of Lord Deputy Strafford, the (established) church recovered the castle of Cloyne with its 600 acres plus 12 acres at Ballycotton and the fishery there. John (fitz Edmond) moved to Ballymaloe which he was to hold on a 60 year lease from Bishop George Synge. John died the following year and his son, Edmond, after the 1641 rebellion had sent Bishop Synge fleeing to Dublin, seized on the Cloyne lands once more. His tenure was a short one; the Cromwellian plantation saw his lands acquired by Lord Inchiquin. Though especially commended (after the restoration) in the declaration of Charles II in 1660 and armed with a decree entitling him to all of his great-grandfather's lands, he was blocked by Bishop Edward Synge who got the lands vested in the bishop of Cloyne and his successors under the Act of Settlement in 1666. Edmond got decrees for about 3,000 acres in Co. Galway under the Transplantation acts.

Other Branches in Imokilly
     The ancestral seat of Inchynacrenagh (Castlerichard) was occupied by a branch nicknamed *geanncach* or snub-nosed. Thomas Gankagh Fitzgerald of Inchynacrenagh was frequently mentioned in Elizabethan Fiants. 'He was son of James — probably James the Dean. After the Cromwellian wars John Fitzgerald 'als Glanckogh' forfeited Inchinocrinagh and Carrigarostig, lands which were then granted to Col. Richard Fitzgerald who had forfeited Castlemartyr. Richard's youngest brother, Maurice, was put in possession and his descendants remained at Castlerichard until it was sold by Richard Fitzgerald in the mid-19th century. This family had the hereditary custody of the Imokilly amulet, the *cloch ómrach* which was reputed to cure both murrain and hydrophobia.
     Edmond Óg Fitzgerald of Culogorie who was pardoned in 1577 was a brother of Sir John fitz Edmond of Cloyne. He made his will in 1618, requesting that he be buried in Cloyne Cathedral. His son, James, was succeeded by Edmond (commonly known as Éamonn Chúil Ó gCorra) who was living there in 1648. In 1704 James Fitzgerald and his son, William, then living at Glenane, sold the Coolegorragh estate to Captain James Uniacke who renamed it Mount Uniacke. James Fitzgerald's son, William, was also of Glenane, and held the castle and lands of Dungourney on a mortgage from the Barrys. The murder of Robert Barry in 1696 led to charges against William and his sons but these were dropped when the Fitzgeralds gave the Dungourney title-deeds to Sir Alan Broderick of Ballyannon who in return had William Fitzgerald knighted! A younger son of Sir William, also named William, married Margaret Barry of Ballydona on the Dungourney estate. He died in 1757 and his headstone may still be seen in Dungourney graveyard together with those of a son, James of Ballymartin (1786) and a grandson, William of Ballydona (1823).
     To his third son (Thomas) John fitz Edmond of Cloyne in 1594

conveyed the castle and lands of Rostellan on the eastern shore of Cork harbour, an estate which he had purchased from Gerald fitz James Mac Sleyney in 1565. Here in the summer of 1617 Thomas entertained Sir Walter Raleigh who was destined to be executed the following year. They rode together to Cloyne for a day's hawking. In his will (1628) Thomas left Rostellan to his son, James, who in his will (1635) desired to be buried in Cloyne and appointed his cousin, Sir John Fitzgerald of Ballymaloe, his sole heir and executor. Richard and Garrett fitz Edmond of Rostellan (probably brothers of Sir John) were outlawed in 1643 and Sir John's widow (Lady Ellen) was there in 1645 when the castle was captured by Lord Inchiquin who afterwards acquired Rostellan for himself.

Richard Fitzgerald, brother to old Sir John fitz Edmond of Cloyne, had a son, John fitz Richard, who in 1612 took a lease of the lands of Lisquinlan from Sir Richard Boyle. (These lands, east of Ladysbridge, had formerly been Geraldine property; they were forfeited by Richard mac Maurice after the Desmond rebellions.) John was succeeded by William who died in 1656. William and his son, Garrett, claimed to have been 'innocent Protestants' during the 1641 rebellion. Garrett was not only restored to Lisquinlan but was also granted the castle and lands of Corkbeg. This estate, near the mouth of Cork harbour, had been purchased by Sir John fitz Edmond from William Condon in 1591 and mortgaged by his grandson to Sir Robert Tynte of Ballycrenane. Garrett's heir was Robert Fitzgerald who was M.P. for Youghal and also for Castlemartyr around 1700. On his death in 1718 Lisquinlan and Corkbeg were bequeathed to his grand-nephew, Robert Uniacke, on condition that he assume the name of Fitzgerald. The Uniacke Penrose Fitzgerald family continued to reside until the present century at Corkbeg House, now superseded by the storage tanks of an oil refinery.

A pedigree in the *Leabhar Muimhneach* shows the Fitzgeralds of Baile Uí Chríonáin to have been related to but distinct from the Fitzgeralds of Castlemartyr and Cloyne, being descended from Nicholas, grandson of the first seneschal of Imokilly. In 1588 John fitz Redmond of Ballycrenane and Ballykinealy was attainted for his part in the Earl of Desmond's rebellion, but seems to have retained his lands. His son, Redmond, was living at Ballycrenane in 1622 and, according to Richard Boyle, Earl of Cork, 'was turned pirate for the third time, God damn him!' His brother, Gerald, who was taken captive by the Moors, wrote to the Earl on 1st September, 1622, imploring a ransom of £200. Lady Honora Fitzgerald gave Redmond a minion or brass gun for his ship which he was fitting out with the aid of Sir Robert Tynte of Youghal. (This was probably the Lady Onoria – daughter of James Fitzmaurice and married successively to John fitz Edmond, seneschal of Imokilly and to Edmond, son of Sir John of Cloyne – who presented to the Dominicans of Youghal, the silver gilt shrine for the image of

'Our Lady of Graces' now kept at St. Mary's Church, Pope's Quay, Cork.) Later the Tyntes took over Ballycrenane (on a mortgage) while the Fitzgeralds moved to Ballykinealy (near Knockadoon). Although this was forfeited by John, son of Edmond, after 1641, their friendship with the Earl of Cork, who acquired it, enabled them to continue in residence there, even after Redmond Fitzgerald of Ballykinealy was outlawed in 1691 for supporting King James – along with the Fitzgeralds of Glennageare, Ballycullane, and Ballydaheen. John fitz Redmond's great-great-grandson was the celebrated Irish poet, Piaras Mac Gearailt (1702-1795), who was educated at Cadiz where his uncle was an extensive wine-merchant and an important link in the smuggling trade between Spain and Ballykinealy. Piaras' home was a regular meeting place for local poets. His own best-known poem is the rousing *Rosc Catha na Mumhan*. His great-grandson, Michael Fitzgerald, was living at Ballykinealy up to the beginning of this century.

In nearby Ballymacoda lived a Fitzgerald family with the title of Mac Robiston or Mac Robinston. Garrett fitz John alias Mac Robinson of Ballymacoda was attainted in 1588 but was pardoned in 1601. He died thirty years later leaving Edward as son and heir. After 1641 Edmund Fitzgerald alias Roberson forfeited 309 acres of Ballymacoda.

It is clear that there was quite a network of Geraldine proprietors in Imokilly in the 17th century. Twenty three of them were listed among the forfeiting proprietors of 1641 (as against five in the remainder of Co. Cork). These included the Fitzgeralds of Ballymaloe, Ballymacoda, Rostellan, Ballymartin, Ballyre, Ardra and Ballinwillin. What the position was in 1659 is not known as the census returns for Imokilly are not available. In the rest of the county there were but two 'tituladoes' – Thomas Fitzgerald, gent., of Ballyheedy and Jordanstown (par. Ballinaboy) and William Fitzgerald of Castledod (Ballyhay).

Orrery and Kilmore

This is the only barony where Fitzgerald families (nine) were recorded. One family stronghold in the area was Castle Lishen or Castleishen in the parish of Kilbolane. In 1600 the 'Súgán' Earl of Desmond was imprisoned in this castle through the treachery of Dermot O Connor. Pierce Lacy with 4,000 men besieged Castle Lishen and set the prisoner free. As we have seen, both Castle Lishen and Kilmaclenine were listed among the possessions of Sir John fitz Edmond of Cloyne in 1613. Maurice Fitzgerald was the owner in 1641 and one of his tenants deposed that he had seen Maurice in command of an Irish company at the battle of Liscarroll. Accordingly his lands were confiscated and granted to Henry Tynte and others. After the restoration, however, Sir Edmond Fitzgerald, knight, of Clonglish, Co. Limerick, established himself at Castle Lishen. James Fitzgerald of Castle Lishen was outlawed in 1690 for supporting King James but both he and his son Maurice were restored by the Court of Claims in 1694 and their descendants continued in possession up to the present century. David Fitzgerald, gent., of Castle-ishen, became a Protestant in 1751.

Castle Dod, at Ballyhay, was part of the Earl of Desmond's lands confiscated in 1583. After changing hands several times in 1641 it was occupied by Richard Fitzgerald who married a sister of Sir Philip Percival and took the English side during the rebellion. His son, William, was a commissioner for poll-money ordinance in 1660 and his grandson, Robert, M.P. for Charleville, 1703-1713. Later in the 18th century Castle Dod became the residence of the Harrison family who renamed it Castle Harrison.

Kinnatalloon

According to Dr. Smith, this small barony in east Cork was, in the 15th century, assigned by way of mortgage to Thomas, 7th Earl of Desmond, by Lord Barry, on the occasion of Thomas' marriage to Elizabeth Barry. Smith adds that Mogeely castle was the Earl's principal seat in the barony. Conna castle, together with the former Cogan castle near Mourne Abbey (now Barrett's castle), was in the mid-16th century given by James, 15th Earl of Desmond, to his eldest son, Thomas (Rua), whom he had disinherited in favour of another son, Gerald. Thomas later had to mortgage Castlemore (Mourne Abbey) but continued to reside at Conna until his death in 1596. His son, Sir James fitz Thomas, known as the 'Súgán' Earl, was one of the principal rebels in Munster during the period 1598-1600. Conna castle was dismantled by Lord Essex in 1599 and Fitz Thomas, later captured, as related under Ó DUBHAGÁIN. In 1602 Queen Elizabeth granted a lease of Conna to Sir John Fitzgerald of Cloyne, but in 1610 it was granted to Richard Boyle by King James. Another confiscated Geraldine stronghold was Aghern castle, west of Conna.

Mallow

The manor of Moyale, a strategic crossing-point on the Blackwater, was, according to an inquisition of 1282, acquired by Thomas fitz Maurice (*Tomás an Ápa*) from Henry de Rupe in exchange for lands in Connacht. James, the 'usurper' Earl of Desmond, in the 15th century assigned to Maurice, son of Earl Thomas, the manor of Moyallow as well as those of Kilcolman and Broghill. At the time of the Desmond rebellion, it was held by a brother of the Earl, Sir John Fitzgerald, who was slain in a skirmish near Castlelyons in 1581. The castle and lands were then confiscated and passed to Sir Thomas Norreys who replaced the old castle with a new building, the extensive ruin of which may still be seen. Norreys' only daughter married Captain Jephson, ancestor of the Jephson family of Mallow castle. In 1612 James I granted to Sir John Jephson the lands of Killagrohan (in Mallow parish) otherwise known as Begg's land after its former owner, Morrice Gerald, otherwise Morrice Begg.

The associated castles of Kilcolman and Broghill (Ballyhay) likewise passed out of Geraldine hands. Kilcolman with over 3,000 English acres was granted to Edmund Spenser in 1590. Raymond Fitzgerald of Broghill was executed for treason and his property later gave title to one of Richard Boyle's sons. The Geraldine connection seems to have been finally severed in 1690 with the outlawry of Maurice and Redmond Fitzgerald, esq., of Moyalloe.

But Mallow was later to be the birthplace of the most renowned eulogist of the Geraldines, namely, the poet-patriot Thomas Davis who in his romantic vein wrote:

Those Geraldines, those Geraldines; rain wears away the rock,
And time may wear away the tribe that stood the battle's shock;
But ever, sure, while one is left of all that honoured race,
In front of Ireland's chivalry is that Fitzgerald's place.

MALLOW CASTLE *(O'Callaghan Newenham, 1826)*

Ó FLAINN

Ó FLOINN   (O) FLYNN

Flann, which originally meant 'ruddy' or 'blood-red', was a popular personal name in Ireland, and so families of Uí Fhlainn (Uí Fhloinn) arose independently in several parts of the country. In Co. Cork there were at least two such families.

Muskerry was the home of one of these. This barony, which formerly did not extend south of the Lee, took its name from a pre-Eóganacht tribe known as Múscraige Mittaine. A pedigree of the chieftains of this tribe is to be found in the *Book of Leinster*. When it was being compiled, the next in line for the kingship was Flann, son of Blathmac. It must have been from his descendants that the tribal area took its alias of Múscraige Uí Fhlainn ('Musgrylin').

Ó Huidhrín's poem names Ó Floinn as king of Múscraighe Mittaine with Ó Maoil Fhábhaill as one of its lesser lords. The *Annals of Inisfallen* record the slaying 'through enmity' of Ua Maíl Fhábaill of Múscraige by Mac na Sethar (surname obliterated) in 1208. This was Mac na Sethar Ua Flainn who four years later was slain by Cormac Liathánach Mac Carthy whose first exploit it was on becoming king of Desmond. The account of this slaying fits in with the tradition (as given in O Brien's *Irish Dictionary*, 1768) that Ó Floinn was king of Muskerry until treacherously put to death by Mac Carthy, although O Brien's dating, namely, the beginning of the 14th century, is a century too late. Furthermore, O Brien credits Ó Floinn with having built the castle of Macroom – in 1199 – and claims that it was known as Caisleán Uí Fhloinn. We have no proof that this was so, as there are no historical references to the O Flynns of Muskerry after 1212, but quite a few relating to the other family of that name in Co. Cork.

Ó Flainn Arda
According to the Genealogy of Corca Laoighdhe, three of the principal families of that race – Ua hEdersceoil, Ua Cobhthaigh and Ua Floinn Arda – were descended from three sons of Maicniadh. In another part of the genealogy, Flann Arda is given as seventh in descent from Maicniadh. Flann's descendants are described in Ó Huidhrín's poem as follows:

> Uí Fhloinn Arda as úr fiodhach,
> buidhean as geal geiniolach,
> radhamna gach fear dá bhféin,
> Uí Bhadhamhna as eadh iaid-séin.

(The O Flynns of Arda of the wooded land; a company of illustrious genealogy; there is great material in every man of their sept; these are the Uí Bhadhamhna.)

It is generally believed — on the authority of O Brien's *Irish Dictionary*, followed by John O Donovan — that the Ardagh in question is the site of an old castle to the west of Lough Hyne. There seems to be no evidence for this identification; on the contrary, it is highly unlikely that the O Flynns could ever have been in possession of a castle in the heart of O Driscoll's country. Both the Genealogy and O Huidhrín's poem associate the O Flynns with the Uí Bhadhamhna whose territory, judging from the present barony of Ibane (and Barryroe), lay to the east of Rosscarbery, on the peninsulas at either side of Clonakilty Bay. Of the several Ardaghs in west Cork the one most likely to have given its name to the O Flynns is Ardagh in the parish of Ross.

The first reference to the family in the annals actually mentions Ross. In 1057, according to the *Annals of Inisfallen*, Ua Mútáin, erenagh of Cork and lector, was slain at Ros Ailithir by Ua Flainn Arda, presumably as the result of an ecclesiastical dispute. In 1103, the same annals tell us, 'a house was burned over Ua Flainn Arda, and many fell therein, including his wife and the master of that house'.

In 1345 Thomas Offlyn was one of the named leaders of the army assembled by the Mac Carthys and others to aid the Earl of Desmond's insurrection through an attack on such places as Robert de Barry's lands at Clontead.

For the next two centuries there are but a few scattered ecclesiastical references to the family. Cornelius Offlayn was abbot of Gill Abbey, Cork, around 1482. His successor as vicar of Clonmeen (Duhallow) was Dermit Ysflayn, priest, while Donatus O Flynn was vicar of Kilshannig in 1499. William Oflioyn was parish priest of St. Catherine's (near Shandon) in 1523.

After the reformation, Ruricus O Flynn was vicar of Inishkenny in 1581 and of Kilbonane ten years later. Edmund Flinn was vicar of Ballyclogh also in 1591.

As usual, the Elizabethan Fiants provide the most detailed information on this family. Oddly enough, none of the O Flynns pardoned in them appear to have lived in west Cork, but were scattered throughout the northern and eastern areas of the county. Several were followers of the O Callaghans of Clonmeen — Teige mac Donogh O Flywyn (1573), Conogher O Floyne (1576), John rwo O Flyne (1577), Dermod mac Thomas O Floine (1601), Conoghor O Flyn (1601), and Dermod mac Thomas mac Melaghlin O Flyn (1602). In the Roche country were Donogh (1573) and David O Flyne (1577) of Cregg, and Donald mac Thomas O Flyn of Garrymacwhny, kern. Further north were Teige mac Conoghor O Fleine of Mitchelstown and Dermod O Floine of Kilbolane, smith, in 1601. There was another smith to be found among a group of O Flynns living, apparently, on the coast of Imokilly in 1585:

Darby O Flin mac Morietagh, smith
Edmond O Flin mac Thomas, husbandman
Daniel O Flin fitz Thomas, fisherman
Darby O Flin fitz Thomas, fisherman.

Some of those listed in the Fiants may have been descendants of Muskerry O Flynns forced eastwards centuries earlier by the Mac Carthys. But they may also have moved westwards from Co. Waterford, where in 1659 there was a very large concentration of the name, far stronger than in Co. Cork where O Flynns were spread over the eastern half — Youghal 4, Barrymore 14, Orrery and Kilmore 12, Cork city and Liberties 21. Some of the last-mentioned group may have had their burial-ground at Carrigaline where there are several 18th century Fling or Flynn headstones, as well as one dated 1695 and bearing an unusual O Flynn crest. In 1686 Will O Fling of Old Court, Rochestown, was accused by the churchwardens of Carrigaline of not paying the church rates.

In the *Book of Fermoy* there is a poem addressed to two Mac Carthy ladies (connections of the Roches of Fermoy), the poet being Muircheartach Ó Floinn. But the best-known of the name in Irish literary circles was Donnchadh Ó Floinn (1760-1830) who was born in Carraig na bhFear and spent the greater part of his life in Mallow Lane (Shandon St.) in Cork. Donnchadh was a noted scholar and poet and had for a time portion of the *Book of Lismore* in his care. He also searched diligently for records of his family using the works of O Brien, Vallancey and others. Before his death, he composed the 16-line Irish epitaph which may still be seen on his headstone in Dún Bolg graveyard.

Ó HAODHA

O HEA   HAYES

Since Áed (Aodh) was the most popular of all personal names used in early Christian Ireland, it is not surprising that families named Ó hAodha and Mac Aodha, under a variety of anglicized forms, are to be found all over Ireland.

In Co. Cork alone there is evidence of more than one such family. The people of Múscraige Trí Maige in the Orrery and Kilmore area of north Cork were known for a time as Múscraige Áeda while some of the kings of Múscraige in the first half of the 11th century were surnamed Ua hAeda — Muiredach Ua hAeda (d. 1010) and Muirchertach Ua hAeda (d. 1029). After Muirchertach's death, his son Donnchadh acted treacherously towards the two sons of his brother, Cenn Faelad, thus instigating, no doubt, the family feud which led to the slaying, twelve years later, of Donnchadh's son, Muiredach Ua hAeda. In the genealogy of Múscraige Trí Maige, Áed, the eponymous ancestor of the Uí Áeda, had a son Donnacán, and later kings bore the surname Ó Donnacáin while the tribal area became Múscraige Ua nDonnacáin (Muskerry-Donegan). The Uí Áeda are not further heard of in this district.

Duan Catháin has a reference to an Ó hAedha family connected with the Uí Chochláin who in turn were of Clann Sealbhaigh, a family group with strong episcopal connections. It may be that Gregory Ó hAedha, bishop of Cork, 1172-1182, and Murchadh Ó hAedha who filled the same position, 1192-1206, were of this family.

However, for the source and origin of most west Cork O Heas, we need go no further than the Genealogy of Corca Laoighdhe. Here we are informed that Ua hAedha of Cluain Dá Mhael was one of the hereditary leaders of Tuath Ó nDúngalaich, a district which lay east and west of where the town of Clonakilty now stands, an area later known as Ibane and Barryroe — the very district which was the stronghold of the O Heas in later centuries. In fact, their ancient seat of Cluain Dá Mhael may be identical with Aghamilla, the site of the principal O Hea castle up to the 17th century.

It may well have been these Uí Áeda who, according to the *Annals of Inisfallen*, had a slaughter inflicted on them by one of the Mac Carthys in 1194. We do know that shortly afterwards Norman families such as Arundels and Hodnetts began to penetrate into O Hea territory and that the Barrys (Roe) eventually became chief lords, forcing the O Heas to pay them a head-rent. John de Barry, according to the Justiciary Rolls for 1295, was pledge for Royry O Hethe to whom (in

156

company with O Donovans and O Cobhthaighs) suit of peace was granted for 40s. – and also for Fyngola Ynynyethe (*Finnghuala inion Uí Aedha*) wife of Nicholas Magnel, who got suit of peace for 20s. Thomas O Hethe was also pardoned. Apparently Rory did not pay up, since some of his property was later confiscated and Robert de Arundel, coroner of Obathem (Uí Badhamhna or Ibane), was directed to deliver same to John de Barry. As for Thomas, he was in trouble again three years later when he was a member of a group of O Donovans and others who owed the sheriff over £36 for having the king's peace.

Still, the O Heas remained firmly entrenched in what became known as Pobal Uí Aodha ('Pubble-O Hea'). They supplied many clerics to the diocese of Ross as well as to the local religious foundations. Dermit Oheda, scholar, was assigned the rectory of Templeomalus in 1433 and later became a canon of Ross while Nicholas Oheda was elevated to the abbacy of St. Mary de Fonte Vivo (Abbeymahon) in the same year. In 1469 a complaint was made that Donatus Ohega had assumed the priorship of the Benedictine abbey of Rosscarbery by force some twenty years earlier. John Ohega was vicar of Ardfield and chancellor of Ross in 1485. Maurice O Hea was bishop of Ross diocese from 1559 to 1561. (Another of the name, Dr. Michael O Hea, was bishop of Ross from 1858 to 1876.) After the reformation, a John O Heyes was chancellor of Ross and vicar of Ardfield between 1591 and 1615.

Friar Moriartus O Hea of Timoleague, a holy and simple priest, was credited with having miraculously cured a sick man whose life was despaired of, in 1595. Friar James O Hay of Youghal was 'examined' by Pelham in 1580, having come from Spain as James Fitzmaurice's standard-bearer and having been taken in the skirmish near Kilmallock. Another account says that he was captured in 1587 and thrown, seriously wounded, into prison but survived the ordeal to live another thirty years.

The Elizabethan Fiants contain a number of O Hea pardons. In 1573, Shane mac Conoghor Iea (*Uí Aodha*) and Shane mac Rikyrde Iea, of Courte, were pardoned. This was in the east Cork lands of the Barrymores which had by then been taken over by the chief of the Barry Roes (see BARRY). It was probably the second Shane's family who were pardoned in 1601, namely, Morris mac Shane mac Rickard O Hea of Carrygane-ny-grane (Carrigane, par. Carrigtwohill) and his brother, Rickard. Shane O Hea of Ballyvodock (par. Mogeesha) was also pardoned. (A tombstone in Carrigtwohill graveyard was erected by John O Hea, Esq., of Carrigane, in memory of his wife who died in 1800.)

In west Cork a pardon was granted to Teig O Hea of Ballyduvane (near Aghamilla), yeoman, in 1573, while William mac Dermod I Ea of Rathe (Rathbarry), yeoman, was pardoned three years later, but in 1582 James O Hea, styled *netyraghe*, languished unpardoned in Dublin Castle. During the months leading up to the battle of Kinsale, pardons were issued to Donogh O Hea of Dromrevin, Mahowne mac Conoghor y Hee of Rathbarry, Donell mac Dermodie O Hea of Kilruane (par. Ross), Teige mac Donnell O Hea of Ballyvackey (par. Kilkerranmore), William roe mac Teig O Hea of Carrigroe (par. Rathbarry) and Thomas fitz William O Hea. The following November (1602), John fitz William O Hea of Timoleague was pardoned — perhaps the Shane O Hey, 'a man from Mounster', suspected of treason overseas in 1607. A report from the Protestant bishop on Timoleague friary in the same year stated that 'in this abbey is chief Rory O'Tamy Murriertaghe (O Hea), Shane O Hea, his brother, with others. They be sturdy fellows, well-fed and warm'.

(It is noticeable that the O Heas used Norman-type personal names — John, William, Thomas etc. — almost as frequently as the traditional Tadhg, Domhnall and Diarmaid. This may have been due to their long association with the Barry Roes.)

The inquisitions of the early 17th century yield further information regarding the O Heas. According to one, Thomas O Hea of Aghamilla castle (described in a funeral entry of 1636 as son of Cormack son of Thomas son of Teige Duff O Hea) died in 1590. His son and heir, Teige O Hea, was then forty years old and married. The castle and lands of Aghamilla were held of the Barrys of Rathbarry by knight's fee and by service but there were also certain rents and services due to Mac Carthy Reagh, lord of Carbery. The lands included Aghamilla, Ballydwane, Carhoo, Carrigroe, Knockaphonery, Creagh Beg, Creagh More, Maulycorcoran, Curragh, Kilruane, Derryduff, Gobborussine and Kilmacadarrie. This presumably was Pobal Uí Aodha, centred around the castle of Aghamilla.

Tadhg, son of Thomas, died in 1637 aged about 87 years. His son and heir, Donogh, having died three years earlier, his grandson, another Tadhg, then became O Hea of Aghamilla. This Tadhg was married to Ellen, daughter of Florence Mac Carthy of Gortnaclohy (Skibbereen). Donogh and the elder Tadhg were buried in Timoleague friary.

Several inquisitions taken in 1632 dealt with other branches:

Mahoune mac Conogher O Hea of Carrigroe, deceased. His heir was his grandson, John mac Teige. The lands were held of the manor of Rathbarry but a small annual rent was also due to Teige O Hea of Aghamilla.

Teig mac William O Hea of Carrigroe, deceased. Donogh his son and heir.

Connogher mac Dermid O Hea of Creagh Beg, deceased. Donogh his son and heir. William mac Shane O Hea of Cruary and Teige O Hea of Aghamilla had a claim on the lands.

Donnell O Hea of Creagh Beg, deceased. Dermod his son and heir.

Teige mac Mahown O Hea of Knockaphonery, deceased. John his son and heir.

In 1633 it was found that William fitz John O Hea had died seised of lands in Cruary, Ballymacwilliam, etc., also that John mac Mahowne O Hea had died seised of Killinemcidarrie, Maulycorcoran, etc. Donell mac Shane O Hea was John's heir.

All these landed family groups were radically affected by the rebellion of 1641. Sir William Hull of Leamcon castle made a deposition regarding the losses suffered by him since December 1641. He claimed that the Barrys, Teig O Heay of Kilgarriff (Aghamilla is in Kilgarriff parish) and Thomas mac Mahowne (O Hea), gents., took away over £250 worth of his farm animals and property from the island of Inchydoney. He suffered similar losses in Clonakilty. Among the 'principal culprits and actors' were 'Teig O Heay of Heay's castell in the parish of Kilgarriff, gent., Daniell O Heay and his brother of Ballinaten' (Ballinatona).

Another account, this time by Arthur Freke who had acquired possession of the principal Barry Roe castle of Rathbarry, describes the siege of that castle by the Irish in 1642 at a time when numerous English refugees had flocked inside its walls. His nearest neighbour was Thomas mac Mahony (probably a son of Mahowne mac Conogher Y Hee of Rathbarry who was pardoned in 1601). Thomas wrote to him offering his services if he (Thomas) and his son Mahowne mac Thomas were admitted to the castle. Freke then held a conference with the O Heas and the Barrys who informed him that unless some Irish gentlemen were in charge of it, the castle would be besieged by the rebels, but he refused to make any agreement with them. On the morning of the 14th February, 1642, the O Heas (now including the chief, Teige O Hea) and the Barrys with 800 men appeared before Rathbarry and in the evening captured Dundeady castle. Later they took Dunowen. Freke accused the O Heas of the murder of several Englishmen. Rathbarry castle held out until October when a relieving army conveyed the besieged occupants to Bandon, having first burned the castle behind them.

In July 1643 Colonel Myn led an English army through Ibane and took the castles of Aghamilla, Rathbarry and Timoleague as well as the town of Rosscarbery. A local tradition which tells of how Aghamilla castle was battered by the cannon of 'Cromwell's forces', relates that the people were assembled to dance on a Sunday evening, when the battering commenced from a hill on the other side of the castle and that the walls fell almost immediately, being very ancient. Only the foundations of the castle now remain, standing on a rock above the ancient ford of Aghamilla, about a mile to the north-west of Clonakilty.

The following O Heas — all described as gentlemen — were outlawed in 1643: Thomas of Aghamilla, Donogh and John oge of Carrigroe, Donogh of Shanacoole, Mahowne of Kilkerran, Teige of Corrabally, Thomas and William oge of Pallas. Most of these — along with Teige of Aghamilla, John oge of Timoleague, Daniel of Killine and others were listed as 'forfeiting proprietors'. As a result of the

Cromwellian confiscations, Teige O Hea alias O Hea) forfeited Agha-milla, Carhoo, Creagh More, Ballydwane, Curragh and Derryduff; William O Hea lost Carrigroe, Daniel O Hea lost Killeen and Daniel mac Cnoghor O Hea part of Creagh Beg. The lands were acquired by Admiral Sir William Penn. His son, William, founder of Pennsylvania, on a visit to his father's lands, wrote in his journal on 27th May, 1670: 'I gave George O Hea a note for £4 per annum, and young T. O Hea forty shillings'. Edmund O Hea's part of Creagh Beg went to the Duke of York.

Sir William Penn also annexed Kilkerranmore forfeited by Thomas O Hea — perhaps a son of Owen mac Cnohor O Hea of the same place whose will was proved in 1640. Thomas O Hea's part of Corbally (Ardfield par.) passed to the Earl of Barrymore. Penn and the Earl jointly acquired the lands of John óg O Hea in Ardfield parish — Bally-bane (? Ballyva), Creboy and Farran m'Shonick (Farran), while Daniel O Hea's lands of Pallas fell to the provost and burgesses of Bandon. Penn also got John óg O Hea's lands at Ballymacredmond (par. Lislee).

John óg continued to reside in Timoleague town, where, according to the census of 1659, John O Hea, his son John and John O Hea Mac Murtagh were 'tituladoes'. (The will of John oge Hea of Timoleague was proved in 1690 and that of William O Hea of Timoleague in 1729.) 'Tituladoes' were people of note, usually landowners or landholders, and despite all the confiscations there were several others of the name in Ibane and Barryroe in 1659 — Dom. mac Thomas O Hea in Ardfield parish (Pallas, Brittas and Garrymore) and Matthew, Thomas and James Hea in Kilkeran (beg) in Rathbarry parish. Even among the people of lesser note O Hea was the most numerous of the surnames in the barony (45 families). There were also ten O Hea families in Kilbrittain, 24 in East Carbery, 13 in West Carbery, 11 in Barrymore and 9 in Orrery and Kilmore. (These last may have constituted a remnant of the former chief family of Múscraige Áeda.)

The accession of James II brought several of the name into public life. Four O Heas were among the burgesses named in the new charter given in 1687 to Clonakilty by the Earl of Tyrconnell, acting for King James. In Browne's infantry in the Jacobite army William Heas was a captain and James and William Heas were lieutenants. In 1690 those outlawed for adherence to King James included Daniel O Hea, Leamon (? Leamcon), gent., William Heagh, Baviden (?) Esq., and James Hea, merchant, of Cork city.

Following on the Jacobite debacle, although O Heas remained numerous in Pobal Uí Aodha in the 18th century, only the O Heas of Kilkeran (par. Rathbarry), who had conformed to the Protestant religion, maintained their position among the landed gentry. They also used the family tomb in Timoleague friary as well as the title 'The O Hea'. Kilkeran was formerly known as Kilkerranbeg to distinguish it from Kilkerranmore (parish) nearby. The Mahoune O Hea of Kilkeran who was outlawed in 1643 and the Mathew Hea who was a 'titulado' there in 1659 may have been one and the same since Mathew was used as an anglicized form of Mathghamhain. There was another Mathew O Hea there in 1720. Mathew (mac Thomas) O Hea of Kilkeran had a daughter Ellen who married William fitz James Barry, and their son, James Barry, married Helen O Hea, daughter of Cornelius O Hea of 'West Barryroe'. This must be the 'Mathamhuin Ó hAodha ó Chill Chiaráin' for whom the early 18th century poet, Séumas Mac Gearailt, composed an elegy of 24 stanzas. Another elegy was written on the death of Donnchadh mac Mathghamhna Uí Aodha who had served in the army of King Louis, but he does not seem to have belonged to the Kilkeran family, as he was buried in Caheragh (*a tteampcioll Catharach*).

Up to 1720 the head of the family was James O Hea. James was related to the ill-fated Sir James Cotter with whom he corresponded in an endeavour to be of assistance during the latter's imprisonment. Although twice married (firstly to Margaret Gold who died in 1687 and secondly to Mary Donovan) he had but one child, a daughter named Mary who married Martin Meade of Tisaxon. She died in 1757 and in the following year Kilkeran was advertised for sale by Lucy O Hea, widow and administratrix of Mathew O Hea. However, the property seems to have remained in the family. Captain John O Hea, who fought with the North Cork Militia in 1798, settled down there and was accidentally drowned while fishing on the little lake near Kilkeran House. His son, James O Hea, a barrister, became a Young Irelander and friend of Thomas Davis while his grandson, John Fergus O Hea was a noted cartoonist and illustrator, best remembered for his cartoon of Davis, Dillon and Duffy planning the birth of *The Nation* in the Phoenix Park. Unusually, the drawing is signed in Irish − S. Ó hAodha.

Little is known of other branches of the O Hea family in the 18th century. Wills were registered for Denis O Hea of Lisduff (1763), James of Camus (1768) and James of Clonakilty (1796). A Fr. Francis O Hea was Superior of the Irish College at Toulouse between 1751 and 1771. He was a native of Little Island in the parish of Ardfield.

There is no record of the fate of Teige O Hea of Aghamilla castle. He may have been transplanted to Clare where there was a Teige O Hea, a 'titulado', in the barony of Burren in 1659. He may have gone to Spain where a Don Tadeo O Hea (? a descendant) was an army cadet in 1725. Or he may have simply sunk into obscurity. According to a family tradition, Tadhg's descendants were tenant-farmers on the Hungerford estate at Cahermore near Rosscarbery. One of this family, also named Teige, went to Salamanca in Spain to study for the priest-hood and being at home on leave in 1798, took part in the battle of the Big Cross, where he was wounded. Afterwards, he settled down in Ireland and taught school in Clonakilty until his death in 1830. His descendants gained prominence in the medical and legal professions and one of them, Patrick O Hea, was a Parnellite M.P. at Westminster.

Ó HAONGHUSA

(O) HENNESSY

Families of Uí Aenghusa (descendants of Óengus) evolved independently in various parts of Ireland — for example, among the Uí Failghe and the Dál Cais — and there were two such families in Co. Cork with, apparently, separate origins.

Taking the west Cork one first, we find in the Genealogy of Corca Laoighdhe that Ó hAenghusa was the hereditary chieftain of Tuath Ó n-Aenghusa which extended from Fearsaid Ruis (the sand-bar of Ross) in the east to Góilín na Gaethneamhtha (Dirk Bay — Red Strand) in the west, and from Dún Déidi (Dundeady) in the south to Béal Átha na Leice (? Curraghlicky, par. Drinagh) in the north. Fourteen lesser families are named as being under the overlordship of Ó hAenghusa; the territory was called 'Ihanegus' in a document of *c*. 1230. Yet no further records of this west Cork family survive. Some members may have moved into Muskerry where there is a townland called Bally-hennessy in the parish of Donaghmore. It was written as Ballyenisy in 1588, i.e. *Baile Uí Aonghusa*.

There are, however, many references to Uí Aenghusa of Críchad an Chaoilli (in the Fermoy region) who occupied Baile idir dá Abhainn in Tuath Ó Conaill, to the west of the Fermoy-Mitchelstown road. This *baile* is now confined to Ballyderown townland (par. Kilcrumper) which has a ruined castle overlooking a ford at the junction of the Araglen and Blackwater rivers, but in earlier times it included Uam Cróine (probably Cronohill, par. Leitrim) and adjoining areas. The Uí Aenghusa were also connected with St. Molaga's church of Aghacross, while in the life of Colmán mac Luachain one of the name was said to be erenagh of Cill Úird (Kilworth).

The inroads of the Normans which caused so much scattering and relocation elsewhere seem to have left the O Hennessys as occupiers of their original patrimony. In Elizabethan times their lands in the Glanworth-Kilworth area acted as a buffer zone between the powerful Roches and their bitter enemies, the Condons. In 1260 Cathel Ohanegus and others were charged with having disseised Adam de Cauntincton (Condon) of 10 acres in Mathuehenan. In 1295 Tathbeg and Nyvin Ohengus, with other men of Baldewin son of Philip, were charged with receiving the O Keeffes and other malefactors of Desmond. (Baldwin was from Co. Waterford. A Nicholas Hennessy was appointed bishop of Waterford and Lismore in 1480. He had previously been abbot of St. Mary's, Fermoy, and because he could speak no English he was disliked by prominent citizens of Waterford. Hennessy was listed among the principal Irish families in the barony of Decies in 1659.) In 1313, Nicholas (son of the above Baldwin) was charged with aiding and abetting the larcenies of Maurice O Henwys, Donald O Henwys, Padin O Henwys and two of the O Dooleys. The charges, which related to Co. Cork, were not proved and Nicholas was acquitted.

A Donaldus O Henos in the Doneraile area is mentioned in the Pipe Roll of Cloyne, *c*. 1366, while William Ohenassy held the vicarage of Kilcrumper and Macroney a century later. He was also a canon of Cloyne in 1480 as was Tatheus Ohenesa, prebendary of Glanworth, in 1489. Theobaldus Ohenyssi was vicar of Monanimy in 1494.

In a pardon dated 1551 which was granted to David son of Lord Roche and to Richard Noglay (Nagle), gent., we find among their followers Donagh and Richard mac David O Henassa, Thomas og O Henassa, Bryan mac Sheane Y Henassa, David mac Thomas Henassa and David mac Philipe Y Henassa, all 'horsemen'. Followers of William Synane of Doneraile included Donagh mac Thomas Henassa alias mac Y Photery and Philip mac Thomas Henessa alias mac a mheiyr, horseboys; Bryan mac Thomas Y Henassa, William mauntaghe O Henassa, John a churry O Henessa, Philip mac David og O Henassa and David og O Henasa, alias Fear Ryata, kerns.

The aliases used indicate a completely Gaelic-speaking environment although the personal names are mainly of Norman origin due, no doubt, to the influence of the Roches, Nagles, etc.

During the reign of Elizabeth many similar pardons were granted to members of the O Hennessy sept, very often as followers of the Roches. One in 1561 was issued to John mac Donogho mac Da O Hennes of Downemaghen, 'especially for the death of James Condon'. Dunmahon is a parish and townland south of Glanworth in the Roche-Condon marchlands. It has a ruined keep or tower-house which may have been occupied by the Hennessys at this period though there is no evidence that it was built by them. In 1573 John of Dunmahon and his brother David were again pardoned, while a third pardon was granted in 1575 to 'John fitz David O Henose of Dunmaghen, gentleman' in company with Theobald Roche of Cregg, gentleman. (The lands of Dunmahon were leased to Theobald Roche of Cregg in 1574.) There is a reference (by James Terry, Athlone Herald, in 1712) to a Maria Hennessy, daughter of John Hennessy, Knight, lord of Dunmahon.

Curraghoo (par. Glanworth) which has a similar tower-house, must have been another stronghold of the O Hennessys. In 1573 John fitz David mac Donough O Henous, Thomas ny Kartyne O Henous, Richard fitz David O Henous and Thomas fitz Richard O Henous, all yeomen of Curraghoo, were pardoned. Some of those were again pardoned ten years later. In 1621 Thomas O Heanessy of Curraghoo granted to Morish Nugent of Ballygown the lands and tenements called Garryen vodyge (near Castlekevin) 'now or lately occupied by Morish Ruo O Heanessy alias mc david napadery'. Morish Ruo was still tenant there in 1633.

Several of the pardons mention Donogh dwilleagh (*Donnchadh doicheallach*) O Henois of Farahy, yeoman, his sons – including David of Dannanstown, horseman, – and his grandsons, – including David of Castlekevin, yeoman.

Others of the name to be pardoned were John O Henesy alias Y tleya (*a'tsléibhe*) of Castletown, David O Henesy alias Yrwan and Engertach O Henesy of Oldcastletown, Thomas fitz David and his son of Caherduggan, John mac Donogh Y Enisie, late of Crahmerie (? Connaberry), and John O Henoys of Ballymcwystell, yeoman.

This was not the the Mitchelstown we know today but a townland in the parish of Castletownroche; the name is no longer extant. It was still a family seat at the time of the 1641 rebellion. The only one of the name in Co. Cork to be outlawed in 1643 was William O Henessy of Ballymistealy, gent. William was probably the Sergeant-Major Henesy named in a contemporary account of the battle of Liscarroll (1642) as one of the 'lords of Munster' almost all of whom were on the Irish side. (Lord Roche was one of the principal Confederate leaders in the county.) The sergeant-major must have gained promotion, if indeed it is the same officer who is referred to in Lord Castlehaven's account of his campaign in east Cork in 1643. In it he tells of a castle – probably Mogeely – which had surrendered to him upon quarter. As it was a fine day, Castlehaven went hunting, leaving Colonel Henesy to see the quarter made good. Some of the soldiers decided to plunder the castle, as was their usual custom. To prevent this outrage, Colonel Henesy and several other officers joined the garrison and successfully defended the castle until the return of Lord Castlehaven who summarily punished the mutineers, executing two of them. Colonel Henesy's regiment was later prominent in the siege of Dublin in 1649.

After the war had ended, William Hensey, 'Irish Papist', saw his 97 acres of BallymcMichtall confiscated and given to John Hodder and Richard Hull. In their place he was allotted 40 acres (Irish) in the barony of Inchiquin, Co. Clare. Also listed as 'forfeiting Irish Proprietors' were Donogh Henesy, John Henesy and Thomas Henesy, but there are no records of lands forfeited by them. Some of the name may have managed to retain some property; there is a record of an inquisition held in 1662 into the lands of Capt. Charles Henesey.

One branch of the family settled at Ballymacmoy near Killavullen. Prior to 1641 these lands belonged to Pierce Nagle and following the confiscations they were granted to Capt. John Blennerhasset. But James Hennessy, who was married to Helen Nagle, is subsequently found in possession. He had a son named George. In 1690 George Hensey of Moyalloe (Mallow) esq., and Garrett Hensey of Ballydamon, esq. were outlawed as supporters of King James, but in August 1699 George Hennessey of Ballymacmoy was successful in his claim for restoration under the articles of Limerick. Whether there were two different Georges –

or even three, as the Capt. George Hennessy in Colonel John Barrett's Infantry may have been a third — is not clear. (Several others of the name served in the Irish Brigade in France, including Lieut. Robert O Hennessy who was wounded at Fontenoy.) At any rate, George of Ballymacmoy had two sons, — James, his heir, who married Catherine Barrett, and Charles of Brussels and Ostend who married Margaret O Murphy.

James' eldest son, George, was next in line at Ballymacmoy, while his second son, Richard, served in the Irish Brigade in France and was the founder of the well-known Hennessy family of Cognac where he settled in 1765. He married his cousin, Ellen Barrett, widow of James Hennessy of Brussels; his son James (Jacques) married one of the Martell family and became a member of the Chamber of Deputies. A later descendant, George Richard James Hennessy, was a prominent figure in the British military and political establishment, and was created Baron Windlesham in 1937.

Other branches of the Hennessys remained as substantial landholders in north Cork in the 18th century in such places as Castletownroche and Mourne Abbey. Maurice Hennessy had a thriving salt business in Cork city until his saltworks in Dunscombe's Marsh were burnt down in 1768.

The Hennessys of Ballymacmoy lived in their old residence until 1818 when James Hennessy had the present Ballymacmoy House built in Killavullen about a mile down-river from the old one. This remained the family residence until the early years of the present century. It was purchased by James Hennessy of the Cognac family in 1932.

Ó HEACHTHIGHEIRN

Ó HEICHTHIGHEIRN   Ó HEACHTHIGHEARNA
Ó HEACHIAIRN   AHERN (E)
AHEARN (E)   HEARN (E)

Two families of Uí Eachthigheirn receive mention in the genealogies, and both belonged to the Dál Cais in north Munster. One family was said to be descended from Echtigern who was a son of Cennétig and a brother of Brian Boru. The other derived from Echtigern son of Ailill whose sub-sept was known as Uí Rónghaile. It was probably this latter family that Ó Huidhrín named as lords of Uí Chearnaigh, a district in Co. Clare between Sixmilebridge and Limerick, east of the river called Owenogarney (*Abhainn Ó gCearnaigh*) which flows by Bunratty Castle. Five chieftains of the Uí Echthigirn were slain in 1151 at Móin Mhór (near Mourne Abbey) while aiding Toirdhealbhach O Brien of Thomond in a sanguinary battle.

Yet the census of 1659 does not mention the surname as being one of the principal Irish names in Co. Clare; in fact the only one of the name referred to there was Morish Agherin, gent., in the parish of Desert, barony of Inchiquin, – and he may well have been a transplantee. All the Aherns listed in that census were either in east Cork or in Co. Waterford. This shows that the whole sept must have migrated at some period. Fr. Woulfe was of the opinion that they were driven out by the Mac Namaras about 1318. A few attained high clerical rank. Alan O Hathern or O Hachierane was bishop of Kerry from 1336 to 1347, Dennis Ohachigerna a canon of Limerick *c*. 1400, and Eugene Ohachyerryn a cleric of Cloyne diocese *c*. 1489.

We have, however, no other record of their activities in Co. Cork until the 16th century when the Fiants provide us with an extensive list of Aherns, as follows:

1553: Pardon to Maurice Roche, Lord Roche, . . . Maurice Leaghe mac William mac Owen Iagheren, Owen mac William Iagheren.

1567: Pardon to Maurice Y Agheren fitz William of Mogeely, gent., Thomas Y Aghern fitz William alias Cowcallen, Gerald fitz William Y Agheren, Thady Downy alias Teige mac William of Mogeely, horseman.

(The nickname 'Cowcallen' seems to be that of the legendary hero Cúchulainn. Perhaps it was he who was mentioned in a document of 1585 '. . . one Cuchelayn was attainted and executed at Cork for taking *shrach* (i.e. an exaction in money) for the Earl of Desmond in Kerrycurrihy'.)

1573: Pardon to Thomas fitz Morish lye O Haghiren of Castelrwane (obviously a son to Maurice *liath* of 1553); Thomas fitz Owen fitz William O Haghierin of Glanworth; Donald Farsing fitz William mac Morish, Gerald fitz William mac Morish Iagherin, Conogher Keaghe O Haghierin of Clashganniv (par. Rathgoggan); Thomas mac William mac Morish Iaghierin, of same, and Teig andwna (*an dúna*) fitz Morish Iaghierin, horseman.

1574: Pardon to James Roch, alias ny geyllaghe, of Old Castleton, gent., . . . John mac Morish O Haghierin, of same.

1576: Pardon to Maurice mac Shane y Agherin of Mogeely, Margaret ny Morghe y Agherin of Ballynamuddagh (par. Leitrim), Gerald fitz William y Agherin of Ballycullane (par. Mogeely), horseman. Sir John of Desmond's men and (pardon) granted at his suit.

1577: Pardon to Gerald mac William y Ogheren of Acharren, horseman. (This place is Aghern near Conna, a name which bears a remarkable resemblance to the surname Ahern but is in fact derived from the ford, *Áth an Chairn*.) Owen mac Morish mac Owen I Agheren of Ballenishiry, Gerald mac William mac Morish Y Eogheren of Ballymurphy (par. Knockmourne) and John mac Gerald mac William alias Johne ne Gehe (*Seán na Gaoithe*).

1583: Pardon to Maurice Roch, Lord Roch of Castleton, Co. Cork . . . Thomas mac Owen Iacherin of Johnstown, William mac Owen Iacherin, of same.

1584: Pardon to Thomas of Desmond, knight . . . Morice og mac Morice I Aghierin, Owen mac Morris, Thomas fitz Morris and John mac Morris I Aghierin; Morice and Daniel mac Shane mac Therelgh I Aghierin, Therelgh mac Teig I Aghierin, Morogho mac Teig I Aghierin, Donnell mac Donogho I Aghierin . . . James fitz Thomas of Desmond's men.

1587: Pardon to Ellen ny Owen ny Agherin, Morroghow mac Teig I Agherin; Thomas fitz Morrice fitz William Aghiern, late of Ahicarne (Aghern).

1601: Pardon to David mac Thomas Iaghieren, Morrice oge O Haghierin, Thomas and Owen mac Morrice O Hagheirin, Owen mac Morrice mac Owen O Haghierin, Tirlagh mac Teige O Haghierin (all in east Cork). Morrice fitz Garrett I Agherin of Ballymacsimon (par. Aghern), Morreghy mac Owen mac Donnell Iagheren. Shane mac Morris mac Owen Iagherie of Tuocusheen (par. Knockavilla).

Much useful information regarding the Aherns may be gleaned from these pardons. They were obviously domiciled in east Cork and equally obviously were devoted followers of the leading Norman lords of the area — in particular Lord Roche and the Fitzgeralds of Desmond. They were especially prominent in the small barony of Kinnatalloon which was then Geraldine territory. The castle of Conna was granted by James, Earl of Desmond, to his eldest son, Thomas

Rua, in the mid-16th century, while Mogeely castle was occupied by another son, Sir John of Desmond. The Maurice fitz William Ahern of Mogeely who was classed as 'gentleman' may well have been regarded as chief of his name. Many other Aherns lived in the parishes of Mogeely, Knockmourne and Aghern. Their close association with families of Norman extraction influenced their choice of personal names and even caused them to use *fitz* in place of the more usual *mac*. Maurice — a favourite with both Geraldines and Roches — became the most popular Ahern personal name. William, John, Thomas and Gerald were also well to the fore, but a residue of their Dalcassian origin may be traced in the occasional use of such names as Toirdhealbhach and Murchadh. In the main they were classed as 'horsemen' (a designation only slightly lower than 'gentleman'), or as yeomen (substantial farmers). It may be that they originally came from Co. Clare to act as professional soldiers or gallowglass — like the Mac Sweeneys and Mac Sheehys. This would explain the frequency with which they find mention in the Fiants.

A few of the name settled in the city of Cork. Richard Walshe of Cork in his will (1583) bequeathed to his daughter Ellyne 'the meane profits of a parcell of said parke (in Dungarvan near the North Gate) which parcell is now in the tenure of her fosterfather Conoghor O Hahyrny'. There was a Morgan (? *Murchadh*) O Haherine's tomb in St. Peter's churchyard in Cork, according to a document of 1609. John O Haherin was owner or occupier of some waste pieces of ground ('whereon was a cabbin') in Spittle Street in the south suburbs of Cork at the time of the Civil Survey. Over a century later, in 1788, Maurice Ahern lived in Cove Lane and had a malt house at Blackpool, but his business failed.

In Youghal we find Donell mac Owen O Herne (1617) and David fitz Philip Hagherne, cooper (1636). John fitz Morrish Hagherin lived near Ballymaloe in 1642. Murtagh Hagherin was Protestant vicar of several parishes in Cloyne diocese between 1615 and 1637 — 'a reading minister, an honest man and readeth Irish'. William fitz Morish O Hagheirin and David O Hagheirin were acting in a land transfer at Innygraga (par. Midleton) in 1616.

Owen fitz Morris Haghierin of Carrignashinny (par. Mogeely) and Morris fitz Thomas Haghieren of Rochestown were named in a defeazance action of 1641. Previously Maurice had witnessed a lease by John fitz Edmond Fitzgerald of Cloyne in 1616 and Owen a similar one in 1634.

The only landed Ahern to be outlawed in Co. Cork in 1643 was Morris mac Shane Agherin of Gregg, gent. He appears to have been the then occupant of Cregg castle, a Roche castle three miles west of Fermoy. He may, perhaps, have been the Morrish O Agherns who was a 'titulado' in Castleishen (par. Kilbolane) according to the 1659 census. The only other Ahern of note then in Co. Cork was Bryan

Agharne of Glenatore in the parish of Knockmourne. According to the same census there were 55 of the name among the 'principal Irish families' in Co. Waterford and 20 in the barony of Barrymore, Co. Cork. (Perhaps the thirteen 'Mac William' families in Kinnatalloon were also Aherns.)

The Earl of Clancarty in his will, made in 1665, named among his legatees one Captain Owen Hagherin. This Capt. Owen, described as of Rochestown, Co. Cork, made his own will three years later.

Among the entourage of James II when he sailed from France for Ireland in 1689 was a Major Simon O Haugherne. Simon had held several military commissions from 1683 onwards and joined the Irish Brigade when it was formed in France in 1689, later becoming Major in the King's Foot Guards. He seems to have survived until 1750 as in that year a Simon O Haugherne living in France applied for and received a grant of arms from Ulster's office. He was stated to be son of William son of James son of Maurice son of William O Haugherne of Carrigirea in Munster (perhaps Carrickarea in the parish of Stradbally, Co. Waterford.) Edmond Hagherin of Garrancorbally, Co. Waterford, gent., was outlawed for (Jacobite) treason 'beyond the seas' in 1691.

After the Treaty of Limerick we find Aherns in various places, both at home and abroad. In Kinsale William Haghearne or Hagheron was constable of Ringcurran in 1692, as was another William Aheiron – perhaps his son – in 1734. Maurice Ahern, a captain in Brigadier Whetham's regiment, had his will proved in 1709. Don Patricio Aghcarn was a sub-lieutenant in the Spanish army in 1715 while Don Bernardo Hearne was a cadet in 1759. A Timothy Ahern of Co. Cork fought at Bunker Hill in 1775 during the American war of independence.

In the 18th century there were several Irish poets of the name, e.g. Muiris 'Múinte' Ó Heichiaruinn whose poem in 1709 deplored the act of parliament which decreed that registered priests should be compelled to take the oath of abjuration. The death in Castleyons of Donnchadh Ó hEichthiaruinn was lamented by the poet Éamann de Bhál in 1728. Domhnall Ó Heachiarrainn composed a lament on the death of the Knight of Glin in 1737 while a priest-poet was An t-Ath. Seán Ó Heichthigheirn. The complexities of spelling the surname are well illustrated in a manuscript compiled in 1823 by David Ahern who spelt his name variously: Ó Achaiarainn, Ó Athiaruin, Ó Achhiarinn, Ó Achuirionn, Ahearne, Ahearn. Another manuscript prayer-book was compiled by Seán Ó Dreada for *Micheál Ó Eichiaruinn san Oileán Beag* (Little Island) in 1824.

Ó HÉALATHAIGH

Ó HÉALUIGHTHE   Ó HÉALAITHE   HEALY   HELY

Éladach or Éalathach was a personal name in frequent use among the Uí Echach of Munster (see Ó MATHGHAMHNA). The *Annals of Inisfallen* record that Éladach son of Dúnlang was killed in a battle in Muskerry in 828. According to the genealogies he was of the kingly line of the Uí Echach, one branch of whom was known as Clann tSealbhaigh, being descended from Sealbhach. According to Duan Catháin, Sealbhach had four sons, one of whom was Cochlán and another Éalathach. Since Ua Selbhaigh and Ua Cochláin were names prominently associated with the see of Cork, it is likely that the Uí Éalathaigh were of the same group, especially since they too functioned as a hereditary ecclesiastical family later on − though in the diocese of Cloyne.

The parish of Donaghmore or Donoughmore (*Domhnach Mór*), whose patron is Laichtín, lies on the southern slopes of the Boggeragh mountains. It is now partly in East Muskerry and partly in Barretts barony, in the former Múscraighe Mittaine territory. Much of the land in Donoughmore belonged to the church, having, apparently, been donated by the Uí Éalathaigh. They, in turn, were entitled to be *airchinnigh* or erenaghs of the church, i.e. laymen who cultivated the church lands as freeholders and who were responsible for the upkeep of Laichtín's church.

In 1301 Thomas Ohellethi was vicar of Donoughmore while John Ohellethi and Nicholas Ohellechi were clerics also in the diocese in Cloyne. A royal pardon granted in 1317 to Dermot Mac Carthy, chief of the Irish of Desmond, included the names of Thomas (deacon), Gilbert and Gregory Ohelehit. Around 1366, according to the Pipe Roll of Cloyne, Master Gilbert Ohelghy, Patrick Ohelghy, Malachy Ohelghy, Philip Ohelghy, Nicholas Ohelghy, Matthew Ohelghy, John Ohelghy and four others were the tenants of the Lord Bishop of Cloyne at Donoughmore. They swore on oath that they were 'true men of the Blessed Colman of Cloyne and that so were their ancestors, and that they cannot be moved from the land of the church itself without leave of the Bishop.' The preponderance of Norman personal names is probably due to the influence of such families as the Cogans, the overlords of Muskerry in the 13th century.

Master Gilbert Ohelghy (who was probably vicar of the parish) also held half a carucate in Balytayg near Donaghmore while Cornelius Ohellohy held one messuage, five acres, near the church.

Not unexpectedly there were many clerics of the name in the diocese of Cloyne. Philip O Haylle was one in 1406, and in 1414 Thomas O Healghy was a canon of Cloyne. A petition by Maurice Yhelayd, cleric of Cloyne, in 1461 stated that a canonry with the prebend of Domnachmore was vacant by the resignation of the former canon, Thomas Yhelayd. But whether Thomas had resigned or had been forced out is debatable. In 1473 Thomas Ohelay, clerk, got a mandate to have a canonry of Cloyne and the prebend of Donaghmore, detained for fifteen or twenty years by Maurice Ohelay, clerk. Possession seems to have been nine points of the law, as eight years later Thomas Ohelahy got another mandate to be put in possession of Donaghmore, now being held by Donatus Ohelahy, priest, 'from fear of whose power the said Thomas cannot safely meet him in the city or diocese of Cloyne'. In 1492 Johannes Ihellahyg was a canon of Cloyne diocese and occupied the prebend of Donaghmore – a prebend which seems to have been exclusive to the family.

After the Mac Carthys became lords of Muskerry in the 14th century the O Healys were forced to pay them a head-rent. A list of the lord of Muskerry's lands in 1600 included four 'countries in Muskrye' – O healiey, O herliey, O longe, O cromin – all apparently with ecclesiastical connections. The O Healys are recorded as holding 12 ploughlands. When an O Healy chief was inaugurated, he had to pay £4-9s to Mac Carthy.

In the Elizabethan Fiants are recorded pardons granted to numerous O Healys of Donoughmore, usually as followers of the Mac Carthys of Blarney or of Carraig na Muc (Dripsey). In 1601, for example, Sir Cormac Mac Dermod's followers included Thomas oge O Hialihie, alias O Hialihie, of Donoughmore – apparently the then chief of the sept. Along with him were pardoned Denis, Donnell, Morrice, John, Philip, John oge, William, Dermod and Donogh O Hiallihie, all of Donoughmore and all described as 'gentlemen'. Later in the year, it was reported that Donnough O Healey was in the army of Spain.

Followers of Callaghan mac Teig of Carraig na Muc in the same year included Donell mac Morrish O Hialeigh of Donoughmore, John mac Thomas oge O Haleighie of Kilcullen (par. Donoughmore; he was probably a son of the chief; Dermod mac Thomas oge O Hyalyhy of Ballycunningham was pardoned in 1577), Morris mac Shane mac Thomas, of same, Morris mac Shane O Hialaii of Carhoo (par. Magourney), John oge beg O Hallihey of same, and John oge O Hallihie entarmyn of Donoughmore. The soubriquet *an tearmainn* means 'of the termon', i.e. church lands of sanctuary. This may be the John O Hiallihie of Donoughmore who in 1588 sent a petition to the Privy Council seeking pardon for the 'poor and ignorant offenders in those parts' for their share in the rebellion of the late Earl of Desmond.

A John O Healy, 'one of Cormac's old thieves', was also mentioned in connection with Cormac Mac Carthy, lord of Muskerry, who was imprisoned at Cork in 1602. John was appointed to go to England in order to bring home Cormac's eldest son from Oxford. Carew got wind of the plot and O Healy was captured on board ship before leaving Cork — but not before he had thrown all his letters and money overboard. Because he would not confess as to the letters and money, he too was lodged in Cork gaol. When Cormac was eventually pardoned in March 1603, his loyal follower 'John Hialihy, of Blarney, gentleman', was pardoned along with him.

Inquisitions of the early 17th century show us that the O Healys were still flourishing in Donoughmore at that period. One was taken in 1625 into the lands of Donald O Healehie of Ballycunningham, Kilcullen and Coolmona, who died in 1619. John was his son and heir. The lands were held of Cormac óg Mac Carthy (late of Oxford). Donald O Healehie of Kilcullen and Oliverius O Healy of Fornaght laid claim to the lands. (Donald may have been the Donell O Healehy of Fornaght pardoned in 1591 while Oliverius was probably the Oliver Healy, gentleman, mentioned in the marriage settlement of Cormac óg's daughter and Sir Valentine Browne). Another inquisition, dated 1638, dealt with the lands of Thomas mac Meater O Healyhy and Johanna ny Meater O Healyhy, alienated to Viscount Muskerry, and one in the following year dealt with lands which Thomas O Healihy of Gowlane alienated to William O Riordan of Clodagh.

Certain difficulties arose with regard to former church lands after the reformation period. A document in Brady's *Records* describes Donaghmore as the most considerable episcopal demesne in the diocese — excepting Cloyne itself. It was one of the see's earliest possessions and was let on lease as a fee farm to the O Helihies (now Helys) at 6s.8d per plowland, who tenanted part and let out the rest to the chiefs or heads of clans 'in that part of the country which comprehends the Bogra mountains, the wildest and most uncivilized district in the county of Cork'. Bishop Lyon (1583-1617) instituted a suit against its possessors but nothing came of the negotiations. Bishop Synge (1638 - 1652) renewed the suit against the tenants of the whole eighteen ploughlands. The bishop's plea was that the Pipe Roll of Cloyne reckoned Donaghmore expressly as the bishop's manor and that Bishop Bennet soon after 1500 lived in the manor house there; that as the English were lords in chief, the O Helihies who were *hibernici* could only have been tenants at will or *villani*. The Helys on the other hand contended that their land was freehold and had continued in their family for 500 years, that they owed suit and service not to the church but to Lord Muskerry, and that they paid composition to the king which no church land ever did.

This was in 1639 and eventually one of the O Healys agreed to take a lease from the see, delivering up to the bishop the celebrated shrine of St. Laichtín's arm which was the symbol of power in the manor. (This is now in the National Museum, Dublin.) The 1641 rebellion, however, put an end to further suits and Lord Muskerry retained his overlordship. At least one of the family, William Healy, became a Protestant clergyman (though a MS of 1615 says of him: 'William O Hialyhy noe graduate; his wife and children goe to Masse'). He became chancellor of Cork diocese from 1610 to 1632 and resided at Athnowen (Ovens). His example was not followed by Patrick O Healihy, a priest, who with six others in 1628 attacked and beat Edmund Murphy or Murfield, servant to the Protestant bishop, who was endeavouring to collect tithes at Dunisky in Muskerry. O Healihy called him 'a devilish heretical churl and the servant of the devil'! A John Hialihy was sworn a freeman of Cork in 1631 — perhaps a son of the Thomas O Hyalliyhie who had a house in Cork in 1582.

The Civil Survey gives us full details of the O Healy lands in Donoughmore parish in 1641. Thomas mac Daniel Healihy, Irish papist, of Gowlane, held Gowlane, Lackanbane and Ballygirriha, 880 acres in all, but mortgaged to Lord Muskerry for £400. On the lands was 'an old decay'd House, with a ruinous grist mill' which perhaps indicates the site of a former O Healy castle. Fornaght was held by Oliver Healihy but West Kilclogh (par. Matehy) had been purchased from John Healihy fitz Philip by Zachariah Travers of Cork. Lower Kilmartin belonged to Maurice mac Thomas Healihy and Upper Kilmartin to Dermod O Healihy, deceased. Donogh mac Thomas Healihy held Ballykervick and Monataggart while Thomas mac Meater held Barrahaurin. Coolmona ('both Coolmonys'), Killeenleigh, Ballycunningham and Kilcullen all belonged to Daniel mac Shane Healihy. In every case a chief rent was payable to the lord of Muskerry.

All of these O Healys must have joined Lord Muskerry in the 1641 rebellion since the entire group (described as 'gentlemen') were declared outlaws in 1643, together with John of Castlemore, Thomas of Mashanaglass and Donogh O Hialighy of Ballyburden (near Ballincollig), 'a doctor of Physic'. At the end of the war an allegation was made that Dr. Healy was involved in the deaths of English settlers who formed part of a convoy from Macroom to Cork in 1642. Even after the rebellion had ended and the plantations were completed, a contemporary account listed 'all the Hialihyes and their children, brethren and followers' among those who were 'plotting for troubles'. They were given as 'in carbry' — possibly in error for Muskerry.

As we might expect, the O Healy lands were declared to be forfeited during the Cromwellian period but when Charles II was restored in 1660 Lord Muskerry (now Earl of Clancarty) had his estate restored, with a proviso enabling him to grant leases at low rents to the representatives of those freeholders who had 'gone out' with him in 1641. Thus leases were granted to Morris Healihy (Kilmartin Upper), Daniel Healehye (Kilcullen) and to Dermot and Donnogh Healihy (Coollicka). However, the confiscation to the crown of the Clancarty estates after the Williamite wars set aside these leases. In 1697 the Protestant bishop of Cloyne again laid claim to the lands of Donoughmore but to no avail. Finally, in 1703, Bishop Crowe purchased the lands for £4,020 and leased them to suitable tenants.

One of these was Mathias Earbery of Ballincollig who took a lease of Gowlane. His daughter, Prudence, in 1719 married Francis Healy of Gertrough — perhaps Gortroe in the neighbouring parish of Kilshannig. Francis seems to have conformed to the established religion. Their son, John Healy or Hely, a barrister, in 1751 married the grandniece and heiress of Richard Hutchinson of Knocklofty, near Clonmel, and changed his name to Hely-Hutchinson. He was M.P. for Cork from 1761 to 1790 and became Secretary of State for Ireland. His eldest son and heir, Richard Hely-Hutchinson supported the Act of Union and was created Earl of Donoughmore. In the House of Lords the Earl supported Catholic Emancipation while his brother, Christopher, championed the Catholic cause in the House of Commons. It was a later Earl of Donoughmore who moved the ratification of the Irish treaty of 1921 in the House of Lords.

The rest of the now landless clan scattered to various parts, many joining the Wild Geese abroad. John Healy, born in Donoughmore, was in 1690 in O Mahony's Dragoons and later a Major-General in the Spanish army. A Captain Healy of the Irish Brigade was wounded at Fontenoy and a Lieutenant Healy wounded at Laffeldt. Don Francisco Haly was a sub-lieutenant in the regiment of Ultonia in Spain in 1718 while Don Tomas (1725) and Don Guillermo Healy (1759) were cadets in the same regiment. Among the Co. Cork gentlemen outlawed in 1691 for 'treason beyond the seas' (i.e. adherence to King James) were: Daniel Heally, Kilneally, called heir of land of Kilcullen; Thomas Mac Morris Healy, Kilmartin, called heir of land of Upper Kilmartin; John mac Thomas Healy, Barrahaurin; William and Maurice Healy, Ballygirriha; John Hely, Fornaght; William and John mac Oliver Healy of Gortacrohig (par. Aghabulloge).

A Thomas Healy of Muskerry in the 19th century settled in Bantry where he taught Greek and Latin. He also taught his children that their family had been despoiled under the Penal Laws and that the bronze reliquary of St. Laichtín's hand had been in the guardianship of his people. His grandsons, Tim and Maurice Healy were noted Irish members of the Westminster parliament around the turn of the century and Tim Healy was chosen to be the first Governor-General of the Irish Free State in 1922.

Ó HEIDIRSCEOIL

Ó DRISCEOIL   O DRISCOLL

Few family groups maintained such a lengthy and unbroken association with their native place as did the O Driscolls, the chief family of Corca Laoighdhe, to whom reference has been made in the introduction. These remained the strongest grouping in west Cork even after the Eóganacht conquest of Munster. As they were too numerous and too powerful to be ignored, the genealogists eventually brought them into the fold by providing mythical Goidelic ancestors to disguise their Ernean origin. Accordingly, Ith (son of Bregon) who was credited with being an uncle of Míl (*a quo* the 'Milesians') was declared to have been the progenitor of Corcu Lóegde, one of Ith's descendants being named Lugaid Lóegde. From Lugaid's great-great-grandson, Óengus Bolg, was derived a segment called Uí Builg and their leading family in turn were the Uí Etersceóil, named either from Óengus' grandson, Eterscél, or from a later descendant, Eterscél son of Finn, whose *floreat* was in the mid-11th century.

A grandson of the latter, Mac Raith Ua hEitirsceóil, erected (according to the Genealogy of Corca Laoighdhe) the cathedral of Rosscarbery (*teampull mór Fachtna i Ros Ailithri*) but the first of the name to receive mention in the *Annals of Inisfallen* was Conchobar Ua hEtersceóil who died at Ros Ailithir in 1103. Although not listed in the genealogies, he is described as king of Corcu Lóegde. Ciarmhac Ua hEtersceóil died in 1126, and in 1155 Amhlaoibh Ó hEidirsgeóil, king of Corcu Lóegde, was killed at the door of the church of Bréanainn of Birr. It is not stated what he was doing so far from home but it is clear that at this period there was severe pressure on Corcu Lóegde as a result of the movement of Eóganacht Caisil families into south Munster. This pressure increased after the Norman invasion; in 1178 Muirchertach Mac Carthaigh was slain by Ua hEtersceóil at Móin Cluana Cuarbáin (Clooncorban par. Kilmeen). In the following year, the son of Finn Ua hEtersceóil was slain and in 1196 Mac Con Ua hEtersceóil died. The name Finn occurs frequently in the early genealogical lists but was replaced in the 14th century by Fíngen or Fínghin (sometimes anglicized as 'Florence') probably due to the influence of Mac Carthy and O Sullivan neighbours. Mac Con was another old and unusual personal name, one which remained in use up to the present century. (Two ladies of the family in the 14th century bore the musical names Finnuala and Dirbhail).

By the 13th century three distinct divisions of the O Driscolls had evolved. The main line was represented by Donnchadh Mór, king of Corcu Lóegde, who died in 1229. His youngest brother, Aedh, known as *Garbh* (the rough), moved into the Béarra peninsula apparently as the result of a dispute. He was killed 'by his own people' in 1213. 'It is from him are sprung the people of Béarra and Ua hEidirsceóil of Béarra with their correlatives.' They were later superseded in that region by the O Sullivans, although O Clery's genealogy traces seven descents from Aedh Garbh and Ó Huidhrín's poem (*c*. 1400) names Ó hEidirsceóil as lord of Béarra. (It is of interest that in the 13th century there was a parish named Baile Uí Eidirsceóil (Baliederscolle) in Ardfert diocese, probably the modern parish of Ballinvoher on the Dingle peninsula.)

The third branch was founded by the youngest son of Donnchadh Mór, namely Amhlaíbh, known as *An Gascunach* (The Gascon) for the following reason. At the age of twelve Amhlaíbh was given as a pledge for a cargo of wine to the crew of a merchant ship from Gascony. He remained in that country and was put to caring the vines which flourished without defect during his time. This proved that he was of noble blood and he was conveyed back with honour to his own country. (Ascribing the fruitfulness of the earth to a good king was a well-known motif in Irish literature. Eoin Ua Maethagáin, lamenting the death of Diarmuid Ó hEidirsceoil in the early 16th century remarks that:

'The fruit is scarce on account of Conchobhar's son,
And scarce is the milk with milch cows',

while a century later, Tadhg Ó Dálaigh, with reference to the demise of Sir Fínghin O Driscoll, tells us that:

'The pure soil had been fruitful
From the eye that has just been clouded'.)

The Gascon, whose descendants were known as Uí Eidirsceóil Óig, was himself slain at the side of Diarmaid Mac Carthy and many of the nobles of Munster while fighting against the Anglo-Normans at Tralee in 1234. This was two years after Domhnall God Mac Carthy had defeated the O Mahonys and made himself lord of Carbery, when apparently he acquired the allegiance of the O Driscolls. From then until the late 16th century it was customary for the chieftain- elect of the O Driscolls to receive his rod of office from Mac Carthy of Carbery. In 1421 Fínghin, son of Aonghus Ó hEidirsceóil, was killed at Carrigrohane while aiding Mac Carthy Riabhach, and in the 16th and 17th centuries we find details of levies payable by the O Driscolls to the Mac Carthys. There were, of course, warring factions among the Mac Carthys themselves. The *Annals of Inisfallen* tell us that in 1268:

On the first of August the sons of Domhnall Gall Mac Carthaig and the Uí Eterscéoil and the Corcu Laígde fought at sea, and that was the hardest and most triumphant battle ever fought in

Ireland, for only the night parted them from each other after many on both sides had been drowned.'

It is hardly surprising that the O Driscolls, in their rocky sea-girt patrimony with Carbery's hundred isles spread out before them, had become expert seafarers and were not averse to a bit of plunder or piracy on the side. For some reason they allied themselves with the Powers, Barons of Dunhill, and kept up a recurring feud with the merchants and burgesses of Waterford city over several centuries. Among the Carew manuscripts are stories of such encounters. In 1368 a pitched battle between the Waterford merchants and the Powers occurred at a place called Glenoradmore, the Powers being aided by 'Raymond O h-Edriscoll, with his Galleys and men'. The Mayor, Sheriff and Justice of the Peace with about 100 men were slain and on the other side the Baron of Dunhill and his brother 'with divers of the Powers and of the O h-Edriscolls'.

In 1413 another Mayor of Waterford, Simon Wicken, sailed to 'Ballintimore' where he landed at supper-time on Christmas Day and gained entrance to O Driscoll's great castle by pretending he had not come 'more than to daunce and drinke and so to departe'. But before their departure the Waterford men made prisoners of O Driscoll, his son, and other relatives 'saying unto them they should go with him to Waterford to syng their carroll'. O Driscoll's fate is confirmed by an entry in the *Annals of Connacht*:

A.D. 1414. Ó hEitirsceóil Mór was craftily killed by the crew of a merchant ship.

The annals record the death, four years later, of Mac Con Ó hEtersceóil and of his brother, Bishop Matthew Ó hEtersceóil. (At the time Matthew became archdeacon of Ross in 1394 it was stated that he had studied canon law at Oxford and at Vienna for many years. Another of the family, Odo O Driscoll, was bishop of Ross at the end of the 15th century. He it was who became involved in the dispute with (Blessed) Thaddeus Mac Carthy who was consecrated bishop of the same diocese in 1482 on the erroneous assumption that the see was vacant.)

In 1450 a statute was enacted as a result of numbers of the king's subjects being slain by 'Ffynyn Ohedirskoll, chieftain of his nation, an Irish enemy', to the effect that no person of the southern ports was to fish at 'Korkly Balthymore', and the town that received the said Ohedirskoll should pay £40 to the king!

In 1461 the O Driscolls landed at Tramore, again on the invitation of the Powers, and battled with the citizens of Waterford at Ballimacdare (?Ballymacaw). The Carew MSS account gives victory to the Waterford men who made prisoners of 'O h-Edriskoll Oge with vi of his sonnes, which were then brought to Waterford with three of their Gallyes'.

Nor were the O Driscolls strangers to the continent of Europe. In 1472 the annals record the death of Fínghin Ó hEidirsceóil (Mór) and of his son, Tadhg, after their return from the pilgrimage of St. James, at Compostella in Spain.

On the 20th February 1537, Fínghin O Driscoll, chieftain of Inishircan (Sherkin), captured a Portuguese ship with a cargo of wine consigned to Waterford, and distributed 72 tuns of wine among his neighbours. Burning with indignation, the citizens of Waterford besieged and captured the castle of Sherkin, destroying all the villages of the island, as well as the friary and the mill. (This Franciscan foundation was due to an earlier Fínghin O Driscoll, around 1460.) They also destroyed the adjoining island of Inchipite (Spanish Island) 'where Fineen has his most pleasant seat in a castle, adjoining to a hall, with an orchard and grove', and finally they attacked the burned Baltimore and broke down 'Teig O Hederischol's goodly castle and bawn'.

Baltimore (*Baile an Tighe Mhóir*) was named after O Driscoll's 'great house'. Its original name of Dún na Séad indicates that the stone castle was preceded by an earlier fortification. The first castle on the site was built probably by an illegitimate son of Robert Fitzstephen in the period when a chain of Norman castles was being constructed around the south-west coast prior to 1214. After the battle of Callann (1261) most of these castles fell into the hands of the Gaelic Irish, and Baltimore became the principal seat of O Driscoll Mór. The O Driscolls also fortified their island properties with stone castles – Dún na Long on Sherkin, Dún an Óir on Cléire (Cape Clear), Dún na nGall on Ringarogy island and another on Spanish Island. Also at various times they had castles at Castlehaven, Castlenard, Lettertinlish, Rincolisky (Whitehall), Oldcourt (near Skibbereen), Aghadown, Lough Hyne and Ardagh.

By the 16th century the O Driscolls of Béarra had long since succumbed to the O Sullivans while pressure from the Mac Carthys, O Mahonys and O Donovans had confined O Driscoll Mór and O Driscoll Óg to the areas known as Collymore and Collybeg, respectively. *Princeps Cothliae* is how Philip O Sullivan Bear describes O Driscoll; 'Cothluighe' is perhaps a corruption of Corca Laoighdhe. At this period Collymore contained 63 ploughlands, 25½ of which were on the islands. Its land boundary on the north-west was a line from the river Ilen near Skibbereen to the sea near Toe Head, so that the mainland part embraced the parishes of Tullagh and Creagh. Collybeg, O Driscoll Óg's territory, had 34 ploughlands, mainly in Aghadown parish, while Glanbarraghan (Castlehaven) with its 5½ ploughlands was owned by Sliocht Taidhg, descended from the Tadhg O Driscoll who died in 1472.

Although O Driscoll Mór was generally regarded as an independent chieftain, Mac Carthy Riabhach claimed an annual *cuid oíche* which amounted to £4.13.4 in cash. In 1575 the O Driscolls were listed among the followers of the Mac Carthys to whom they could supply a force of six horsemen and 300 kern. The Earls of Desmond, in turn, claimed overlordship over and rents from the Mac Carthys, including an annual rent of eight beeves (or eight nobles sterling) payable out of the O Driscoll territories.

The audacious attempt by Sir Peter Carew to take over large sections of Munster and Leinster in the late 16th century also involved the O Driscolls. On Carew's list were 'Collymore, Collybeg; Odriscolmore and Odriscol oge holdeth; 2 horsemen, 40 footmen' — and the chieftain, Fínghin, ('whose ancestors never came to any Deputy') was among those who conferred with him. The takeover bid collapsed but an obviously worried Fínghin travelled to London in 1573 to make a surrender of his lands and obtain a regrant from the queen. Three years later he swore allegiance to Sir Henry Sidney and in 1583 called upon the Privy Council in London. As a reward for his loyalty he was knighted, being henceforth known as Sir Fineen. By taking letters patent for his lands from Queen Elizabeth he ended the Irish custom whereby Mac Carthy Riabhach presented the ceremonial rod of office to the chieftain-elect of the O Driscolls. He also, of course, acquired title, in his own person, to all the sept-lands of the O Driscolls.

In return, Sir Fineen remained constant in his loyalty to the English crown and interest, even when his son was killed early in 1599 by a force of 400 Connachtmen, headed by William Burke, who were ravaging Carbery in order to enforce support for O Neill. A naval force with a similar aim was defeated by the O Driscolls. Only when the arrival of the Spaniards at Kinsale enhanced the prospects of the northern earls did Sir Fineen's loyalty waver and, rather reluctantly, he joined other west Cork chieftains — Mac Carthys, O Sullivan and O Donovan — in the rebellion. His two eldest sons, Fínghin and Conchobhar, came to Don Juan de Aguila to offer their assistance. Sir Fineen himself 'who never in the course of his whole life had been tainted with the least spot of disloyaltie' handed over to Pedro de Zubiaur his castles of Baltimore and Dún na Long (Sherkin) while Donnchadh O Driscoll and his brothers (of the Slíocht Taidhg) did likewise with Castlehaven, which the Spaniards made their chief base in west Cork. An English fleet under Sir Richard Leveson attacked Castlehaven but was driven off with severe losses. Two days after the Kinsale disaster, Red Hugh O Donnell arrived at Castlehaven and immediately set sail for Spain, accompanied by the Spanish commanders de Zubiaur and de Soto as well as O Sullivan Bear's son and Domhnall O Driscoll, son of Sir Fineen.

In February 1602, as the Spaniards were preparing to surrender Castlehaven to the English, the O Driscolls by a ruse regained possession of the castle and were holding it against the Spaniards when English ships under Captain Roger Harvey appeared. They then abandoned Castlehaven for the last time. Harvey continued on to Baltimore and the castle there was handed over without incident as was Dún na Long where Harvey was feasted by the governor, Andreas de Aervy. Dún an Óir on Cléire, garrisoned by Capt. Tyrell's men, held out for one day but was then abandoned. Sir Fineen immediately submitted himself to Capt. Harvey as desired by Carew who wrote '. . . the poor old man was over-ruled by his son, and hath no disposition to be a traitor, but his son and heir called Connor O Driscoll is a malicious rebel and lies in wait to take the castle from his father to deface it'. O Sullivan Bear in a letter to de Zubiaur, took a different view '. . . I know you will pity old Sir Fineen, forced by this composition to yield his body to the merciless butchery of our heretical enemies'.

In March, among those who accompanied Don Juan to Spain from Kinsale was Dermot mac Conougher O Driscoll of Castlehaven, with his brother and son. Dermot with Bishop Mac Egan sought and obtained aid for O Sullivan Bear, now the leading rebel in Munster, and arrived at Ardea (Co. Kerry) on 5th June with a shipload of supplies and money. By this time O Sullivan's chief stronghold, Dunboy castle, was being invested by Carew who on his way there encamped 'near unto Kilcoa being a castle wherein the Rebell Cnoghor, eldest sonn to Sr. Ffynine O Driscoll, Knight, held a ward'. Conchobhar O Driscoll had placed another garrison of 60 men with three pieces of Spanish ordnance in a fort on Dursey island; this was taken by Capt. Bostock (assisted by Owen O Sullivan) and the survivors executed at Dunboy. After Dunboy itself had fallen an assault was made on the last stronghold held by Conchobhar of Castlehaven and his brothers, a promontory fort called 'the Downings' (probably Dooneendermotmore at Toe Head). A 'great boat' belonging to Tadhg was captured, his brother Dáire slain and a few days later the fort was taken. On his way home from Dunboy Carew captured and burned the castle of Lettertinlish which belonged to Sir Fineen and had been garrisoned by his son, Conchobhar. Capt. Harvey was given orders to burn Dún na nGall, Dún an Óir and the Downings but the castles of Dún na Long, Dún na\ Séad (Baltimore) and Castlehaven were respited pending further orders.

With his castles fallen and all hope of further resistance faded, Conchobhar (son of Sir Fineen) along with the Jesuit, Fr. Archer, set sail from Ardea for Spain on 6 July 1602. Accompanying them were Donnchadh, the former owner of Castlehaven with his brother, Domhnall; three brothers, Mac Con, Tadhg and Muircheartach, described as 'Mac Iffie O Driscolls'; one of the sons of Gulleduffe of Clear; Dermott oge mac Dermody O Driscoll; and nine-year old Connor óg, son and heir of the rebel Conchobhar O Driscoll. Conchobhar received a pension in Spain and was from 1607 to 1616 captain of a company in the Spanish army in the Low Countries. (One of the sergeants in his company was Macon O Driscoll who got licence to return to Ireland in 1608.) In 1614 an act of attainder was proposed to disinherit him as well as other fugitives abroad. His son, Connor óg, became an ensign in the Spanish navy and was killed in an engagement with the Turks in the Mediterranean in 1618. The other O Driscoll emigrants along with the son of O Sullivan Bear were treated with the greatest consideration by the Count of Caracena. Dermicio son of Donnchadh became a Knight of Santiago, as did his cousin, Daniel son of Diarmaid. Denis O Driscoll, son of Tadhg of Castle-haven, became archbishop of Brindisi in Italy from 1640 to 1650.

There remained, of course, many of the name at home in Corca Laoighdhe. Among the O Driscolls who received pardons in 1601 (before the arrival of the Spaniards) were Eneas Mac Con of Dún na nGall, Fynen of Rincolisky, Teige mac Conoghor of Lackoone (? Leighcloon), Teig mac Dermod of Baltimore, Conoghor mac Donogh of Inishbeg, Conoghor mac Donogh mac Donell roe of Ardraly, Dermod mac Cragh of Collybeg, Dermod mac Morierty of Dún na Séad, Dermod Mac Con of Drishane (par. Creagh), Teige mac Morierty of Collymore and Donogh mac Fynine of Inissircane (Sherkin).

But the planters were waiting to move in on O Driscoll lands, remote though they were. In 1606 John Kinge of Dublin was granted the castle and lands of Glanberighan (Gleann Bearcháin or Castlehaven) as well as Island-Molloe (? Horse Island), the former estate of Donoghue mac Connoghor O Driscoll, attainted. Always alert to danger, Sir Fineen immediately applied for a 'surrender and regrant' of all Colly-more, mentioning, in passing, how he had maintained the castle of Baltimore against his eldest son until he handed it over to Carew who put a garrison in it. But, he added, the garrison pulled down much of the timber of the said castle for fuel, so that a great part of the stone frame was now fallen.

This regrant would help to solve another problem for Sir Fineen. Although living at Baltimore and generally regarded as O Driscoll Mór, he was in fact genealogically junior to the O Driscolls of Dún na Long and Dún na nGall (known as *Carrach* or rough-skinned), who were entitled to half of the rents from the O Driscoll lands as well as half of the royalties from the harbour of Baltimore. On the death of his cousin, Conchobhar, Sir Fineen took both halves for himself and held it until his right was challenged by Conchobhar's son, Fínghin Carrach. But Fínghin failed to regain possession before he died in April 1600. In August of the same year, Sir Fineen, his wife (Ellen Mac Carthy Riabhach) and Walter Gould, a merchant of Cork (probably a mortgagee), assigned the whole lordship to one Thomas Crooke, apparently on an extensive mortgage. In 1604 Sir Fineen paid a bond of £500 to have his castles of Donoshee and Dunolonge, to be retained as long as he remained a good subject. The following year, Domhnall Mac Carthy Riabhach assigned his rights in Colly-more to Sir James Lancaster (who appointed Thomas Crooke as his attorney), and in 1606 Sir Fineen and Walter Gould again assigned their rights to Thomas Crooke (described as of Dromea).

In the Summer of 1607 Sir Fineen and Crooke jointly surrendered all the lands to the crown in order to obtain a royal regrant, but the regrant was to Thomas Crooke only; he was then described as of

Baltimore. In the following year an inquisition was held to define the extent of O Driscoll's country. Mention was made of the dispute with Donnchadh Carrach (son of Fínghin Carrach) which had been arbitrated on, the arbitrators decreeing that Sir Fineen should continue to hold Downysheade with the various rents appertaining to it while Donnchadh Carrach should have Dún na nGall, 'the little Illande with the Castle of Innyspicke', and rents from the islands.

The inquisition provides a complete picture of the lands and rents of O Driscoll Mór. Of special interest is the schedule of harbour dues levied by the lords of Baltimore, including such items as four gallons of wine out of every butt landed, fishery payments and all wrecks along the coast. Several sub-septs of freeholders are named — Sliocht Dhonnchadha Uí Dhrisceoil, Sliocht Dhiarmada Uí Dhrisceoil, Sliocht an Easpaig, Sliocht Mhic Aonghasa, Sliocht Uí Fhithcheallaigh, etc. (Part of the island of Cléire was known as Sliocht Aodha.) One of the arbitrators mentioned was Sir Walter Coppinger of Cloghane who from then on obtruded himself more and more on O Driscoll affairs. Coppinger, an expert in land transactions, amassed a huge amount of land throughout Co. Cork, principally by way of mortgages. At the outset, on 1st March 1609, he purchased Donnchadh Carrach's rights to Baltimore and its surrounds for £300, having, apparently, spied some legal flaw in the settlement (arbitrated on by himself and by O Donovan of Castle Donovan) and so became a co-partner with Crooke and Sir Fineen. In June 1610 the trio leased the castle, lands, rents, etc. to Thomas Bennett for 21 years at a rent of £50 per annum.

On 10th July 1610 Crooke got a royal licence to alienate the lands of Collymore to Sir Fineen, Walter Coppinger and Donnchadh Carrach and twelve days later (with Sir Fineen's assent) he granted to Walter Coppinger the reversion in fee expectant upon Bennett's demise for a sum of £185-10s. In April of the following year, Sir Fineen released his rights to Coppinger, but in November he and his wife — plus Thomas Crooke who was probably the prime mover — paid off the mortage on the lands. A few days later Crooke again released all his rights to Coppinger but it is noticeable that Sir Walter's 'surrender and regrant' of 1615-16 makes no mention of Baltimore or its lands though it does include such places as half of Inishidriskell and halves of several townlands in Collybeg.

Crooke was now firmly established at Baltimore, which on 26 September 1612 received its official charter. Thomas Crooke was himself appointed as the first sovereign while the first twelve burgesses all bore English names — Bennett, Hoskins, Salmon, Carter etc. A whole new English town had been established. Though Crooke prospered and was created a baronet in 1624 shortly before he died, there is every indication that he was deeply involved in piracy, a trade which brought retribution on the town in the shape of the notorious sack of Baltimore by Algerian pirates in 1631. (Incidentally, the reference in Thomas Davis' romantic ballad to the capture of 'O Driscoll's daughter' by the Algerians is entirely fanciful; in fact, in the year previous to the sack of Baltimore, the mayor of Waterford (an ancient adversary) warned the Earl of Cork that Cornelius O Driscoll, an Irish pirate with his rendezvous in Barbary, was in the neighbourhood with a ship of 200 tons and 14 guns.)

After Crooke's death, Sir Walter Coppinger got possession of the old castle at Baltimore while the English planters, after some legal proceedings, were allowed to remain in undisturbed possession of their property.

Sir Fineen, now 'of great and decrepide age' and living at Bally-island (par. Creagh), attempted to regain his estates in 1629, his agent being his son, Donogh. Arbitrators were appointed and accepted Sir Fineen's statement that he never intended his conveyance of his estates to be absolute, but that the payment of £1,693 was by way of mort-gage. Their award decreed that if Sir Fineen repaid £1,300 to Coppinger he could recover his estates. They further stated that Donogh O Driscoll had 'calamniously slandered the said Sir Walter in the pleadings.' Obviously Sir Fineen was unable to repay such a substantial amount, so neither he nor his descendants ever occupied Dún na Séad again. He died soon afterwards – in England according to some sources, but a local tradition says that he died in the castle known as *An Clochán* on Castle Island in Lough Hyne. It seems quite likely that this picturesque spot was the Ballyisland residence of Sir Fineen's declining years.

Incidentally, Sir Walter Coppinger had a brother named Richard whose daughter married Tadhg Carrach O Driscoll and to their son (his own grandson) Richard bequeathed the castle and lands of Dún an Óir in Cléire in 1651.

The O Driscolls Óg still flourished in Collybeg, which lay to the west of the Ilen. Their principal residence was at Castlenard (Ballinard) where Diarmaid mac Conchobhair O Driscoll died in 1629. The previous year he had mortgaged some of his lands to John O Crowley of Gortard. His son, Conchobhar Óg, mortgaged more lands to Tadhg O Donovan of Drishane in 1629, 1635 and 1638 while Conchobhar's son and heir, Donnchadh, in 1670 finally sold Ballinard to Tadhg O Donovan's son.

The castle of Oldcourt was another O Driscoll stronghold. In 1612 Murtagh O Driscoll mortgaged it to Sir Walter Coppinger for £60 and in 1630 Dermott mac Murtagh mac Brien O Driscoll obtained a further advance of £40 on it.

Then there were the O Driscolls Carrach. Fínghin Carrach, who died in 1600, was married to an O Hurley (*Onóra Ní Raghnaill*) and assigned the castle of Dún na Long to the O Hurleys for her lifetime. His sons Conchobhar and Donnchadh succeeded him. Donnchadh died about 1647, his son, Conchobhar, having predeceased him and Conchobhar's widow (Catherine Mac Carthy) and young son, Donogh, were expelled from Dún na nGall and their estates as a result of the Cromwellian confiscations. After the Restoration, they petitioned for the recovery of their lands, maintaining that Donnchadh, the grandfather, had behaved innocently and inoffensively during the rebellion. Their claim to the castles of Dún na nGall and Dún na Long with most of the island of Sherkin appears to have been unsuccessful and the lands were retained by Henry Beecher and Captain Jarvoys.

There is but little information regarding the activities of the O Driscolls during the rebellion which began in 1641. Tadhg Carrach and Donnchadh Carrach were named as early supporters of Lord Muskerry. We know that seven were outlawed in 1643 – Cornelius and Donough of Dún na Long, Teige and Florence or Fyrmyn of Ballymacrown (par. Tullagh), Donogh of Glannemonfoyne (? Glanna-feen, par. Tullagh), Fyrmyn mac Enyste of Ballyn Iteragh (? par. Creagh) and Dermott of Couldrout (?), all described as gentlemen.

In 1650 F. (? Fínghin) O Driscoll entered into a covenant with Mac Carthy and O Donovan to resist jointly any attack on Clancahill, Clandermot or Collymore. Cornelius O Driscoll (described as of Dones-aide) raised a regiment of foot at his own charge to fight for King Charles. Though 'of tender years when the commotions began in Ireland' he himself was colonel of the regiment and was wounded in action. One of the last to surrender to the Cromwellians, he after-wards served in the Duke of York's regiment abroad, to which he brought five entire companies of foot. In 1660 King Charles II ordered that he be restored to his estates, but though his petition extended to 2,382 acres of ancestral lands, including Baltimore, Ballymacrown and Ballylinchy, he had to be satisfied with 337 acres in Ballymacrown, land which had been confiscated from Francis (? Florence) Driscoll.

Practically all the O Driscoll landowners had been swept up in the net of confiscation at this stage. Teige O Driscoll als. O Driscoll lost Ballyisland and other parts of Creagh parish (to James Coppinger). His title indicates that he was perhaps a grandson of Sir Fineen (who used to reside at Ballyisland) but there was also a Donogh O Driscoll als. O Driscoll who forfeited Inispike als. Spanish island, three small islands near same and Dongall island. Donogh Carrach lost Dún na Long on Sherkin as well as parts of Castlehaven parish. (A Donogh O Driscoll of Inishirkane had his will registered in 1670.) The whole island of Cléire (Cape Clear) which prior to 1641 was occupied entirely by O Driscolls – Teige Carragh (of Dún an Óir), Erevan (*Eireamhón*) óg., Knogher mac Erevan etc – was acquired by Sir Algernon May and his wife.

The 1659 census shows that O Driscolls were still numerically strong in West Carbery; there were also eight families then in Kinalmeaky. A Donnogh O Driscoll, Esq., was a 'titulado' in Coologory, parish of Tuamgraney, Co. Clare – presumably a Cromwellian transplantee.

The ancient family estates were now occupied by the Bennetts, the Beechers and their friends.

Colonel O Driscoll returned to active service in the war between William and James. In 1690 he was governor of Castle Park at Kinsale where he was killed when the fort was captured by Williamite forces under Marlborough. Another and younger Colonel O Driscoll was killed a month later while leading an attack on Castletown House, in their ancient patrimony of Castlehaven. The two O Driscoll colonels were listed among the Jacobites attainted in 1690. One was described as of Ballynronane (probably Ballymacrown) and the other as of Cotty (? Cothluighe or Colly). There was a Capt. Cornelius O Driscoll alias Curragh (*Carrach*) of Cotty on the same list — probably the Capitaine Cornelius Q. O Driscoll who was in the Irish Brigade in France in 1693, and later Lieutenant-Colonel in the regiment of Dragoons of the famous Count Daniel O Mahony. Also attainted were Cornelius and Thady (alias Curragh) of Sherkin; Dermott alias Durig, Canme (? Mac Con) and Daniel son of Canme, all of Baltimore; Florence alias Finen of Ballyisland; Denis of Ballyherard (? Ballinard); Michael and Murtagh mac Browne of Oldcourt. (There was a Finnin mac Brown of the O Driscolls who went to Spain in 1602).

It is not to be assumed that all of these were landowners in the places named to identify them, but any who were would have forfeited their lands. In 1694 Dennis Driscoll of Ballynegornagh (Barleyhill, par. Ross) was successful in his claim for restoration (as was Michael Driscoll of Limerick in 1699) but the castle, town and lands of Ballymacrown belonging to Col. Cornelius were in 1703 sold to the Hollow Sword Blades Company.

Henceforth the O Driscolls were but tenants on their ancestral lands, however noble their lineage. Rickard O Donovan, writing at the time of the Famine, referred to the many members of the clan then striving to keep alive in the workhouses of Skibbereen and Schull. He mentioned one William O Driscoll (son of Denis O Driscoll of Greagh Court) then aged 84 and living in England ('in his youthful days a most magnificent specimen of the old Irish chieftain race') who claimed the title of 'O Driscoll' as a descendant of Col. Cornelius. Since his only son was unmarried, however, this branch appeared likely to become extinct, and the title would then devolve on cousins in Charleston, U.S.A., although, O Donovan adds, 'according to a wild tradition in the country, there are fishermen on Cape Clear and on other islands off the coast of Carbery, who are lineally descended from the youngest son of Sir Finghin, or Florence of 1602.'

Ó HÉIGEARTAIGH

(O) HEGARTY

Because of the existence of a well-known sept of Uí Éigeartaigh in Ulster (Donegal-Derry) it has often been assumed that a branch of this family at some period settled in Co. Cork. There is, for instance, an interesting traditional account of his ancestors given in an auto-biography *Is Uasal Ceird* by a west Cork teacher, Diarmaid Ó hÉigeartaigh (whose son, Diarmuid O Hegarty, was secretary of the first Dáil Éireann and later private secretary to W.T. Cosgrave). According to this version, the first of the family in west Cork was a soldier in Hugh O'Neill's army who, instead of returning to his native Ulster after the battle of Kinsale, settled in Carrigillihy in Myross parish where he was the first to use a horse-drawn plough. In Cromwell's era, two des-cendants, Tadhg and Domhnall Ó hÉigeartaigh, were farming in Cloghane in the parish of Caheragh, and from these he traced various branches in the parishes of Aghadown and Skibbereen as well as in the parish of Caheragh where his own family lived.

The early part of this account obviously belongs to the realm of folklore rather than of genealogy, though the mention of Carrigilihy may be of some significance, in view of the O Donovan connection which will be noticed further on. It is certain that the O Hegartys were well-established in Carbery long before the battle of Kinsale and they were probably of local stock, unconnected with the O Hegartys of Ulster. Écertach was a personal name used in Munster before the adoption of surnames, among both Eóganacht and Dál Cais. One branch of the Eóganacht — Clann Cerbaill — when its genealogy was being compiled in the early 11th century, had a chief named Écertach, whose son (Conall son of Écertach, royal heir of Cashel) was slain in battle in 1027 according to the *Annals of Inisfallen.* It is quite possible that the O Hegartys of west Cork are descended from this Écertach; Mac Fir Bhisigh in his *Book of Genealogies* states that both the Uí Éigeartaigh and the Uí Chearbhaill are descended from him.

As early as 1295 the surname appears in official records in Co. Cork when Gillyse O Hegerthy (*Giolla Íosa Ó hÉigeartaigh*) was pardoned for various misdemeanours committed in company with a miscellaneous group of Barretts, O Donovans, etc.

Almost two centuries later, in 1475, the name turns up at Kinsale, where Thadeu Ohegertha resided with his wife, Margaret Galway. In the following century, a Dermitius O Heagerty owed ten cow-hides to Richard Ronan of Kinsale, in 1579. Among the clergy we

186

find Donaldus O hegeritaide as vicar of Kilmaloda, near Timoleague, in 1484. (Later, in 1689, we find a Fr. Hegartie as chaplain of Clancarty's regiment in King James' army.)

Coming down to Elizabethan times, one Dermot roe O Hagirtie was pardoned in 1577 in company with a group from the Dunmanus-Kilcrohane area but a later pardon places him (if it be he) elsewhere. This pardon, dated 14th May 1601, is the only one to list a large group of the name in Co. Cork. It appears also that they were followers of O Donovan of Castle Donovan, chief of Clancahill. Dermod roe O Heagirtie, a name already mentioned, is given as of Castledonovan, but the chief member of the clan apparently was Dermod O Heagirtie alias Heagirtie of Girrane, which seems to be Garranes (north and south) in the parish of Drimoleague. Several others lived at Girrane — Donogh mac Donnell mac Reirie, Rorie mac Donell O Heagirtie, Moriertagh mac Donell mac Fynine, Conoghor mac Deirmodie gire O Heagirtie, Dermot duffe mac Sheanteige and Donell mac Teige gir O Heagirtie. Also in the parish (of Drimoleague) were Donell O Heagirtie of Deelish, Conoghor O Heagirtie of Loughcrot and Rickard mac Conoghor of Balliatrassie. Not far away were Conoghor oge O Heagirtie of Killicogh (Kilcoe) and Katherine ny Heagirtie of Glanycronie (*Gleann an Chroim*).

The evidence of the Fiants would lead one to believe that the O Hegartys were to be found only in the Drimoleague-Dunmanway area, but other sources show that this was not so. In 1602, for instance William O Hegerty, of Blarney, smith, paid a fine of 20s to have a pardon, on condition that William and his son Robert appeared within 20 days. Again, the census of 1659, while giving thirteen O Hegertie families to West Carbery, also mentions ten such families in Barrymore in east Cork.

In 1694 Teige Heagartie was one of the band of rapparees in the mountain fastnesses of west Cork for whose apprehension large rewards were offered by the lords justices. Others had, no doubt, joined the 'Wild Geese'. Don Guillermo Hegarty was a captain in the Spanish army in 1715. In the Irish Brigade in France there was a Lieut-Col. O Hegarty (of Lally's regiment) who was wounded both at Fontenoy and at Laffeldt while a Capt. Hagarty was also wounded at Fontenoy and another Capt. Hegarty killed at Laffeldt. A Lieut.-Commander Hegarty fought in the frigate *Le Tonnant* in the naval battle of Quiberon Bay, 1759. We cannot, of course, be certain that these were Co. Cork O Hegartys.

In the 18th century Pádraig Ó Héigeartaigh was one of the minor poets of Co. Cork while Maitias Ó Héagarta was a poet of local fame in the Killarney area. Several of the name were prominent in the independence movement of the present century, particularly the brothers Séan and P.S. O Hegarty of Cork city and Diarmuid O Hegarty of west Cork.

Ó HIARLAITHE

(O) HERLIHY

Though no genealogies of this family survive, or indeed any records of the name prior to those of the 15th century, there is no doubt but that Iarlaithe is as ancient a personal name as any in Ireland. The patron saint of Tuam in Co. Galway was named Iarlaithe ('Jarlath'). In the period when family names were beginning to come into use an Iarlaithe was chieftain of Uaithne, a tribal territory on the borders of Limerick and Tipperary. Perhaps the family originated here. It is recorded that the O Briens invaded Owney in 1313 and slew many of its inhabitants, and it may be that some members then fled to Desmond. Though the O Herlihys of the 16th century — and perhaps for long before that — had a close association with the church lands of Bally-vourney, there is no mention of them in the 14th century Pipe Roll of Cloyne.

Throughout the entire 15th century, however, clerics of the name were prominent in the dioceses of both Cloyne and Cork. The following were among those listed:

1417: Gillebert Ohiarlaythe, a canon of Cork — possibly the same man who died (prior to 1458) prebendary of Killaspugmullane (north-east of Cork city).

1427: Donald Ohyarlathy, a clerk of the diocese of Cloyne.

1445: Maurice O herlathy, clerk, rector of Ballynoe in the diocese of Cloyne.

1465: Donald O hiarlachaig, canon of Cork.

1471: Donatus (*Donnchadh*) and Nicolaus Ohyerlathy, priests of Cloyne diocese.

1479: Rinaldus Yherlathy, *de facto* vicar of Clondrohid.

1481: Maurice O hyerlaydh, prebendary of Inishkenny (Waterfall).

1484: William O hirlathi, canon of Cloyne.

1485: Johannes Ohyerlay, junior, appointed treasurer of Cork diocese in place of John Ohyerlahy the elder. Although not yet ordained he was given a canonry and the prebend of Desertmore, in order that he might engage in the study of letters.

1487: Donatus Oherley, canon of Cork.

1496: John Hyerlachy, dean of Cork.

In the early 16th century there was a noted Franciscan, Fr. David O Hierlaithy (d. 1544), who was twice provincial of his order. (It may perhaps, have been the same Fr. David who was credited with the rebuilding of Bantry friary in 1482.) Even after the Reformation, in 1591 David (Juvenis) O Hearley, who was a layman, held the vicarage of Ballyvourney until deprived of it for his 'manifest contumacy'.

But the most celebrated cleric to bear the family name was the saintly Thomas O Herlihy who was appointed bishop of Ross in 1561. He is said to have been born in Kilmacabea parish (Glandore-Leap area) though no doubt connected with the Ballyvourney O Herlihys. The Barberini acts state that he was a canon of Cork while the Corsini acts refer to him as *Thomas Hierllahius, de nobili genere ex utroque parente procreatus, vita et scientia idoneus*. Six months after his consecration Bishop O Herlihy was in attendance at the Council of Trent, one of only three Irish bishops who attended. On his return to Ireland he zealously promoted the decrees of the council until forced to take refuge on an island off the coast where he was arrested in 1571 by one of the O Sullivans and handed over to Sir John Perrott. He was confined in the Tower of London along with Primate Creagh but rejected all pressures to make him renounce his religion until eventually his release was secured by Cormac Mac Carthy, lord of Muskerry. Refusing to live in Cormac's castle he built himself a small hut in Muskerry — tradition says at Carraig an Easpaig in Sleveen near Macroom — where he continued to minister to the people until he died in 1579. His burial-place is in Kilcrea friary.

All of Muskerry was, of course, part of the Mac Carthy domain. An account of the lord of Muskerry's lands in 1600 lists 'O Herliey' as one of the 'countries in Muskrye' (those with ecclesiastical connections). The family group then held ten or eleven ploughlands. The head of the family, 'Daniell O Herlihie de Ballyworny, Gen.,' was in 1576 one of the jurors in an inquisition held after the death of Sir Donogh Mac Carthy Riabhach of Carbery. In a pardon granted to Cormac Mac Carthy of Blarney and his followers in 1573 we find the names of David óg, Connogher and Shane, yeomen, sons of Da (i.e. David) O Hierlyhy of Ballyvickydy (Ballymakeery). Others pardoned in the Elizabethan Fiants were:

1577: Thady mac Thomas O Hyerlyhy and John O Hyerlyhy of Ballyvourney, yeomen. Shane mac Donald Y Hierllithe of Ballyvourney, soldier. John O Herlehey ny baghley of Banduff (par. Clondrohid), yeoman.

1579: Donald O Hierlyhy of Ballyvourney, yeoman.

1585: Thomas mac Davy Y Herlihy of Ballyvourney, kern.

1601: William O Hierlihie of Ballyvourney, Shane mac Ranell I Hirleighey of Ballyvourney, John mac Donell I Yerleghy of Ballyvourney; Cnoghor O Hierlihie of Dunbeacon, husbandman; Cnoghor mac Hurly Hierlihie of Dundirig (Dundareirke); John O Hierlihie of Ballyowcane (? Ballyourane, par. Caheragh); Teige and Donogh mac Morrice O Hierlihy, Morrish fitz John O Hierlihie, Thomas and John mac Connoghor O Hierlihie, Thomas mac Teige O Hierlihie.

William oge mac William mac Teige O Hierlihy of Ballyvourney, head of the family, died in 1614. An inquisition (taken in 1625) into his lands found that he had owned Shanacloon, Gortnafunshion, Gortnatubbrid, Murnaghbeg, Derrylahan, Cappagh and other town-lands in the parish, but the heirs of Thadeus O Hierlihy claimed Cappagh and Currinclogh (? Coomaclohy). In 1608 he had granted lands to Daniel mac William O Hierlihy. This was presumably the Daniel O Hierlihie alias O Hierlihie of Ballyvourney, gent., who died on 2nd March 1637. He was described in his funeral entry as eldest son and heir of William, eldest son and heir of Daniel, eldest son and heir of William, descended (presumably on the maternal side) from the house of O Donoghow More of Onaght Idonoghow, Co. Kerry. He had been twice married (to Gyles, daughter of Art O Leary of Carrignaneelagh and to Síle, daughter of Maolmhuire O Mahony of Gurtinroe, Co. Kerry, gent.), and had twelve sons and twelve daughters. He was buried in the old church of Ballyvourney; the O Herlihy tomb was on the north side of the altar. His eldest son and heir, William, married Ellen, daughter of Callaghan Mac Carthy of Claraghbeg (par. Drishane), gent.

The Civil Survey makes it clear that in 1641 the heirs of Thadeus O Hierlihy (David mac Teige Hurlihy and Daniel oge Hierlihy) held Cappagh West only (Cappagh East was held by Thomas O Hierlihy). William, the chief of his sept, held Inshynogugalin (? Inchamore) where he lived, as well as Slievereagh (which had on it 'the foundation of the stump of a small castle' — perhaps the original family home — and a demolished mill), Shanacloon (mortgaged to Oliver Hierlihy), Killeen, Derreenaling, Coumaclovane, Fohiribany (Fuhiry), Derry-lahan, Gortyrahilly, Derrynasaggart, Gortnafunshion, Coolea, Gort-nascarty, Coolavokig, Murnaghbeg and Gortnatubbrid. This com-prised practically the whole of Ballyvourney parish, apart from a section in the east which belonged to the Mac Carthys.

As usual, the landowners of the sept incurred outlawry in 1643 — William and John O Hierlighy of Ballyvourney, gents, Thomas of Cappagh, gent, and Donnogh (? Daniel) oge, gent. So when the war had ended, over 12,000 plantation acres of O Herlihy lands in Bally-vourney lands were confiscated and set out under Cromwell to John Colthurst. Up to 1691 there remained a slight hope that the O Herlihys might recover their lands, a hope that was terminated by the Treaty of Limerick. A John Herrlohy of Tuogeage (?), Co. Cork, gent., was attainted as a Jacobite supporter in 1691 and Capt. Daniel O Herlihy served in Boisseleau's infantry in King James' army at the same period. Following the treaty the authorities in Dublin castle proscribed certain individuals in Cos. Cork and Kerry, threatening with imprisonment any who harboured them. Amongst the suspected harbourers were O Hierlihy of Ballyvourney, David Baccoh O Hierlihy and Daniel mac William Hierlihy.

Dáibhidh Bacach O Hiarlaithe was a well-known local poet at whose house in Ballyvourney the *cúirt éigse* used to assemble. But he appears to have been ousted from there and forced to remove to Glenflesk, an event deplored by a fellow-poet:

Is cás liom cill bhláfar na dtriatha suilt
Gan fáilte ruim tháintibh dá dtrialladh ann
Ó tiománadh ár n-ardflath fá iarthar cnoc
'Sé Dáth geal mac Pádraig Í Iarlaithe.

Dáibhidh had two sons who became priests – An t-Athair Uilliam and An t-Athair Pádraig – and both were poets as well. Quite a number of O Herlihys composed poems in Irish in the 18th century, several of them, no doubt, in the Ballyvourney area where O Herlihys must have remained on as tenants after the Cromwellian plantation though we have no evidence of this in the 1659 census from which returns for Muskerry are missing. The census, in fact, does not list O Herlihy as a principal Irish surname in any of the baronies of Co. Cork although there were twenty families of the name 'O Herlyhy and O Helyhy' in the barony of Connello, Co. Limerick.

An old man in Cork city in 1706 told Bishop Dive Downes that at one time he used to receive the bishop's rents for Bishops Boyle and Synge (who occupied the sees of Cork, Cloyne and Ross between 1660 and 1678) and that he received £7 per annum chiefry out of the 12 ploughlands of Ballyvourney from the Hierlighys during all that time.

John Richardson in *The Great Folly, Superstition and Idolatry of Pilgrimages in Ireland* (1727) wrote thus of the much-venerated oaken statue of St. Gobnait in Ballyvourney:

'The image is kept by one of the family of the O Herlihys, and when anyone is sick of the Small-Pox, they send for it and sacrifice a sheep to it, and wrap the skin about the sick person, and the family eat the sheep. But this hath now much lost its Reputation, because two of the O Herlihys died lately of the Small Pox.' The O Herlihys continued as guardians of the statue until 1843 when the hereditary representative on the female side, an O Brien of Dunmanway, fearing for the safety of the statue, handed it over to the parish priest of Ballyvourney where it is still resorted to for cures.

In the mid-19th century on the Colthurst estate (which was the old O Herlihy estate) there were five O Herlihy tenant-farmers while several others of the name lived in the parish, including the schoolmaster John O Herlihy who even before the founding of the National school system taught 68 scholars aided by a £20 subscription from Sir Nicholas Colthurst. Even today, Ballyvourney is still redolent of the family name. One of the traditional 'stations' in the round performed there is the 'Priest's Tomb' at the right corner of the east gable of the ruined church, the burial place of Fr. O Herlihy. The graveyard also contains one of the very few mid-19th century gravestones to bear an inscription in Irish, as follows:

> *Uam adhlaicthe Ui Iarfhlaithe*
> *taiseach tuatha Baile Mhuirne*
> *Or̃ f anm̃ na treibhe.*
> *Or̃ f anm̃ Seain mic Tadhg*
> *do ecc san mbl. 1864*

(The burial-place of O Herlihy, lay chief of Ballyvourney. Pray for the souls of the sept. Pray for the soul of Seán son of Tadhg who died in the year 1864.)

Ó HIONGARDAIL

Ó HÚRDAIL   HARRINGTON

For many centuries the name Harrington or Ó hIongardail has been associated with the baronies of Bear and Bantry. Yet the only family group of the name to receive mention in the genealogies belonged to the Fir Maighe Féne (Fermoy). The name Ingardal or Indardgal is itself a very rare one in the old genealogies. In the period to which *Críchad an Chaoilli* relates, the Uí Ingardail were no longer in the Fermoy area; the former *tuath* of Íbh Ingardail with its chief residence, Conbaidh (Conva, par. Ballyhooly) then formed half of the *tuath* of O Quain.

Perhaps by that time the Uí Ingardail had already migrated — either by choice or from necessity — into west Cork. The townland of Kippaghingerghill (? *Ceapach Uí Ingarghail*) in the parish of Kilmocomogue (Bantry) may have been an early settlement of theirs. There are no early records of the name; the first reference to it in west Cork occurs in 1518 when Donaldus Yhyngardeyll, parish priest of Kilmackillogue (Co. Kerry) became P.P. of Killcaslain and Kadmarra in the dioceses of Ross and Ardfert, — probably Kilcaskan and Kenmare.

Practically our only source for the history of this family is in the Elizabethan Fiants. The first pardon, in 1576, is to Dermod oge O Hingerdell and to Donoughe mac Dermod oge, Donald mac Dermod oge and Dermod oge bege. In the following year, among pardons granted to a group of west Cork chieftains (Mac Carthy, O Mahony, O Driscoll, O Donovan, etc.) we find Thady O Hingerdell, called O Hingerdell. He was chief of his name and obviously of some importance politically. A later pardon (1584) gives his place of residence — Teig O Hingerdell *alias* O Hungerdell of Bantry. His son, perhaps, was the John mac Teige O Hengerltye *alias* Harrengton of Downebechane, gent., who was pardoned in 1577. Dunbeacon was then the site of an O Mahony castle. This is the earliest evidence we have of the transposition of the family name to 'Harrington'. Apparently the name Ó hIongardail — it had not then been modified to the modern Ó hÚrdail — was found difficult to pronounce by English officials, and somebody must have suggested an English alternative. Harrington bears little resemblance to Ó hIongardail but the choice may have been influenced by the fact that Sir Henry Harrington was a leading figure in Elizabethan Ireland. (His son, James, was slain at the Yellow Ford in 1598.)

Others of the name pardoned in 1577 were Thady O Hingirdill of Cahermuckee (par. Kilmocomoge) and John O Hingerdell of Carre-

193

brie, gent. In 1585 pardons were issued to Shane O Hungerdill (in company with the O Sullivans), also to Donell and Teige mac Philip O Hungerdill, Philip mac Teige oge O Hungerdill and Teig mac Diermot mac Teig, all described as 'Sir Owen O Swylyvan's tenants'. In 1587 a pardon was granted to John O Hingerdell of Monaster de Beantry, gent., – perhaps the John mac Teige referred to above. The old friary of Bantry, founded by the O Sullivans, formerly stood in the Abbey graveyard, to the west of the town. In 1597 Nicholas Browne listed the followers of O Sullivan Bear as: Odonogan, Olnichehan, Olinigetdell, Olinche (Ó Donnagáin, Ó Loingseacháin, Ó hIongardail, Ó Loingsigh).

Further pardons were granted in the 1590s: Shane roe mac Conogher mac Philip I Hindergell of Bantry, Philip mac Conogher oge mac Conogher mac Rory I Hindergell, John mac Donell O Hengerdell of Bantry, John mac Teige oge O Hingerdle, John O Hengerdell, merchant.

But by far the largest number received their pardons on 9th May 1601, due to the government's pacification policy in the period which preceded the battle of Kinsale. Almost all were in the Bantry area. In Killaningi (prob. Kealanine, par. Kilmocomoge) were Deirmod mac Shane O Hingerdle, Teige Mergagh O Hingerdle and Shane mac Awlive O Hingerdle. Donell mac Teige mac Shean O Hingerdle was from the same area while Donogh O Hingurdle alias Duony was from Whiddy. A large group were followers of Owen O Sullivan of Carriganass: Deirmod ruo mac Connoghor O Hingerdle, Ellis ny Shane, his wife, John mac Donell O Hingerdle, Teige mac Philip O Hingerdle, Donell mac Teige O Hingerdle and More ny Deirmodie, his wife, Owen mac Teige O Hingerdle, Onora ny Donell, his wife, Teige merigegh mac Donell O Hingerdle, Dermod oge beg O Hingerdle, Gillichrist and John mac Deirmod oge O Hingerdle, Teige, Owen and Gillechrist mac Donogh O Hingerdle. At Rossmackowen on the Béarra peninsula there was another large group: Philip O Hingurdill, Donell O Hingurdill, Donogh O Hingurdle, Conoghor mac Teige stuogaghah, Donell mac Donogh O Hingurdle, Philip Vohny O Hingurdle, Donogh mac Philip, Shane mac Teige mac Deirmodie, Teige O Hingurdle, Connoghor mac Teige oge. In the same area were Reirie mac Connoghor O Hingirdle, Philip mac Conoghor O Hingerdle and John ruo mac Conoghor O Hingerdle.

This list shows that Tadhg was the most popular personal name, followed by John, Diarmaid, Domhnall and Philip – the last-mentioned possibly because of O Sullivan influence. The agnomen 'Vohny' is of particular interest since up to quite recently *Uaithne* (Green) was used as a family name in Béarra to the complete exclusion of Ó hÚrdail or Harrington. 'Cáiscí' is a similar name which has only recently been rendered into Harrington and may likewise date back several centuries. In 1694, Teige na Caska and Daniel na Caska of Coomhola, along with Daniel, John and John oge Harrington of Bearhaven, were suspected friends and harbourers of Tories.

One who did not seek a pardon was Donogh O Hinguerdel, a follower of Donal Cam O Sullivan Béarra. During the epic retreat of 1603 O Sullivan fought a major engagement against the Burkes at Aughrim, and here Donogh saved the life of Captain Maurice O Sullivan by cutting off Richard Burke's right hand with his sword.

Two of the 1601 pardons indicate an eastward trend — Shane mac Donnell y Ingerdell of Killmidie (Ballymartle) and John Hingardell of Ballyvoyrane (Ballyvorane, par. Nohoval). The Teig mac Donell (Merigagh) who was a follower of Owen O Sullivan in 1601 turns up some years later paying a levy on property in Kilmichael parish. In 1659 there were six Ungerdell families in the barony of Kinalmeaky — the only ones recorded in Co. Cork. Further east, there was a miller in Youghal in 1629 named John O Hungurdill and the name appears again there in 1642. A rebel Thomas O Hingerdell in March 1644 in company with Thomas Barry and Cosny mac Kegan gained possession of the castle and lands of Templeconnell (near Buttevant) by means of a ruse. Even in Co. Tipperary there was a William O Hingerdell of Ballydoyle in 1593. Pádraig Ó hIongurdail was a minor poet in the Whitechurch-Carraig na bhFear district around 1841.

But the majority of the Harringtons remained, and are still to be found, in their native Bear and Bantry. Tim Harrington (1851-1901), who was born in Castletownbere, was in his time the best-known of his name, being M.P. for Westmeath and later for Dublin, secretary of the Land League and Lord Mayor of Dublin. He and his brother Edward were among the small band of M.P.s who remained loyal to Parnell after the 'split'.

Ó HIONMHAINÉIN

Ó NÚNÁIN   Ó NUANÁIN   NOONAN   NUNAN

The only family of Uí Ionmhainéin mentioned in the genealogies were the descendants of Ionmhainén son of Faelchad who belonged to a segment of Dál Cais, according to *An Leabhar Muimhneach*. From the beginning the name became associated with a variety of ecclesiastical positions; the prebend of Inishcarra, for example, was held by Philip O Hynovan *circa* 1300. A more unusual post was held by the holy monk, Donnsléibhe Ó hInmainéin, who was chief master-carpenter of the monastery of Boyle until his death in 1230. Somewhat earlier, around 1100, another outstanding craftsman, Cúdulig U Inmainen, with the help of his sons, fashioned at Armagh the exquisite shrine of St. Patrick's bell, now one of the treasures of the National Museum. The *Book of Lismore* contains a poem by another of the name – Flaithbertach Ua Hinmhoinen.

But earlier still, in 1059, the *Annals of Inisfallen* record the death of Dúnadhach Ua hInmainéin, erenagh of Tulach Léis, and it is with Tullylease (near Freemount in north Cork) that this family name is inseparably linked for centuries afterwards. The ancient church of Tulach Léis and other ecclesiastical remains in the parish have always been associated with the Saxon saint, Berchert; in fact the district as a whole was often referred to as Tuath Saxan. It was in Berchert's church that the Uí Ionmhainéin held the position of *airchinnech*, an office which had become secularized by the 11th century so that the erenagh was often a hereditary lay abbot. Subsequently the family title was *comharba* (coarb or successor) and the O Noonans were regarded as hereditary wardens or protectors of the church.

In 1305, the *Annals of Inisfallen* inform us, Tairdelbach O Brien violated the sanctuary of Berchert (and died as a result) while Ó hInmainéin, a noble and pious coarb, was taken prisoner by the Uí Chuiléin and Uí Chlainne Inneirgi, and put to death. This may have been either Maurice Ohynnevan, senior, or Maurice, junior, both of whom were among the clergy of Cloyne diocese in 1301. The background to the killing may have been the claim that Tuath Saxan was part of the Uí Fidgeinte septlands rather than part of the surrounding territory of Múscraige Uí Dhonnocáin. The western section of Uí Fidgeinte were known as Uí Chonaill Gabhra whose ruling family at this time were the Uí Chuiléin. Later in the same year (1305) some of the O Donegans set out to avenge on the Uí Chonaill the death of their coarb but on their way Mílis Ó Donnocáin and his kinsman were slain by Sir Henry de la

Chapelle, a Norman knight. Strangely, too, in the very next year the church of Tulach Léis was burned by lightning!

The Norman presence obviously affected the O Noonans. Adam O hynevan was hanged in 1311 for being in rebellion with the Condons. Thirty years later, William Ouhynounan rose to be the king's surgeon, achieving fame as the man who cured Lionel, the third son of Edward III. Tullylease itself was, in the 14th century, held of the bishop of Cloyne's feudal manor of Kilmaclenine. In 1364, according to the Pipe Roll of Cloyne, Donald O Henwonhan acknowledged that he held of the lord the seven carucates of Tullylease by the service of two marks yearly. (He also admitted that he was obliged to do in all things as Maurice Chapel should do, and his tenants as the tenants of the said Maurice — who was, no doubt, of the same family as the above-mentioned Sir Henry.) Some years later Richard Ohenwonham was paying 6s 8d for one carucate in Tullaghles. Another of the name, Donatus Ohenwonham, was a tenant in the parish of Lackeen (near Liscarroll). Odo Ohenwonham was a monk in the Cistercian monastery of Fermoy in 1402.

Ó Huidhrín's topographical poem (*c.* 1400) contains a reference to:

Tuath Shaxan an oirir fhinn
as d'Ua Ionmhoinéin áirmhim.

(Tuath Shaxan of the fair territory I reckon as belonging to Ó hIonmhainéin.) This follows a verse which names the O Donegans as lords of all Múscraighe Trí Maighe. Incidentally, there was also a Múscraighe Uí Núnáin (written Muskreenowaine in the mid-17th century) which included the townlands of Gardenfield East, South and North in the parish of Drumcollogher, Co. Limerick. Another Irish poem, a mid-15th century eulogy on David Roche, extols the lord of Fermoy for an attack on the sept of Ionmhainén (*Fine Unmhaineáin*) whose king he held as a hostage.

In 1459 the perpetual vicarage of Tulachleys 'long void by the death of Philip Ohyminayn' was assigned to Thomas Ohyminayn, clerk, of the diocese of Cloyne. It would hardly have been practicable to appoint a member of any other family in view of the all-pervading O Noonan presence there. As Dr. O Brien, 18th century Catholic bishop of Cloyne, noted in his *Irish Dictionary* (1758): 'The O Nunans, an ancient stock, were hereditary Wardens or Protectors of St. Brendan's Church at Tullaleis in Co. Cork, and proprietors of all the lands of Tullaleis and Castle Lissen, under obligation of repairs and all other expenses attending the divine service of that church, to which these lands had originally been given as an allodial endowment by its founder.' Near the churchyard in former times stood a building known as the Comharbach, i.e. belonging to the Coarb.

Even at the time of the dissolution of the monasteries (1540) the rectory of Tullylease was said to be 'unlawfully detained by the Coorbe

of Tollelyche'. Around 1581 Dominus Corcalius Y Newnane was deprived of the vicarage of Kilshannig. Sir William Noynyn, priest, was one
of the witnesses of the will of Cormac mac Teig Mac Carthy of Blarney
in 1583, and was probably chaplain to the lord of Muskerry.

Also in 1583, a Fiant was issued granting a pardon to David mac
Edmund Yonnonan of Castleton. Two years later similar pardons were
granted to Donell mac Conoghor O Hynownayn and to William *bacach*
mac Dermody O Hinownan, both of Co. Cork. These pardons obviously
had a connection with the Desmond rebellion. But the chief of the
name, Donagh O Hynowan alias O Hynowan, then residing at Castleishen, went unpardoned. Castleishen or Castle Lishen, in Kilbolane
parish, seems to have long been an important family seat. (John Barry
of Leamlara is said to have married a daughter of O Nunane of Castle-
ishane in the early 15th century.) We learn of Donnchadh's attainder
in 1597 when a grant of his former estate was made to George Isham of
Brianstown, Co. Wexford. As well as the castle and lands of Castleishen
itself, the estate also included Cloonsillagh, Cloonee, Cooles, Curra,
Dromsharule and Gleatan (?) and Delliga (beg) — but not perhaps the
whole of these lands. When the estate was being re-granted in 1605 (to
Theobald Bourke, Baron of Castleconnell) only five or ten acres were
reckoned in each ploughland, making a total of ½ carucate. It had, no
doubt, been pointed out in the meantime that the chief of the name
was not the full legal owner of the sept lands. Another undertaker,
Robert Stroude, in 1593 received a grant of Muskereye Nownan, 4½
quarters of land in the parish of Ballicastilane (Co. Limerick), late the
lands of Donogho O Nownan, attainted.

More pardons followed in 1601 — Mullmorie fitz Morish I Nownane,
yeoman; Richard and Donell mac Shane O Hununane; David mac Morish
O Hononain, Edmund and Shyvery (*Séafraidh* or Geoffrey) O Hononane,
Dermod mac Gilly O Hononane, Dermod en Downey (?), Morrish
fitz William; Conoghor mac Donogh I Hononane of Kilbolane; David
mac Dermod, Morish mac Donogh and Dermod mac Teig O Honane,
all of Bowles; Donell O Hononane of Castell ni Lyshine (Castleishen),
Riccard, Teig mac Connor and Donogh mac Dermod O Hononane, of
same.

Little seems to have been recorded of the activities of the O Noonans
in the early 17th century. Whether or not they took part in the rebel-
lion of 1641, they certainly suffered the fate common to all Irish
Catholic landowners, namely, total confiscation of their lands. The O
Noonan landowners, all in Tullylease parish, were as follows: Teig O
Hunan, Dermot mac David Hunan, Morris mac Richard Hunan, Dermot
oge O Hunan, Donogh mac Dermot O Hunan and Teige mac Patrick O
Hunan, all described as Irish papists. The lands they forfeited comprised:
Pollere, named as part of Tullylease (? Poulavare), Dromanig, Cloon-
gown, Raheen and Cahernagh, a total of 2,218 acres. The spoils were
parcelled out among Lord Kingston, Sir George Hamilton, Col. John

Hamilton and Lewis Craig.

Presumably, the plantation did not entirely wipe out the O Noonans in Tullylease but we have no 1659 census returns for Duhallow. We do know that there were then twelve families of the name in the barony of Connello, Co. Limerick (probably around Drumcollogher) and a further six in the barony of Coshmore and Coshbride, Co. Waterford. In the census the name is spelt O Nonane and Nunane, showing that by the mid-17th century the shortened version of the surname had been fully accepted – no doubt as a parallel to the development of the word *ionmhain > ionúin.*

One who succeeded in his claim for restoration in 1699 (after the Williamite wars) was Edmond Nownane of Ballylagh (? Ballagh, par. Tullylease). Maurice Nunan of Curra (par. Kilbolane) sold lands at Curra and at East Knockaneglass (par. Tullylease) to Denis Nunan of Keeltane (par. Tullylease) in 1783. Others of the name were scattered throughout Cos. Cork and Limerick. There was a Denis Noonane at Ballynoe in 1721, and 18th century Noonan headstones may be seen in the graveyards of Kilcully and Carrigaline, north and south of Cork city.

Nevertheless, in the middle of the 19th century the Noonans were still numerically strong in the vicinity of Tullylease, and retained their right of burial in the chancel of the ruined church. One of them still prided himself on inheriting the guardianship of the edifice. There is a tomb in the middle of the choir erected to commemorate Philip O Nunan who died on the 30th April, 1752, aged 90 years. He must have been born just after the assignment of the family patrimony to strangers. His sons' names were Denis and David. A nearby headstone was erected by Edmond Nunan of Clounrus (? Cloonroosk) in memory of his father, Francis Nunan (d. 1843) 'of the Bolough (? Ballagh) family the Rickards and Neds'. Further memorials – to Bartholomew Noonan (1820) and to Cornelius Nownan of Castleishen (1780) – may be seen within the ruined church in the old graveyard of Dromcollogher.

KINGSTON

CINNSEAMÁN

This surname at the time of its first appearance in Ireland in the 13th century was written 'de Kyngeston', indicating that it derived from a place called Kingston, but as there were many such places in England the name may well have had several distinct points of origin.

We have a record of one Thomas de Kingesdon in Ireland as early as 1277 and of a Richard de Kyngeston in Dublin twenty years later. At the beginning of the 14th century frequent mention is made of William de Kyngestoun in Co. Meath while the first of the name recorded in Co. Cork was John Kingstoun who was appointed chaplain of Holy Trinity (Christ Church) in Cork in 1381. The name came into prominence in the city again in 1785 when the mayor of Cork was James Kingston.

But today Kingston is generally, and correctly, regarded as a west Cork family name, and we can trace its origin there to the aftermath of the Cromwellian plantations in the mid-17th century — though there was a Richard Kingston in Bandon in 1619. The only one of the name to acquire confiscated lands in west Cork was Samuel Kingston who in company with James Draper got 118 plantation acres of Skeaf East in the parish of Kilmaloda, near Timoleague. This townland which had a total of 215 plantation acres (371 acres today) was, prior to 1641, the property of Tadhg óg O Crowley.

We know that the new owners settled there because the 1659 census listed as 'tituladoes' in East Skeaf the following: James Draper, Joseph, his son; Samuell Kinstone, John Kinstone, his son. The census also recorded that in the townland as a whole there were six English and nine Irish. A marriage between John Kingston (son of Samuel) and Joane Dobson took place in 1666. (Between then and 1750 twenty-four Kingston marriages were recorded in the diocese of Cork and Ross.) A latter-day descendant, Dr. Richard Kingston, in a recent article in the *Journal of the Cork Historical and Archaeological Society* has traced many modern branches of the family back to Samuel Kingston of Skeaf who must have lived to a ripe old age since his will was not registered until 1703. A few miles to the north-west, in the townland of Cashel Beg (par. Desertserges), lived Paul Kingston whose will was registered in 1683.

A short account of the Kingston family in west Cork was published in a Cork diocesan magazine in 1893 and republished in Armagh in 1929. It is mainly derived from the oral narrative of Paul Kingston of

Lissangle as recorded by Rev. J.S. Reeves, rector of Caheragh from 1853 to 1890. According to this source, the first of the family in Ireland was a Colonel James Kingston from the west of England who accompanied William of Orange to Ireland in 1690 as colonel of horse, as did his two sons, James and Paul, who were captains of foot. Although this information conflicts with the evidence from official sources as to the first bearers of the name in west Cork, the account is, nevertheless, worth quoting as an authentic family tradition, much of which is undoubtedly based on fact: 'Besides Colonel Kingston, King William had two other Colonels — namely, Stawell and Honor. With these he fought the famous battle of the Boyne, in which Colonel Kingston saved King William's life by giving him his horse when his own refused to take the water.

'After the battle was over and peace restored, King William gave his Colonels and Captains land for their service both at the Battles of Boyne and Aughrim. About which time, a little after the battle of Aughrim, one of Colonel Kingston's sons, Paul, died of fever in the camp at Dundalk, so that all the land of the three Kingstons — that is, of the father and two sons — came to Captain James Kingston. Captain James Kingston had several sons and four daughters. The person who tells this only remembers the names of three of them. One lived in Ballycotton House; another, George, lived in Barleyfield; another, Sam, lived in Skave. The latter married first a Miss Cooke, and then a Miss Blood. (Ballycotton is Ballycatteen, par. Rathclarin; Skave is Skeaf, already mentioned. There is, in fact, a record of a marriage between Samuel Kingston and Alice Blewytt in 1712.) Jerry Kingston was the youngest and his own (i.e. Paul Kingston's) great-grandfather. His four daughters married — one a Mr. Laughton, another a Mr. Maylor, another a Mr. Elbery and another a Mr. West Allen. Jerry Kingston, the great-grandfather of Mr. Paul Kingston, who relates this, settled in a farm in the parish of Kilnagross, which he rented from one of the Stawels, who was then a great friend of his, on account of the two families coming over at the same time. This was in the year 1715, the year of the great snow. His son Paul and grandson Sam lived and died there and there he himself was born.'

Gradually the Kingstons began to establish themselves throughout many of the parishes of west Cork. James Kingston of Rathclarin parish had a will registered in 1729. We find Thomas Kingston in Lislee (will, 1773) and William Kingston of Knockeenbwee in Drimoleague parish (will, 1778). It was in this latter parish that the family name proliferated to the greatest extent. The family narrative already referred to claimed that at one period of the 19th century the sixty children on the roll of Meenies N.S. in Drimoleague parish — and their schoolmaster — were all surnamed Kingston, and even if the claim is over-stated, it is not too much of an exaggeration. So prevalent had the name become in the parish that it was found necessary to affix such titles as 'Richard

Sally Sam' and 'Richard Mary Sam' to distinguish various members, using the personal names of the parents and grandparents after the Irish fashion.

The Irish form *Cinnseamán* was, according to Fr. Woulfe, sometimes used for Kingston. There are no townland-names derived from it; Kingston's-fields in the parish of Litter near Fermoy obviously takes its name from the Earls of Kingston (of Mitchelstown) whose family name was King. Neither is there any connection with the Kingstones of Mosstown (near Kenagh, Co. Longford) whose original name, *Mac Clochaire* or Cloughrey, was construed as *Cloch Rí*, 'King's stone'!

Being of solid yeoman stock and concentrating almost entirely on farming, the Kingstons found no difficulty in living in accord with their Catholic neighbours, and never lost their original attachment to the land. In 1875, of 33 prominent Kingstons listed in Co. Cork by Guy's *Directory*, no less than 19 were given as 'landholders'.

Ó LAOCHDHA

LEAHY

There are no genealogies or references in the annals to help us trace the origin of this family. The personal name Láegda (heroic) appears only in the genealogy of the Uaithne, a non-Goidelic tribe who in historic times were located in the north-east of Co. Limerick (Owneybeg) and the adjoining part of Tipperary (Owney and Arra). From there Uí Laochdha may have been dispersed in a southward direction; the only 13th century reference to one of the name was in 1295 when suit of peace was pardoned to Hugh Olyethe for all trespasses. This happened in Co. Waterford, and later sources indicate that the surname was indigenous to east rather than to west Cork, even though the only townland in the county which appears to embody the name is Gortyleahy (? *Gort Uí Laochdha*) in the parish of Macroom. Fr. Thomas Oleghe was a cleric of the Cloyne diocese in 1420.

The Elizabethan Fiants show that there were O Leahys scattered throughout the eastern half of the county in the late 16th century. In 1573 a pardon was granted to Donill O Leighy of Cregg (the site of a Roche castle on the Blackwater) and another to Teige O Leaghie of Cregg in 1602. Thady or Teige bane mac Thomas I Laghkey, a follower of John Barry of Castlelyons, got his pardon in 1577; there was a David mac Shane Lehe in Lord Barry's garrison at Annagh in 1598 while his brother William was in the garrison at Barryscourt. In 1585 William mac Donagh Y Leighie of Leitrim (in Condon's country) was pardoned and in the following year Donell O Leaghe, a husbandman of Ballygilleghcane – possibly Ballygrillihan in Castletownroche parish. In 1601 pardons were issued to Ririe O Leaghie of Ballinedirrie (? Ballinterry, par. Gortroe) and to Dermod O Leaghie of Garranejames (par. Mogeely). The name was also to be found in Youghal town, as for instance, William Leaghie, tailor, in 1615 and David Lehie, husbandman, in 1639.

The Lee valley, too, sheltered several O Leahys, among whom were Dermod mac Donogh Ileaghe of Coolacullig (par. Magourney), Dermod oge O Leaghie of Murragh, Teig O Leaghie of Knockowrane (Mountmusic, par. Kilmichael) and Shane mac Dermod O Leahy of Castleinch, all of whom were pardoned in 1601.

Generally speaking, the O Leahys of that era appear to have been of farming stock, and a particularly prosperous group settled in the Carrigaline-Ballygarvan-Tracton area to the south of Cork city, where they may have originally come as followers of the Mac Carthys of

Ballea. In 1584 a pardon was granted to Teige O Lyegh of Tracton Abbey and at the time of the Cromwellian confiscations we find John and Helena O Leah listed as forfeiting proprietors in Kinalea. In April 1657 an inquisition was held before John Hodder into lands held by John Leaghie of Robertstown and Ballinluig (pars. Carrigaline and Ballyfeard). He was found to be an Irish papist who went into rebellion and his lands accordingly became the property of his Highness, Oliver (Cromwell), Lord Protector of the Commonwealth, who bestowed them on Alexander Codner, 'a souldier'. But the Book of Survey and Distribution shows that the 196 acres of John O Leigh at Robertstowne eventually came into the possession of Lord Shannon.

Conogher fitz (or mac) David O Leighye was pardoned twice – at Kilnahone, near Ballygarvan, in 1575, and at nearby Killanully ten years later.

In Kilmoney the first to be mentioned was John oge O Leighie in 1585. He – or possibly his son – was pardoned three times in 1601-2, being described variously as John oge O Leaghy, John oge mac John O Leaghie and John oge O Leaghy, junior, gent. John oge's will was registered in 1627; other 17th century wills were those of Donogh O Lehie (1631), John mac Dermod O Lehie (1639), David Leaghie of Corke (1642), and John Leahy of Currabeg (1681). Besides John oge, other Leahys in Kilmoney in 1601-2 were Owen O Leaghie, Donogh O Leaghie, Teige O Leaghy and Guilleashias O Leaghie.

This last name (*Giolla Íosa*) in the shortened form of 'Gully' re-appears several times in the 17th century. Gully O Leachy paid a levy on his lands in Cork in the early years of the century. In 1609 these lands were at Ballinvrinsig in Inishkenny parish – a little to the south of the viaduct on the main Cork to Bandon road. In that year he was one of the freeholders brought within the new boundary of the 'County of the City of Cork'. Around the same time (according to an inquisition taken in 1630) John O Leyhye, gent., held for a time a mortgage on some of the Cogan lands in Ballinaboy parish – Liskillea, Knocknalyre and Ballintannig – for which he paid an annual rent. He was succeeded by Gilly O Leighye, gent., who let the lands to another branch of the Cogans. In 1610 Richard Barrett mortgaged Ballyshoneen (par. Inish-carra) to Oliver Terry of Cork and Gallye O Leighie of Ballinvrinsig, gent. As a Catholic landowner, Gully's lands were liable to forfeiture after the 1641 rebellion. His 355 acres in Ballinvrinsig and in nearby Kilmurriheen went to William Finch and others.

In the North Liberties of Cork city at the time of the Civil Survey, Daniel O Leaghy (with Daniel O Cromyne) had one ploughland at Bayanvarrig (probably Ballinvarrig, par. Whitechurch), while Dermod O Leaghly had half a ploughland at Boolybeg in the same parish. The census of 1659 shows that there were 15 Leehy and O Leaghy families in Cork city and liberties at that period; there were eight in Kinalea, seven in Kerrycurrihy and thirty in Barrymore – a distribution similar to that of the time of the Fiants. There were also nine families of the name in Magunihy, Co. Kerry. Only one is recorded as having gone overseas — Thomas Leaghio, lieutenant in Captain William Hurley's company in the Spanish army in Flanders. He got leave to return to Ireland in 1660 after his company had been disbanded but appears again in the Spanish Netherlands in 1663 as Don Tomas Olechie. Some of the name were merchants in the city of Cork in the late 18th century, and in the early 19th a prosperous branch resided in Shanakiel House. David Leahy (d. 1820) and his son Daniel (d. 1855) were of this family and acted as land agents for the Earl of Cork.

Seadhan Ó Laochadh compiled and transcribed an Irish prayer book in the mid-18th century while the name of Uilliam Ó Laochadh, an Irish scribe and translator, is found in a Co. Cork manuscript of the early 19th century.

Leahy gravestones from the 18th century onwards are most numerous in east Cork, with eleven in Midleton (old graveyard), eight in Churchtown North, five in Gortroe and four in Kilcredan.

Ó LAOGHAIRE

Ó LAOIRE   (O) LEARY

Cois abhann Ghleanna an Chéime
In Uíbh Laoghaire 'sea bhímse.

So sang the poetess of the O Learys, Máire Bhuí Ní Laoghaire, after the 'Battle of Céim an Fhia' in 1822. To her, as to many generations before and after, Uíbh Laoghaire meant the parish of Inchigeelagh, for long the patrimony of the O Learys. It was not, however, the original habitat of either of the Uí Laoghaire septs in Co. Cork. In the Fermoy area, Uí Laoghaire were chieftains of Hi Bece Abha (in the Awbeg river-basin) and their chief stronghold was Dún Cruadha, now Castletownroche. After their displacement by the Cambro-Normans, the sept is not heard of again, though members of it may have given their name to Ballyleary (*Baile Uí Laoghaire*) in Carrigtwohill parish and to another Ballyleary on the Great Island.

The genealogists derive the O Learys of Uíbh Laoghaire from the Corca Laoighdhe of west Cork (see Ó HEIDIRSCEOIL), giving them a common ancestor with the O Driscolls, i.e. Maicnia, sixth in descent from whom they put Laoghaire, whence Ó Laoghaire. These Uí Laoghaire were chieftains of Tuath Ruis or Tuath in Dolaich, a stretch of coastal territory on the peninsula between Rosscarbery and Glandore, from which they were known as Uí Laoghaire Ruis Ó gCairbre. An early 13th century document mentions Doleht Ilecheri (*Dolach Uí Laegairi*) as territory granted by Henry Pincerna to David de Barry. Perhaps the townland-names Derryleary (*Doire Uí Laoghaire*) and Scrahanyleary (*Screathan Uí Laoghaire*) in Schull parish derive from their west Cork sojourn. There was a John Olaegere, rector of Kilmoe (Goleen), who was made Chancellor of Ross in 1448, while Matheus Olaure was chancellor in 1485. Dermitius Olaegary vacated the parish of Brinny (near Bandon) in 1499.

Unfortunately, apart from their genealogy, we have no other records of the O Learys prior to the 16th century. The Irish annals and official records are alike silent as to their activities, so we do not know exactly when they forsook the rocks of Carbery for the mountainy fastnesses of Iveleary. John O Donovan believed that it happened about the time of the Norman invasion, and this belief is strengthened by a statement in the *Calendar of State Papers* (1589) to the effect that the O Learys were freeholders and 'older in the country' (i.e. in Muskerry) than the Mac Carthys themselves.

The extensive parish of Inchigeelagh, comprising 118 townlands (45,415 statute acres), is now in the barony of Muskerry (West) with the exception of a small portion in the south which is part of Carbery and does not concern the O Learys. After Diarmaid Mór Mac Carthy became lord of Muskerry in 1353, the Mac Carthys demanded 'chief rents' from the smaller clans who were followers of theirs or who had been there previously. Only the O Learys and O Mahonys claimed to be freeholders in Muskerry. However, the lord of Muskerry exacted a yearly rent of 24 beeves and £7 2s 3d sterling out of 19 ploughlands in Iveleary, and his *tánaiste* or 'crown prince' had, by Irish custom, the right to 'refection' in Iveleary for two days and nights four times a year. When, in 1578, Cormac mac Taidhg Mac Carthy got an official grant of practically the whole of Muskerry, it was disregarded by the O Learys, who continued to regard themselves as freeholders.

In Elizabethan times, when we begin to get records of the O Learys, the chief was Art Ó Laoghaire, whose genealogy is traced back through about 25 generations to the original Laoghaire. Art resided at Carrignaneelagh castle — Carraig na nGeimhleach, a name obviously associated with Inse Geimhleach. This castle has long since been demolished, but on the Ordnance Map its site is marked near Kilbarry House. 'Arthur O Leary of Carignygyelagh, Co. Cork, gent.,' received a pardon in 1573 after the first Desmond rebellion and was similarly pardoned in 1584, 1585 and 1587. In 1585 he was described as 'Art O Lerie alias O Lery of Yvelerie, gent.'. He died in 1597 leaving at least two sons (Tadhg and Domhnall) to succeed him.

A second O Leary castle was at Carrignacurra, near Inchigeelagh. The ruins of this castle still stand on a rock overlooking the river Lee. It is also known as Castle Masters, from a modern proprietor. In 1584 a pardon was granted to Dermod oge O Lery of Karignekorie, gent., and to Teig mac Dermod Y Lery of same, gent. An inquisition held at Shandon castle in Cork in 1588 found that Diarmaid Óg, (among others) had been involved in the Earl of Desmond's rebellion. Presumably the pardon received in 1584 saved his lands from confiscation for we know that his son Tadhg (Meirgeach) O Leary of Carrignacurra castle died in 1615 leaving Conchobhar (Meirgeach) as son and heir. Also pardoned at Carrignacurra in 1601 were Arte Mac Dermody O Leary, gent. and Firganenem (*Fear gan ainm*) O Leary.

Dromcarra castle, somewhat further east, was a third O Leary castle. Although it lay in ruins after the 1641-52 wars, the castle remained standing until 1968 when it was pulled down because of its unsafe condition. The first owner we can trace is Donnchadh O Leary who died in 1637 and was buried in the parish church of Inchigeelagh. He was married to Ellice Crowley of Toom (par. Fanlobbus) and his son and heir was Amhlaoibh, who was married first to Ellen O Leyne of Jordanstown and secondly to Shily O Donoghue of the Glens. A second son, Conoghor, married Onora, daughter of Art O Leary of Gortatanavally.

As mentioned earlier, Art of Carrignaneelagh was chief in the 1580s but before his death in 1597 he may have become incapacitated. Around the year 1592 (according to an inquisition taken in 1604) an assembly of the chief men of Muskerry elected Amhlaoibh O Leary of Mannen as chieftain of Iveleary and he was given the white rod of office by Cormac Mac Dermod, lord of Muskerry. He was probably the Owlise rwo mac Conoghor O Lery of Carrignaneelagh who was pardoned along with Art in 1584 and was, in all probability, a brother of Art. Mannen seems to be Magninenagh (also spelt Maginenagh, Maughinmugh, Maghinniaghs) held by Connor mac Auliff O Leary in 1641, an obsolete townland between Garryantornora and Tooreenalour on the northern slopes of Shehy Mountain.

Amhlaoibh proved to be a fiery leader, and joined O Neill's rebellion at its inception, taking the field with William Bourke and others. In 1600 he led his followers on a *creach* or cattle-raid on the lands of Donnchadh Maol Mac Carthy of Phale near Ballineen (much to the delight of the English, since both were supporters of O Neill). The Mac Carthys followed the raiders and recaptured their cattle. The O Learys in turn pursued the others and overtook them at Ahakeera in the parish of Fanlobbus where a pitched battle took place. Though Mac Carthy's brother, Fínghin, was dangerously wounded, the O Learys seem to have come off worse, losing, it is said, 'O Leary, the head of the sept and ten others the chief of his family'.

His son, Donnchadh, must have taken Amhlaoibh's place, since in 1601 a pardon was granted to 'Donnogh O Lerie alias O Leyerie, of Manen'. Another pardoned was Teig mac Awliffe O Lerie of Mannan, while in the following year Donnogh Ingearhie (*Donnchadh an Ghaorthaidh*) O Leary of Maninge was pardoned.

After the battle of Kinsale, Maghan mac Donogh O Lery, a follower of Barry Oge, was one of those who sailed for Spain with Don Juan d'Aguila in March 1602. In October of that year, one of the conditions of Cormac mac Dermod Mac Carthy's pardon was 'that you have brought in the O Learies and other loose and suspected people, inhabitants of Muscry, and put in assurance for their subjection to her Majesty'.

As was to be expected, the chiefs of the O Learys were attainted for their part in O Neill's rebellion, and an attempt was made to confiscate their lands. A list of crown lands drawn up in 1606-7 includes 'Maymen in Muskerry, late possession of Awliffe O Flerry (*sic*), chief of his sept, attainted'. Also listed were the lands of Carrignaneelagh of Teige mac Arte O Learie, attainted; Carrignacurra, of Teige Merrigough O Learie, attainted; and Carrickleevan (?) of Donell mac Dermott O Learye, attainted. The lands of Iveleary, including Maninge, Carrignacurra and Carrignaneelagh, 'parcel of the estate of Dermot oge O Learie, attainted, and of Awliffe, Conogher, Teige, Donell and Teige mac Art O Learie, slain in rebellion', were later conveyed by King James I to Francis Gofton who enfeoffed Richard Boyle, the notorious landshark. Boyle in turn enfeoffed Donoghe and Cnoghor O Leary by way of mortgage. Boyle was also involved in the lands of Teige O Leary of Carrignacurra and Dermod mac Teige mac Fynin O Leary of Coornahahilly. We know too that Sir James Craig got a royal grant of a fair at Dromcarra with licence to create a manor out of the lands of Iveleary, on 20th March, 1622.

These legal dealings failed to dislodge the O Learys from their patrimony. Iveleary remained remote and inaccessible to the servants of the crown until the time of the Cromwellian confiscations. We are fortunate in having (in the Civil Survey of Muskerry) a full list of the 35 or so O Leary proprietors of Inchigeelagh parish in 1641. All are described as 'Irish papists' and at the time of the Civil Survey (1654-5) most of them were already deceased. The following is a list of those proprietors, with the townlands they occupied (in modern spelling when identifiable):

Daniel mac Arthur O Leary, als. O Leary of Carrignaneelagh (Gortsmoorane, Kilbarry, Coolnacranagh, Rossmore, Cloonshear West, Derrineanig, Carrigleigh, Currahy West, Kilmore, Gortnamona, Derreenlunnig, Illauninagh West and Carrignamuck). (It will be noticed that the chieftaincy had reverted to the Carrignaneelagh branch; Daniel was probably son of the Art who was chief before 1592.)

Cnogher Merigah O Leary of Carrignacurra (+ Inchigrady, Cloghbarra, Cloughboola, Tooreenalour and Farranmaryne).

Auliff mac Donough O Leary of Dromcarra (South Dromcarra – 'on the premises is a demolished castle' – North Dromcarra, Inchineill, Cleanrath, Currahy East, Dromanallig and Dirineveigh).

Arthur O Leary of Teergay (+ Cornery).

Cnogher mac Aulif O Leary of Gorteenakilla (+ Millinavarodig (? Milleen), Cloonshear West, Diryargid, Inchibeg and Inchimore).

Teige mac Donnell O Leary of Turnaspidogy (+ Glassynamolgum (? Glasheen)).

Lisagh O Leary – (Inchinaneave and Gortnaclodige (? Derreenclodig)).

Donough mac Auliff O Leary of Cloonshear East.

Ferdinand O Leary of Rathgaskig.

Conor mac Donough O Leary of Graigue East (+ Gortinorogy and Dirineknockroe, Carlecask, Illauninagh East, the two Kealvaughs, Cooragreenane West and Derrygortnacloghy).

Teige mac Dermot O Leary of Derryvane.

Dermot O Leary of Tooreenlahard.

Finnin mac Dermot O Leary of Derreennacusha (+ Coomroe).

Donogh mac Conor O Leary of Garrynapeaka.

Conor mac Dermot O Leary of Inchircoongwogane. (This obsolete townland, also spelt 'Inchirninggwogane', 'Inchyrwoangogan', which seems to have 'Gougane' as its last part, is now part of Derreennacusha.)

Dermod oge O Leary of Dromcotty (+ Derreenglass).

Teige mac Dermot O Leary of Coornahahilly (+ Derreendonee). (According to the Book of Survey and Distribution he held Derreendonee, Inchibeg, Inchimore and 'Cooganborrogh' *i.e.* Guagán Barra.)

Finine mac Donell O Leary of Gortaneadin (+ Tooreennanean).

Donogh mac Auliff O Leary of Tooreenduff.

Laurence O Leary of Inchinossig.

Teige mac Dermot Roe O Leary of Glassynabulgum (Bargarriff and Dooneens).

Conor mac Arthur O Leary of Gorteenadrolane (+ Derryleigh, Gortatanavally, and Dirineveluesty).

Dermod mac Finnin O Leary of Gortnalour (+ Derryriordane South).

Donogh mac Dermott O Leary of Monvaddra (+ Derryriordane North).

Dermod oge O Leary of Teeranassig (+ Derryvacorneen).

Cnogher O Connell of Garryantornora. (*B.S.D.* informs us that Cnogher held Garryantornora and Cornery jointly with Art mac Cnogher O Leary, whose brother-in-law he may have been.)

Connor mac Auliff O Leary of Gorteenakilla (Maughinmugh).

Daniel mac Teige mac Dermott 'Boyder' (or 'Buy') of Gortnarea.

Cnoghor mac Dermott mac Cnoghor O Leary of Cooragreenane.

Finine mac Teige O Leary of Monvaddra.

Donogh mac Connor oge O Leary of Kealeriheene.

Dermod mac Connor O Leary of Coolroe.

Finine and Daniel mac Teige O Leary of Ratheahiff.

Daniel mac Donogh O Leary *als.* Dulagh of Gortnalour North.

Donogh mac Shane O Leary of Cappanclare.

Reading between the cold lines of official statistics, we catch here a glimpse of what must have been one of the most tightly-knit and deeply-rooted of the old Gaelic clans to have survived into the mid-17th century. These 35 were, of course, the landowning aristocracy and no doubt there were many O Leary families of tradesmen and workmen as well. Their most favoured Christian names were Conchobhar, Diarmaid, Donnchadh, Tadhg, Fínghin, Domhnall, Amhlaoibh and Art, in that order. It is remarkable that only once do we find a name of Norman origin (Seán). 'Lisagh' and 'Laurence' are probably both anglicizations of Laoiseach, while Ferdinand probably stands for 'Fear' or 'Fear gan ainm', another unusual O Leary name. Both names are to be found in *Caoineadh Airt Uí Laoghaire* where Eibhlín Dubh addresses her late husband as *A Airt Uí Laoghaire mhic Conchobhair mhic Céadaigh mhic Laoisigh Uí Laoghaire aniar ón nGaortha* (the last-named being perhaps the Lisagh O Leary of Inchinaneave listed above) while her baby son was *Fear Ó Laoghaire*.

Sixteen of the O Learys including Art of Carrignaneelagh (probably son and heir of Domhnall) were outlawed in 1643 for their part in the 1641 rebellion, and the whole lot became 'Forfeiting Proprietors' after

Cromwell's victory. All the lands of Iveleary were confiscated under the Act of Settlement but after the Restoration passed into the possession of the Earl of Clancarty because of his claim to the overlordship of all Muskerry. An unusually large number of O Learys were, however, granted leases by the Earl. Daniel O Leary, als. O Leary (perhaps son of Daniel mac Arthur of 1641) obtained a 99-year lease of Gortsmoorane, Kilbarry, etc., in 1677 but his lease was disallowed at Chichester House in 1700. Kedagh O Leary (perhaps the Céadach son of Laoiseach and grandfather of Art Ó Laoghaire mentioned above) in 1688 held over 5,000 acres on 99-year leases, plus another 1,000 acres for which no tenure was specified. Helen O Leary had about 3,000 acres while Arthur, Daniel mac Teige, Katherine, Teige, Cornelius mac Auliffe and Dermod mac Daniel held about 2,600 acres between them. Some must have been transplanted to Co. Clare, as in 1659 we find Daniell O Leary, gent., and Dermott mac Daniell as 'tituladoes' in BallyMcDonellane while Teige Leary, gent. was in the townland of Killclogher in that county. Daniell Leary was a 'titulado' in Dromdisart, Co. Kerry, and there were seven families of the name in the barony of Trughanacmy in that county. The only 'tituladoes' in Co. Cork (Muskerry not being found in the census) were Teige O Leary and Dermod his son in Reenydonagan near Bantry. Perhaps it was from this branch that the townland of Cooryleary (*Cuar Uí Laoghaire*) took its name. There was a Humphrey (Amhlaoibh) Leary of Dromclogh whose will was proved in 1764; all three townlands are in Kilmocomoge parish. In 1659 also O Leary families were plentiful in Cork city and liberties (15), Kinalmeaky (21), Ibane and Barryroe (8), Kilbrittain (14), East Carbery (42) and West Carbery (11). These latter may largely have been descended from O Learys who never migrated from their Corca Laoighdhe homeland.

The Williamite wars and the subsequent confiscation of the Earl of Clancarty's estates scattered the O Learys still further. As one might expect, they were fervent Jacobite supporters. Arthur mac Daniel Leary of Drishane, gent., (who was either brother or son to The O Leary of Gortsmoorane) and Daniel Leary of Aghane, Co. Cork, were outlawed on this account in 1690. In the same year King James II's retinue in Ireland included Major-General Leary, one of the many O Leary officers in the Jacobite army. Kedagh Leary — perhaps the Céadach previously mentioned — was a lieutenant in Sir John Fitzgerald's Regiment of Infantry. In 1699, as Capt. Keadagh Leary of Carrignacurra, he was successful in his claim for restoration. About five years previous to this there were seventeen O Learys residing in Gougane Barra and Iveleary who were suspected friends, relations and harbourers of tories. Some bore nicknames — 'Mughory', 'na Ganny', 'Meriga'. A robbery warrant was executed against one Keadagh Leary in 1712. A lament on the death of Céadach Meirgeach Ó Laoghaire was composed by Domhnall na Tuile Mac Carthaigh in 1723. One of the tory leaders in the West Muskerry mountains was Dermod Leary of

Iveleary. He led a band of about forty tories in an attack on the custom-house of Skibbereen, in which two revenue officers were killed, and for this they were proclaimed by the lords justices. Other outlaws in 1694 were Teige, John and Dermot Leary, alias Baroole, late of Ive-leary, and Daniel and Teige oge na Ganny.

Again while many O Learys spread their wings with the Wild Geese — eleven are listed among the officers of the Spanish army in the early 18th century — yet several managed to retain some hold on their Iveleary homeland. Amongst those who successfully claimed restoration of their estates in 1699 were Capt. Keadagh and Capt. Cornelius Leary of Carrignacurra, Capt. Daniel O Leary of Inchigeelagh, Ensign Arthur Leary of Derryargid and Teage O Leary of Millinavarodig — as well as John Leary of Noddstown, Co. Tipperary, Ferdinand O Leary of Cume, Co. Kerry and Dermod Leary of Kilbeene, Co. Kerry. (If this last place be Killeen near Killarney, then Dermod was dead since 1696, the year in which he was lamented by Aodhagán Ó Raithile.) Wills proved in the 18th century include those of Dermod Leary of Inchideraille (1700), Timothy Leary of the Acris (? Augeris) (1772), and Cornelius Leary of Cooldorragha (par. Kilmichael, 1756). Carrig-nacurra seems to have remained, at least partly, in O Leary occupation also; Cornelius Leary (1699) and Cornelius O Leary (1753) are both described as of there.

However, the chief of the name (of the Carrignaneelagh family) removed to the Millstreet area. This was Arthur mac Daniel O Leary who, when outlawed in 1691, was described as of Drishane. His move there was porbably due to the fact that his sister, Juliana, became second wife of Colonel Donogh mac Owen Mac Carthy of Drishane. Donogh was a veteran of both the Williamite and Cromwellian wars, being aged 106 years at the time of his death in 1725. In his will, he left a life interest in his property to his wife, Juliana, with bequests to her nephew (Arthur's son) Daniel Leary, of Millstreet, gent., and to Daniel's son, Denis. But Drishane had by then been purchased by the Wallis family. so the O Learys continued to reside at Millstreet.

Daniel's son, Denis, who died in 1783, was known only by the name 'O Leary' and was a well-known character in Millstreet. Though his house was small, he kept up the tradition of open hospitality to every guest at every season. His cellar was never locked but secure by reason of deference to his sway and respect to his person. Being a very athletic type who always carried a long pole which he knew how to use, his very appearance at fair or meeting was sufficient to quell any distur-bance or faction fight. His only daughter, Helen, married Denis Mac Carthy of Glynn, Dooneen and Kilcorney (a descendant of Donogh mac Owen) and resided at Coomlegane. Denis was a widower when Helen married him and she made his son, Denis, her heir, on condition that he assumed the name of Mac Carthy-O Leary, which he did.

An outstanding folk-hero of the Penal days was Art Ó Laoghaire, the *caoineadh* or lament for whom, already mentioned, is familiar to generations of students. Art's father was Conchobhar or Cornelius O Leary of Ballymurphy near Crossbarry who, in 1753, was nominated as one of the executors of the will of Cornelius O Leary of Carrignacurra, gentleman. This shows a connection with the leading O Leary families of Iveleary, a connection underlined in Eibhlín Dubh's lament, but Cornelius seems to have come to Ballymurphy from the Kenmare estate in Co. Kerry, where Ferdinando O Leary had a lease of Coumnahavanistragh in 1681 ('Cume' in 1699). By 1765 the O Learys were living at Raleigh (*Ráth Laoich*) just west of Macroom. Art is said to have been in military service on the continent in his youth, and returned home in 1767 aged about 21. His remarkable physique and athletic appearance caught the eye of Eibhlín Dubh Ní Chonaill (aunt of the Liberator and a young widow at the time) one day in Macroom. *Thug mo chroí taitneamh duit*, she said, and shortly afterwards the two were married despite the disapproval of Eibhlín's relatives. For a brief five years Art, with his proud and fearless bearing, was a thorn in the flesh of the local Protestant ascendancy. A bitter quarrel between himself and Abraham Morris of Hanover Hall culminated in the fatal shooting of Art by a soldier at Carriganima on 4th May 1773.

He was buried in the family tomb at Kilcrea. His two young sons were named Conchobhar (Cornelius) and Fear. Of the younger we hear no more, but Cornelius later married and had two sons, Cornelius Ferdinand and Goodwin Richard Purcell O Leary. The latter became Professor of Materia Medica in Queen's College, Cork and was a welcome guest at the Courts of Sweden and Denmark on account of his offer to bring a hundred Irishmen, mounted and accoutred, to the aid of Denmark, then threatened by the might of Austria and Prussia. After he died in Manchester in 1876 his remains were brought home to be laid in his grandfather's tomb in Kilcrea.

Another 18th century Arthur O Leary achieved fame in a different sphere — Rev. Arthur O Leary, the Capuchin friar. He was born near Dunmanway but spent much of his childhood with relatives in Inchigeelagh parish. Ordained at St. Malo in Brittany in 1758, he was transferred in 1771 to Cork where he straightaway set about building a new church in Blackamoor Lane (off Sullivan's Quay). He became nationally known as a preacher and as a writer of controversial tracts.

A grand-nephew of Fr. O Leary was the celebrated General Daniel Florence O Leary (1801-1854) principal aide-de-camp of Simon Bolivar, hero of the South American war of liberation. Another noted O Leary revolutionary in the 19th century was John O Leary, the Fenian, who was born in Co. Tipperary. He it was who evoked the oft-quoted lines of W.B. Yeats:

Romantic Ireland's dead and gone
It's with O Leary in the grave.

The only noted 18th century Gaelic poet of the name was Donnchadh Dall Ó Laoghaire who extolled the virtues of the Mac Carthys. In our own century a new generation of writers in Irish was inspired by the work of An t-Athair Peadar Ó Laoghaire who in his autobiography *Mo Scéal Féin* traces his descent from Diarmaid and Conchobhar of Carrignacurra castle and recounts the wanderings of his ancestors until they settled at Lios Carragáin in the parish of Clondrohid.

Ó LEIGHIN

(O) LYNE LANE LYONS

Families bearing the various forms of this surname are plentiful in Co. Cork today and appear to have been equally numerous in the 16th century, according to the evidence of the Fiants. But there are no extant genealogies of the Uí Leighin; in fact Leighen as a personal name does not appear at all in the genealogies.

The place-name Carraig Uí Leighin (Carrigaline, bar. Kerrycurrihy) seems to indicate a family connection with this part of Co. Cork in pre-Norman times. Also in Carrigaline parish is the townland of Ballin-lining (written Ballinlynigh in 1601 — obviously Baile an Leighnigh) but it is more likely that this derives from the Norman name Leynagh. (In nearby Killanully, Donell mac Shane O Leyn, tailor, and Robert Leynagh received pardons in the same Fiant in 1584.) In view of the fact that Carraig Uí Leighin was the principal strongpoint in the territory of the Ciarraighe Cuirche, it is tempting to postulate a connection with Co. Kerry — where Lynes are numerous and well-established — seeing that the Ciarraighe Cuirche were of the same stock as the Ciarraighe Luachra.

However, this may be just a coincidence, and there is a strong possibility that Leighen may be a derivative of *liaigh*, a leech or physician, since the Uí Leighin, in the 15th and 16th centuries at least, were numbered among the hereditary medical families of Ireland. (Another medical family name directly derived from *liaigh* is Mac an Leagha, *anglice* Mac Alee or Lee.) Still, accepting that Leighen was an occupative personal name brings us no nearer to fixing a point of origin for the surname; there could have been more than one.

One area with which the family name had constant association over several centuries is the north-eastern quarter of Co. Cork. As early as 1295 when Philip le Blund, apparently from the Fermoy district, was being pardoned for his trespasses, his followers included John Oleyn, Dermod Oleyn and Gillekeran (*Giolla Chiarán*) Oleyn. In 1344 Magnus Olyne was named among the followers of Adam de Barry of Rath-cormack who rebelled against Barry Mór of Castlelyons. (This last place had no particular connection with the Uí Leighin; in Irish it was known as *Caisleán Ó Liatháin*.) An 18th century Irish scribe from Castletown-roche named the composers of the saga *Tóruigheacht Conaill Gulban* and described one of them, Mleachloinn Buidhe Ó Leighinn, as *adhbhar leágha* (medical student).

The family name Lyon was in evidence in Kinsale in the late 14th century, although we cannot be sure that this represents the Gaelic

215

'Ó Leighin'. A grant of property there was made to John Lyon in 1398 and the same property was granted by Thomas Lyon to William Any twenty-five years later. In Cork city there was a bailiff named David Leyne in 1341.

The medical dimension becomes apparent in the 15th century. Aedh Buidhe Ó Leighin was the scribe of a herbal in a manuscript (H.3.22) now in Trinity College, Dublin, and dating from 1415. Domhnall and Donnchadh Ó Leighin compiled other medical manuscripts, now in the British Museum collections. In 1459 Cormac Mac Duinntsléibhe (again a member of a hereditary medical family) translated into Irish, at Cloyne, a section of a well-known medical tract, *Rosa Anglica* . . . 'for Diarmaid mac Domhnaill hí Leighin. May it prove of value to him and to his family'.

A scholarly branch of the family found favour with the Roches of Fermoy. It was Domhnall Ó Leighin who in 1461 compiled for Dáibhidh Mór Roche, lord of Fermoy, a list of the townlands which were Roche property, with their extent. This list was transcribed into the Book of Fermoy about a century later, one of the witnesses present being Diarmaid Ó Leighin, *ollamh an Róidsigh*. (One of the ploughlands of Lord Roche in 1611 was Ballinleynig, now apparently part of Castle Wrixon, par. Imphrick, but again this name may derive from one of the Leynagh family.)

Bridgetown Augustinian priory near Castletownroche functioned under the aegis of the Roches and it was probably this influence which caused Dermit O Leyni (perhaps the Dermit who was a canon of Cloyne diocese between 1461 and 1467) to be appointed prior there without canonical title, an appointment which led to a Papal inquiry in 1486. About this time also was built the Dominican priory of Glanworth, the site for which was donated by John Fitzgerald, knight of Kerry, though it lay in the heart of the Roche territory. It is interesting that the only family who appear to have had burial rights within the church precincts there were O Leynes. In the south corner of the choir may still be seen the now desecrated vault and 18th century mensal slab commemorating Kennedy O Leyne and his wife, Elizabeth. Also in Roche territory is the small parish of Carrigdownane where Thadeus Oleyn was *de facto* vicar in 1477. Another Thadeus O Leyn was executor of a transfer deed (Barrett to Mac Carthy) of Cloghphilip near Blarney in 1488.

The Elizabethan Fiants between 1567 and 1602 provide numerous though scattered references to the O Leynes and some interesting patterns emerge. For example, John or Seán was the most popular first name but practically the only one of Norman origin — apart from a few Thomases. Otherwise they favoured Domhnall, Donnchadh, Conchobhar, Tadhg and Diarmaid as did so many other Gaelic families, but they also used some more unusual ones — Amhlaoibh, Muircheartach, Maolsheachlainn and Aonghas (Aeneas). Mathghamhain (Mahon) was a particular favourite.

The only one of the name classified as 'gentleman' in the Fiants was Awliff Lyne of Jordanstown (near Ballinhassig). Two were described as 'horsemen' – one step below a gentleman. They were probably father and son – Mahoune O Leyne of Kilvolen (1567) and Awlyve mac Mahoun O Leyne of Balentobrede (1586). Although these two Fiants deal mainly with Muskerry, Kilvolen seems to be Killavullen in Roches country while the second place may be the Ballyntybrod which formed part of an estate around Rathgoggan (Charleville) in 1587. With Awlyve there was also pardoned Mahoune oge O Leyne (possibly his son) of same place, yeoman. Three others were classed as yeomen, two as husbandmen, with one tailor, one labourer and one kern.

However, in keeping with the tendency noticeable in the previous century, the most numerous classification was that of 'chirurgeon' or surgeon. These surgeons were:

Dermot O Leyne fitz Ennys of Glanworth (1573).
John O Leyne mac Ea (East Cork) (1579).
Donell O Leyne of Ballyvaran (Ballyveerane, Macroom) (1584).
John O Leyne of Ballyveiran (physician) (1601).
Eneas O Lyne of Castletowne (Roche) (1602).

Also, Donoghow mac Conor y Lean of Killumney (1585) was described as 'sergeant', probably in error for surgeon.

The indications are that O Leynes were the hereditary physicians of more than one family. It is almost certain that they doctored the Mac Carthys of Muskerry. Two, perhaps three, of the medical men listed above resided in Muskerry. Furthermore, a document dated 1600 listing the septs and followers of the Lord of Muskerry includes:

'Aulyves als. O Leavies, 3 ploughlands, they are surgeons.'

Since there is no trace of any family of O Leavies, surgeons or otherwise, in the Elizabethan Fiants relating to Co. Cork, it is more than likely that 'Aulynes' (i.e. O Lynes) was intended.

The Fiants also indicate that O Lyne families were surgeons in Co. Kerry and in King's Co. (Offaly).

This predilection for medicine did not disappear with the breaking up of the clan system. There are numerous later references to O Lyne medical men both in Cork and in Kerry; even in Spain in the late 17th century there was a Dr. Guillermo de Leon who came originally from Co. Cork – probably an O Leyne.

The same tendency is noticeable in modern times. A note in Mrs. O Connell's *Last Colonel of the Irish Brigade* traces a century and a half of Dr. Leynes in Tralee, ending with Dr. Jeremiah Leyne who died in 1872. The professor of medicine in the Catholic University medical school in Dublin was Dr. Robert Dyer Lyons (1826-1886), son of William Lyons, merchant, who was mayor of Cork in 1848-49. In 1870 Dr. Lyons was invited by Gladstone to act on the commission of inquiry into the treatment of 'treason-felony' prisoners, and was described by O Donovan Rossa as 'one of the fairest-minded Englishmen (*sic*) I have ever encountered'. Furthermore, the name Lane has for many generations been associated with the traditional skill of bonesetting in Co. Cork.

In respect of geographical distribution, the O Leynes of the Fiants appear to fall into four main groups — those of north-east Cork, already referred to, those in O Sullivan Bear's country, a large but scattered group in Muskerry and a small but influential group in the western parts of Kinalea-Kerrycurrihy.

There were many O Leynes on the Béarra peninsula in Elizabethan times, including five on Whiddy island. They may have served as physicians to the O Sullivans Bear; Aulibius Olleinus (*Amhlaoibh Ó Leighin*) was Domhnall Cam's chief physician in Spain in the early 17th century. Donna Eleysica Leyn, widow, whose husband had been tutor to Domhnall Cam's son was in receipt of a pension at Santiago in 1610. The surname is, of course, well-known in Co. Kerry, where it is usually spelt Lyne and from where it may have spread to contiguous areas of Co. Cork. Mr. Gerard J. Lyne (*Journal of the Kerry Arch. and Hist. Soc.*, 1976) states that all the Lyne families now resident in the Lauragh and Bearhaven areas are, with one exception, descended from a physician named Dermot Lyne who settled in Ardgroom around 1680. Dr. Lyne, who was a Catholic landholder of considerable influence during the Penal times, may have originally come from the Dunkerron area in Co. Kerry.

Those in Muskerry were obviously followers of the ruling Mac Carthy family, being concentrated mainly around the strongholds of Blarney and Kilcrea. In 1599 when the English under the Earl of Essex raided the friary of Kilcrea, all the monks escaped except Fr. Matheus O Leyn who because of his age and feebleness was overtaken and slain on a ford on the river Bride. (Frs. Malachy Lein, Cork diocese, and Cornelius Leyne, Cloyne diocese, were ordained at Bordeaux in 1619.)

When some of the Mac Carthys were imprisoned by the sheriff of Co. Cork in 1564, Mahon O Lein was in prison along with them. Again, in 1602 when Cormac Mac Carthy of Blarney was in Cork jail, it was his trusty attendant, Maghon óg O Lyne who, according to *Pacata Hibernia*, broke the window of the cell overlooking the street, thus enabling Cormac to escape. There was a John O Leyne who paid a levy on property in Desertmore parish in the early part of the 17th century. In 1702 when the estates of the Earl of Clancarty were being sold at Chichester House, among his tenants in the Macroom area were Daniel Lyne, gent., (Kilbarry, Knockacareigh and Rosnascalp) and John Leyne (Rahalisk).

The O Leynes of Ballinaboy parish, in the western portions of Kinalea and Kerrycurrihy, are first mentioned in 1573 when Mahon O Leyn of Knockygogany was pardoned. Mahowne O Lenie of Jordanstown died in 1579 leaving Awliffe as his son and heir. A claim to the lands was made by Matheus (i.e. Mathghamhain or Mahon), son of Mlaghlin O Leine. Knockygogany (now Gogganshill) was named after the Goggans or Cogans; at this period William Cogan of Barnahely was overlord of much of Ballinaboy parish. But part of the parish was in Barry Óg's territory. In 1589 Sir Thomas Barry Óg mortgaged Bally-jourdan, Rathroe and Knocklucy in Ballinaboy parish to Auliffe O Layne. In 1601-2 Awliff O Lyne, gentleman, Donnell O Leyne, Thomas O Leyne and Joan ny Lyne, widow, received pardons at Jordanstown or Bally Jordan. (This townland no longer exists, but was certainly in Ballinaboy parish and adjoined Ballyheeda. It may now form part of Rigsdale, par. Dunderrow, as it was acquired by Edward Riggs in the Cromwellian plantation.) In March, 1602 Mahowne mac Donnough O Lyne (dwelling under Barry Oge) sailed for Spain from Kinsale with Don Juan de Aguila.

In 1606 William Cogan enfeoffed James oge fitz Walter Cogan and Richard fitz James Cogan with the lands of Knockanevarrodige (Barretts-hill) and Ballineboy. He appointed Awliffe O Leyne of Jordanstown as his attorney. Because Awliffe was brother-in-law to James Cogan, in 1619 James granted him the lands of Ballinaboy in trust for the use of his (James') son and heir. Awliffe's daughter, Ellen, married Amhlaoibh O Leary of Dromcarra castle.

Awliffe himself died in 1637; an inquisition was held in the following year into his lands on which head-rents were payable to Philip Barry Óg, lord of Kinalea. His heir was named as Auliffe oge O Lyne of nearby Annaghbeg, but he too must have died shortly afterwards as his will was proved in 1638. His heir must have been Melaghlin as in 1643 among those outlawed for rebellion was Melaghlin O Leyne of Jordanstown, gent. But in the Book of Survey and Distribution Aulife O Line is given as the owner (in 1641) of Jordanstown whose 200 acres were acquired by Edward Riggs. (An Auliffe O Leyne had a will proved in 1652.) Melaghlen must have died in or before 1661 in which year the will of 'Mc Laughlen O Lyne of Gurtnaglogh' was proved. Gortnaclogh is adjacent to Ballinaboy. But there was another Melaghlan O Leyne who witnessed an assignment of lands in 1677.

One of these may have been the man referred to in a letter written by Cornelius Donovan, of Mishells, Bandon, to his son in America in 1898, relating the traditional history of his ancestors. According to Cornelius, one of those ancestors was Maolsheachlainn Ó Leighin:

'. . . a tall strong bold determined man; proverbially so, and the same determination ran in all his descendants both men and women. They were remarkable for a half turned up nose and a strong tuft of black hair standing up straight on the front of their heads. He was the owner of all the land from Ballinhassig bridge to Brinny bridge at the south side of the river; he kept three mansion houses, he was an officer in Charles I's army and was considered the best shot in Ireland.'

Cornelius recounted a story of how Maolsheachlainn fired a shot from his house at Annagh at a horseman descending Killeady hill, a mile away, thinking that it was Cromwell. The bullet struck the horse, but the rider turned out to be 'Mac Carthy, Lord Muscry', who, however, took the incident in good part with the remark *A Mhleachlainn, do bhí an dearmhad ann*! Maolsheachlainn's son, Mahon, lived at Mishells. 'He was remarkable for his great activity, swiftness and nimbleness of foot.' Mahon married Mary 'daughter of Capt. Cornelius O Mahony of Kilmore, also an officer in James II's army'. He later moved to Finis, where his son, Cornelius ('a man of gigantic stature') succeeded him. This Cornelius had three daughters, one of whom married John Donovan, great-grandfather of the writer of the letter.

The census of 1659 (from which both Fermoy and Muskerry are missing) enumerates 18 O Line families in Orrery and Kilmore and 11 in Cork city. There were 28 of the name in Co. Kerry and 30 in Co. Limerick, while Teige Line, gent., was a 'titulado' in Co. Clare. About this time also, an anonymous list of those 'plotting for troubles' includes, in Carbery, 'all the Hialihyes (Healys) and all the Leyns there'. This could be in error for Muskerry. In Youghal there was a David Leyne in 1618, John Leyne (constable of the south gate) in 1629 and an Edmond O Lyne in 1649.

The form Lane began to appear in the 17th century. John Lane of Carrigrohane served on a jury to examine the survey of the south Liberties of Cork in 1655. Richard Lane of Cork had a will proved in 1662, as had John Lane of Laragh five years later. The introduction of some English Lanes in Cromwellian times may have had an influence here.

Early in the 1800s Seághan Ó Leighin worked in Cork city as an Irish scribe while later in the century, Denny Lane, whose forbears came from the Matehy district in Muskerry, emerged as one of the noted 'Young Ireland' poets of the *Nation*.

Ó LOINGSIGH

LYNCH

This is a surname which originated independently in several parts of Ireland and there was also a de Lench family of Norman origin which became famous as one of the 'tribes' of Galway. The Uí Loingsigh of west Cork, however, were a distinct family group belonging to the Corca Laoighdhe. Again, *Duan Catháin* claims them as an offshoot of the Uí Eachach but with even less credibility than usual, since the compiler appears to have overlooked having assigned to the Uí Loingsigh in the earlier part of the poem an ancestor named Loingsech mac Donnghail, and so gave them another and completely different derivation (from 'Loingsech mac Loingsigh na laoch') at a later stage.

Accepting then as more authentic the account in the Genealogy of Corca Laoighdhe, we find that Ó Loingsigh was among the hereditary leaders of Tuath Ó nDunghalaigh, an area in the vicinity of where the town of Clonakilty now stands. At a later stage the family must have moved into Béarra, accompanying, perhaps, the branch of the O Driscolls who were lords of Béarra before the O Sullivans came there. The surname is recorded in Co. Kerry in 1480 when John Oloynsigh of Ardfert diocese obtained the vicarage of Kilcummin in the diocese of Aghadoe.

In 1597 O Linche was listed as one of the followers of O Sullivan Bear. Another sept in O Sullivan's following was that of O Linchehan (*Ó Loingseacháin*), some members of which may afterwards have shortened their name to Lynch. (It is rather confusing to find that in the *Book of Survey and Distribution* Ó Loingseacháin is rendered 'O Lynchigh' while Ó Loingsigh is written 'O Linty'. Similarly, Ballylinchy near Baltimore, which one would expect to be *Baile Uí Loingsigh* was, in the 17th century, known as Ballylynshighane, i.e. *Baile Uí Loingseacháin*. In 1302 Pilib Ó Loingsecháin, erenagh of Kilcatherine in Béarra, died.)

A survey made about 1597 tells us that O Linchigh's land was valued as 3½ quarters, and paid a sorren yearly, or in lieu thereof eighteen ounces of silver, valued at two shillings and two white groats the ounce, 40s in all. This was payable to Mac Carthy Mór as chief overlord of the area, but in 1611 the O Linchighs were also paying a yearly chief rent of £4.13.4 to O Sullivan Bear. Their lands were mainly in the parish of Kilcaskan, as we learn from an inquisition into the property of Dermod O Linshie of Kilcaskan who died in 1622. Dermod, presumably chief of his name, held 1½ carucates at 10s per annum, and also paid a head-rent to O Sullivan Bear. His son and heir was named John. Another inquisition was taken in 1637 on the lands of Thaddeus mac Conohor Bane O Lynchy of Derrymore in the barony of Bear, apparently a junior branch of the family.

In the year of the rebellion, 1641, the chief of the O Lynches was Dermot, who must have been either a son or brother of the John O Linshie mentioned in the inquisition into the lands of his father. When the war ended, Dermot O Linty, alias O Linty (i.e. *the* Ó Loingsigh) forfeited up to 3,000 (Irish) acres in the parish of Kilcaskan, that mountainous and infertile but highly scenic area between Glengarriff and Hungry Hill. Dermot, the spelling of whose name seems to have given much trouble to officialdom – he was described this time as 'Dermott O Leiny, Kilcuskane, Gent.,' – was among those listed as outlaws in 1643. However it made no difference whether or not Dermot had been in rebellion, since O Sullivan Bear, the overlord, had, and so Kilcaskan parish became the property of the Earl of Anglesey, a highly-placed Cromwellian official.

The dispossessed chieftains, though now landless and impoverished, continued to live in their beloved Béarra, preferring the constant grief of seeing their ancient patrimony in the hands of a stranger to the utter misery of never seeing it at all. When Dr. Dive Downes, Protestant bishop of Cork and Ross, visited the area in 1700, he found O Sullivan Bear living in a cabin at the foot of Hungry Hill. He also spoke to the old chief of the Uí Loingsigh; if this was Dermot, he must have been in his eighties, if not older, by then: 'Old Linehey (*recte* Linchey) of Kilcaskin, saies he formerly paid to the Bishop of Corke a chiefry of 5s per an. for 9 gneeves of Dromfennagh, the other 9 gneeves are held it is said by patent.' In 1694, Dermot Linchy, John Linchy and Finin Linchy of Clanlaurence (in Béarra) were suspected friends and harbourers of tories.

The Elizabethan Fiants show that Lynches were to be found in other parts of Co. Cork besides Béarra around 1600. Those pardoned included:

1587:   Donnogh mac Dermody Lynsey, yeoman.
1600:   Teige mac Donogh O Lenshye of Ballincollig, yeoman.
1601:   Gulissie (Giolla Íosa) O Lenshie, Donell O Linshie, Dermot O Lwensie, Teige O Lenshie, Dermot O Linshie of Nadrid, Teige O Lynsey of Killaconenagh, Moriertagh O Lynshy of Dunboy, Dermot O Linsie of the Downinges, Donell O Lenshie of Cloentean (Cloonteens), Donogh oge O Lenshie of Carrigbuy, Dermot O Lwenshie of Dundirig (Dundareirke) Donogh and Teig mac Teig y Lenshie of Annahala.
1602:   Dermod mac David I Lenshy of Dromsicane, labourer.

This list shows a concentration of the name in the barony of Muskerry. There is a record too of a Teig O Linsy who paid a levy on lands in Kilmerty (? Kilnamartery) in the early 17th century. A Thady mac David Linch had a will proved in 1670.

Muskerry is not represented in the census of 1659 which lists Lynch as a 'principal Irish name' in the barony of Kerrycurrihy only. Killingley graveyard (near Ballygarvan) in the heart of this barony has been the burial-place of Lynch families from 1727, if not earlier. In nearby Tracton parish Daniel Linchy of Gronig (Granig) had a will proved in 1772. He was, no doubt, ancestor of Diarmuid Lynch (1878-1950) of the same place, a noted I.R.B. leader and a staff captain in the G.P.O. in the 1916 rising. In his book (*The I.R.B. and the 1916 Insurrection*) he informs us that old neighbours of his boyhood days used to tell him that he was of the ninth generation of the Lynches in Granig.

A contemporary fellow-Republican was Liam Lynch (1890-1923) born in Anglesboro, Co. Limerick and buried at Kilcrumper near Fermoy. He was O/C of the North Cork Brigade (I.R.A.) and later chief of staff of the Republican forces during the civil war, at the end of which he was killed in action.

Another Lynch to have made his mark in national politics is Mr. Jack Lynch, T.D. Though born in Cork city his family origins were in west Cork and he became the first Corkman to attain the position of Taoiseach which he held from 1966 to 1973 and again from 1977 to 1979.

Ó LONGAIDH

Ó LONGAIGH   LONG

There is nothing to indicate the origin of this mid-Cork family, apart from a reference in *Duan Catháin* (a poem dealing with branches of the Uí Eachach) — *Fine Longaidh ó Longadh*. But as this Longadh is said to be son of the mythical Corc mac Ughoine, the reference is of little value since family names were not derived from ancestors so remote. In fact, all that it tells us is that the surname Ó Longaidh was known in Co. Cork in the 14th century.

Cannaway or Canovee parish in Muskerry (south of the Lee) was for long the family base of the Uí Longaidh. Like the O Healys and O Herlihys, they were 'erenaghs' or hereditary occupiers of church-lands, so it is not surprising that there were many clerics among them in the 15th century. In 1401 Laurence Olongscyg (probably for 'Olongayg'), priest of Cork diocese, was assigned the perpetual vicarage of Cluechyg (? Macloneigh) long void by the death of David Olongayg. In 1413 Andrew Ylongayg resigned from the vicarage of Ballymodan. A papal mandate of 1457 assigned to Donatus O Longayd, clerk, the vicarages of Cannaway and Magourney formerly held by Dermit O Longayd, clerk, and Donatus Olongayd, priest.

At this stage the old Gaelic names seem to have replaced the biblical-style personal names used earlier in the century; an unusual one, also found in 1457, is that of Lattinus Ylongaych who held the vicarage of Aghinagh. (Lactinus or Laichtín was patron of Donoughmore and of the O Healys, and the adoption of his name underlines the ecclesiastical status of the O Longs.) Two years later, Gilbert ylongaygh was vicar of Aglish and Clondrohid in the united dioceses of Cork and Cloyne. In 1484 Dermitius Long was a priest of the Cork diocese while in 1591 another Dermitius Long, the Church of Ireland diocesan treasurer, held eight livings, including Cannaway, before he was suspended from office.

In Elizabethan times the O Longs held 4½ ploughlands in Muskerry, for which they paid an annual head-rent of £4.10.0 to the lord of Muskerry. These lands were obviously in Cannaway parish and their ecclesiastical connection is evident as late as 1700. In that year, according to Bishop Downes, '. . . the Prebendary of Killaspugmullane has half the tithes of the four plowlands and a half of Cannaway'.

In 1576 a pardon was granted to Donogho roo O Longe of Cannaway, yeoman, and three years later one to an O Long with the unusual personal name of Gyllebryaned. In February 1601, among the chieftains of Muskerry who got pardons was Dermod Longe alias O Longe of Canwey (Cannaway). Others pardoned in the same year were Morris O Longy and Patrick Longe of Cannaway, Donogh and Dermot O Longe of Macloneigh and Donogh O Longie of Enniskeane. These pardons were designed to lessen support for Hugh O Neill's rebellion, but at least one O Long fought at Kinsale. Dermond O Longy, of Muskerry, sailed for Spain with Don Juan de Aguila from Kinsale in March, 1602. Also Maurice Longe (who served in the wars in his own country in defence of the Catholic cause) joined the regiment of Colonel Henry O Neill in Spanish Flanders in 1604.

Dermot, the chief pardoned in 1601, died on 2nd March, 1623. An inquisition taken after his death found him to have been the owner of Clashy, Inshymore, Gearymore, Knockmore, Carrykippagh, Dromkeill, Cwillnyhahy and Cwildrome. All these were presumably in Cannaway parish, though only the first and last (Classes and Cooldrum) are recognizable there today. John Long, Dermot's son and heir, was then 25 years of age and married. Another inquisition, taken in 1636, found that John possessed Cowlenehay, Cowleenacarrigy (Coolnacarriga) and Clashyfadda, with the antique bawn of Cannaway, Cooldrum and Carra. At the time of the Cromwellian surveys he also owned Coolnasoon, Monallig, Inishmore, Killinardrish and a small townland in the neighbouring parish of Moviddy called Garran I Longy (*Garrán Uí Longaidh*). In Cannaway parish, the Civil Survey tells us, on the north side near the river Lee stood the walls of a large ancient house which belonged to the chief proprietor of the said island (Cannaway island) being of the family of the Longs. As well as the head-rent payable to the lord of Muskerry, a sum of £1.2.6 was paid annually to the bishopric of Cork. (In the 1670s Bishop Synge's agent used receive £7 per annum out of the *tuath* of Cannaway in Muskerry from the family of the Longs 'who were proprietors'.)

For his part in the 1641 rebellion John Long was outlawed in 1643. He was dead at the time his lands were surveyed and confiscated. Under the Act of Settlement, Lord Muskerry (now Earl of Clancarty) had all his estates restored to him, including those of former freeholders such as the O Longs. In his will the Earl instructed his executors to deal justly with the former freeholders, and so some Longs were enabled to get leases of their ancestral lands. One of these was Darby Long, counsellor-at-law, who was appointed a magistrate and recorder of Cork in 1687. He was also an M.P. in James II's parliament. John Long had got a lease of Cooldrum and other lands in Muskerry in 1674, but after the Williamite confiscations his claim to the lease was disallowed. There was some property in Kilbonane parish on which Philip O Longy paid a levy in the early 17th century but we hear no more of it.

In 1700 Bishop Downes visited Cannaway parish and found that 'Counsellor (Darby) Long's lands bound upon it (the church) . . .

the Earl of Clancarty had and Counsellor Long has, an estate in this parish. No other proprietors'. In 1702 Darby's claims to leases of Lehenagh, Killinardrish and Coolnacarriga were disallowed, but his claim to a lease of Monallig for 99 years from 1674 was allowed. His daughter, Ellinor, in 1706 married Daniel Fitzgerald of Ballinruddery, Co. Kerry, son to the Knight of Kerry, and the lands were later sold by the Fitzgeralds, thus breaking the ancient link between the Longs and Cannaway parish.

Mountlong in the parish of Kilmonoge, east of Kinsale, was the seat of another branch of the family, whose founder was Dr. Thomas Long, a doctor of both canon and civil laws and author of several Latin treatises. His original residence seems to have been at Clodagh in the parish of Kilmurry. A pardon granted to a number of Muskerry men in 1577 (including Donogho mac Shane I Longha of Macloneigh, yeoman) was at the suit of Dr. Long. He must have been one of the Cannaway Longs; in 1620 Dermitius O Longy of Cannaway in a marriage settlement enfeoffed Dr. Thomas' sons with lands to be held for the use of his (Dermot's) son and his son's wife. Also, in 1641 John Long of Mountlong held the lands of Lehenagh in Cannaway parish.

In June 1589 Sir Thomas Barry Óg of Kinalea granted to Thomas Long, 'doctor of both laws', the lands of Kilmohonoge alias Oyster Haven and seven other small townlands adjoining. In the same year he released to Thomas Long the castle of Twolleymohelly (now Ballyhandle), Ballymurphy, Lissagroom and Crossbarry mill, all in Knockavilla parish. These lands were later held by James Long (perhaps the younger son of Dr. Thomas) according to an inquisition held in 1639. James had enfeoffed Philip and James Long (presumably his sons) with some of the lands. In a short time the Longs in Kinalea acquired a status comparable to that of Barry Óg. In 1590 William Lyon, Protestant bishop of Cork, complained that Dr. Long and Capt. Long were seeking to deprive him of his bishopric in favour of another. In September 1592, Henry Barry oge and Thomas Long were the chief compositors for cess in Kinalea. Dr. Thomas died on 30th March, 1603.

His son and heir, John, was then 14 years of age. In 1604 Robert Morgan was granted the wardship of 'John Longe, son and heir of Thomas Longe, late of Cloghdea'. John was to be educated in the English religion and habits and in Trinity College, Dublin, from the 12th to the 18th year of his age. He came of age and got livery of seisin in 1610. In a chancery commission for defective titles in 1618 it was agreed that John Longe of Rynynyan (Ringnanean, par. Kilmonoge) was entitled to his lands and to a manor of 600 acres, with a creek and bay called Oyster Haven. Here in 1631 John built an imposing castellated mansion overlooking the peaceful waters of Oysterhaven creek, and five years later he was granted permission to create the manor of Mount Long and to empark 1,000 acres.

His idyllic sojourn lasted but a decade. Having shed the 'English religion and habits' of his upbringing he threw all his weight behind the Catholic cause in 1641 and as he was High Sheriff of Co. Cork at the time he was quickly accepted as a leader. He formed a 'rebel camp' at Belgooly which, his enemies believed, was intended to besiege Cork, Kinsale and Bandon at one and the same time. Barry Óg was also in the camp and they were joined by the doughty warrior, 'Captain Sugán', brother of Mac Fínghin Mac Carthy of Ardtully. They received supplies from the 'Popish inhabitants' of Kinsale until English reinforcements landed there, after which the rebel camp was broken up. Tristram Whitcombe of Kinsale wrote to his brother that on the 25th May, 1642 '. . . we marched forth, about 300 men, to besiege Mountlong castle' (which they found empty) . . . 'It is a very stately building, and the like cannot be built for £2,000 . . . But my Lord President . . . hath given order to demolish it; but till then we keep a ward in it of 32 muskettiers'.

John Long was, of course, outlawed for his activities, as were his sons John (junior) and James and also James Long of Tullymoghelly. In 1652 when the war had ended, 35 persons were put on trial and condemned to death — 'some of note, one of whom hath been Sheriffe of the county'. Shortly afterwards John Long was executed, at Cork. He had made his will in 1649, probably while in prison, commencing it with 'In the first year of the reign of our sovereign lord King Charles II of England', and leaving everything he had to his son and heir John (junior).

The will proved of little value as the estates of the Longs in Kinalea were carved up and distributed among the victors. Giles Busteed got Mountlong, Knockleigh and Carrigeen. Killehagh and Knocknahowla went to Thomas Knowles and others. Edward Riggs got Knocklucy and Ballyheedy; John Stepney got Clogheenduane and Skehanagh west. The Earl of Cork, as usual, got his share — Lissagroom, Killeen and James Long's lands at Ballyhandle and Ballymurphy. Others got Annaghmore and Willowhill. Some of the Long estates (Ringnanean and Ballingeemanig) eventually came into the possession of the Duke of York (later James II.)

The Longs never recovered any of their lands. John (junior) got his father's will proved in 1661 and received royal permission to retain possession of his father's lands if he was able to compensate the adventurers in possession — a most unlikely event! He was allotted 800 acres in Co. Clare but does not appear to have settled there.

In 1690 two of the Longs were outlawed for supporting King James. One was John Long, esq. of Ballyhandle; he was probably son of James Long of Ballyhandle but it is unlikely that he was the occupant. The other was Thomas Long, gent., of Knockballyvornane.

After this the Uí Longaidh were scattered throughout Co. Cork — but not in Co. Kerry where Long is an anglicized version of Ó Lúing.

Among the Gaelic poets of Co. Cork in the late 18th and early 19th centuries was Diarmuid Ó Longaidh. One of his poems was an *aisling*, written in 1784, praying for the success of Charles Stuart, while another was a lament on the death of Dr. Florence Mac Carthy, bishop of Cork, in 1810.

Ó MATHGHAMHNA

Ó MATHÚNA   (O) MAHONY   (O) MAHONEY

An influential segment of the dominant Eóganacht people in Munster was Eóganacht Raithlenn, also known as Uí Echach Muman. These were subdivided into Cenél Lóegaire – whose chief family, the O Donoghues, later moved into Co. Kerry – and Cenél Áeda who gave their name to the barony of Kinalea which in earlier times extended to the Kinsale, Courcies and Kilbrittain areas. On the introduction of surnames the ruling family of Cenél Áeda took theirs from Mathghamhain (son of Cian) who was born in the late 10th century. Mathghamhain, which is an Irish word for a bear, had not previously been in use among the Uí Echach; an explanation for its appearance may lie in the fact that (according to 17th century sources) Cian married Sadhbh, daughter of Brian Boru. Mathghamhain was frequently used by the Dál Cais, Brian himself having an older brother of that name.

As it happened, this Mathghamhain of the Dál Cais and Cian's father Mael Muad contended fiercely for the kingship of Munster in the late 10th century. Mathghamhain proved the stronger for many years but was eventually killed by Mael Muad in 976. Mael Muad then became 'King of Cashel' but two years later was slain by Mathghamhain's brother, Brian (Boru), who later extended his power over all Ireland. Mael Muad's son, Cian (from whom, it is said, Inis Céin or Enniskeane is named), was slain together with two of his brothers in the same year as Brian (1014) in an internecine battle between Cenél Áeda and Cenél Lóegaire.

Although the Dalcassian power was weakened after the battle of Clontarf, the southward thrust of Eóganacht Caisil into Desmond soon began to affect the Uí Echach and from the early 12th century onwards the Mac Carthys emerged as the recognized kings of Desmond. Cenél Áeda, now becoming known as Uí Mhathghamhna, were eventually confined to two separate areas of Co. Cork. One was the district around Mizen Head which became known as the Ivagha (*Uíbh Eachach*) peninsula. In 1062 two of the Uí Fháilbi, royal heirs of Corcu Duibne, were slain in Dursey island by the Uí Echach, whose settlement in west Cork may have had a connection with this event. The other O Mahony territory was around the present town of Bandon and became known as Cineál mBéice (Kinalmeaky) after an ancestor named Bécc.

Both the *Annals of Inisfallen* and Mac Carthaigh's Book make frequent references to the activities of the O Mahonys in the 12th and 13th centuries. Mathghamhain had a son named Brodchú and his son, Cú

Mara, was slain by the son of Mael Muad son of Matudán — perhaps a relative — in 1108. Cú Mara's son, Donnchadh Donn, died in 1119. His successor, Cian, was among the Munster chieftains who deposed Tadhg Mac Carthaigh from the kingship of Desmond (in favour of his brother, Cormac) in 1123. Twelve years later Cian was killed while on a foray with the same Cormac near Mountrath, Co. Laois. The O Mahonys again assisted Cormac Mac Carthy against the men of Thomond at Waterford in 1137 and gave refuge to Cormac's son, Diarmaid, in 1151.

A kingship dispute, of the type that bedevilled so many Irish clans, then hit the O Mahonys. In 1161 Domhnall son of Mael Muad — described as king of Cineál mBéice and a contender for (the kingship of) Uí Echach — was slain together with his son, by the Uí Mhathghamhna, who were, presumably, the O Mahonys of west Cork. This wiping out of a rival dynasty must have been carried out by the son of Cian, known as Donnchadh *na hImirche Timchill* ('of the roving around') whose son Conchobhar was ancestor of the later lords of Cineál mBéice who bore the title Ó Mathghamhna Cairbreach. From Conchobhar's three great-grandsons were named the minor septs of Clann Maghnusa, Clann Conchobhair and Clann Domhnaill of Gort Mór.

Then the Normans arrived on the scene. When Dermot Mac Carthy submitted to Henry II at Waterford in 1171 he was followed by Domhnall Mór Ó Briain and by Donnchadh Ó Mathghamhna. Their submission did not secure Henry's protection for them as they had hoped it would; soon afterwards Henry bestowed the 'kingdom of Cork' on de Cogan and Fitzstephen, to whom succeeded the de Courcys and Carews. Long years of conflict and turmoil ensued. In 1201 Donnchadh Ó Mathghamhna assisted the Mac Carthys against William de Burgo's army at Kinneigh and five years later was involved in the deposing of Fínghin Mac Carthy in favour of Diarmaid, a dissension which caused the annalist to remark: 'the whole of Desmond was destroyed by them and by the grey foreigners'. Donnchadh died in 1213 probably as a result of his imprisonment by Cormac (Liathánach) Mac Carthy.

Mac Carthaigh's Book records (*s.a.* 1214) the building of a ring of Norman castles around the coast of Desmond. Robert Carew (whose mother was a Mac Carthy) built the castle of Dunnamark near Bantry and the Carews thereafter laid claim to the western peninsulas, including Ivagha. According to Sir George Carew's pedigree of the O Mahonys (in Lambeth), 'Dermod O Mahon married a daughter of Carew Marquis of Cork, and had in marriage with her Inisfaddo and Calloghe-Chrage by Skulhaven (Long Island, Colla and Croagh); she married secondly Donal Cham Mac Carthy Reoghe, a quo the branch of Mac Carthy Reoghe.' Some confirmation of this may be found in the Plea Rolls for 1290 when Maurice de Carreu was impleading his tenants of Catherach Cro and Inysfade. These included Donenold, Donethud, Mathawen and Ricardus Omathawen. Eight years later the O Mahonys were again sued by Maurice who claimed that his grandfather, Robert de Carew, had held these lands until expelled by Diarmaid Mac Carthy.

The O Mahonys found themselves once more embroiled in Mac Carthy dissensions in 1232 when Domhnall God Mac Carthy plundered Ó Mathghamhna's land and slew three of his sons. Because of this Domhnall gained the epithet *Cairbreach* (of Carbery) and from him were descended the Mac Carthy lords of Carbery. The O Mahony who was plundered was named Muircheartach, a chieftain who, perhaps because of the wiping out of his family, does not figure in the genealogies. In these, the successor to Donnchadh na hImirce Timchill was his son, Diarmaid Mór, mentioned in the annals in 1233 and again on his death four years later. Diarmaid's heir was his son Tadhg; two other sons gave their names to Clann Domhnaill an Ghuibín (Gubbeen near Schull) and Clann Ricard. The name Ricard may derive from Richard de Carew whose daughter is said to have been wife of Diarmaid Mór. A fourth son, Mac Raith, ancestor of the branches known as Clann Fínghin and Clann Rua, was slain in 1258 by Fínghin Mac Carthy (the victor of Callann) in retribution for the killing of An Crom O Donovan. His son (Donnchadh) was, in 1282 'treacherously slain together with five nobles of his people at Innishannon by the foreigners' — probably the Barrys. Retribution for these slayings was exacted in 1304-5 when the sons of Fínghin son of Mac Raith (called 'Clann Fínghin' in the annals) killed first Tadhg Rua Mac Carthy and then Geoffrey óg de Carew.

Meanwhile, in the main line, Tadhg had four sons — Donnchadh, his successor, Mathghamhain from whom descended Clann Mic Céin Rua, David from whom came Clann Mic Dauith and Tadhg Rua from whom came Clann Mic Taidhg Rua. Donnchadh, styled 'of Rath Dreoáin' died in 1297 leaving three sons — Diarmaid Mór (II), Tadhg an Óir (from whom descended the O Mahonys of Uí Flainn Lua) and Tomás. In the year 1315 they were attacked by four of Fínghin's sons who came with four long ships from Béarra and encamped on Carbery island in Dunmanus Bay. There they remained for most of the summer, a thorn in the side of Diarmaid Mór and Tadhg an Óir. One reason for the attack may have been that the invaders' grandfather, Mac Raith — and not Tadhg — was, according to one genealogy, the eldest son of Diarmaid Mór I, so entitling them to be regarded as the senior line. Eventually Diarmaid Mór's son, Fínghin, hauled a boat from Ballyrisode strand across the ridge of the peninsula to Dunmanus and from there ferried out his forces in relays to Carbery island by night. When dawn broke he attacked and defeated the sons of Fínghin, two of whom were killed and the other two taken prisoner.

The O Mahonys' close involvement with the Mac Carthys led to much conflict and dispersal. In 1283 one of the Carbery Mac Carthys and his Uí Echach supporters who had been in rebellion made peace with Mac Carthy, king of Desmond. The O Mahonys included Cian son of Mael Muad and the sons of Domhnall son of Lochlainn. 'And the king's land was given to them', say the annals. Two years later Domhnall óg Mac Carthy (Carbery) was released from imprisonment on condition that he handed over a large contingent of the Uí Mhathghamhna to John de Cogan, but most of the hostages were later released unharmed.

The successor to Diarmaid Mór II (in the main line) was Fínghin. He had two brothers, Domhnall and Diarmaid, to whom, it is said, their father willed Rossbrin and eighteen ploughlands besides, but when Fínghin refused to give them possession they departed in anger. Diarmaid became a follower of Mac Carthy Mór in Kerry and was ancestor of the Sliocht Meirgeach O Mahonys, chief stewards of Mac Carthy Mór. (One branch of these was, in the 17th century, in possession of Kilmeedy castle in Drishane parish.) Domhnall moved to Barrett's country (then under pressure from the Mac Carthys) where he founded the Kilnaglory branch of whom we have little information apart from a genealogy which traces their descent down to Dáibhíth son of Conchubhar, their chief representative in the 17th century. Another of Fínghin's brothers, Donnchadh, was styled Ó Mathghamhna Donn.

It would appear, then, that there was a castle or stronghold at Rossbrin in this era. (Ros Broin may have taken its name from Bron or Bran, great-grandfather of Mathghamhain.) Obviously it was not the residence of the chief but of his *tánaiste* or some other relative. The chieftain in 1473 resided at Ard an Tennail (Ardintenant or White Castle near Schull). This could hardly have been erected before the 14th century since Donnchadh, who died in 1297, was styled 'of Rath Dreoáin' — probably the strongly-fortified ringfort which gave name to the townlands of Rathruane near Ballydehob. Other O Mahony castles, whose picturesque ruins still adorn the western headlands, were erected at Dún Locha (Three Castle Head), Leamcon (Black Castle), Dunmanus, Dunbeacon, Ballydevlin and Castle island (formerly Meán-inis). There were twelve in all, according to Sir Richard Cox, who wrote in the 17th century. Others may have been at Lissagriffin, Knockeens, Crookhaven and Castle Mehigan. This last was probably granted to the O Mehigans by the O Mahonys, perhaps in return for literary duties. Eoin Másach Ua Maethagáin composed an elegy on one of the O Driscolls in the 16th century.

On the political scene the Mac Carthys and O Mahonys were in the forefront of the supporters of the first Earl of Desmond's rebellious acts in the 14th century. About fifteen O Mahony leaders are listed as having been attached to the Earl's army when in 1345 he attacked Norman settlements in various parts of Co. Cork. They bore such names as Omaghoun Keen, Mac Loghlyn Omaghoun, Conghir Brak' Omaghoun and Omaghoun Fynith Mc Conghir. They do not appear to include the lord of *An Fonn Iartharach* (as the western lands were then known) who should probably have been Domhnall son of Fínghin. But a 15th century genealogy states that a second cousin of his, Diarmaid Ó Mathghamhna Buí, was lord over *An Fonn Iartharach* (as well as over

Uí Flainn Lua, a fact confirmed by other genealogies). There must have been a succession dispute, resolved, no doubt, by allotting to Diarmaid Buí's branch a section of the western lands; in the 16th-17th centuries these included Bawnshanaclogh, Shanavagh, Coosane, Colla, Ballyrisode and Rathruane. Separated as they were from Uí Flainn Lua, the proprietors of this area became an independent sub-sept, known as Sliocht Taidhg − named perhaps after their ancestor, Tadhg an Óir. In 1599 the lands of O Mahony Fionn were estimated at 105 ploughlands and those of Sliocht Taidhg at 36.

The setting up of Diarmaid Mór Mac Carthy as lord of all Muskerry in 1353 must have led to conflict with the O Mahonys who were settled there. In 1367 Diarmaid Mór was slain by Clann Fínghin O Mahonys at Inse Aille (? Inchaleagh, par. Aghinagh). Later we find Clann Fínghin settled in the parishes of Aglish and Moviddy, apparently accepting the overlordship of the Mac Carthys. Another Diarmaid, of the Mac Carthy lords of Desmond, was slain (treacherously according to the *Annals of Ulster*) by the O Mahonys of An Fonn Iartharach in 1381.

In the lordship of An Fonn Iartharach Domhnall (son of Fínghin) was succeeded by Diarmaid Runntach, 'a truly hospitable man who never refused to give anything to anyone', who died in 1427 'after a victory of penance', as did also his son Conchobhar Cabach in 1473, in his own fortress of Ard an Tennail. The lordship was then taken by Conchobhar's brother, Donnchadh, while a third brother, Fínghin, became *tánaiste*. Fínghin resided at Rossbrin castle and was one of the foremost scholars of his day in Munster. Among his literary works was an Irish translation of 'The Travels of Sir John Mandeville'. He was also the chosen patron of another learned scholar-historian and alumnus of Oxford, Donal O Fihelly, who dedicated to Fínghin his Annals of Ireland, probably the work now known as 'Mac Carthaigh's Book'. Donnchadh Ó Duinnín compiled a manuscript for Fínghin in Rossbrin castle in 1465. (Another scribe of the same period wrote on the manuscript in O Mahony's house at Bel na Duiblinne or Ballydevlin.) It is likely too that in Fínghin's time was compiled the genealogical account of the O Mahonys known as the 'Psalter of Rossbrin', which, unfortunately, has not survived. After Fínghin had succeeded his brother Donnchadh as chief his death in 1496 was recorded in several of the books of annals: 'Ó Mathghamhna of An Fonn Iartharach, that is, Fínghin, a jubilant universal protagonist of the hospitality and valour of west Munster, the man most accomplished in Latin and English of all his contemporaries, died this year.'

Following on Fínghin's death a succession dispute arose between the families of the various brothers and eventually the son of Conchobhar Cabach became chief. He was known as *Conchobhar Fionn na n-each* ('Fair Conchobhar of the steeds') and after his time the title 'O Mahony Fionn' was adopted. He was succeeded by his two brothers, Fínghin Caol of Leamcon (from whom came the O Mahonys Caol) and Diarmaid of Dún Locha but the chieftaincy then reverted to his son, Conchobhar Fionn *na gcros*. At this period the O Mahonys and O Driscolls were closely linked. A daughter of Fínghin of Rossbrin married Fínghin O Driscoll of Collymore, and their son, Conchobhar O Driscoll, married Jane, daughter of Conchobhar Fionn O Mahony. Jane married secondly O Mahony Carbery and was the mother of Fínghin O Mahony of Castle-mahon who, accordingly, was half-brother to the father of Sir Fínghin O Driscoll.

The O Mahonys first experienced the era of Elizabethan conquest in 1562 when Donal O Mahony of Rossbrin, great-grandson of Fínghin the scholar, was seized in Cork city, charged with piracy, condemned and hanged. The citizens of Cork then fitted out an expedition to capture Rossbrin castle. In this they claimed to have been successful but — whether through agreement or otherwise — the chief, O Mahony Fionn, got possession of the castle and lands. In 1571 Sir John Perrott took the castle and put in a garrison of Mac Sweeney gallowglass. A year later, these were fined 60 cows for 'rebellious practices' and in 1576 were pardoned along with Teig mac Conor O Mahony, gentleman, for 'conspiracy, confederation and rebellion.' Eventually, in 1578, Conogher O Mahony, brother of the attainted Donal, was given a lease of Rossbrin and its lands at a nominal rent. He must have died soon afterwards and his son and heir, Donal Mac Conor, became involved in the second Desmond rebellion. Inevitably there followed the confiscation in 1584 of Rossbrin with 1,080 acres adjoining, 'parcel of the possessions of Donal O Mahony, of high treason attainted'. The lands were leased to Oliver Lambert and sold in 1602 to Robert Morgan. The O Mahonys never subsequently recovered Rossbrin though an attempt was made by Donell mac Teig O Mahony, son of Tadhg 'Spáinneach' — so-called because he entered the Spanish service after his father's execution in 1562. Pensioners in the Spanish army in 1605 were Teig (na Bally), Donnel and Conogher O Mahowny.

Another castle confiscated was Dunbeacon, whose owner, Donal son of Fínghin, had also taken part in the Geraldine rebellion. In 1588 the O Mahonys attacked and burned Dunbeacon, following the line of action taken by their namesakes in Kinalmeaky.

At this period Conchobhar Fionn III had succeeded his father in the chieftaincy. It was probably he who in 1574 in Cork city attended on Sir Peter Carew, cousin of Sir George Carew and a descendant of their ancient adversaries in Ivagha. Sir Peter was reviving the Carew claim to half the kingdom of Cork but died before making much progress. A year later, O Mahony was back in Cork to join in the festivities at Sir Henry Sidney's Christmas party. So it is no surprise to find that he refused to take part in the Desmond rebellion, even though he had his lands spoiled by Sir James of Desmond for his refusal. In financial difficulty, he mortgaged Inis Fada (Long Island) and 'Callacrowe' to Richard Roche of Kinsale. Then in 1592 he applied for and got a 'Surrender and Regrant' of all the O Mahony Fionn lands. A few weeks later he was dead, leaving a young family to mourn him. Sir Geoffrey Fenton, in 1597, obtained the wardship of his son and heir, Donnchadh. When in March 1600 the O Mahonys visited O Neill in his encampment at Inishcarra, their visit was avenged by government forces under Captain Flower who 'took a great prey and killed divers of the O Mahons' in April. Carew, who wrote that 'O Mahon Carbrey and O Mahon-Fin' were among the disloyal friends and supporters of Florence Mac Carthy, continued the harassment in the following month. The result was that the O Mahonys and O Crowleys sued for peace, which lasted until the arrival of the Spaniards at Kinsale.

In June 1602, just before the siege of Dunboy, a section of the Earl of Thomond's army, accompanied by the sons of Sir Owen O Sullivan, surprised and captured the O Mahony castle of Dunmanus, killing four of the guards. After Dunboy had fallen, Capt. Roger Harvey's company captured Leamcon castle, belonging to Conogher O Mahony, grandson of Fínghin Caol. In July, Conogher was among those who set sail for Spain from Ardea, but subsequently he received a pardon. Dunmanus, too, was recovered by the O Mahonys. Fynine mac Thaddeus Gankagh O Mahony died there in 1634 leaving a son and heir, Thaddeus.

In March 1602, Donogh O Mahony of Ardintenant, the heir to the chieftaincy, died and was succeeded by his brother, Donal, also a minor, whose wardship had been granted to Sir George Carew. His inheritance included the castles of Ardintenant, Ballydevlin and Dún Locha with 'chiefries' from the occupiers of the other castles. In 1607 he let Ardintenant and ten ploughlands to Thomas Hollander and later to Sir Geoffrey Galway, making Ballydevlin his own residence. In 1616 Dominick Roche of Kinsale got a royal grant of Ardintenant (with licence to empark a manor there), part of Dunbeacon and chief rents out of Ballydevlin, Dún Locha and other lands. (Philip Roch was a 'titulado' in Ardintenant in 1659.) In 1627 Dún Locha was let to Dermot Coghlan through whom Richard Boyle (Earl of Cork) gained an interest in it.

Boyle was also involved in a takeover of the lands of Sliocht Taidhg. Of the 36 ploughlands, Donogh O Mahony of Skeaghanore (par. Kilcoe) held 22 and Teig O Mahony of Ballyrisode held 4. After Donogh had died, leaving a six-year-old son and heir, Dermot, the lands were seized in 1615 by Boyle on the pretext of a title purchased from Donogh Mac Carthy who claimed to have bought the lands from Donogh's uncle. Boyle's tenants were sued for possession by young Dermot O Mahony of Skeaghanore in 1623. Dermot's long-drawn-out suit was unsuccessful but in 1634 he mortgaged several thousand acres to the Coppingers. (The castles of Dunbeacon, Dunmanus and Leamcon, together with many townlands in Ivagha were mentioned in Sir Walter Coppinger's 'regrant' in 1615.)

At Leamcon, the representatives of Conor O Mahony in 1622 leased the lands to Sir William Hull, then occupying the confiscated castle of Dunbeacon. After the outbreak of the rebellion Hull wrote (on 22 October 1642) regarding his losses: 'The firste Robbers wer great O Mahowne als O Mahouon Foone of the parish of Kilmoo, gent, . . . Dennis Roagh O Mahowne, Lord of the Castell of Donmanos and his sonn Daniell mc Donnogh O Mahowne, gents., Dermond O Glack (als Dermond Cartye) of Donbeacon castell, gent., Cornellis O Mahowne, Fynnon oge O Mahowne, Dermond O Mahown and their other two brothers, all of Lymcon, gents., Mahowne Merriga (als Mahowne oge O Mahown), Dermod Merriga (als O Mahowne) Teig O Mahowne, all of the Gubbyn, yeomen . . . with 7 or 800 other Rebells came about Christmas last and besieged the castell and town of Crookhaven, seised on all the Inhabitants' goods . . . in this company were Teig Merriga of Kilmoo and his son, yeomen, Dermond O Mahowne and his brother Cnoghore of parish Kilmoo, gents.'

With a recommendation such as this there was no difficulty in having the O Mahonys outlawed in 1643 — apart from getting their names right. The chief ('O Mahowney Ffound') is named as Donnell (who had died more than ten years previously leaving Conchobhar as heir) and his residence as 'Carignaghy'. Also outlawed were Connor of Leamcon, Cnogher (Mac Fínghin) of Gurteenakilla, Connor (alias Mac Idwyla) of Ballyrisode, Fínghin of Arderrawinny, Keane of Geary (? Gerahies, par. Kilcrohane), Donnell and Keane of Ballniskeagh (?) and Dermott alias Muskrigh of Skeaghanore. (*Muscraigheach* because he was of the Sliocht Taidhg who were descended from the Uí Flainn Lua O Mahonys of Muskerry.)

The next step was confiscation. Conchobhar O Mahony Fionn, the chief, had his castle of Ballydevlin and 718 acres confiscated. A similar fate befell the O Mahonys of Dunmanus (1594 acres), Dermod of Skeaghanore (1567 acres), O Mahonys of Leamcon (1244 acres), Mac a'Deile of Ballyrisode and Durrus (1210 + 646 acres), Knoghor O Mahowny of Coolagh (751 acres) and Dermod na Buolly of Kilcrohane (282 acres).

The new landowners in Ivagha bore such names as Sir Richard Hull, Lord Kingston and Sir William Petty. But because of the remoteness of their newly-acquired estates, they appear to have been willing to accept the former owners as lessees or tenants. So in the census of 1659 we find classed as 'tituladoes' Dermod and Donnogh O Mahony at Coolagh, Teige mac Cnoghor at Gurteenakilla, Connor at Kilbronoge, Connor at Derryconnell and Finnine at Arderrawinny. In Kilmoe parish Donnogh was at Cloghanacullen and David at Callaros Oughter. One of the named transplantees from Co. Cork (to Connacht) was Finine oge O Mahowny of Ivagh — probably Leamcon.

A sad little postscript is found in the will of Kean O Mahon son of Dermod of Skeaghanore who lived on a farm at Ardura (par. Kilcoe), part of the former Sliocht Taidhg lands. He bequeathed to his children 'the Irish interest I had in this ploughland if it ever be restored' — which inevitably it was not.

The last despairing effort of the sept in supporting King James resulted in the outlawry in 1690 of the following O Mahonys: Florence O Mahon, Leamcon; Thady mac Dermott, Derryleary; Cornelius, Dermot and Thady oge mac Tage, Dough; David mac Cnogher oge, Cullishagh (? Callaros); Florence mac Cnogher Oge, Nagholerragh (? Scrahany-leary); Donat mac Teige, Cooradarrigan; Daniel mac Teige, Dunmanus; Daniel, Ballydevlin; Darmit oge, Dumyone (? Dunbeacon); Darmitt Darreagh, Colla; Cornelius Spaine and Daniel Spaine, Caher. All are described as either 'gent' or 'esq'. Not one was restored to his patrimony by the Court of Claims.

O Mahonys of Kinalmeaky

Although its very name, Cineál mBéice, links this barony with Bécc, a remote ancestor of the Uí Echach, there are no records of O Mahonys occupying it in the early Norman period. In 1300 'Kinalbek', including what is now part of East Muskerry south of the Lee, contained many Norman *villes*. It formed part of Milo de Cogan's grant which descended to the de Courceys. In 1372 an inquisition following the death of Miles de Courcey found that the cantred of 'Kinalbeg and Flanlow' was let by de Courcey to Philip de Barry (óg). However, the Gaelic resurgence of this era must have brought the O Mahonys back to Kinalmeaky. Paradoxically, they came to be known as the O Mahonys *Cairbreach* (of Carbery) while those who actually dwelt in Carbery were not! The genealogies trace their origin to Conchobhar son of Donnchadh na hImirce Timchill of the western O Mahonys. It may well be that they repossessed Kinalmeaky in the time of Diarmaid Cairbreach who was fifth in descent from Conchobhar and who flourished probably in the late 14th century.

Kinalmeaky was for long the farthest east territory of a Gaelic sept in Co. Cork as all of east Cork was in the possession of lords of Norman descent. It was a small compact lordship estimated in Elizabethan times at 63 ploughlands. The earliest chief's castle is said to have been at Caisleán na Leacht (Castlelack) but this was replaced — possibly in the 15th century — by Caisleán Uí Mhathghamhna (Castle Mahowney) near the present town of Bandon (formerly known as Droichead Uí Mhathghamhna). Ó Huidhrín's early 15th century poem describes Ó Mathghamhna's territory as:

> *Cinél mBéce, the land of cattle,*
> *Around the Bandon of fair woods.*

Not until the 16th century do we get official notices of this sept. A State Paper of 1515 named 'O Mahund of Kynalmeke, Chief Captayne of his nation' as one of the independent Irish chieftains. Sixty years later, Sir Henry Sydney described O Mahony, who came to visit him in

Cork, as 'a man of small force, although a proper countrie'. The chief at that time was Fínghin — 'Florence O Mahony, alias O Mahony Carybry, of Castell Mahowny'. In 1570 he and his son (another Florence) were pardoned in company with Mac Carthy Reagh of Kilbrittain. Seven years later one of the Florences was again pardoned, together with Dermod O Mahown (also of Castlemahown) and 25 of his men (at the suit of O Mahown Carbry). They included Cornelius O Mahown, Teig *na reilige* O Mahown and Morriertagh Mac Dowling, all of Kinalmeaky. These were three brothers, sons of Muircheartach O Mahony and nephews (as well as possible rivals) of Florence. An earlier Fiant of the same year (in which the third brother is named as Moriertagh oge O Mahowny mac Moriertagh) describes them as of Castlemahowne — from which they may later have expelled Florence.

Next we have a State Paper of 25 July 1580 which informs us that '. . . one Conogher O Mahowne, being a rebel, and kept 40 men always attending upon him, was killed by two cousins german of his own — which are sons to O Mahowne that now is — and his head sent hither to Cork — which Conoghor was brother to Teige Mc Relagey, who is also come in upon protection'.

So far, this appears a mere family quarrel over the chieftaincy, so frequent in Elizabethan times. But now came a more sinister development. An inquisition held at Cork in 1584 found that the slain Conogher was seized of Castlemahowne and of the lands of Kinalmeaky, and that he went into rebellion at Ballyhoura on the 9th August, 22nd year of Queen Elizabeth. (This should read 21st Eliz., i.e. 1579, just after the return of James Fitzmaurice from the continent.) It must have come as quite a shock to the sons of Florence — among whom Maelmhuadh seems to have been the recognized leader — to discover that their reward for having slain their rebellious cousin was a declaration that Conogher had been the legal owner of the Kinalmeaky lands all of which were now confiscated. This shameless piece of legalized landgrabbing was completed soon afterwards by the allotment on 14 March 1586 of over 30,000 acres of Kinalmeaky to three English 'undertakers' — Phane Beecher, Hugh Worth and Michael Sydnam. (Worth sold his share to Sir Richard Grenville not long after.) And it was not just the chief of his name who was dispossessed on this occasion. Undertakers were so called because they undertook to fulfil certain conditions, in particular the planting of English Protestant families on their estates. Beecher was one of the few who fulfilled his undertakings to the letter and he built houses for 91 English families. The result was that none of the O Mahony name was even allowed to remain as tenant on the land of Kinalmeaky.

Not unnaturally, the O Mahonys protested vehemently. A 1587 account of 'Land in Munster allotted to undertakers, claimed by the Irish' included: 'Claimed by Mac Carthy Reagh and by one of the O Mahownies in Kinelmeky — Kinelmeky the country of Conogher O

Mahony, containing two seignories and a half'. The O Mahony in question was Domhnall *Gránna*, son of Maelmhuadh and grandson of Florence, the chieftain of 1570. Mac Carthy Reagh was Sir Owen, an uncle of the famous Florence Mac Carthy (the prisoner in the Tower) who in one account was accused of fomenting Donal Gránna's rebellion. Donal may have hoped that Mac Carthy Reagh's influence might assist in the recovery of his lands, but an inquiry held in Cork in 1588 rejected the claim, maintaining that 'O Mahony was as ancient in Kinalmeaky as Mac Carthy Reagh in Carbery, and that he was never known nor heard of to be either appointed or displaced by any Mac Carthy'.

Donal Gránna made at least one journey to London to press his claim but to no avail. A local tradition pictured him as disdainfully rejecting a settlement which would allow him half his lands, either north or south of the river. His reply gave rise to an old saying – *I dteannta a chéile is fearr iad, mar a dúirt Ó Mathghamhna leis an bhfear gallda* (It is better to have both, as O Mahony said to the foreigner).

Finding all legal avenues closed, O Mahony took the obvious course. He entered into rebellion and startled the undertakers of Munster by burning Castle Mahowne of which Beecher had taken possession. 'The whole nation of O Mahons is to be suspected', wrote Beecher's attorney, 'for they do pretend title and are brothers and cousins of the traitor, Daniel Graney O Mahon'. Another report complained that 'he walketh by night and often by day in Carbery at his pleasure'. For several years Donal kept up this guerrilla warfare, making life miserable for the undertakers and their tenants until his death – probably in action – in 1594. The leadership was then taken by 'Dermod O Mahowne, alias O Mahowne Carberie' – perhaps an uncle of Donal. In the same year, Fr. (now Blessed) John Cornelius O Mahony, S.J., born (in Cornwall) of noble parents and of the illustrious family of the O Mahonys of Kinalmeaky, was hanged at Dorchester.

In 1595 as a result of Florence Mac Carthy's representations on behalf of Dermot O Mahony in which he again asserted that the rebel Conoghor had never been seized of Kinalmeaky, the Privy Council contemplated holding another inquisition, but following vehement protests from Henry Beecher (son of Phane) abandoned the idea and decided to let sleeping dogs lie.

So it can hardly have been a matter of great sorrow for the O Mahonys when, in October 1598, Hugh O Neill's army sent the undertakers of Munster scuttling to safety, abandoning their seignories with unseemly haste. The Beechers fled from Castle Mahon which was, no doubt, exultantly re-occupied by its former owners. Around this time, Dermot O Mahony was succeeded by Maelmhuadh, seemingly a brother of Donal Gránna (whose father was also named Maelmhuadh). In March 1599 Sir Thomas Norreys burned the corn and spoiled the country of the O Mahonys in Kinalmeaky. A repetition of these tactics by Carew forced the O Mahonys into submission but in October (1599) Essex received a report that O Neill had assured to David O Mahowny and the rest of his sept the lands of Kinalmeaky, and when O Neill arrived at Inishcarra in January of 1600 the O Mahonys visited his camp there. In November of that year, the English garrison from Kinsale took a prey of 200 cows from Kinalmeaky but when they attempted a second prey a month later they were met by a force of 300 foot and some horse led by Maelmhuadh O Mahony and his cousin, Dermot Maol Mac Carthy, and were driven off without any booty.

Eventually, however, Carew's spoiling and burning tactics forced almost all the Munster chieftains into submission. On 14th May 1601 Maelmhuadh (described as Moelmoe O Mahowny alias O Mahowny of Castlemahowny, Co. Cork, gent.), his son Cian, and their followers, received official pardons. It is significant that Maelmhuadh was described as 'of Castlemahowny', and the addresses of his followers – most of them in Kilbrogan parish – show how quickly the O Mahonys had repossessed their lands. These followers included: Connoghor O Mahowny of Coolfadda, gent., Fynen mac Connoghor mac Donnell Y Mahowny of Gurtynymahowny (*Goirtín Uí Mhathghamhna* now Gurteen), Teige mac Connoghor O Mahowny alias Teige ny Sawny of Fynagh (? Shinagh), gent., Donoghe mac Moielmoe O Mahowny of Farranthomas, gent., Shane ladir O Mahowny of Laragh, gent., Teige and Donogh mac Shane ladir Y Mahowny of Carhoon, yeomen. (These last two, in February 1602, after the battle of Kinsale, were resident in Tracton parish, according to a Fiant of that date, in which they are described as 'gentlemen'.)

Not content with these precautions, Carew went a step further. In July 1601, he lured to Cork and there imprisoned the three leaders he considered the most dangerous in the county. Two of these were Mac Carthys and the third was Maelmhuadh O Mahony. So when O Neill and O Donnell encamped in Kinalmeaky on their route to Kinsale the chief was not there to greet them. Still his people remained rebellious. Even after Kinsale, in the Autumn of 1602, Captain Flower burned all the O Mahonys' corn in Carbery and that of other rebels. And in one of the last skirmishes of the rebellion in January 1603 at Grillagh near Ballineen, Thaddeus (Teig) son of O Mahony Carbery fought at the side of Bishop Owen Mac Egan. He was later captured and put to death.

Finally, in June 1603, Maelmhuadh O Mahony was released from Cork prison on condition that his son and heir, Cian, remain in custody as a pledge for his father's loyalty. The old chief now bowed to the inevitable and took a lease of the lands of Killowen from the new owners for his own lifetime. We know that in 1611 when trees were being commandeered 'for His Majesty's shipping' eight hundred were demanded from 'Moyle More O Mahowne's' wood of Killowen.

After his death we hear no more of the O Mahony lords of Kinalmeaky. One pedigree names Mathghamhain son of Cian (and nephew of Domhnall Gránna) as a 17th century head of the now landless family. A traditional *rann*, said to have been composed on the occasion of a meeting between the representatives of the two ancient lordships, expresses well their new condition:

> *Ó Mathghamhna an Iarthair, agus tiarna Chineál mBéice,*
> *Beirt do bhí i dtiarnais 's anois ag iarraidh déirce.*
>
> (O Mahony of the west lands and the chief of Kinalmeaky;
> Two who once were lordly but now for alms are seeking.)

The name 'Mealmo O Maghoone' recurs in 1685 when one of that name was appointed constable of Ringrone by the corporation of Kinsale. Prouder titles, however, were borne by two others who, five years later, were outlawed for supporting King James II. They were: Colonel O Mahon, Kinalmeaky, and Florence O Mahon alias O Mahon, Castlemahon, esq.

Old memories die hard. Even though their former castle was completely reconstructed by the Bernard family in the early 18th century and renamed Castle Bernard, the old name lived on in the minds of Irish speakers. O Donovan Rossa in his *Recollections* recalls how one day (in the mid-19th century) he met a man with a car-load of hay as he rode into Bandon. *'Go d'aon caisleán é sin thall ansann?'* he enquired. *'Caisleán Uí Mhathúna'*, came the reply.

O Mahonys in Muskerry

At least three minor septs of O Mahonys settled in the territory south of the river Lee which became part of Muskerry when the Mac Carthys took the lordship of that area in the 14th century.

Clann Fínghin, whose origin has already been referred to, eventually settled in the Farran-Crookstown area. They were also known as Clann Fínghin na Ceitherne. One of the O Mahony supporters of the Earl of Desmond's rebellion in 1345 was named 'Omaghoun Gillenegill Okerny' – possibly the origin of the later O Mahony Kearneys. Mathghamhain Ó Mathghamhna, lord of Clann Fínghin, died in 1466. Diarmaid Dorcha, son of Conchobhar, became chief of Clann Fínghin after his elder brother, Donnchadh, had been hanged at Cork for his involvement in the second Desmond rebellion. In 1609 the king granted to Francis Gofton all the lands of Clanfineene, parcel of the estate of Donogh mac Connoghor, attainted. In the 17th century, Clann Fínghin were represented by Diarmaid son of Tadhg, the last to be named in the genealogy. He held Farnanes in the parish of Moviddy and in 1617 successfully defended his right of inheritance against Lord Muskerry. He was outlawed in 1643, but restored before his death in 1663. Then came the Williamite wars and a further confiscation. In 1700-1 a claim was lodged on behalf of one 'Darby Mahony, an ancient poor gentleman, grandson and heir of Dermot mac Teig Mahony', who had held the two half ploughlands of Farnanes until dispossessed by Thomas Crook who claimed them as part of the confiscated Clancarty estate. Darby never recovered an acre.

Incidentally, the adjective *rua* (red-haired) was of such frequent occurrence in this line that in the 16th century a segment became known as An Chlann Rua.

Clann Chonchubhair were a branch of the O Mahonys Carbery of Kinalmeaky and held 14 or 18 ploughlands spread over the parishes of Kilmurry and Kilmichael. Their genealogy ends with the two sons of Conchubhar, namely, Donnchadh and Fínghin. Another son of Conchubhar may have been the Dermod mac Cowhore mac Fynine O Mahowney, who along with Coomaryve or Cuvarryve mac Donogh mac Fynine was attainted in Elizabethan times, and their lands – Dunmarklum, Ballytrasna, Knocknaneirk, Lissarda, Ballymichael, Poularick and other townlands in Kilmurry parish – granted to Thomas Roper in 1612. Fínghin may have been the Finin Roe O Mahoon who at his death in 1628 held the townland of Poularick in Kilmurry as well as Derragh and Lack Beg, both in Kilnamartery, apparently mortgaged to him by Lord Muskerry. His son and heir was Donogh, probably the one who forfeited Knockaurane (Mount Music) and Gortinerig in Kilmichael parish as well as Teereeven in Kilmurry after the 1641 rebellion. Another son, Conor, forfeited Ballymichael (near Kilmurry) granted to him by Lord Muskerry in 1618. Still, at the time of the Civil Survey, a Donough O Mahony held a lease of Cloghmacow in Kilmurry parish.

The sept of Uí Flainn Lua (from whom were descended the Sliocht Taidhg) held the western part of Kilmichael parish – though undoubtedly Uí Flainn Lua itself covered a wider area in former times. In 1604 the entire 28 ploughlands, '. . . the lands of Donnell mac Connoghor O Mahony, late of Ichouloe, gentleman, for high treason attainted', were granted to Sir William Taafe. (Their genealogy derives later chieftains not from Donnell but from Donnchadh, son of Conchubhar an Chróchair ('of the bier') – perhaps his brother.) It is not clear what happened to the lands subsequently, but they seem to have been appropriated by Lord Muskerry. However, their title lived on in the popular mind and in 1719 Cian an Chróchair, fourth in descent from Donnchadh, was extolled in a poem by Domhnall na Tuile Mac Carthaigh (*Tá Uibh Fhloinn Luadh le suairceas lúthgháireach*). Cian was buried in Kilmichael graveyard. His son, Cornelius, like so many of his name, obtained a commission in the Spanish army and died in 1776. The executor of his will was Count Demetrius O Mahony (of the Kerry branch) whose father, Count Daniel, gained renown as the defender of Cremona in 1702, being immortalized in the lines of Thomas Davis:

> *At the head of the regiments of Dillon and Burke*
> *Is Major O Mahony, fierce as a Turk.*

An O Mahony from Muskerry, Fr. Conogher O Mahony, S.J., was

the author of a controversial work *Disputatio Apologetica* published in Lisbon in 1645. It was considered so extreme (e.g. in proposing that the Irish drive out the English completely and choose a king of their own race) that the Supreme Council of the Confederation of Kilkenny ordered that it be burned. (Fr. Francis O Mahony, O.S.F., Guardian of the Franciscan house in Cork city, was tortured and hanged in Cork in 1642.)

At home, several O Mahonys were poets and scholars. Donnchadh Caoch Ó Mathghamhna, a contemporary of Aodhagán Ó Raithile, was probably the best-known of the poets, while a Domhnall óg Ó Mathghamhna was both physician and poet to Dr. Tadhg Mac Carthy, bishop of Cork, in the early 18th century.

The most widely-known of the clan in the 19th century was John O Mahony (1815-1877) who was born near Kilbehenny where the counties of Cork, Limerick and Tipperary meet, an area in which his family were for long regarded as the natural leaders of the people. John O Mahony was a noted Young Irelander and one of the founders of the Fenian movement; it was, in fact, he who first suggested the use of the name 'Fenian'.

O Mahonys of the present day are served better than most in the preservation of the traditions of their ancestors, mainly due to the inauguration in 1955 of the O Mahony 'clan rallies' by the legendary Eoin ('The Pope') O Mahony.

Ó MURCHADHA.

Ó MURCHÚ   MURPHY

Out of every thousand people in Ireland today, approximately thirteen are surnamed Murphy, the most numerous of all our family names. One reason for its prevalence was the widespread popularity of Murchadh as a personal name, so that families of Uí Mhurchadha evolved independently in all the four provinces. Of these the best-known were the Uí Mhurchadha of Uí Felmeda in Co. Wexford, and in the absence of an alternative genealogy, literary men of the name in 18th century Co. Cork — Seán na Ráithíneach in particular — tended to derive their descent from this family.

It is, however, unlikely that a segment of a Co. Wexford sept settled in Co. Cork in the 13th or 14th century. Two possible sources may be found much nearer home, one being the Múscraighe Mittaine who populated Muskerry before the coming of the Eóganacht. Their ruling family group (at the time their pedigree was being compiled, probably in the 11th century) included Murchú son of Blathmac son of Scandal and Murchú or Murchad son of Fintan son of Scandal. From either of these may have sprung the Uí Mhurchadha of Muskerry — just as from Flann, eldest son of Blathmac, came the Uí Fhlainn (whence the name Múscraighe Uí Fhlainn).

Alternatively, they could have been of the Uí Chonaill Gabhra who formed the western portion of the dominant Uí Fidgente in the Co. Limerick area in the 7th and 8th centuries. Scanlán, a king of Uí Fidgente who died in 786, and six of his brothers are named as eponymous ancestors of various families there. One of the brothers was Murchad — ó tát Huí Murchadha (from whom descend the Uí Murchadha). Ballymurphy (Baile Uí Mhurchadha) near Croom may have been their residence for a time, but during the 12th century they could have joined in the southward migration of such Co. Limerick families as the O Donovans and the O Cullanes.

Since the Mac Carthys were supreme in Desmond from the early 12th century, it is not surprising that from the 14th century onwards almost all references to the Uí Mhurchadha involve the Mac Carthys. When Diarmaid Mór Mac Carthy established himself as lord of Muskerry in 1353 the Uí Mhurchadha became loyal followers of his branch of the family. After two sons of Diarmaid Mór — Tadhg and Cormac — had been slain, a third son, Feidhlime, became 4th lord of Muskerry, and to ensure his position engineered the slaying of his nephew (Diarmaid son of Tadgh) by the Barretts, a killing which disqualified Feidhlime's descendants from ever becoming lords of Muskerry. It also brought retribution from the Uí Mhurchadha; in 1382, according to *An Leabhar*

Muimhneach, Feidhlime was slain in Muskerry by Muinntir Mhurchadha. Later, when the Mac Carthys were at war with the Barretts in East Muskerry, Andrew Barrett was killed by the Uí Mhurchadha, in 1404, an event recorded in the *Annals of Connacht*.

The Mac Carthy expansion continued during the 15th century and by 1475 Mac Carthy Riabhach was in control of the southern bank of the Bandon river, opposite Innishannon which was in the territory of Barry Óg of Kinalea. As Innishannon parish embraced both sides of the river, a petition was sent to the Pope by Cormac Mc Carryg and Cornelius Y Murchw (*Ó Murchadha*), cleric, asking that a separate parish be set up on the southern bank. Cornelius (who was rector of Rathdrought, now part of Ballinadee parish) was described as being precentor of Cork and 'of noble birth'. This statement may be a mere formality or it may indicate the existence of a senior line of the family, which certainly existed a century later, at Knockavilla.

The Barrys erected the castle of Dundanier ('Downdaniel') in an attempt to stem the Mac Carthy onrush, but in vain. In the early 16th century, Barry Óg was described as a vassal of Mac Carthy Riabhach, while Cormac Láidir Mac Carthy of Muskerry extended his sway to the shores of Cork harbour for a time, erecting the castles of Blarney and Kilcrea as well as several religious houses. Many areas once held by families of Norman origin were overrun. Accompanying the Mac Carthys came the O Riordans, O Murchadhas, Clancallaghans, and later the Mac Sweeneys, four families mentioned in a document of 1600 as 'followers in Muscreye'. The Uí Mhurchadha appear to have been allotted four ploughlands and these were almost certainly in the parish of Knockavilla.

Cnoc an Bhile ('hill of the sacred tree') is a noticeable eminence a few miles north-east of Bandon. It was an ancient church site which gave its name to the surrounding parish. In the 14th century it was Barry Óg territory but here again the Mac Carthys took over much of the parish and settled some of their followers. It is likely that Cormac Láidir's 15th century penetration resulted in the renaming of over 1,000 acres just north of the village of Crossbarry as *Baile Uí Mhurchadha* (Ballymurphy North and South). Part, at least, of this was previously known as Ceathrú Liath. By Elizabethan times, however, the Barrys must have regained that townland as the Uí Mhurchadha were then concentrated in the western half of the parish. The chief individual of the name was described in 1584 as 'Teige mac Dermond mac Donnell Y Morohow of Knocyvillie, gentleman' (i.e. *Tadhg mac Diarmada mhic Dhomhnaill Uí Mhurchadha*). In 1586 Thomas Barry Óg mortgaged to him Tuocusheen and Killeadyne (? Killeady). We know that one of the Barry Óg connections, James Barry of Brinny (d. 1618), was married to Ellen, daughter of Daniel Murphy of Knockavilla, gent.

This, no doubt, was the Donell mac Dermodie mac Donnell, gent., of Knockavilla, who was pardoned in 1601. He was probably a brother of Tadhg. So also it seems, was Dermod oge mac Dermod mac Donell I

Morhow of Knockavilla who received a pardon in 1603, and who leased Cnockyrussealige from Cormac Mac Carthy of Ballea in 1634. (Cnoc an Ruiséalaigh or Russelhill was named after the Russell family; Tadhg's wife was Catherine, daughter of James Russell, as appears from a pardon granted to both of them in 1604. Five years later Tadhg and Thomas son of Maurice Russell were acting as joint trustees on behalf of Ellen Mac Carthy, wife of Thomas Goggane of Barnahely.) Tadhg Ó Murchadha was one of four appointed in 1604 to arbitrate on a dispute between rival Mac Carthy chiefs. He appears to have lived then in the castle of Tuocusheen.

In this townland also in 1601 were pardoned Teige mac Donnell mac Teige O Morghow, Shean mac Donell O Moroghow and Conoghor O Moroghow, while in the neighbouring townland of Lissanisky were Dermod, Owen and Conor, sons of Murrihirtagh O Murroghow, and Teige mac Donogh O Moroghow, yeoman. Ten others of the name are recorded in the Fiants as having received pardons in Knockavilla parish. So permeated with the Uí Mhurchadha was the whole parish that it is difficult to visualize the principal location of the sept as having been anywhere else but here. Even today, Murphy is the surname most frequently inscribed on the headstones of Knockavilla graveyard, where deceased members of families from such places as Rearour, Corravreeda, Ballygroman and Killumney were brought to be buried in their ancestral graves.

Raheen (*Ráithín*) is another townland in the parish, one which gave its name to the branch of the family whose best-known representative was the poet Seán na Ráithíneach Ó Murchadha (1700-1762). In an elegy on Diarmaid Ó Murchadha who died at Knockavilla in 1754, he tells us that Diarmaid was son of Diarmaid son of Tadhg son of Seán who fought in the service of the Mac Carthys. The Murphys of the Kiskeam-Boherbue area, according to family tradition, also originated in Knockavilla. One Tadhg Ó Murchadha and his followers in the 17th century settled, it is said, first in Glenville and later in the Sliabh Luachra area, and Tadhg's son, Domhnall, eloped with Sadhbh, daughter of O Keeffe, an elopement which led to a battle between the two families.

The Fiants of Queen Elizabeth record the names of approximately 360 of the Uí Mhurchadha in Co. Cork, the occupations of about 100 being listed. Just over half of these are described as 'yeomen' (i.e. substantial farmers). Three (including one lady) are described as 'gentlemen'. Four were 'horsemen' (and four 'horseboys'), fourteen were 'husbandmen', while at the bottom of the social scale were twenty 'kerns'.

Their Christian names, when analysed, show that Domhnall (Donnell) was the most popular, being used by one in every six. Next in order of popularity were John, Donnchadh, Tadhg, Diarmaid, Conchobhar, William, Edward and Thomas. Nicknames used in the Fiants included *bán, dubh, rua, óg, maol, ciotach, riabhach*, and *caoch*. One interesting name is Dermot Barrie O Morowe of Kilcrea (1601), the earliest occurrence of a name well-known on the hurling-fields of Muskerry. A headstone in Kilcrea records three successive John Barry Murphys of Coolmackee, the earliest having died in 1818. This stone is said to have been preceded by one commemorating Dermod Roe Murphy, 1710, believed to be the Derby Murphy who in 1703 was tenant of Coolmucky, Ballinguilly, Rathfelane etc. Earlier still, a Shane mac Donell Imureghu of Coolmackee was pardoned in 1601.

Kilcrea provides a typical example of the habitat favoured by the Murphys – a tract of fertile farmland dominated by one of the foremost Mac Carthy castles in Muskerry. No fewer than 25 of the name are recorded in the Fiants as living in Kilcrea and the Murphys still form the largest name-group buried in the old friary there.

A similar position obtained wherever a Mac Carthy castle stood. Twelve Murphys are named in the Fiants as being of Blarney. In 1635 John mac Donell O Morrogho, of Blarney, gentleman, acted as attorney for Cormac óg Mac Carthy, Viscount Muskerry. Perhaps he (or his son?) was the Don Jean de Morphie or Morfi, colonel of an Irish regiment in Spanish Flanders between 1646 and 1659, who in his will dated 1669, desired that his wife should go to reside in Blarney Castle '. . . which is cordially offered her by my lady, the Countess Dowager of Clancarty'. His estate (willed to his eldest son, Charles, with remainders to his other sons, John, Dermot and Morogh) included rent charges on the lands of Macroney and Mashanaglass. Don John's widow may have been the Maria de Margarita de Murphy who in 1700 claimed the benefit of a judgement debt affecting the estates of Donogh, Earl of Clancarty, only to have her petition dismissed.

Another John O Murphy, of the parish of St. Mary, Shandon, Cork, gent., had four sons – John, Cornelius, Darby and Richard – who at the end of the Jacobite wars in Ireland (1691) sailed for France. Cornelius Nicholas O Murphy became captain of a frigate with the East Indian Co. and later settled in St. Malo. Another exile, Eugene-Charles O Sullivan of Brussels, traced his descent (on the maternal side) from William O Murphy of Moellan (Meelin), Co. Cork, whose will was registered in 1685.

Thadeo O Mouroghu (son of Edmundo O Mouroghu of Ross, Co. Cork) arrived in Portugal in 1622 with his wife, Mariana Mac Carthy of Manch, who gave birth to a son. The son, Domingo, was brought up by the queen of Spain and was a page to the king. Later he became a high-ranking officer in the king's household and a knight of the military order of Calatrava in 1663.

There was also a Connor Murphy of Blarney, gent., who was outlawed for his part in the 1641 rebellion. Incidentally the Blarney estates included Coolymurraghue (*Cúil Uí Mhurchadha*, formerly *Currach Uí Mhurchadha*), the name of which indicates a connection with the family.

Murphys were numerous around Cloghroe, Ballea, Dripsey, Macroom, Drishane, Kanturk, Lohort and other Mac Carthy strongholds — but not at Dundareirke (par. Kilnamartery) where the Mac Carthys of Tuath na Dromann (descended from the Feidhlime slain by the Uí Mhurchadha in 1382) held sway. It is noticeable too that although Murphy is the most numerous surname on the gravestones of Kilcrea, Knockavilla, Athnowen (Ovens), Kilmurry (south) and Donoughmore, there are only four Murphy headstones in Kilnamartery, none earlier than 1842.

Outside of Muskerry, the name was, and is, well-known in most parts of Co. Cork. There is another Baile Uí Mhurchadha in east Cork (Ballymurphy, Upper and Lower, par. Knockmourne) dating back to the 16th century if not further. Murphys were to be found in Murragh and Enniskeane as well as in Bear and Bantry. Most of the latter would have been tenants of O Sullivan Béarra, but near Bantry in the townland of Breeny lived a more independent branch of Murphy (Óg). Dermod Mac Donogh O Murroghoe of Brinnagh who died about 1620 was succeeded by John Oge Murfie als. O Murroghowe of Bryny, gent. John died in 1636, leaving an infant son of the same name who died a year later. His cousin, Donnchadh, then inherited the property, but was outlawed seven years later for taking part in the 1641 rebellion. It may have been the same Donogh (Oge Murphy) whose 56 acres in Knockmacool (par. Desertserges, bar. Carbery) were confiscated.

No landowners of the name are to be found among the Jacobites outlawed in 1690, but there were three from Cork city listed, namely, William Murphy, wool-merchant, Denis Murphy, boatman, and Richard Murphy fitz John, merchant. In 1699 Capt. Dennish Murphy of Lismeelcunnin (near Kanturk) submitted a claim for restoration of his property under the articles of Limerick.

Even after the various upheavals and resettlements, the Murphys are often found as loyal followers of the Mac Carthys. All the surviving poems of Diarmaid óg Ó Murchadha, who flourished in the late 17th century, extol the Earls of Clancarty, while Seán na Ráithíneach, already referred to, was a faithful eulogist of the Mac Carthys of Carraig na bhFear and their relatives all his life. Others were to be found in Clancarty's regiment in the Irish Brigade. A Cornelius Murphy was major of the regiment in 1691 while the quartermaster in 1703 was also a Murphy. Some became rapparees, like 'John Murphy Roe, late of Toames' one of a band of outlaws for whose apprehension large rewards were offered in 1694. (The outlaws derisively issued their own counter-proclamation two weeks later 'given at the Councell Chamber at Annahally Bogg'.) Seán Rua, who seems to have spent a period in the Irish Brigade, was highly regarded in local song and story.

The majority, however, remained on as tenants on the same estates as formerly, but under new landlords. The rough census made about 1659 lists Murphys for most of the baronies in Co. Cork, but the returns for Muskerry have not survived. Murphy was then the most numerous surname in Kinalea, Kinalmeaky, Barretts and the Liberties of Kinsale. In East Carbery there were 37 named 'Murphy and Murphy Oge'. In Kinalmeaky there were 25 Murphys and 11 O Morohows, which shows that the new 'English' form was taking over. The 'ph' sound in the name appears to have originated in the Kilkenny area in the 16th century, due to a tendency there in the spoken Irish to change a medial 'ch' to 'ph'. From there it spread to Co. Cork in the early 17th century.

A handful of the name in the 18th century were of sufficient importance to have their wills registered – John Murphy of Ballyndanagh, gent. (1734) William Murphy of Mitchelstown, gent. (1766) Michael Murphy of Ballynabearna (1775), Michael Murphy, Newtown (Bantry) gent. (1779). Some Gaelic poets of the name were also to be found in Co. Cork in that period – Donnchadh (*an Phuisín*) Ó Murchadha, Tadgh Ó Murchadha of Kanturk etc. That the work of these and of many other Gaelic poets was preserved is due to the diligence of another of the name, Dr. John Murphy, Catholic bishop of Cork from 1815 to 1847, who salvaged numerous Irish manuscripts for posterity. Members of his family, whose burial-place is at Carrigrohane, were prominent in the literary, political, ecclesiastical and industrial life of Cork city in the 19th century, and they also founded a brewery and distillery.

By then, of course, there were scores of family groups in various parts of the county, often distinguished by nicknames such as Dubh, Bán, Bog, Stuac, Buidhe, Caol, Pound, Doirbh, etc. The last-mentioned name was prominent in the parishes of Kilmurry and Kilmichael in the 18th century. A 1752 headstone in Kilmurry (South) bears the name Dennis Murphy, alias Dorriffe.

There is no lack of descendants of these families on the fertile lands of Muskerry today – or indeed in Co. Cork as a whole, where only the O Sullivans outnumber the Murphys.

Ó MURTHUILE

Ó MUIRTHILE   HURLEY

The most curious fact regarding this family name is that it should never have been anglicized Hurley at all but rather Murley. The surname Hurley properly belonged to the Uí Urthuile of Knocklong, Co. Limerick, who are given a Dalcassian descent by the genealogists, though they may have been descended from Aurthuile of Uí Chonaill Gabhra (bar. of Connello, Co. Limerick).

Unfortunately the pedigree-compilers of the 19th century united the two family groups by making Randal Ó Murthuile – whose initials, R.M. (not R.H.), appear on a window-embrasure in Ballynacarriga castle – a son of Thomas O Hurley of Knocklong. There may well have been a marriage connection, if Lodge was correct in stating that Juliana, daughter of Dermod O Hurley of Knocklong, married Edmund Oge de Courcy of Kinsale, since we know that Edmund's grand-daughter married Randal Oge Duff Hurley of Ballynacarriga, but otherwise the two families were not connected. (Even among the 18th century poets there was a Seán mac Donnchadh Uí Mhurthuile with surname distinct from that of Seán mac Muiris Uí Urthuile.)

The surname Ó Murthuile existed in west Cork several centuries before Ballynacarriga castle was built but its origin is not adverted to by genealogists except for the early 14th century *Duan Catháin* which derives 'the nobles of the Uí Mhuirthile' from one Murthuile Mór (described as 'the pupil of Colman') of Uí Eachach stock. The suggested origin is, however, extremely dubious, since Murthuile Mór's father, Duilghín, is named elsewhere as son of Beannt, progenitor of the Beanntraighe, a sept nowhere else regarded as connected with the Uí Eachach. (There was, incidentally, an Ó Muirrthaili family name among the Fir Sceinde of Connacht but it is unlikely that any of these came as far south as Co. Cork.)

As early as 1260 Gillerenav Omurthyle (*Giolla-na-naomh Ó Murthuile*) accompanied Fínghin Mac Carthy of Carbery in a raid on Norman lands.

The name was prominent in ecclesiastical circles during the following centuries. In 1391 John Omurchily, a priest of Ross diocese, was declared to be in wrongful possession of the vicarage of Lislee. In 1411-13 mention is made of Renaldus Omurchali (O Murrchuyle), a canon of Cork diocese. This name Raghnall (Randal) was the favourite personal name in the family for long afterwards. In 1421 Donaldus Omurchile who had, apparently, transferred to Killaloe diocese, nominated his relative, Johannes Omurchile as vicar of Fanlobbus parish (Dunmanway). John died in 1464, in which year Reginald Imurhyle, who had lectured in canon law at Oxford University for over a year and a half, was reinstated as rector of Cursruhara (probably Ballymoney). No doubt he was the Renaldus Omurhily who was a canon of Ross in 1469 and 1471 – and a canon of Cork in 1470! In 1494 Reynaldus Ymirtaly was perpetual vicar of Fanlobbus and in 1510 Renaldus Ymurhuly, junior, was a canon of Cork, while John and Donaldus Ymurli held several benefices in the diocese. From 1517 to 1519 John O Murrilly, who had previously been abbot of the Cistercian Abbeymahon, was bishop of Ross. John was nephew of the previous bishop, Edmund de Courcy, who resigned in his (John's) favour. Bishop O Murrilly was buried in Timoleague friary.

A friar named Donatus O Muirhily was sacristan of Muckross friary, Killarney, in 1589. Hearing of attacks on other abbeys, he hid some of the sacred vessels on an island in Loch Léin. He and a companion were later captured but though tortured to death refused to reveal the hiding-place of the valuables.

It is interesting that a Raghnall Ó Murthuile was rector of Ballymoney in 1464 since the castle of Ballynacarriga is in that parish and the Ó Murthuile owners of the castle appear to have always been Randals. Béal Átha na Carraige, the castle site itself, seems to have been originally in the townland of Ardea – referred to as 'Ardea Ranell oge' in a Mac Carthy document of 1593 (there being a head-rent on it payable to the lord of Carbery). In 1633 it was called 'the castle and 2 plowlands of Ardea, alias Bealnicarrigie.' Later, however, it became a townland in its own right.

The first of the family mentioned in the Fiants was Randolph O Hurrely of Nedineagh, gent., pardoned in 1576. This is also the first time we notice the 'Hurley' version of the surname although it was presumably the same Randal who, nine years later, put his initials, R.M., on the newly-built Ballynacarriga castle. The full inscription is '1585 R.M.C.C.' The C.C. refers to his wife, Catherine O Cullane of Ballincourcey. Randal appears to have resided at Nedineagh (par. Fanlobbus) prior to the building of the castle. Florence Mac Carthy of Enniskeane married Marianne, daughter of Randal Hurley of Nedineagh. In 1615 Randal Óg Hurley was granted the right to hold a fair at Nedineagh More on 25th July and the day following. This became the celebrated fair of Béal Átha Buidhe, formerly known as *Aonach Randal Óg*.

Also in the 1576 Fiant two of the sept were pardoned at Ardea – Donald mac Teige mac Coyne, yeoman (later described as Donell roo mag Teig mac Qwyne y Hurrily, kern) and Cormac mac Conoghor mac Ronell. By 1584 Ranell Oge O Hurley was described as of Ballynacarriga; Donell roo and Dermod mac Shane mac Hurryly, kerns, were also there. Presumably this was while the castle was in the course of erection; it was completed by 1585. Another pardon was granted in 1587 to 'Ranell Hoorley, junior, gent'. But we cannot be sure that this was a son of Randal of 1576 since his father may also have been Randal. There is a reference in 1594 to 'Reynold oge O Hurley, th'elder' who was a follower of Florence Mac Carthy.

A branch at Phale (also in Ballymoney parish) retained the Ó Murthuile form somewhat longer. Thady mac Donoghe lea (*liath*) and Donald mac Donogho lea O Murhillie were there in 1579 with Donogh roe mac Donoghoe lea at nearby Enniskeane. In 1584 we have Donell leigh mac Diermod O Huryly but two years later Dermott mac Donell oge O Murhilly.

Fínghin (Carrach) O Driscoll, who died in 1600, was married to an O Hurley (*Onóra Ní Raghnaill*) and in the year before he died he entrusted to David Hurley of Ballynecurrigg (? Ballynacarriga) — probably her brother — the castle of Dún na Long for the use of Onóra.

Quite a number of O Hurleys received pardons in 1601 (before the battle of Kinsale). These included a contingent from Ballynacarriga — Ranell oge O Hurlie, Ranell oge beg Morhelly, Donell mac Donogh O Morhelly, Teige row O Morhellie, Donogh mac William, Donell mac Teig O Murhely, John mac Teig O Murhely, Donogh mac Donell oge O Murhely, Donell roe mac Teig O Murhely, Dermod mac Donell oge O Murhely. There was a further group in Templebryan, headed by William mac Ranell Hurlie and his wife, Ellen ny Learie. Others were to be found in the Kilbrittain area — Kilbrittain, Ratharoon, Garranereagh, Ballynabooly (near Sandycove), Carriganass and even Dundanier (Downdaniel near Innishannon) where there was a Leaffe mac Conoghor mac Teige Murly. These, no doubt, were followers or tenants of Mac Carthy Reagh.

Yet despite their submission, Carew had no scruple in instructing the Earl of Thomond as follows on 9th March 1602: 'If Teg O' Norsy's castle (Togher) and Rannell Duff's shall in your opinion be meet for the service, do you take them into your hands and have wards in them; But let not your intent be discovered until you be possessed of them.'

The O Hurleys do not seem to have suffered any loss of lands at this time, although mention is made (in an inquisition taken in 1631) of a royal grant of the lands of Ballynacarriga to Arthur Chichester of Belfast. Reinald Hurley and William Hurly were among the freeholders of Carbery who protested against the exaction of the 'Earl's Beeves' tax in 1610. In 1615 Randal Óg of Ballynacarriga, in company with Florence mac Donell Mac Carthy of Benduff (par. Ross), assignees of Sir James Semple, as a result of a 'surrender' received a grant from James I of extensive lands in Carbery, including those of several of the O Crowleys of Kiltallowe and the castle of Dún an Óir on Cléire. Later it was discovered that much of this land had previously been alienated to them by the O Crowleys and they had to pay fines to receive pardons for same.

This Randal Óg is also credited with the building of Ballinvard castle, near Rossmore. That castle was occupied in 1641 by William mac Randal Hurley who in his will, dated 11th August of that year, named William Óg as his son and heir. To his second son, David, he left Cashelisky, Letter and Cahirconvoy (Caher), with further bequests to a third son, Maurice, with his six daughters and wife. Another son, James, he disinherited. He desired to be buried in the parish of Kilmeen, and while this wish may have been carried out, his heirs never enjoyed their inheritance since all the estates were swallowed up in the Cromwellian confiscations. Ballinvard castle is said to have been garrisoned by the English and subsequently dismantled by order of Cromwell.

Randal Óg was dead by 1631, the year in which an inquisition was held into his lands. These included the castle and town of Ballynacarriga. Randal Óg (II) was declared to be his son and heir. It was probably this second Randal Óg who, in 1620, married Ellen, daughter of John Lord Courcy (by Mary, daughter of Cormac O Crowley). Their fathers drew up an indenture to the effect that Ellen was to have the use of the lands of Buddrimeen and Kilcaskan (par. Ballymoney) and Ardcahan (par. Fanlobbus). But Randal mortgaged the lands to William Wiseman and in 1633 Ellen's brother, Gerald Lord Courcy, made him sign a bond to hand over for Ellen's use the castle and lands of Ballynacarriga in the event of his not redeeming the mortgage within three years. Randal must have failed to redeem his mortgage since after his death in 1637, Wiseman (a crown official who operated from Bandonbridge) was found to be still in possession of the lands in question. It was in 1633 also that the couple presented to the church a chalice with the inscription 'Dns. Ranaldus Hurly et Dna. Eulina de Curcy'. It is now kept at St. Mary's Cathedral, Cork. It is interesting that the de Courcy connection was kept up a century later, when during the Penal days in 1731, it was reported that Teige mac Shane O Murley, priest, was maintained by the Lord Courcy.

The 1633 bond was signed by, among others, Randal Óg, Donell mac Dermod Hurley of Cloonkirgeen and Donoghe mac Donell Hurley of Bunanumera. This latter place, near Manch Bridge, was the seat of another branch of the family. Donoghe was the son of Donell mac Teige who in turn may have been a son of the Teig Hurley of Carbery, said to have been 'prejudicial' to Florence Mac Carthy in 1614.

The Kilbrittain branch was also prominent in this period. In 1626 Daniel Mac Carthy Riabhach of Kilbrittain granted a 21-year lease of lands in Ballymore (par. Kilbrittain) and Carriggynigary to Daniel Oge Hurley, gent., and in 1634 a similar lease of Ratharoon East to Dermod mac Owen Hurley and Cnogher mac Owen Hurley. This last-named had been pardoned in 1624 for his part in breaking into Barry's castle of Timoleague in 1620, an offence for which he was outlawed and attainted.

Inevitably the Hurleys were swept into the maelstrom of 1641. Among the outlawed in 1643 were Randal and Randal oge Hurley of

Ballynacarriga, William of Ballinvard, Donogh mac Donell of Bunanumera, Donnell oge of Kilbrittain, William of Liscubba (par. Kilmeen),
James of Grillagh (par. Ballymoney) and James of Ballinbride – all
described as gentlemen; also Ellen Hurley, widow, of Grillagh Ighteragh.
It was inevitable too that all of these would suffer confiscation of their
estates once the war had ended. Randal Óg lost his castle and lands of
Ardea als. Ballynacarriga, as well as Cloonkirgeen, these going to Ben-
jamin Crofts – as did Donogh mac Daniel's lands of Bunanumera. William
oge Hurley forfeited Ballinvard castle which was acquired by the archbishop of Dublin. He also lost Lisnabrinny, Lissinroe and part of
Knockea while others of the family lost Liscubba, Kilmeen and parts of
Letter and Caher, all in the parish of Kilmeen. Other Hurley lands were
confiscated in the parishes of Kinneigh, Fanlobbus, and Inchydoney,the
total confiscated being 3,830 plantation acres.

These were acquired by men such as Crofts, Richard Dashwood,
John Freke, Francis Beamish, etc. No Hurley proprietors were left in
Carbery. According to the 1659 census the only 'tituladoes' of the name
left in the county were John Hurley and Florence, his son, of Gortna-
horna in Kilbrittain cantred (Barleyfield, par. Rathclarin), tenants of
James Coppinger.

One branch may have got a tenancy of some of their former lands,
only to lose them again. For supporting King James in 1691 Arthur
Hurley of Grillagh was attainted. Three years later we learn that John
Hurly, late of Grillagh, and Dermot mac Maurice Hurly were members
of a band of rebels 'on their keeping' in the mountains of west Cork,
for whose apprehension large rewards were offered.(In 1731 James Cox
and Gilbert Mellefont were paid £10 for the capture of two notorious
tories, John Hurly and Hugh Hurly.)

According to Cronelly, the Randal Óg who was outlawed with his
father in 1641 was succeeded, in turn, by four further Randals, the last
of whom was succeeded by John Hurly who emigrated to America with
his family about 1810.

According to O Hart (1883) the Ballynacarriga O Hurleys were then
represented by the O Hurleys of Drimoleague, but he also derived the
Hurly families of Ballynacarriga and of Farranhavane (near Bandon)
directly from the lords of Ballynacarriga castle and says they were
styled *na carraige*.

Many traditions of the Ballynacarriga O Hurleys were recorded by
Rev. P. Hurley over seventy years ago. One such tradition related to the
time when the castle was occupied by Cromwellian soldiers anxious to
capture a noted rebel named *Crothúr a'ghleanna*. Although they took
his mother prisoner, Crothúr's marksmanship intimidated them into
setting her free again. (There may be a confusion here with a later
popular hero of the Williamite wars, Séamus 'Atroher', i.e. *An t-urchar*
or the marksman.)

According to Fr. Hurley, the Randal Óg of that period fought at

Limerick and was later buried at Clogagh graveyard near Timoleague. He left six sons, two of whom were priests. Perhaps one of these was the 'Popish priest John Hurly' for whose delivery to Cork in 1715 Maurice Stack was paid six shillings (or 30p!). Randal's brother was the father of seven sons and three daughters. Two of the sons, James and Jeremiah, were in Limerick during the Williamite siege. James (*an t-urchar*) is credited with having shot six troopers who were sent to arrest him at his house. One of James' sons was Randal who as parish priest of Clontead was responsible for renovating the graveyards of Clontead, Kilmonoge and Ballyfeard where his name is still to be seen inscribed on the gate-pillars. Descendants of James' other sons lived at Desertserges and at Clonakilty.

(DE) NAGLE

NANGLE   DE NÓGLA

Jocelyn de Angulo (i.e. of Angle in Pembrokeshire) was one of the warriors who served Hugh de Lacy, first Norman lord of Meath. An Irish genealogy claims that Jocelyn was son of Ludovicus, 'the French knight', who was son of 'the Duke of the city, i.e. Ludarius, son of the king of France'. The family name afterwards became de Naungle and de Nangle. De Lacy bestowed Navan on Jocelyn, and the Nangles were afterwards barons of Navan. To Jocelyn's son, Gilbert, he gave the barony of Morgallion. But Gilbert was outlawed for taking service under Cathal (Crobderg) O Connor who granted him lands in Connacht. He seems to have been the first of the Norman lords to adopt Irish ways, being styled in the Irish fashion 'Mac Oistealbh' (Jocelyn's son) from whence derived the surname Mac Costello or Costello.

According to the *Annals of Inisfallen*, another 'son of Jocelyn' was slain during an incursion into Desmond led by William de Burgo in 1201. However, despite statements by D'Alton, O Hart and others, there is no firm evidence of a connection between the Nagles of Co. Cork and the descendants of Jocelyn. The Justiciary Rolls show that around 1300 there were Nangles to be found in various counties of Leinster and Munster. A few legal cases indicate that the surname had been introduced to the north Cork area by then. In 1301 Christiana le Nangle was murdered by John Scorlag who fled to the church of Mallow for refuge. In 1307 Thomas del Naungle was a defendant in a case concerning a freehold at Buttevant. In the same year Alan de Naungle was found guilty of taking from Moinmor two mares belonging to Henry le Blound. Perhaps a son of his was the David son of Alan de Nangle who in 1309 held the knight's fee of Moynamny for which he paid an annual rent of 13s 4d to James de Keting. *Móin Mhór* was the name given to the moorland between Mourne Abbey and Rathcormack, the area afterwards known as 'Nagle's Mountains'. Moynamny or Monanimy, where David settled, later became the chief seat of the Nagle family. It may have been the same David who was a juror at an inquisition in Cork in 1331.

While any or all of these could have been descended from Jocelyn de Angulo, they do not appear to have been persons of wealth and influence. Later in the century, one of the name did achieve a certain notoriety. In 1376 justices were appointed to investigate the crimes of David Naungle in the counties of Cork and Limerick, and to 'clear the gaol of him according to law', and to receive from him a reasonable fine, half of which was to be paid to John Grassebek for the expenses of his capture and the other half into the Exchequer. Maurice Nangle was in better favour in 1423 when the king gave a licence to him and to John Roche to buy four weys of corn in Ireland and to transport it in a ship to Kinsale.

According to O Hart, there was a David Nagle of Monanimy in 1451 whose daughter Margaret, married John O Connor, lord of Ciarraighe Luachra and founder of Lislaughtin friary. On the other hand the 'Roche charter' of *c.* 1460 indicates that the lordship of Móin Ainmne was largely Roche property but that there was a William Nagle (*Uilliam do Nócla*) who held lands in the district.

There is evidence too of the name in Cork city in the early 16th century. Thomas Nogull was a merchant in Cork in 1518-19 while Dominus David Nogla (also Dawye Nagle) was chaplain of Holy Trinity (Christ Church) between 1543 and 1552.

It is only in the latter half of the 16th century that we get any real records of a cohesive family grouping of Nagles centred around their stronghold of Monanimy. This castle stands on the north bank of the Blackwater, opposite Killavullen, though the main part of Monanimy parish lies south of the river, reaching up the slopes of Nagle's Mountains. In 1551 a pardon was granted to Richard Noglay of Monanimy, gent., and to David Noglay of the same, horseman. Again, in 1573, when the first Desmond rebellion had ended, a pardon was issued to what was practically the whole Nagle sept 'in consideration of their having released all debts due to them by the crown, and all exactions and cesses for the Queen's service in Munster which had been taken from them' – a rather nice touch of legal blackmail! Those pardoned were: Gybon Nagill fitz Richard of Carrigacunna, gent., James Icollyn Nangle fitz Richard of same, Maurice ny cargy (*na carraige*) Nagill fitz Richard of same. (Carrigacunna castle was built in the mid-16th century according to an O Keeffe pedigree which states that Siobhán O Keeffe of Glenville was the wife of Nagle '. . . *agus isí do thóguibh Caisleán Charraig an Chunna.*) Gerot roo fitz Richard Nagell of Carganduff (? Carrigduff, par. Mourneabbey) and John ny Killy Nagill of same, gentlemen, Maurice ny cargy fitz John Nangle of same, yeoman; David fitz John Nangill of Ballygriffin (birthplace of Nano Nagle); Klyny Nagyll of Ballynegaraghe (Mount Nagle); John Nagill fitz Gerot of Glanmore, yeoman, David Nagill fitz Morishe, George Nagill fitz Morishe, Gerot beg Nagill of same; Gerot Nagill fitz Richard of Monanimy. Finally the chief of his name was pardoned – John Nagyll fitz Richard of Monanimy, gent.

James Nagle 'alias ykhollen' of Carrigacunna was again pardoned in 1575, as were Gerot Nagell of Monanimy, gent., Gybbon roo Nagle of Monanimy and Edmond Nagle of Monanimy, kern. Richard Nagle 'alias ny Counte', yeoman, was described as of Monanimy in 1575 and of Carrigacunna a year later. (Carrigacunna is close to Monanimy but on the south bank of the Blackwater.) In 1583, after the second Desmond rebellion, Maurice Nagell fitz Gerrot and William Nagell, both of Monanimy, were pardoned, as were, in the following year, David Nagill and Brien mac Donell, gent., both of Monanimy and described as Lord Viscount Roche's men. Brien mac Donell may have been a Mac Sweeney constable in Monanimy castle.

Richard Nagle of Monanimy (1551) is described in a pedigree compiled in 1638 as son of John son of Richard son of John son of Richard son of John Nagle of Monanimy. If this be correct, the last-named John must have been at Monanimy in the early 15th century. Richard's eldest son was also named John, as we have seen in the Fiant of 1573. This John died without heirs and the chieftaincy then passed to his brother David, probably the one mentioned in 1584. His jury service in 1604 proved a costly experience for David. On trial was William Meagh, the recorder of Cork who led a revolt against the Crown in Cork city, and because they found him not guilty of treason the jurors were sentenced 'to wear papers on their heads declaring their offence in the face of the four courts to be held at Drogheda' while David was also fined £500. However, David served again on a jury in Mallow in 1611; in that same year three ploughlands of Monanimy formed part of a regrant to Lord Roche by James I.

David Nagle was married to Ellen Roche of Ballyhooly and they had ten sons and nine daughters. The eldest daughter, Ellin, married Sylvanus, eldest son of Edmund Spenser, the poet. In 1613 Sylvanus Spencer of Kilcolman and David Nagle of Monanimy jointly demised to Ion Grove the townland of Rossagh in Doneraile parish. When David died in 1637 he was succeeded by his son, Richard, who must have died soon afterwards. All we know of him is that he married Ellen Barry of Rahanisky. His eldest son, John, was outlawed in 1642 (along with James Nagle of Glanworth) and was killed at Monanimy in the course of the rebellion, according to an inquisition taken in 1653.

After the war had ended, Monanimy (along with Killissane, Ballygriffin, Killavullen, Ballymacmoy, Cappagh, Carrigacunna and Ballincurrig) was forfeited by Pierce Nagle, 'Irish papist'. It is not clear whether Pierce was son or brother of John. Shanballyduff (mod. Ballyduff) was forfeited by Edmond Nagle. Although Captain Pierce Nagle of Monanimy was among those specially decreed to be in the grace and favour of Charles II at the restoration in 1660, both Monanimy and Carrigacunna ended up in the possession of the Earl of Clancarty while Ballygriffin went to Sir John St. Leger and Killissane to John Blennerhasset. But the trafficking in land was not all in one direction. Richard Nagle acquired Ballincurrig (forfeited by Pierce) as well as some Roche lands in surrounding parishes and some belonging to the Walls of Wallstown.

This, no doubt, was the subsequent Sir Richard Nagle, second son of James Nagle of Annakisha. A James Nagle (along with Ulick Roche) had forfeited Clenor (par. Clenor) in the Cromwellian confiscations but appears to have taken leases of lands (including Annakisha) in the same parish. At any rate James Nagle in his will dated 1676 (he died in 1678) is described as of Annakisha, and this became the chief Nagle seat in the 18th century. James' eldest son and heir was Pierce, but his second son, Richard, achieved greater fame.

Born in 1636, Richard Nagle was at first educated for the priesthood but afterwards studied law, in which profession he made rapid progress. Both Richard and Pierce married daughters of James Kearney, of Rathcoole, Co. Tipperary. After living for a time at Carrigacunna Richard moved, in 1684, to Dublin where two years later he was knighted and appointed attorney-general. He was also chosen speaker of the House of Commons. (His brother, David of Carrigoon, was M.P. for Mallow in King James's parliament.) Being an ardent Jacobite he played a prominent part in the war between William and James. Military orders to commanders of regiments signed by King James were countersigned by Sir Richard Nagle, as chief secretary. After the Boyne disaster, Sir Richard was one of those consulted by King James in Dublin. Their decision was that James should lose no time in going to France accompanied by Sir Richard who continued to fill the office of Secretary of State for Ireland at the Court of St. Germain. His loyalty to James brought about his attainder by William and he forfeited all his estates in Cos. Cork and Waterford. Carrigacunna was acquired by Henry Viscount Sydney who sold it to the Mitchell family. Sir Richard died in 1699 leaving seven sons and six daughters.

His brother, Pierce of Annakisha, who had been High Sheriff of Co. Cork in 1689, forfeited his estates as well, but acquired new leases of Annakisha and lands nearby. His son and heir, James, was educated in France, and married a daughter of Alderman Stephen Gould of Cork, thus connecting the Nagles with the Coppingers of Barryscourt and Garrancloyne. A half-brother of James, named Richard, made his residence near Annakisha, in a townland called Ballynegaraghe or Ballingeary which he renamed Mount Nagle. Richard's grandson, another Richard, was created a baronet in 1812. James of Annakisha's son and heir was Pierce who settled for a time at Naglesborough in the parish of Castletownroche. The last of the line to reside at Annakisha was another Pierce, in the 19th century. His lands were sold in the Encumbered Estates Court in 1851 and the house fell into ruins soon afterwards.

The Nagles of Annakisha were one of the few landed Catholic families in Co. Cork during the Penal days. A brother of Pierce and Sir Richard, Fr. Garrett Nagle, joined the Capuchin order and died in France. Fr. James Nagle was parish priest of Kilworth *c*. 1704-1722. The executors of his will included his cousins Joseph Nagle and Richard Nagle fitz Pierce. The Nagles built a Catholic chapel (thatched) near their Annakisha residence and this was used as a chapel of ease to Killavullen until the new church at Clenor was built about 1876.

The census of 1659 does not list Nagle as a 'principal Irish name' in any of the baronies in Co. Cork, probably because the returns for

Fermoy are lacking. The only 'titulado' mentioned is John Nagle, of Youghal, where the name was fairly prevalent. There was a Nicholas Nagle there in 1585. In 1611 James and John Nagle were tuckers in the town. William Nagle was bailiff there in 1613 and Nicholas Nagle in 1636. In King James' time in 1688 Andrew Nagle was mayor of Youghal, Sir Richard Nagle and Pierce Nagle, merchant, were aldermen and William Nagle, gent., a burgess. Andrew and Sir Richard were outlawed by the Williamites.

The Nagles of Garnavilla, near Cahir in Co. Tipperary, were descended from James, a brother of Sir Richard. At Chichester House in 1702 James was allowed a lease of Garnavilla. His grandson, another James, was tried for and acquitted of suspected Whiteboy activities in 1767, the year after Fr. Sheehy was hanged at Clonmel. This James' granddaughter was the lovely 'Kate of Garnavilla' celebrated in verse by Edward Lysaght. (At least one of the Nagle family, Éadbhard de Nógla, was a well-known Irish poet of the 18th century.)

From another brother of Sir Richard, namely David (M.P.) of Carrigoon, were descended the Nagles of Ballygriffin near Monanimy. David's son, Garrett of Ballygriffin, married Ann Mathew and their eldest daughter was Nano Nagle (1719-1784), foundress of the Presentation order of nuns.

Yet another branch flourished in the parish of Templeroan. Supporters of King James outlawed there in 1690 included Garrett Nangle of Daumstown (? Dannanstown), gent., and Richard son of Garrett Nangle of Shanballymore. (This Garrett was a near relative of Sir Richard, according to his tombstone inscription at Templeroan.) Garrett was later in possession of Clogher and Shanagh which were leased to his son David and sold to Arthur St. Leger in 1700 for £650. But the Nagles must have continued in residence as Garrett and David Nagle, gents., were at Clogher in 1713 while in 1731 Edward and Edmond Nagle were paying £58 rental half-yearly to St. Leger. Edward Nagle of Clogher died in 1757. A month later Garrett Burke purchased a lease of the lands from Edward's nephew, Garrett Nagle, the Nagles continuing to live at Ballinamona castle. (This castle and the now demolished castle of Shanagh are believed to have been built by the Nagles.)

Garrett Burke was brother to Edmund Burke, the statesman, the most celebrated connection of the Nagle family. Their mother was Mary Nagle, daughter of Garrett Nagle of Ballyduff near Mallow. (Garrett of Shanballyduffe was successful in his claim for restoration in 1699.) Mary married Richard Burke in 1724. According to one account, the young Edmund Burke spent five years of his childhood at Ballyduff and received his early education at a hedge-school in the ruined castle of Monanimy. He often revisited the area in later years and his elder son was named Richard Nagle Burke.

MAC OITIR

MAC COITIR   COTTER

Despite the number of Nordic settlements on the Irish coast during the Brian Boru era when family names were being adopted in Ireland, surprisingly few names can be traced to Viking ancestors. Coppinger and Skiddy were names once influential in Cork city and believed to derive from Danish sources, but they have become progessively rarer so that the only family name of Viking origin now numerous in the Cork area is that of Cotter. The modern form of this name is derived from the Irish word *mac* (which supplied the initial 'C') and the Norse personal name *Otr* or *Ottir* (otter). That the Viking ancestry of the family was still remembered in the 18th century is shown in the lament composed by Seán na Ráithíneach Ó Murchadha on the death of his fellow-poet, Liam Ruadh Mac Coitir, in 1738:

Niadh de bhorbfhuil Lochlann laochta anall
(A champion descended from the hardy race of heroic Lochlann.)

Ottir was a name in frequent use among the Vikings, both in Ireland and outside it. The *Annals of the Four Masters* record the death of Oitir who sailed from Loch Dáchaoch (Waterford) to Scotland in 916, and in 1142 the taking of the kingship of Dublin by Ottir, grandson of Ottir, of the Hebrides.

A family manuscript claims the last-mentioned as ancestor of the Cotters of Cork, stating that his grandson, Therulfe mac Thorfin mac Cotter, settled in Cork after the Norman invasion. It is more likely that any Norse chieftains would have been forced out of Cork city at this period when Cork became an Anglo-Norman stronghold. The same manuscript names 'Famry Cotter' or 'Farrenmaccotter' as the first known residence of the family, but the only Farrancotter in Co. Cork is in Buttevant parish and likely to have been a later settlement.

All the indications are that the family originally settled in the barony of Imokilly, between Cork harbour and Ballycotton. In 1301 the only townland bearing their name was Balymaktocyr in Imokilly (presumably Ballymakcotyr was intended). While one might take this to be the modern Ballymacotter in the parish of Ballintemple on the coast of Imokilly, its position in the 1301 list indicates that it was, in fact, the 17th century Scart Mac Cotter, now Dunsfort near Midleton. Another townland called Dooneenmacotter (*Dúinín Mhic Oitir*) is near Shanagarry in the parish of Kilmahon. A 16th century roll of the lands from which the seneschal of Imokilly claimed rents and services included

261

'Clan Cottir's lands', namely: Dunnyne Mac Cottir, Ballyandryne, Ballyvicotter, Cnock capuyll, Ballymattley and Scart Mc Cottir. Elsewhere, Clancotter's lands were given as Balincopinera (Coppingerstown) and Cnockanacrushy. There was also a Carrige Cotter amongst the lands of the bishop of Cloyne.

The polarization of the inhabitants of Ireland in the 13th century into 'English' and 'Irish' created some difficulties for those of Norse extraction. In 1290 Maurice Makotere protested, on behalf of 300 of his race, at being treated like the native Irish (i.e. being killed or plundered at pleasure) when they were not Irish, his ancestors having purchased the rights of Englishmen for £3,000. He wrote 'from the world's end', a place rather difficult to identify. The king decreed that Maurice Makotere was, like his ancestors, 'a pure Englishman', and was to enjoy the same liberty and customs as his other English subjects. About the same time there was a Reginald Mac Cotir in Co. Tipperary who seems to have been a moneylender.

There is a reference to a member of the family at Castlecorth (Midleton) in a law case of 1307 when the court had to decide 'if Hugh le Copyner disseised Thomas Mc Ottir of his freehold in Castlecorth, 9 acres'. Perhaps this was the Thomas Mc Cotir who was a juror at an inquisition in Cork in 1331. It is rather ironic that Coppingerstown castle (near Midleton) later became one of the principal residences of the Cotters. The name 'Macodrys' appears several times in the mid-14th century 'Pipe Roll of Cloyne'. In 1354 Maurice Macodrys was a juror at an inquisition taken in Midleton. From another source we learn that 'Mac Cottyr' had the ancient privilege of presenting prebendaries to the church of Caherlag (near Glanmire). Thomas Maccotyr held the archdeaconry of Cloyne up to the time of his death c. 1350.

By 1400 the family had several offshoots – at Farranmaccotter (Farrancotter near Buttevant), on Inis Mór (Great Island in Cork Harbour) and the senior line in Coppingerstown castle near Midleton. In 1585 John Cotter of Coppingerstown, having land to the extent of 174 acres, made it over on his son, Edmund fitz John Cotter, on condition that he should divide and share it with his cousins after the manner of their predecessors. (This stipulation may explain why the Cotters never built up a centralized family power-base.) In 1610 Edmund's son, James mac Edmond fitz John oge Cotter of Coppingerstown, gent., received a pardon from King James, as also did another son, John. William son of Edmund Cotter forfeited his estates following the 1641 rebellion. His lands of Knockanegeragh and Cnocknegaple (now Gearagh, par. Midleton) passed into the possession of Sir William Penn. Coppingerstown went to Walter Scudamore. After William Cotter died without issue, the Cotters of the Great Island became the chief representatives of the family.

These were known as the Cotters Buidhe or 'Yellow Cotters', according to the family manuscript, other branches being distinguished as 'the Black Cotters', 'the Red Cotters' etc. Deeds of 1572-3 relating to lands on the Great Island mention James son of Maurice Mac Cotter, Gerald son of William (*juvenis*) Mac Cotter and Edmund Boy (Buidhe) Mac Cotter. One is a deed of conveyance by Edmond Hodnett of Belvelly castle, chief of his nation, to Gerald fitz William Juvenis Mac Coter, of one carucate called Hodnett's Wood, south of Belvelly.

In 1642 Edmond Cotter of Innismore or 'Barry's Island' removed to Ballinsperrig (near Carrigtwohill) which he had leased from Lord Barrymore. This residence became known as Cotter's Lodge, but is now called Anngrove. Other lands on the Great Island which Edmond purchased in 1665 from a lessee of Lord Barrymore's led to a series of lawsuits in the 18th century between the Cotters and the Barrymores, the final hearing being at the Bar of the House of Lords in 1732. Edmond died in 1660 and was buried in the family vault at Carrigtwohill.

His son and heir, James, for his services to King Charles II received a ring and other marks of royal favour. These services included the hunting down and assassination of the regicide, Col. John Lisle, in Switzerland in 1664. James later fought at Sedgemoor under James II who bestowed a knighthood on him. In 1689 Sir James Cotter was appointed governor of the city of Cork and of the Great Island and was also M.P. for the city. He was in command of the Jacobite troops at the battle of Bottle Hill, between Cork and Mallow, in 1691. After the war he was allowed to retain his estates under the articles of Limerick. Although in 1683 he had acquired lands at Ballymagooly (bar. Fermoy) formerly belonging to Theobald Roche, Sir James continued to reside at Ballinsperrig, as did his son, another James, who was the most tragic figure in the Cotter lineage.

Despite persistent efforts to have him brought up in the Protestant faith, the young James remained a champion of the Catholic and Stuart cause during the Penal days. Failing to convict him of Jacobite conspiracy, his enemies managed to have him imprisoned on what is generally regarded as having been a trumped-up charge of having raped one Elizabeth Squibb, a Quakeress. Repeated attempts to secure his release failed and he was hanged in Cork on 7th May, 1720, a deed which threw the Catholic population of the south into turmoil and despair.

The Protestant faction then succeeded in having his son, the third James, brought up in their faith. His mother (James II's widow) remarried and also sold back the leasehold interest of the Ballinsperrig property to the Barrys. James (III) set up house on the Ballymagooly estate, the family mansion there being known henceforth as Rockforest; another family residence nearby was called Cotterborough. James was created a baronet in 1763, and his descendants, the Cotters of Rockforest, continued to live there until the estate was finally sold by Sir James L. Cotter, the fifth baronet, in 1916.

Meanwhile, junior branches of the Cotters had been spreading, particulars of these not being easy to obtain. Among those mentioned in the Elizabethan Fiants are:

1573:   John Og mac Shane Mac Cottier of Inshinabacky, gent. (This is a small parish near Midleton; John was great-grandfather of the William Cotter who forfeited after 1641. A letter from Andrew Skiddy of Cork to Lord Burghley in June 1582, mentions the sad case of John or Shane oge McCotter. Shane complained that he had 100 kine, 40 calves, 28 garrans and a chief horse taken by Captains Rowley and Norreys.)
Robert mac James Mac Cotter of Corbally, yeoman.
Gerald mac James Mac Cottyr of Court, yeoman.

1577:   William mac Edmund Mac Cottier, Gerald and Edmund mac Shane Mac Cottier.

1578:   James balluf mac Shane og Mac Cottir. (*balbh* = dumb).

1582:   William gencaghe (*geancach*) Mac Cottir of Barry's Court, James fitz Gerrot fitz Pers Mac Cottier of same, Edmund mac Shane oge vic Cottier of Ringmeen (Great Island).

1583:   Peter Mac Cotter of Corkbeg.

1585:   William mac Thomas Mac Cotter of the Courts, kern.
James mac Garrett mac Peirs Mac Cotter of Court, yeoman.

It will be noticed that east Cork generally was Cotter territory, and this is borne out in the census of 1659 which lists the Cotters as a 'Principal Irish name' only in the barony of Barrymore, where, with 51 families, it was, after Barry, the most numerous family name. Curiously, it was written O Cotter, an obvious slip of the pen since it never so appears before or after.

As the great majority of these Cotters had long since been absorbed into the Irish-speaking milieu in which they flourished it is no surprise to find that some were Irish poets. It is noteworthy too that the well-known east Cork satire, *Párliament na mBan*, was dedicated to James, son of Sir James Cotter, hero of the Jacobite wars. The young James, whose life was so tragically cut short, has at least one poem ascribed to him, 17 quatrains lamenting the oppression of his country and written when he was but 17 years of age. Upwards of a dozen local Irish poets lamented his unjust execution, foremost among them being one of his own race, Liam Ruadh Mac Coitir (1675-1738), a native of Britway parish and a prolific writer. Liam's brother, Séamas Mór Mac Coitir, and his nephew Séamas Beag, of Curraghdermot, Castlelyons, were also Irish poets.

In a different context, another remarkable bearer of the name was Patrick Cotter who was born near Kinsale in 1761 and grew to a height of 8' 7''. Later styled 'Patrick Cotter O'Brien, the Irish Giant' he became quite a celebrity in Bristol where he died in 1806.

Ó RIAGÁIN

O REGAN

In pre-Norman Ireland Uí Riagáin family groups were to be found in several places — in Meath and in Thomond, for instance — but a separate Co. Cork group existed among the families of Fir Maige Féne in the Fermoy region. There were, in fact, two Uí Riagáin families there, one at Cregg and the other at Kilmaculla near Kildorrery. The family name is preserved in the townland of Coolyregan (*Cúil Uí Riagáin*) in Brigown parish.

Even after the Normans took control, the O Regans remained an east Cork family for several centuries. Among the witnesses to the charter of Matthew, bishop of Cloyne, *c.* 1185, was the 'great priest' U Regan — perhaps the Gilla Colmáin Ua Riacáin, 'a noble priest of the community of Cluain Uama' who, according to the *Annals of Inisfallen*, died in 1208. The same annals record the death in 1261 of Aedh Ó Riegan, treasurer of Cloyne. In 1295 Matthew Oregan and Thomas Oregan were among the followers of Philip le Blund pardoned for their trespasses. A Stephen Oregan, clerk, was involved in an unpleasant matrimonial dispute at Youghal in 1307. Matthew Oregan, rector of Dungourney and vicar of Dangandonovan, died in 1462.

Further evidence of their prevalence in east Cork is provided by the townland-names Ballyregan in Cloyne parish and Ballyregan in Carrigtohill parish. Some O Regan followers of the Condons were pardoned in 1585 — Donell O Reigane, shoemaker, Moreghow mac Dermody O Regan and Ellen oge, his wife. The 1659 census records ten O Regan families living in Barrymore.

By then, however, the majority of the O Regans in the county were to be found in west Cork. There is no firm evidence as to the time of this westward movement but it may have been as early as the 13th century. A legal document of 1295 records 'suit of peace of all trespasses' granted to several west Cork men — O Donovans, O Coffeys, O Hea. Two women were also pardoned; one was Fyngola, daughter of O Hea and wife of Nicholas Magnel, and the other was the wife of Cathal Oregan; her first name (according to another document dated 1302) was Cristok, so that she may well have been of Norman blood. Acting as pledge for all these offenders was John de Barry who at the time held land in Ibane (later Ibane and Barryroe). So it would appear that Cathal Ó Riagáin was domiciled among the O Coffeys and O Heas, which is where the family name flourished in later centuries. There is a townland named Maulyregan (*Meall Uí Riagáin*) in the parish of Ross.

265

(There is also a Ballyregan — More and Beg — in the parish of Ring-curran near Kinsale.)

By the 16th century the name O Regan had become an integral part of the west Cork scene. After Barryroe was raided in 1543 by the citizens of Cork, one of the locals who gave evidence regarding the incursion was Malage O Regan. Further west, a Fiant of 1551 granting pardons to the seafaring O Driscolls of Baltimore included the names of Dermot Ieye Y Regan, Thady mac Richarde Y Regan and Donagh mac Teige Y Regan.

A pardon dated 1577 indicates the residence of the chief of the name — Thady mac Dermod mac Ricard oge of Knockmockfyne, gent. Rickard was a favourite name among the O Regans. The obsolete townland of Knockmockfyne is now included in Tralong and Ballinaclogh in the parish of Ross. When Thady (Teige) was again pardoned in 1601 — together with his son Dermod, his brother Murrehie and his two nephews — he was described as of Ballinaclogh. Another son, John, (Teige's heir), on the occasion of his marriage in 1626 to Ellice Young of Ballyvireen, mortgaged Ballinaclogh to the Youngs and to Robert Coppinger. When John died in 1639 he left an eleven-year-old heir, Teige, who was to gain fame in the service of King James II many years later.

Maulyregan does not seem to have been occupied by O Regans in Elizabethan times but there were several other O Regan seats in the parish of Ross, as for instance, Killeenleigh, where Dermod mac Rickird mac Donell O Regaine was pardoned in 1579 and Donogh mac Deirmody oge in 1601. In the latter year also John mac Morogh O Regaine of Ballynagornagh (Barleyhill) was pardoned. In Ross (Carbery) itself in 1601 we find Maccragh buoy O Reigan and Dermot O Regan alias Mac na Madder. (Conoghor oge O Riegan mac na Madder of Baye was pardoned a year later.) Other 1601 pardons were to Donell mac Ranell O Riegan of Cossrowragh, his sons John, Connoghor and Rickard, his daughter Katherine, and several others of the name; likewise Dermod mac Rickard O Riegan of Glennyrowry and his son Donell. Glennyrowry is now Rouryglen, and Cossrowragh must have been nearby, along the Rowry river. As a result of the land dealings that took place after the battle of Kinsale, Sir Walter Coppinger became overlord of these lands. The O Regans had to pay rent to him and grind their corn at the manor mill (Coppinger's Court) on the Rowry river.

A second influential group flourished in the shadow of the Mac Carthy Riabhach seat of power at Kilbrittain. When Domhnall na Píopaí became lord of Carbery in 1593 he appointed (or re-appointed) William riogh mac Rickard O Regan, gentleman, of Burren (par. Rathclarin) as his chief steward and collector of rents throughout most of Carbery. William and his heirs were to have two pence out of every five groats collected, a commission of 10%. The office was obviously a hereditary one, as reference was made to parts held by other heirs of

William's grandfather's sept which William was to have if they died without heirs. In 1601 William riogh O Riegan, senior, of Burren was pardoned, along with his son Deirmod whose wife was Ellis Mallifont. (Mellifontstown is near Kinsale.) Also in Burren were Teige mac Rickard mac Meloghlin, his wife Katherine ny Callaghan and his son Conogher. If Teige was a brother of William riogh, then William's grandfather was Melaghlin — perhaps the Malage O Regan referred to in 1543. William's son, Teige, was probably the Teige mac William O Regan of Granseur, gentleman (perhaps Grange in Abbeymahon parish), who in 1601 was one of the trustees of John Lord Courcy in a land settlement. Others pardoned in 1601 were Donell, Diermod, Teige and Connoghor rowe mac Donogh mac Teige O Riegane and Teige mac Donell mac Donogh O Riegane, all of Rathclarin.

Further parts of west Cork where O Regans were pardoned in 1601 were Lishane and Cloghane in Caheragh parish, Carrigillihy in Myross, Ballymacraheen in Lislee and even Carriganass in the O Sullivan country near Bantry.

Some there were, however, who refused to be coerced into the Queen's peace. In 1594, among the Carbery followers of Florence Mac Carthy (Mór) who were 'to be examined' were Teig Oreigan and Moroghoe mac Dermod Oregan with his sons, Dermod, John and Donell. Murchadh seems to have been incarcerated, as ten years later, in September 1604, he was released from custody with orders to deliver up his four sons, Shane, Donnell, Donnogh and Teag — or appear himself before the justices. One can only hope he had the good sense to vanish into the wilderness, as did Mortaugh and Daniel mac Shane O Regan, brothers, of Dromgarum (? Dromgarriff, par. Kilnagross) '. . . and other malefactors who had betaken themselves to the fastnesses of the Leap' and on whose heads there was a price of £5 (each) in July 1604. Malachy Riegan 'who served in the wars in Ireland against the heretics' joined the Spanish army in Flanders in 1606; two years later, Dermot Oriegen, Irish soldier, whose right hand had been blown off by a cannonball at the siege of Rheinbergh, got a pension from the king of Spain.

Eventually, most of them settled down to the normal routine of farming and land ownership, buying and selling, frequently in connection with various branches of the Mac Carthys. In 1603 Connogher O Regane of Downmanone (? Dunmanway), gent., was one of the recognizances of Tadhg Mac Carthy of Dunmanway. In 1631 Daniel Mac Carthy (Riabhach) mortgaged to William mac Ranell O Regan and to Connor O Mahony the townlands of Gortroe and Dungannon in Kilmacabea parish. Two years later Teige oge O Regan alias Troha and Donogh O Regan alias Gorm were witnesses to a deed of Dermod mac Owen Mac Carthy.

Although the O Regans must have been involved in the 1641 rebellion to the same extent as their neighbours, only one was mentioned in despatches — William Leagh Regaine who was said to have killed John Ford at Gortbrack near Castlehaven in 1642. It would appear that this William was really Tadhg! In 1620 Teige mac Dermott alias Mac William Reogh Regane alias William Leigh of Burren was outlawed and attainted for breaking into Barry's castle at Timoleague (in the company of Cnogher Hurley). He was pardoned four years later. Three were named as suspected Papist rebels in Carbery — Connor O Regan, gent., Melaghlin and Randal O Regan, yeomen — yet none was outlawed in 1643 though several were listed as liable to forfeiture after the war. According to the *Book of Survey and Distribution,* Joane Reagan of Kilbeloge in Desertserges parish lost her 165 acres which went to Lord Kingston and John Abbot. (Several members of an O Regan family of Knockacullen in this parish were Irish scholars and scribes in the early 19th century.) Daniel oge Reagan's part of Glawn-rooragh (Rouryglen) ended up in the possession of James Coppinger while Daniel mac Rannell Reagan's lands of Knockrudane (Kilfaughnabeg par.) had three claimants — Capt. Morris, James Coppinger and John Murphy. Knockrudane or Knockridane near Leap apparently went with Killeenleigh and what happened here was that the forfeiture was contested on the grounds that in 1641 Daniel oge had conveyed the lands to John Murphy of Leap who assigned them to his son, John, then a student at T.C.D. John (junior) succeeded in getting the lands back and he then restored them to his nephew, Daniel Regan, who was a Catholic. Confiscation again occurred as a result of the Williamite wars, Daniel being a captain in the Jacobite army. However, he got the benefit of the articles of Limerick and was restored once more in 1694. His son, Teige O Regan, was a doctor in Macroom and his grandson, James, a doctor in Mallow. Through marriage the property descended to other medical families, the Cahills and Cagneys in Cork, until finally sold to the occupying tenants under the 1903 land act.

Meanwhile, the chief seat of the family, Ballinaclogh (with Gortnecloghy) had been granted to a Cromwellian lieutenant named Portman but this confiscation was also contested, by Teige mac Shane O Regan, who pointed out that he was only thirteen years of age in 1641. His claim was admitted and he was restored to Ballinaclogh. Tadhg may have been too young for the Cromwellian wars but he was not too old to play an outstanding part in the Jacobite campaigns. In 1690 he was governor of Charlemont fort (Co. Armagh) which lay right in the path of Schomberg's southward march. He refused to surrender the fort to Schomberg until the garrison had no food left, having eaten all the horses but Tadhg's own. He then surrendered on condition of being allowed to march to Dublin unmolested. There he was knighted by King James in Dublin Castle.

At the crucial battle of the Boyne, he again had a significant role; in fact it was held by many (according to James Roche (b. 1771) in his *Essays by an Octogenarian*) that the Irish officer who said 'Change kings and we'll fight you again' was not Patrick Sarsfield but Sir Teige

O Regan. On Sarsfield's recommendation Sir Teige was then appointed governor of the fort and town of Sligo. Here also he held out against superior forces until the 6th August 1691 when he finally capitulated on condition of being allowed to march to Limerick with arms and baggage, having first ensured that the inhabitants of Sligo were guaranteed protection. At Limerick the treaty negotiations had already begun and Sir Teige later accompanied Sarsfield to France where he died. He was unmarried and his lands at Ballinaclogh went to his cousin, Captain Daniel O Regan of Knockridane, already mentioned. Another supporter of King James outlawed in 1690 was Dermot Regane of Skibbereen, gent. Among the Jacobite burgesses of Baltimore in 1689 were Daniel Regane, Timothy Regane and Thady Regane of Ballyvarloghly (?).

By 1659, according to the census of that year, O Regan families were well distributed throughout west Cork, as follows: Kinalmeaky, 19; Ibane and Barryroe, 8; Liberties of Kinsale, 8; Courceys, 5; Kilbrittain, 30; East Carbery (Reagan and Reagan oge) 39; West Carbery, 58.

Ó RÍOGHBHARDÁIN

Ó RÍORDÁIN   (O) RIORDAN   REARDEN

A genealogy in the *Leabhar Muimhneach* derives the Uí Ríordáin from Ríordán, son of Assíd mac Maelchríche and great-grandson of Dúnchad mac Dubhdábhoireann who was king of Cashel in 873. This rather too obvious attempt to attach the family to the main stock of Eóganacht Caisil is not substantiated by other sources — apart from the 12th century Mac Carthy propaganda tract *Caithréim Ceallacháin Chaisil*.

In the early genealogies the personal name Ríghbhardán is found among one group only, namely Éli (Tuaiscirt) who occupied the district between Thurles and Birr, then regarded as part of Munster. O Rahilly considered that the Éli were a non-Goidelic tribe pushed out of the midlands by the Goidelic invaders. Gilla Pádraig mac Cerbaill, king of Éli, died in 1022 — the O Carrolls were prominent in the area later — and a successor was Cerball's great-grandson, Rígbardán mac Con Choirne, who was slain in 1058 at the battle of Sliabh gCrot. It was most probably from this Rígbardán that the Uí Ríoghbhardáin took their name. Mac Firbhisigh, in the introduction to his Book of Genealogies, connects the family with Éile, though apparently he considered them to be the hereditary chroniclers of that area — possibly because Rígh-bhardán could be construed as 'kingly bard'.

It is more likely, however, that they were among the ruling families of Éile. Rígbardán's son, whose name may have been Domhnall, succeeded his father as king of Éile and was slain in 1071. Almost a century later, in 1170, among the Munster nobles who fell while inflicting a slaughter on the overseas men (i.e. Normans) at Waterford, was one named Ragnall Ua Rígbardáin. The fact that he was assisting Diarmaid Mac Carthy and the Desmumu could indicate that by then the O Riordans had already moved into Desmond — and perhaps into other parts of Munster, as the kingdom of Éile was being fragmented by the O Briens. On their way, some may have settled in east Cork where we find the townland of Ballyreardon (*Baile Uí Ríordáin*) in the parish of Templenacarriga in Barrymore. According to the Pipe Roll of Cloyne, one of the tenants of Lackeen (near Liscarroll) in 1341 was Thomas Orewordan.

It is, however, with the western half of the county and in particular with Muskerry, that the O Riordans were later associated. They apparently came as, and remained to the end, loyal followers of the Mac Carthys, though we know little of their activities during the 14th and 15th centuries. Donatus Orywardayn, who died before 1475, originally a priest of Cloyne diocese, obtained the prebends of Desertmore and

270

Inishkenny and became precentor of Cork diocese. In 1492 Cornelius O Riordan, also of Cloyne diocese, obtained the vicarage of Macloneigh. A 15th century Irish scholar was named Tadhg Ó Rigbardáin.

In the 16th century the O Riordans appear to have been particularly numerous around the Mac Carthy stronghold of Macroom. Eight of the name was pardoned there according to the Elizabethan Fiants and it was at Macroom in the year 1540, according to the *Leabhar Muimhneach*, that Muinntir Ríobhardán slew Cormac, the grandson of Cormac Láidir Mac Carthy of Muskerry. This slaying was probably due to a succession dispute and by no means alienated the O Riordans from the lords of Muskerry. At the end of the century, according to one of the Carew manuscripts, the Riordans, as followers of the Mac Carthys in Muskerry, held nine ploughlands – more than the Mac Swineys, Morohoes and Clancallaghans who were also followers.

One might surmise that these ploughlands lay in and around Derry-riordane (*Doire Uí Ríordáin*) in the parish of Inchigeelagh, but that was O Leary territory and the Elizabethan Fiants indicate otherwise. More than one hundred O Riordans are listed in these Fiants, and the greatest concentration was around Carraig na Muc (Dripsey castle), then the residence of the Mac Carthy *tánaiste* of Muskerry. The second largest number was at Banduff in Clondrohid parish and the third at Derryroe in the neighbouring parish of Aghabullogue. One or both of these places – neither of which is a Mac Carthy castle site – may have been the principal seat or seats of the O Riordans. Banduff townland no longer exists in Clondrohid parish; it may now form part of Bawn-more. According to the mid-17th century Civil Survey, it lay between Bawnmore and Caherbirrane.

Daniel O Riordan, who was a captain in Dillon's regiment and aide-de-camp to the Duc de Vendosme, in 1700 obtained a French certificate of gentle birth, being descended on his father's side from O Riordan of Banmor and on the female side from Nolane of Ballinrobe. This seems to have been the Daniel who married Maria, daughter of Col. Charles Mac Carthy Mór, a grandson of the noted Florence Mac Carthy Mór. According to the pedigree Daniel was the son of Donogh More (son of Dermod or Denis son of Daniel). This agrees with the evidence of a claim in Chichester House by Daniel O Riordan who claimed the resi-due of a lease of Derryrue assigned to him in 1687 by Donogh O Riordan. In 1751, a great-grandson of Daniel and Maria, Stephen O Riordan of Nantes, sought and received a grant of arms from Ulster's office. Stephen's grandson, Henry Comte O Riordan, lived at the Chateau de la Tremblaye in Bressuire in 1841.

The pedigree accompanying the grant of arms gives Derryroe (rather than Bawnmore) as the origin of this branch. This could well be cor-rect. In one of the Fiants, dated 1585, we find the name of 'Teig mac Donell mac Rery O Riordane of Direroe, horseman', a horseman being only one step lower than a gentleman. (Three other O Riordan horsemen were pardoned, one at Kilbarry and two at Macroom; the largest section were yeomen or strong farmers, with a lesser number of husbandmen and kerns.) A pardon was granted in 1601 to Donogh Indirrie O Riordan (*Donnchadh an Doire*) of Dyrrie – perhaps Derryroe. The following year Teige oge mac Teige O Riourdane, of Derryroe, yeoman, was pardoned.

A number of O Riordans were followers of Tadhg Mac Carthy of Carrigaphooka castle, while others were to be found in Kilgobnet, in Kilcrea and in various parts of Muskerry. In common with similar Muskerry families, the O Riordans favoured Tadhg, Domhnall, Donnchadh, Diarmaid and Conchubhar as Christian names but a sprinkling of more unusual names is noticeable – Muircheartach, Mathghamhain, Maolsheachlainn, Ruairí, Giolla na naomh (Gullyneofe) and Donnghalach (Donnellagh). One of the Banduff group was Riurdane mac Donogh I Riurdane while one of the Carraig na Muc O Riordans was Raynald duffe O Ryordane, bearing the same personal name as the O Riordan noble who fell at Waterford in 1170.

Also in Elizabethan times there were O Riordans in the counties contiguous to Cork. In 1576 Gaven O Rewrdane was a freeholder in Ely O Carroll (the ancestral home) and one of Sir William O Carroll's most notable followers. After the Desmond rebellions Maurice O Riordan of Castlekippen, Croom, Co. Limerick, was attainted and his lands granted to George Sherlock in 1598.

Not all of the O Riordans pardoned in 1601 remained neutral at the time of the battle of Kinsale. A pardon was granted in August 1601 to Dermod mac I Riourdane, alias Dermod nymrone (*na mbrón*, of the quernstones) and to Owen Mac Donogh ny mrona, of Kilcrea, both of whom must subsequently have thrown in their lot with the Spaniards. After the fatal defeat, among those who sailed for Spain from Kinsale with Don Juan in March, 1602, were Cormock, Dermond and Owen mac Donogh ne mroen Oriardane with Donnell mac Shane Oriardane of Muskerry. There were many of the name in the Spanish army in Flanders in the early 17th century – for example Eugenio Riordan who petitioned the Archduke in 1620 for leave to pass freely through the country and return to Ireland from which the heretics had banished him (together with his wife and children) after they had deprived him of his means of living. Ten years later, Daniel Orierdan 'of good height, pitted with smallpox, aged 22 years' also sought licence for Ireland for one year.

Some of those who remained at home had achieved a higher social standing until the rebellion of 1641 brought ruin and destruction on them. John mac Donnell O Riordan was one who paid a levy on property in Macroom and Clondrohid in the early 17th century while according to an inquisition of 1639 one of the O Healys of Donaghmore mortgaged his lands of Gowlane to William O Ryerdane of Clodagh (par. Kilmurry). Both were listed in the outlawries of 1643 as follows:

John mac Donnell O Ryerdane, Cooleviddane, Gent. (This is Coola-niddane in the parish of Clondrohid; Dermod mac Teige O Riordane of Culnidane was pardoned in 1587.)

William O Ryerdane, Cloghindae (Clodah), Gent.

Also John mac William O Ryerdane, Blarney, Gent., – perhaps a son of William of Clodah. John was commander of Lord Muskerry's garrison in Blarney castle. Capt. Timothy O Riordan commanded the castle and island of Inishbofin (Co. Mayo) until it was surrendered to the Crom-wellians in 1652. Either John mac Donell or John mac William of Blarney may be the 'John Rierdan, gent.' whom we find in the town-land of Killcollum, Co. Clare, in 1659. One of them may also be the John Riordan (described as an Irish gentleman in a low condition) who was one of the chosen companions of James Cotter in the hunting down and killing of the regicide, Col. John Lisle, in Lausanne, Switzerland, in 1664.

We can get a good idea of the distribution of the name at that period from the census dated 1659. Unfortunately, Muskerry is missing from this, but we find O Riordan families in the baronies of Kinalmeaky (7) Barretts (15) Barrymore (18) Orrery and Kilmore (10). They were also in evidence in Co. Kerry: Trughanacmy (8) Magunihy (6) – in Co. Limerick: Small County (8) Connello (13) Coshma (9) – and in Co. Tipperary: Kilnamanagh (6) Clanwilliam (9). But many still clung to the area north of Macroom where quite a number of them obtained leases from the Earl of Clancarty in 1675. These included Donogh O Riordan of Derryroe whose lease later came to Daniel O Riordan but was dismissed at Chichester House in 1700. In Clondrohid parish leases were obtained by Michael O Riordan, Gent. (Gortnagishagh and Carrig-onirtane) William (Liscarrigane) Owen (Ballymacorcoran) and Donogh mac Owen (Caherkeegane). In Drishane parish were Teige O Riordan, Gent. (Caherbarnagh), Michael (Curracahill), Thady (Cloghboola More). In Macroom parish Teige O Riordan, Gent., was assigned his grand-father's lease of Bealick and part of Ballyveerane, and managed to retain it after 1700. Donogh Riordane was allowed the residue of his 31-year lease of Banduff (west), as indeed were most of the other O Riordans in the area. It is of interest to note that the mother of James Barry, the Cork painter, was Juliana Reardon, whose family was said to have been dispossessed of extensive property.

The Jacobite cause inevitably attracted several of the name – as for instance the Capt. Daniel O Riordan already mentioned, and a Major O Riordan of Sir Neill O Neill's regiment. Patrick Riardon, a merchant of Limerick, was attainted in 1691. After the war, two of the Co. Limerick Riordans successfully claimed restoration of their lands, in 1699. So also did Capt. Teige Ryerden of Bealick.

We have but few records of O Riordans during the eighteenth cen-tury, apart from those who gained local fame as minor poets. The best-known of these was Conchubhar *Máistir* Ó Ríordáin who lived around

Macroom in the latter half of the century. Another was Tadhg *na súl mbeag* Ó Ríordáin of Clondrohid, who specialized in composing pithy quatrains. One of these lamented the fate of a group of O Riordans from Rooska (near Durrus) incarcerated in the prison of Cork:

> *Is dúch liom an cúnggrach 'na n-airím iad,*
> *Na húirfhir ón Rúsgaig do bheathíodh cliar,*
> *An chumplacht nár dúnadh a ngeataí riamh,*
> *Is nár túrnadh i súgra ná i ngleacaíocht sgian.*

(Sad am I to hear of the plight of the noble men from Rooska, ever generous to poets; the company whose gates were never closed and who never were defeated in sport or in conflict.)

A modern poet, considered by many to have composed the most outstanding Irish poetry of the 20th century, was Seán Ó Ríordáin who was born in Ballyvourney and died in Cork in 1977.

Seán P. Ó Ríordáin (d. 1957) from Monkstown, Co. Cork, became Professor of Archaeology in U.C.C. and later in U.C.D. For six years he was secretary of the Cork Historical and Archaeological Society and editor of its Journal.

GLANWORTH CASTLE *(O'Callaghan Newenham, 1826)*

(DE) ROCHE

DE RÓISTE

Originally, this family name was written 'de la Roche' in Norman-French and 'de Rupe' in Latin. Both forms signify 'of the rock' — i.e. Roch castle, the site of which is a remarkable rock on a peninsula between Haverfordwest and St. Davids in south-west Wales. The surrounding district, known as Rhos or Rouse was, in the time of Henry I, colonized by Flemings, and it was one of these, Godebert — or his sons — who built Roch castle. One of the sons, Richard fitz Godebert 'a knight of Pembrokeshire', was among the first of the 'Normans' to set foot in Ireland, as he accompanied Dermot Mac Murrough who was returning to Ireland after his visit to Britain, in 1167.

When the real invasion commenced two years later, it was spearheaded by Robert Fitzstephen and Maurice de Prendergast. Maurice was granted territory in Co. Wexford by Strongbow and most of this came later into the possession of Robert fitz Godebert (probably a brother of Richard). Robert's three sons — David, Henry and Adam de Rupe — granted the island of Begerin in Wexford harbour to the Priory of Exeter.

By the beginning of the 14th century there were families of Roches settled in Wexford, Kildare, Louth, Tipperary, Cork and Waterford. In the Justiciary Rolls of 1295-1303 de Rupe appears more frequently than any other Norman name in Ireland. Several of those in Co. Waterford bore Godebert as a personal name, and all appear to have been descended from the sons of Godebert.

Robert of Co. Wexford was succeeded by his eldest son, David de Rupe. David's son, 'Geralt de la Ruchochi, the third best baron in Ireland', was slain in a hand-to-hand encounter with Cormac Mac Carthy, high on the slopes of Mangerton near Killarney, in 1262. Gerald, who was married to a daughter of Thomas fitz Anthony (the custodian of Decies and Desmond), was probably the 'Roidseach' who built the castle at Oirbhealach (Muckross, Co. Kerry) in 1214. From him descended the Roches of Fernegenel, Co. Wexford.

The first mention of a Roche in Co. Cork was in 1207 when King John granted the cantred of Rosselither (Rosscarbery) to David de Rupe. This must have been David of Roch castle in Wales, since the Welsh branch laid claim to lands in Rosscarbery at the beginning of the 14th century.

Another David de Rupe provides the first connection with Fermoy. He was son of Alexander — perhaps the 'Elisron da Roici' who, according to the *Annals of Inisfallen*, had a court at a place called Baile Uí

Dúnadhaigh in 1252. David married Amicia, daughter and heiress of Nicholas de Caunteton (Condon), through whom he gained possession of Glanworth, Licklash, Gurteenaboul and other townlands. Some of these lands he bestowed on his son, Alexander. It is the *Annals of Inisfallen* again which record the death of John de Roche, bishop of Limerick, in 1279, and four years later describe a major assault on the Mac Carthys of Carbery in which both Roches and Condons joined.

This may have been the last occasion that the two families fought side by side since the de Rupes — David, senior, and young David, son of Alexander — between 1289 and 1302 became involved in a series of lawsuits versus Maurice de Caunteton (as described under CONDON). Young David's success in these left him as feudal proprietor of the larger part of the barony of Fermoy. By 1307 he was to style himself lord of Fermoy; in that year also he got permission to exchange lands at the Corran in Fermoy (which he now held of the king *in capite*) for lands elsewhere.

But his legal successes led to many years of violent conflict involving the Condons. 'Great warfare in Laigin between the foreigners themselves', say the *Annals of Inisfallen* in 1309, adding that William Roche's part in the killing of Maurice Condon led to great warfare between Condons and Roches. (There was conflict generally at this period among the great Norman families — including the Roches — over the inheritance of Agnes de Valence, one of the Marshall heiresses.) The war continued into 1311 'with burnings, raidings and killings between them on both sides'. David, lord of Fermoy, was taken prisoner by the Condons who released him to the justiciar on condition of their obtaining the king's peace. William Roche was killed in the same year by an arrow shot by one of the O Briens.

In 1311 also as a reward for their services on behalf of the king against the Condons and the Irish of Leinster, suit of peace for all trespasses and felonies was granted to David son of Alexander de Rupe and all his followers, among whom were over fifty de Rupes. They included David son of Henry de Rupe, knight, Henry son of David, knight, Luke of Awenbeg, Maurice of Dirnetede (*Daire na Teidi*, seemingly in Clenor parish), Luke Duff son of Alexander, William of Dromdowney and Maurice of Condory (? Connaberry, par. Castletownroche).

David's own place of residence is not given, but it could well have been at Castletownroche which later became the principal seat of the lords of Fermoy. In pre-Norman times this place was known as Dún Cruadha. It was called 'villa Castri de Duncrothe' in 1260 and 'Castleton' in 1301. The Roches held land at Duncrothe in 1307.

Following a raid on Cogan lands in 1317 the king ordered David de Rupe to bring to trial his fellow-Roches and their followers who had disturbed the king's peace in Co. Cork. In 1321 Maurice Condon and all his followers attacked Kildorrery, Ballynahalisk and Bern Meic Ímuir (now Farahy), burning thirty houses as well as the church of

Kildorrery and forcing David to give two hostages — Eustace and Gerald de Rupe. Then the Earl of Desmond went into rebellion and the Roches' lands were devastated once again. By 1345 the Earl's rebellious followers had increased in numbers and a large army of rebels which appeared near Clonmel included David de Rupe, lord of Fermoy.

But not all of the name were rebellious. In 1344 William fitz David de Roche of Ballymagooly was made sheriff of Co. Cork. John Roche was bishop of Cork from 1347 to 1358 as was William Roche in the late 15th century.

The David who was knighted in 1365 must have been a son of the earlier David. He married Anna, daughter of Maurice fitz Thomas. In 1374, for whatever reason, he joined a group of *Gaill* in Ulster in an attack on Niall O Neill, but they suffered a grievous defeat which left Roche, the knight (*in Ritiri Rotsich*) and several others slain. In the following year the king took David's widow, Anna, and her family under his protection. He also gave her permission to foster Cormac son of Dermot Mac Carthy, as Dermot was married to David's daughter, Catherine.

David's son and heir, John, was granted the keeping of the peace in 1375 and was made sheriff of Co. Cork seven years later. According to an inquisition of 1377 John fitz David de Rupe and William de Rupe were for a time regarded as heirs of the Cogan lands in Co. Cork after the death of Peter, the last in the direct line of the Cogans, in 1371. (This may have been due to the fact that Isabella, widow of Peter's grandfather, John de Cogan, married (secondly) Gerald de Roche in 1317.) Shortly after this William de Roche was outlawed and in 1405 Maurice de Roche, lord of Fermoy, released to the Cogans all his claims to their lands. Maurice was the son of John who died in 1387 while Maurice was still a minor. His lands were for a period in the custody of Gerald, Earl of Desmond, and he is believed to have married a sister of the earl.

In 1403 Maurice signed an indenture promising not to exact any illicit dues from the Benedictine Priory of Bridgetown and *villa* of Clenor. He must have been the Roche of Fir Mhuighe who in 1421 aided the Carbery Mac Carthys in a battle against some of the Mac Carthys Mór at Carrigrohane near Cork. The Roche of Crích Róisteach, as the annals style him, died in 1448. It is obvious that the family had become well-Gaelicized by then. The next in line, David, was popularly known as Dáibhidh Mór, and for him in 1458 an Irish scribe, William O Hickey, compiled the first part of the manuscript volume known as the *Book of Fermoy*.

This compilation, now in the Royal Irish Academy, was a medieval library in itself, containing the Leabhar Gabhála, mythological tales, etc., as well as historical and genealogical matter with poems in praise of the Roches similar to those being written for Gaelic chiefs all over Ireland. A poem of 58 stanzas lists the achievements and warlike prowess of Dáibhidh Mór who is credited with winning a battle at Áth Glaisi Cró in Co. Limerick and with the plundering of places as far apart as Cashel and Kilbrittain. David's wife was Joan, of the Mac William Burkes — a fact which did not deter the Clanrickard Burkes from raiding and burning part of Roche's country in 1485.

The actual extent of that country in the time of Dáibhidh Mór was detailed by Domhnall Ó Leighin in 1461 and later copied into the Book of Fermoy. Castles are not named but there is a list of townlands, or portions thereof, belonging to Lord Roche. Those which are still identifiable are as follows:

Curraghoo, Ballylough, Ballylegan, Ballykeating, Ballynahalisk, Lisnagourneen, Dannanstown, Carrigleagh, Meadstown, Springvale (*Móin Crubáin*), Farahy, Clogher, Kilconnor, Ballynamona, Shanagh, Ballywalter, Castlekevin (*Caisleán Caoimhín*), Ballygarrane, Ballinvoher, Ballyveelick, Ballydoyle, Ballinaltig, Croaghnacree, Clenor, Ballymee, Caherduggan, Curraghkerry, Doneraile, Castlepook (*Caisleán an phúca*), Carrigleamleary, Monanimy, Ballincurrig.

Before his death in 1488 Dáibhidh Mór received the title of Viscount Fermoy. His successor, Maurice, married firstly Joan, daughter of the Earl of Desmond and secondly, Mór, daughter of Mahon O Brien. Maurice's son, David, married a daughter of Mac Carthy Mór. A panegyric composed by Brian Ó Huigín refers to defeats which David inflicted on his old enemies, the Condons. In 1543 the Lord Deputy, St. Leger, informed the king that he had imprisoned Lord Roche and the White Knight in Dublin Castle 'where now they agree very well together and lye bothe in one bedde that before coulde not agree in a countrey of fourty myles in length betwene them and under ther rule'.

Soon after this David died and was succeeded by Maurice. After Maurice came another David who, as soon as he assumed the lordship, had a copy made of his great-grandfather's list of lands by his scribe, Torna Ó Maolchonaire, in the presence of Diarmaid Ó Leighin, *ollamh* of the Roches and others of the household 'at Castletownroche, the fortress of the authors and ollamhs and exiles and companies of scholars of Ireland'. David also purchased the castle and thirteen ploughlands of Carrigleamleary from a junior branch of the Roches.

Sir Henry Sidney, during his tour of the south in 1566, knighted David Roche, perhaps as a reward for having taken prisoner Domhnall Mac Carthy Mór whom Sidney sent to London (where Domhnall was made Earl of Clancarty by Queen Elizabeth). David's knighthood seems to have ensured his loyalty to the queen despite strong pressure from the Earl of Desmond and others. The Earl of Clancarty and his followers raided Roche's territory in 1568 when 1,500 kine were taken and a great number of men, women and children burnt, along with 7,000 sheep and all his corn. Yet though the Earl of Desmond kept four score gallowglass in Roche's country, David sided with the crown forces when the Desmond rebellion erupted in 1569. For this he received a letter of thanks from the queen in 1572 and in the following year (in consideration of his having supplied 139 cows) a pardon for his followers who included the Roches of Carrigdownane, Ballyhooly, Ballydoyle, Licklash, Ballyhindon, Kilbyrne, Ballylegan, and Castlekevin.

David Roche was one of the great lords of Munster who attended Sidney's Christmas party in Cork in 1575. While they caroused, 24 'notable malefactors' languished in prison awaiting execution. One of them, a younger son of Viscount Roche, got a last-minute reprieve 'for, as the world goes here, his fault was very small'. Some months later, Sidney 'lodged two nights by the way netherwards at my Lord Roche's where I and all my trayne were verie largely and bountifullie entertayned'. David was further rewarded with a lease of the confiscated lands of Bridgetown Abbey.

Yet his loyalty was wearing somewhat thin. He was accused in 1576 of continuing to exact Irish cesses on his tenants and of refusing to allow the queen's cess to be taken. About this time too, it was stated that Lord Roche was one of the thirty 'English' captains following the Irish order and having his own Irish war-cry – *Róisteach abú!* When James Fitzmaurice renewed the Geraldine rebellion in 1579, Roche was still nominally on the queen's side but the presence in that camp of his enemy, Lord Barry, effectively deterred him from giving much support.

David's eldest son and heir, Maurice, took the opposite course to his father. In 1566 he was pardoned for the killing of Gibbon mac Shane mac Irreddery (*Mac an Ridire*) of Clangibbons. His followers included John fitz Edmund Roche of Ballyhindon, James fitz Maurice Roche of Croagh (nacree) and James Roche alias Mac Henry of Corraghmachenry. Maurice was openly on the side of James Fitzmaurice whose sister he had married. In 1580 Sir Walter Raleigh marched to Castletownroche and having gained entrance by a strategem, carried off Lord Roche and his wife to Cork. However, Lord Roche was acquitted of all charges while his son Maurice was later pardoned and reconciled to his father after having alleged that the hard hand borne over him by his father was partly the cause of his revolt.

The year 1582 was a disastrous one for the Roches. Lady Roche was accused of treason by Theobald Roche and others. Two of Lord Roche's sons – Redmond and Theobald – were slain in a conflict with the Condons. When Theobald's wife (Gráinne Ní Bhriain) saw her husband's mangled body she died of grief the same night. Then Maurice Roche was defeated in battle by David Barry. Finally, two more of Lord Roche's sons, John and Ulick, were also slain by the Condons, as well as a great number of Roche followers, so many in fact that Lord Roche and Maurice had to bring in strangers to populate their lands. The following year saw little improvement. Not only did Condon prey again on Castletownroche but, as the *Annals of the Four Masters* record, the deaths occurred of David, Lord Roche, his wife Ellen, and his sister,

'Countess Roche', who was the wife of the Earl of Thomond.

By this time the Earl of Desmond was a fugitive outlaw, abandoned by his supporters. Maurice, the new Lord Roche, joined the rout, informing Ormond on 19th September 1583 that he had captured the Earl's chaplain while 'therle with the rest escaped narowlye with his life'. Thereby Maurice added the spoils of the monasteries of Fermoy and Glanworth to his estate, but after the confiscation of the Earl of Desmond's lands he failed to recover portions of the Roche territory — such as Carrigleamleary — which had been included in the confiscation. (Philip fitz Edmund Roche, alias Mac Myllon of Carrigleamleary and Theobald Roche of Cregg had been attainted for supporting the Earl of Desmond, but Lord Roche would have regarded them as his tenants.) The activities of undertakers such as Edmund Spenser affected Roche's property, and his instigation of a kind of boycott of the undertakers did not help his cause. In 1597 he found himself imprisoned in Dublin castle charged with 'crymes of high nature'. Two base sons of his 'followed by a rabble of loose people' were in arms against the crown and Viscount Roche had failed to deliver them into justice. An account written in that year describes Roche as 'a man of moste enemys in Munster'; these included his uncle, John Roche, and almost all the Roche freeholders, Patrick Condon, a mortal enemy of his, the White Knight and Mac Donogh of Duhallow.

The following year witnessed the ejection of the undertakers from Munster as a result of O Neill's notable victory at the Yellow Ford. David Roche (son and heir of Maurice) promptly joined the rebels and though Maurice himself remained nominally loyal to the crown at first, he too joined in the rebellion in 1599 and successfully defended Castletownroche against the forces of Sir Thomas Norreys. However, later in the year he quarrelled with James of Desmond and came to Essex for protection, receiving a pardon on 24th July.

Roche now vacillated as pressure mounted from both sides. On 14th June Lord Essex lodged at Glanworth, 'a town of the Viscount Roch'. Early in 1600 Hugh O Neill also camped in Roche's country, endeavouring to come to terms with Maurice who, although he rebuffed O Neill, was still suspected by the authorities who were credibly informed that Lord Roche had sent wine and *aquavitae* to the 'traitors'. On the 18th March the Chief Justice of Munster wrote that Lord Roche ('a braynsicke foole') and Cormac Mac Carthy were 'the most cankered subjects that underhand support the rebels'. But when Maurice died later in the year the Irish annals described him as 'a mild and comely man learned in the Latin, Irish and English languages'.

David, the 7th Viscount, immediately proclaimed his loyalty by writing to the queen from Castletownroche. Carew spent the night of the 26 September 1601 in Roche's castle at Glanworth and later, after the battle of Kinsale, wrote concerning Roche to the Privy Council: 'I do not thincke any Noblemen within the Province of Munster to be more assured to the Crowne of England' or as *Pacata Hibernia* put it: 'the Lord Roche was never touched with the least spot of disloyaltie against Her Majesty'. Accordingly, David had little difficulty in securing from James I in 1611 a 'Surrender and Regrant' of his lands which comprised:

The castle and lands of Downegroe or Castletown(roche) with nine ploughlands. The castle and lands of Glanworth with nine ploughlands. The castle and lands of Ballyhay, eleven ploughlands. The castle and lands of Ballymagooly, eight ploughlands. The castle and town of Cregg and the castle and lands of Johnstown. About 140 other townlands were listed. He was empowered to divide the lands into three precincts, of 5,000 acres each, to hold courts leet within the manors of Castletown-roche, Glanworth and Ballyhay, and to empark up to 600 acres of Castletownroche, Cregg, Rahan and Ballymagooly. David assigned to strangers the castle and lands of Ballyhooly (Theobald fitz John Roche, attainted), the lands of Ballydoyle (Morrish and Edmond fitz John Balluff Roche, attainted), and the lands of Kilbrin (Ullick fitz John Roche, slain in rebellion).

Though a Catholic, David remained on good terms with the government until his death in 1635. He was buried in Bridgetown Abbey. Soon afterwards his widow, Jane, sent in a petition concerning the conduct of her son, Maurice, the new Lord Roche. The young man's turbulent, refractory and contentious disposition had fatally brought irrecoverable decay and loss, she said, on that honourable house and shortened his father's days with grief. He was now detaining all her property from her so that weakened by age, she had to live obscurely, beholden for all manner of accommodation to her poor neighbours, without whose help she had not a cup to drink from nor a bed to lie on. In 1637 Maurice was brought before the Star Chamber, fined £10,000 and imprisoned. He was forced to remain in England until given leave to return by the king in 1641. He was then just in time to join the Catholic insurgents and became a member of the Confederate Supreme Council. In 1642 Maurice Roche with Donough Mac Carthy defeated the troops of Lord Inchiquin. For once the Roches and Condons fought side by side only to be eventually defeated by Inchiquin after which Castletownroche was besieged and captured. Rev. Urban Vigors wrote on 16th July 1642 that:

'The Souldiers which doe belong unto the Cundane of Kilgullane Castle, in the parish Marshalstown, and unto Mr. Ulicke Roche, a chief freeholder in those partes, commit many outrages and stealthes. Sir William Ffenton's butler, I heard, killed the young captayne, Mr. Roche's sonne, neere Michealstowne, where hee came in the night with his ragged tren to steal cows from some of the townesmen. I know not well how the old Ulick Roche, of the castle of Balleclogh, doth behave himself. There is a quondam parishioner of myne, one Robert Nixon, in the castle with him. The Lord Roche's castle of Glannor is a strong place yet I heare but a weak ward in it. Our army took his Lordship's castle of Castletowne lately wherein was a thousand people at least; his lady was in the Castle there; they yeelded, as my ffriend, Mr. Rouckhood, of Corke, informeth me, uppon quarter to depart with their lives and wearing apparrell.'

Yet the Roches must have recovered the castle since in 1649 it was again defended by Lady Roche and Cromwell passed nearby without attempting to assault it. After the general surrender of 1652 Lady Roche was brought before one of the 'High Courts of Justice' on a trumped-up charge and condemned to be hanged — *Baintiarna Róisteach mhór na déarca* as the poet Éamonn an Dúna called her.

Maurice Lord Roche, who had been outlawed in 1643 along with 31 other Roches, now saw all his lands and property confiscated while a special act of parliament exempted him from pardon. He and his four young daughters were left destitute, so much so that one daughter died of hardship. Eventually, he was allotted about 2,500 acres in 'the Owles' in Connacht (adjoining Clew Bay, Co. Mayo) to which he travelled on foot, only to find on arrival that it was barren, waste and unprofitable. Even from here he was evicted before he could derive any profit from it. Castletownroche was allotted to Colonel Widenham in 1666; the castle then became known as Castle Widenham.

Maurice died in 1670 leaving a son David, of whom Lord Orrery wrote in 1666, 'I hope you will secure O Sullivan Beare and one Colonel David Roche, son to Lord Roche, for I find a storm a-brewing from such sort of people in this kingdom, as well as from the phanatticks'. David was imprisoned in London in 1681 and died the same year, his brother John succeeding to the title. John and his two surviving sisters, Amy and Blanche, received a pension from Charles II in 1674. John married Catherine, daughter of David Condon (the ancient enemy!). He was a captain in Tyrconnell's Horse in King James' army and died about 1694. His son David, an officer in the British navy, was drowned at Plymouth in 1703. David's brother Ulick, then succeeded and died in 1733, leaving an only daughter, Anna-Maria, who died in 1763. Following 'this there were several unsuccessful claimants to the title of Viscount Roche, the best-known being Sir Boyle Roche, still remembered as the begetter of 'Boyle Roche's bird'.

In 1856 the Right Hon. Edmund Burke-Roche of Trabolgan was elevated to the peerage of Ireland as Baron Fermoy.

Other Roches in Co. Cork

Of the 31 Roches outlawed along with Viscount Roche in 1643 most resided in Fermoy barony — John, Edward, Miles and Theobald fitz John of Castletown(roche), John and Ulick fitz John of Castlekevin, Thomas and William fitz Thomas of Cloustoge (par. Doneraile), David, Theobald and William of Killeagh (par. Glanworth), Edmond and William of Ballylegan, John and Ulick of Ballindangan, John of Ballinamona, James of Cappagh, John of Ballyvolock (par. Glanworth) and

David of Island. Some of the names are not easy to identify — David of Gortinconroe, James of Bally Mchoinkine, Thomas of Aghelenane (? Aghalinane, par Kinneigh), Thomas of Ballincargeagh and Redmond of Garavadrolane. (This last may be the Redmond Roch of Cork, expelled from the Irish House of Commons for high treason in 1642.) Quite a number were from the barony of Kinalea — Adam and William of Ringcurran, David of Ballynalougha (par. Nohoval), James of Kinure, Patrick of Powlenelong (Shippool), Richard of Glinny and Richard of Knocknalurgan (par. Carrigaline).

About three score Roche landowners in almost all the baronies of Co. Cork were listed as liable to forfeiture but even after the confiscations there remained, according to the 1659 census, quite a number of Roche 'tituladoes' (presumably landholders) scattered throughout the county, though Fermoy is missing from the census lists. These were: Edmond Roche, gent;, in St. John's parish, Cork; John Roche, gent., in Inishkenny parish; Richard Roche and Edward, his son, in Innishannon; Maurice Roche, gent., in Ballintubber (Ballymartle par.); Patrick Roche in French Furze (Carrigaline par.); Maurice Roche, Esq. and John Roche in Dunderrow; John Roche in Fanlobbus parish; Patrick Roche in Kilgarriff parish; Adam and Philip Roche in Skull parish.

Again in 1690-1 we have a list of those who were outlawed for their support of King James and who thereby lost whatever they might have retained after Cromwell — David Roche of Aghern, Philip of Ballintlea (Doneraile), Richard and Maurice of Kinsale, Stephen (merchant), Dominick (vintner), and Andrew (gent.), all of Cork city, John and James of Ballydamon (?), John of Skibbereen, James of Kinure, Stephen of Curnarnahy (?), David of Ardlinbridge (?), John son of John of Ballinluig (Ballyfeard), James of Fartha (Ballyfeard), Joaslin of Knocknamanagh (Minane Bridge), Philip and Michael of Poulnelong (Shippool), Patrick of Fountainstown, and James of Island Finch. (A pardon was granted in 1601 to Theobald fitz Morish Doulagh Roche of Ilaneneffyneshine — *Oileán na bhfuinseann*, now Rigsdale, Ballinhassig; Morris Roche fitz John and his brother John of Ellenfinchtowne fought at Kinsale and went to Spain with Don Juan in March 1602.)

At least one of the name, James son of George son of Theobald Roche of Cregg, espoused the cause of King William. He gained the rank of colonel and became famous as the man who penetrated the enemy lines at the siege of Derry and swam the river Foyle carrying a letter of encouragement to the beleaguered garrison. James 'the swimmer' was aptly rewarded with a grant of the tolls of the ferries of Ireland. He was also granted the estate of James Everard in Co. Waterford and was ancestor of the Roches of Woodbine Hill in that county.

The above lists give an idea of how the name Roche had spread throughout Co. Cork, and this dispersion happened centuries earlier as we may deduce from such townland-names as Ardarostig (*Ard an*

Róistigh) par. Inishkenny, Ballinrostig, par. Rostellan, Rochestown, par. Carrigaline, Rochestown, par. Templetrine and Carrigarostig, par. Ightermurragh (Imokilly). By 1300 there were Roche families settled near Mallow and later in the century others held extensive lands in the eastern side of Donaghmore parish. The northern part of Whitechurch parish was included in Fermoy barony in the mid-17th century, in which period it had a townland named Farranaroistigh. An account written in 1597 refers to former 'English' freeholders such as the Roches of Carrignevar (*Carraig na bhFear*) who had been forced by the Mac Carthys of Muskerry to hand over the titles to their lands.

A wealthy and influential branch of the Roches had a long association with Cork city. Maurice Roche became mayor of Cork in 1488 and on several occasions thereafter. From then until the Cromwellian takeover, Roches appear in the list of Cork mayors with unfailing regularity. They were among the dozen or so leading Cork families who shared this privilege. When Maurice fitz Edmond Roche was mayor in 1571 Queen Elizabeth bestowed on him a silver collar in appreciation of his services against the Earl of Desmond. In his will, eleven years later, Maurice asked that he be buried in St. Peter's. (This church is in the North Main Street. There are ancient Roche tombs in Christ Church also.) To his son and heir John he left his principal house, the fourth part of Maghen (Mahon), half the weir of Douglas, all his lands in Lord Roche's country, the manor of Glanmire, one ploughland in Rochestown, certain lands in Corbally, a castle and lands at Classyganny and from the castle south to Maghey-more (this was in the Glanmire area) and half the mill called Myllyn na Karriggy (*Muileann na Carraige*) in Shandon.

Rochestown or *Baile an Róistigh* took its name originally from the Roches of Carrigleamleary, east of Mallow, who bore the title 'Fitz (or Mac) Myllon Roche de Carrick'. (As early as 1375 there was a Milo de Rupe de Carrich in the cantred of Fermoy west, so that Mac Myllon probably means 'son of Milo'.) In 1539 Edmond fitz Philip Roche als. Mac Myllan of Carrigleamleary conveyed Rochestown and other lands to Thomas Ronayne, though the Roches retained an interest in the lands up to 1606.

Alderman Dominick Roche was mayor of Cork in 1609 and M.P. for Cork county in 1639. Two years later the Roches along with other old Cork families suffered a disastrous blow when Lord Inchiquin ordered the expulsion of all the Irish (Catholic) inhabitants of the city. Excluded from this order were Richard, Maurice and John Roche, aldermen, James Roche, sheriff, Edmond and Maurice fitz Edmond Roche, Catherine Roche and Ellen fitz Edmond Roche, widows. Maurice Roche of Cork city had his claim for restoration admitted in 1692. However, under the new regime the Roches and their peers had very little influence in municipal affairs.

Trabolgan, where the names of Roche's Point and Roche's Tower still recall the family, was another seat of the Roches. Edward Roche fitz Maurice fitz Edmund (d. 1626) was father of Francis Roche, of Trabolgan (d. 1669) whose younger son, Edmond, married Mary Archdeacon of Monkstown castle, widow of Maurice Roche of Dunderrow. (He also left a daughter, Ellen, who married Edmond Kearney of Garrettstown.) Edmond Roche was outlawed in 1691 but had his outlawry reversed by special warrant in 1695. He and his wife, Mary, both died at the same hour on 23rd January 1711, and were buried at Dunderrow where an elaborately inscribed tombstone commemorates them.

The Dunderrow Roches were a long-established branch in their own right. A 17th century pedigree names John Roche (known as Jonyne Donydorrowe — *Seoinín Dúna Darmhagha*) as ancestor, the descent being as follows:

Jonyne — Candebek — David — John — Maurice — John — Maurice — John — Richard — Maurice. At this rate Jonyne must have been in Dunderrow in the 14th century. Maurice, the last-named, lived there in 1649, and since he claimed to be a Protestant ('a pretended Protestant' one of his opponents called him) he managed to regain the lands confiscated from his father, Richard. A chalice in Kinsale Catholic church bears the names of Maurice and his wife, Mary, and the date 1664. He died in 1665 (leaving a son, Edward), and his widow later married Edmond Roche of Trabolgan, as already stated. Edmond and Mary were living at Ringabella in 1702 when a new settlement was made whereby Maurice, grandson of Maurice of 1665, inherited Dunderrow. This Maurice's only child, Mary, married Francis Kearney (grandnephew of Edmond Roche of Trabolgan) thus bringing the Dunderrow estates to the Kearney family. An interest in the estate seems to have been retained by a son of Edmond, namely Francis (Squire) Roche of Ballinvarrig or Hollyhill (par. Tisaxon), until his death in 1755.

The de Courcy connection goes back at least as far as the late 15th century when a daughter of Dáibhidh Mór Roche married James de Courcy, Lord Kingsale, while in 1508 his granddaughter married a later lord, David de Courcy.

There was an Edmund Roche in Kinsale in 1488, and John Roche (son and heir of Philip) in 1549. In 1571 a pardon was issued to Patrick, Milo, George and Michael Roche of Kinsale, merchants, arising from their dealings with James Fitzmaurice and other rebels. (Mac Philip Roche of Kinsale was one of three friends who accompanied Fitzmaurice to the continent in 1575.) Philip Roche who was M.P. for Kinsale in 1585 was fined £50 in 1606 for non-attendance at the services of the reformed church. His son James was M.P. in 1613 along with Dominick Roche. David Roche fitz Richard of Kinsale who died in 1637 was seized of the manor of Glinny or Cullen (near Riverstick) and of the castle and lands of Britfieldstown. His son, Richard, forfeited after 1641, Britfieldstown being acquired by Francis Roberts (whence Roberts' Cove).

Patrick and Philip Roche were M.P.s for Kinsale in 1639. Both were sons of Richard Roche of Poulnelong, who was descended from Lucas, 3rd son of Lord Roche. The ruins of the 16th century Poll na Long or Shippool castle may still be seen on the river bank below Innishannon. In 1642 after the Roches had joined in the rebellion the castle was besieged and captured. Patrick's lands were confiscated and later granted to John Herrick and others. The Philip who was outlawed in 1691 (described as of Dublin, Britfieldstown and Poulnelong) was probably a son of Patrick.

Another Roche seat in Kinalea was at Kinure near Oysterhaven. James Oge Roche of Kinure was a member of a jury in 1576. An inquisition into his lands was held in 1633. David, his son and heir, died the following year, leaving a grandson, James oge, as heir. Young James was outlawed in 1643 and Kinure fell to Swithen Walton. James' aunt, Ellen Roche, married Thomas Roche of Fartha (par. Ballyfeard) descended from a 2nd brother of Lord Roche of Fermoy. Thomas died in 1638 and was buried at Kilpatrick near Tracton. Richard, the son and heir, forfeited after 1641, and Fartha went to Giles Busteed. Ballinluig, also in Ballyfeard parish, was the seat of John Roche who in his will, (1663) left extensive lands in Kinalea (settled by his ancestors on the second son of the family of Poulnelong) to his wife Clara (Coppinger) and his son Philip. Philip sold 1412 acres in the Ballyfeard area to James Meade in the 18th century.

Kilpatrick parish too, near Ringabella bay, supported its share of Roches. A pardon was granted in 1601 to Thomas, Peirse and Edmond, sons of James Roche, all of Parkenemaule, a townland (no longer extant) near Fountainstown. A fourth brother, Maurice fitz James Roche, held Kilpatrick, into which there was an inquisition in 1635. James Roche (probably son of Maurice) lost his lands in the Cromwellian confiscations, Kilpatrick going to Lord Shannon and Fountainstown to William Hodder. The older part of Fountainstown House is believed to have been built by the Roches but they never recovered the property, although Patrick Roche who was outlawed in 1691 was, we are told, 'commonly called Roche of Fountainstown'.

Liam de Róiste, elected Sinn Féin M.P. for Cork city in 1918, was born in this townland, though hardly of the same branch since his father came from Cappawhite, Co. Tipperary.

Ó SÍDHEACHÁIN

Ó SÍODHCHÁIN   Ó SÍOTHCHÁIN   Ó SÍOCHÁIN   SHEEHAN
SHEAHAN

While there is no genealogy of this family now extant, there are at least three references to a possible origin to be found in genealogical sources. Two of these are in *An Leabhar Muimhneach*. The more unlikely derivation is one from Mathghamhain, brother of Brian Boru; the other makes them an offshoot of Clann Scannláin. A third source, (in the Book of Leinster) derives Munter Sídecháin from Sídechán, a contemporary (and distant relative) of Brian Boru. All three sources agree that the Uí Shídheacháin were of the Dál Cais and there seems to be no reason for disputing this. There are two Ballysheehans (*Baile Uí Shídheacháin*) in Co. Tipperary, one near Cashel and the other – a former seat of the O Briens – near Clogheen. According to Mac Lysaght, the O Sheehans occupied a portion of Lower Connello in Co. Limerick, from which it is but a short step into north and east Co. Cork where we find them in Elizabethan times.

This movement may have occurred as early as the 13th century as we find Thomas Osithechan a prebendary of Kilcredan parish in Cloyne diocese *c*. 1300. The Pipe Roll of Cloyne refers to an Oshehan in Lackeen parish in 1341. Much later, in 1493, a connection with Kilcredan again appears, when Mauritius Oscyachan, vicar of Leighmoney (near Innishannon), was made responsible for the parish church of Kilcredan as well. During the 15th century quite a number of the name were in clerical positions in Co. Cork, especially in Cloyne diocese. In 1417 Cornelius Osyghichayn, clerk, was made archdeacon of Cloyne. In 1464 William Ysyichayn, vicar of Castlemagner, was granted the nearby vicarages of Subulter and Roskeen, long void by the death of Donatus Ymyrrisey and Cornelius Ysychayn. William – if it was he – seems to have had a long life; there was still a Guillelmus Osichan a priest at Castlemagner in 1513. Around 1465 Thadeus Osychayn was deprived of the vicarage of Inishkenny near Cork, and it was afterwards held by Robert Osyhyhayn. Four years later the prebend of Desertmore, also in Cork diocese, was stated to be long void because of the death of Dermit Osyahcayn, as was Ballyclogh (near Mallow) because of the non-ordination of Denis Osyhytayn. No doubt he was ordained eventually; in 1479 Donatus Oseyn was replaced as perpetual vicar of Clonfert (in Duhallow) by Thateus Oschecayn but two years later he turns up as *de facto* vicar of Roskeen.

Another of the name, David Shyoghan, a servant of Thomas Cromwell (Earl of Essex and secretary of State), was, in 1537, in dispute with Alexander Gough, priest, over certain lands and tenements at

Youghal. The verdict was in Gough's favour. Later in the century Maurice Shighane was private secretary and right-hand man to the rebel Earl of Desmond — 'the cunningest man about the Earl' as one State Paper describes him. He remained faithful to the Earl to the end and afterwards settled at Rathmore, Co. Limerick.

During the 15th and 16th centuries further groups of O Sheehans may have moved into Co. Cork as gallowglass to various lords. The Elizabethan Fiants provide some evidence of this. In 1584, in company with a group of Mac Sweeney gallowglass from the Roche castle of Carrigleamleary, Thady or Teig na Bully (*Tadhg na buile*) mac Daniell O Sheaghann and Dermot ny Bully mac Donell O Shiaghane, of Carrigleamleary, gallowglasses, were pardoned. It so happens that there is a townland named Ballyshehan (? *Baile Uí Shídheacháin*) in the parish of Carrigleamleary. In the same year, William O Shyaghane mac Donoghe was among William Power's men pardoned in east Cork.

In Duhallow in a 1585 pardon granted to O Callaghan of Drominagh and O Keeffe of Dromagh we find the names of Moriertagh O Shighane and David O Shighan of Drominagh. Thady Mac Auliffe's followers in 1578 included Donill oge O Sheihane; later, in 1610, we find Connoghor O Sheaghan, yeoman, settled at Carrigcastle in Clanauliffe. Followers of the lord of Muskerry included, in 1585, Conoghor O Shighane of Blarney, and in 1601, Shane O Shighan, Deirmod O Shiegan of Knockowrane (Mountmusic, par. Kilmichael), Awliffe O Shighan of Dundirig (? Dundareirke) and Dermod O Shighane of Killumney.

In Carbery in 1601 John and William mac Teige O Shighane of Ballyowcane (? Ballyourane, par. Caheragh) were pardoned in company with a group of O Dohertys, Mac Sweeneys and other gallowglasses. With Erivan Mac Sweeney of Enniskean was pardoned David O Shieghan of the same place. There was a scattering of O Sheehans in other areas but only two recorded as husbandmen (farmers) — William O Shiaghane, apparently in Condon's country, and Teig O Sheghan of Liscarroll.

Records of O Sheehans in the 17th century are not plentiful. A Teige O Sheeghane of Cork had his will registered in 1619 — perhaps the Teige Roe O Shigane who in 1617 was admitted a freeman of Cork city 'in as ample a manner as every other tradesman, paying £5'. A house in Cork belonging to Dermod O Shighane is mentioned in 1628. In Youghal John Shyghan carried on his trade as a tailor in 1617 and Daniel O Shehegan lived there in 1628. There was also a William Sheehane appointed town clerk of Youghal when a new (Jacobite) corporation was appointed there in April 1688. Thadeus O Sheaghan was Church of Ireland vicar of Inchigeelagh in 1639, no doubt the same man who had been vicar of Dromtarriff, Drishane and Cullen in 1618.

After the Cromwellian wars and plantations, the distribution of the name in Co. Cork, according to the 1659 census, was still mainly in the eastern half, with 23 O Sheghane families in Orrery and Kilmore and a lesser number in Mallow, Cork city and liberties, Kinalea and Kerrycurrihy. The only part of the western half where the name occurred was Carbery west where there were 18 O Shighanes – and there is a possibility that the original name here may have been Ó Seitheacháin (Hyde).

In 1689 there was a Captain William Sheehan in King James' army. Because of his Jacobite loyalties he was outlawed in 1690, being described as of Ratheenuame (or Rathcumaine) in Co. Cork. This may be Rathcobane in the parish of Templebodan in Barrymore. He (or one of his name – William Sheehane of Ballinamona) successfully claimed benefit of the articles of Limerick in 1699, as did also John Sheeghane of Ballymicen (? Ballyhimikin, par. Garryvoe). But Edmond Sheehane must have lost everything; he was described as a notorious tory or rapparee for whose capture David Donnellan was paid £20 in 1712.

David Sheehan appears to have been a sculptor of some note in the 18th century. The Barrymore monument in the mausoleum erected in 1742 in Castlelyons graveyard is inscribed 'David Sheehan fecit'; John Haughton had a part in it also.

In 1739 Seán na Ráithíneach, the poet of Carraig na bhFear, composed welcoming verses to celebrate the return to Ireland of Fr. Seán Ó Síodhcháin. Later in the century Mícheál Ó Longáin of the same area wrote in praise of one Uilliam Ó Síothcháin. Some minor Gaelic poets of the name flourished, such as Tadhg Ó Síothcháin of West Muskerry – he was born in Cnoc an Chapaill, perhaps Horsemount in Kilcorney parish – and An t-Athair Domhnall Ó Síothcháin who was one of the 18th century east Cork poets. The most famous literary figure of the name was the distinguished cleric and novelist, Canon P.A. Sheehan, who was born in Mallow in 1852 and died parish priest of Doneraile in 1913. Another Canon Sheehan, later elevated to the see of Waterford, was a founder-member and first president of the Cork Historical and Archaeological Society in 1891.

MAC SUIBHNE

(MAC) SWEENEY   (MAC) SWINEY

Along the western isles and promontories of Scotland dwelt a hardy race of mixed Norse-Gaelic extraction whose contacts with the neighbouring Ulster coastline were frequent and often sanguinary. From this source came such well-known Scots-Irish names as Mac Donnell and Mac Dowell, Mac Sheehy and Mac Sweeney, families to whom the term *gallóglaigh* (foreign soldiers) was applied in Ireland. 'Gallowglass' were professional soldiers retained by various chieftains, and the Mac Sweeneys initially took service with the O Donnells of Tír Conaill.

We first meet with the name in the Irish annals when Murchadh Mac Suibhne (who was, in fact, not the son but the grandson of the eponymous ancestor, Suibhne) was captured in Connacht in 1267 and died in prison. His grandson, Murchadh Mer, conquered and settled in the district of Fanad in Co. Donegal, and from him are descended all the Mac Sweeney gallowglass families of Ireland. Murchadh Mer was succeeded by Murchadh óg, whose two sons (Maelmuire and Donnchadh Mór) were the ancestors of Mac Suibhne Fanad and Mac Suibhne na dTuath respectively, these being the two chief lines in Ulster. A strand of each found its way to Co. Cork; those who came to Carbery and Béarra (*Clann tSuibhne Deasmhumhan*) were descended from Mac Suibhne na dTuath while those of Muskerry (*Clann tSuibhne na Mumhan*) were of the senior line.

It was one of the latter who was first to be mentioned in a south Munster context. The reigning grandson of Maelmuire was Toirrdhealbhach Ruadh and one of Toirrdhealbhach's grandson's, Brian, inflicted (according to *Craobhsgaoileadh Chlainne Suibhne*) the defeat of Cnoc na Lurgan on Cormac Dall Mac Carthaigh. This seems to have been Cormac (Riabhach) of Carbery who was involved in a family succession conflict. In 1477 he was captured by Cormac Láidir of Muskerry and later blinded by his own kinsmen. Apparently the lord of Muskerry was assisted by Brian Mac Sweeney on this occasion. The only Knocknalurgan townland now in Co. Cork is in Carrigaline parish but it seems more likely that the battle took place in Carbery.

The same source relates how Brian's son, Maelmuire, assisted Cormac óg, Lord of Muskerry – this time in union with the Carbery Mac Carthys – in inflicting a crushing defeat on the Earl of Desmond at Mainistir na Móna (*Mourne Abbey*) in 1520. Previous to this, in 1498, the annals tell us, one of the Geraldines, Thomas óg, had helped the same Cormac óg become lord of Muskerry when Cormac defeated and killed his uncle, Eoghan mac Taidhg, at the battle of Ceinn bo Cathail. Their combined forces also slew Philip O Sullivan Bear, Brian óg son of Brian Mac Sweeney and two sons of Dubhdara Mac Sweeney, one of whom was named Edmond. (Dubhdara was probably a cousin of Brian's father.) Another son of Brian, namely Maelmuire, was constable to Mac Auliffe of Duhallow and was slain in 1535.

It is obvious then that the Mac Sweeneys first came into Co. Cork in the second half of the 15th century as gallowglass in the employ of Cormac Láidir who greatly expanded the lordship of Muskerry between 1455 and 1494. This is confirmed in a pedigree compiled by Sir George Carew who says that the first of the Mac Sweeneys 'was drawn out of Ulster into Mounster by Cormac'. Carew names the first of them as Edmond (perhaps the Edmond slain in 1498) and continues: 'The Ld. of Muskrye did give unto this Edmond and his posteritie Bonnaght beg (which is a certayne rent of meat and money) upp on every plowland in Old Muskrye, Iveleary, Iflanloghe, Clanconnogher and Clanfinin. Moreover, he had to him and his heyers a quarter of free land, all which the sayed Edmond's posteritie enjoy at this day besides the lands which some of them have sithence that time purchased in Muskyre.'

But Edmond does not seem to have had any posterity. According to the genealogies the descent continued through his brother, Eoin, grandfather of Eoghan an Locha whom we meet later.

Carew also mentions that two other Mac Sweeney chieftains had been hired by Fínghin Mac Carthy Riabhach 'to serve him against divers in Carberrie who would not obey him' — and this again is borne out by a reference in the *Annals of the Four Masters* (1560) to a foray into Carbery by the sons of the Earl of Desmond. An attack was made on the plunderers by Mac Carthy Riabhach aided by 'Turlough the son of Maolmurry son of Donagh son of Turlogh Mac Sweeny of the tribe of Donogh More from Tuaith Tiraidhe with a brave select party of gallowglasses'. This clearly shows the connection between Mac Suibhne na dTuath and Clann tSuibhne Deasmhumhan.

The chief seats of the Mac Sweenys in Muskerry were the castles of Mashanaglass and Cloghda or Clodagh which Carew says they purchased from the Mac Carthys. They also had Carrig Dèrmot óg (Dunisky) for a time and were chief warders of Castlemore near Crookstown.

Mashanaglass is in the parish of Aghinagh, east of Macroom and was a Mac Carthy seat as early as 1237 when Cormac Fionn, king of Desmond, died there. Though in Muskerry it remained the property of the Mac Carthys Mór, the nominal overlords of the Mac Carthys of Muskerry. The existing castle ruins at Mashanaglass date from the late 16th century — perhaps 1584, the year when Cormac mac Dermod Mac Carthy conveyed the castle and lands of Mashanaglass to Donnell mac Owen Mac Swiny, reserving £4 yearly rent, with half the eyrie of hawks and free ingress to the lord of Muskerry and his wife. This may have been in exchange for the manor of Inishkenny near Cork which Cormac

mac Teige had willed to Donnell Mac Sweeney in the previous year. A pardon was granted in 1585 to Donell mac Owen Mac Swynye of Mashanaglass, gent., Ellin ny Donogho (probably his wife) of same and Morogh mac Tirrelagh Mac Swyne of same, gallowglass. Donnell received a similar pardon in 1586 but must have died before 1591 since Neale mac Donell Mac Sweeny is the one mentioned in a pardon of that year. By the end of the century Niall had been succeeded by his brother Owen, who was pardoned in 1601 and 1604. This was the Owen who, according to Carew, purchased Mashanaglass, thus becoming 'a freeholder, to him and his heirs', but whether he did so from the Mac Carthys or from the crown is not clear.

In 1612 James I authorized the Lord Deputy to accept a surrender and make a regrant of Owen's lands in consideration of his 'dutiful and loyal behaviour, and his sufferings, owing to the malignity of his countrymen'. His son, Owen óg, after 1641 forfeited Mashanaglass with 1209 acres ('on the premises is a demolished castle and grist mill') and 114 acres at Aghagandy (? Annagannihy). The lands of Muskerry were restored to the Earl of Clancarty in 1661, and two years later Daniel mac Owen Mac Swiney (eldest son of Owen óg) transferred his rights to Mashanaglass to the Earl in exchange for the lands of Garranereagh, Lackareagh and Killeglasse (par. Kilmichael) and Knocknaneirk (par. Kilmurry).

Daniel died at Knocknaneirk in 1674 and was buried in Kilcrea. He was married to Ellen, daughter of Tadhg Mac Carthy, and had six sons and two daughters. His younger sons inherited land at Kilronane, Coolkelure and Curraleigh while the main estate of Knocknaneirk, Lackareagh and Kilglass went to his eldest son, Owen, who died in 1686 and was succeeded by Daniel. Owen's widow remarried, her second husband being Edmond Murphy (known as 'Guerdol'), a controversial attorney. Murphy set up a title for himself and John Bayley, and was the recognized tenant of the lands in 1702. Young Daniel Mac Sweeney sold his interest to Samuel Swete and John Beamish in trust for himself, but as the trust was illegal Swete ousted the Mac Sweeneys from Kilglass and changed its name to Greenville. His relative, John Beamish, got possession of Knocknaneirk which he sold to the Bernard family. A son of Daniel, Owen, was living in 1733 and kept up the claim to the family lands but to no avail. According to O Hart, a junior branch of these Mac Sweeneys lived for a time at Castlemore and later removed to Dublin.

We now return to Clodagh castle which has an inscription *Anno Dni. 1598 B.M.S.O.G. Decimo Die Julii* on a mantelpiece. The initials are those of Brian Mac Sweeney (brother of Donnell of Mashanaglass) and Onora Fitzgerald, his wife. Presumably in that year, Brian re-erected or renovated the castle. (Carew states that he purchased it.) Brian also held Castlemore (near Mourne Abbey) which had been mortgaged to him for seven score in-calf cows by Sir Thomas of Desmond and his son

James. These Geraldines must have resented their mortgagee's 1598 renovations in conjunction with his lack of support for their cause. This was the year when Tyrell (O Neill's commander in Munster) burned out the undertakers and other opponents of O Neill in the province. So in November of that same year, according to a petition written by Brian in 1611, '. . . James Fitzgerald, attainted, sone of Sir Thomas of Desmond, accompanied by Owney mac Rorie and Captain Terill, took, by force, his castle of Cloghdha, and burned and defaced it, and took all petitioner's goods and cattle, and those of his tenants to the value of £2,000, besides many other preys, spoils, burnings and killing of petitioner's towns and villages'.

He also complained of some alleged harsh proceedings by Henry Beecher, escheator of Munster, against him — not without justification. In the previous year Brian had surrendered his lands to the crown in expectation of the usual regrant but in February 1613 the castle, town and lands of Cloghda, otherwise Clogheendha and Ardra, were granted to Edward Southworthe. Yet the Mac Sweeneys may have remained on as tenants. A Sarsfield inquisition dated 1637 mentions Morrogh mac Brian Mac Swiny of Cloghda castle.

Another castle with which tradition associates the Mac Sweeneys (though not as owners) was Carrig Dermot óg at Dunisky near Macroom, a Mac Carthy castle. Near the castle site is a stone inscribed '1619 E.O.S.'. These are thought to be the initials of Edmond óg Swiney, presumably the Edmond Oge Mac Swyny of Downyskie, gent., who was married to a daughter of David Nagle of Monanimy. (Edmond mac Brien Mac Sweeney of Monanimy was pardoned in 1584.)

There was also a family connection with Castlemore near Crookstown, one of the principal strongholds of Muskerry. Because of their military profession the Mac Sweeneys were frequently appointed warders or constables of castles (*consapal Deasmhumhan*, the *A.F.M.* call one of them). In 1585 a pardon was granted to Rory oge mac Rorie mac Owen reogh Mac Swynye of Castlemore, gallowglass, and to Morogh bullagh mac Tire mac Owen reogh Mac Swynye of same, yeoman. In 1591 Brian mac Tirr Mac Sweeney was at Castlemore, but no Mac Sweeneys are recorded there in the 17th century. In 1666 the castle and lands (1,800 statute acres) were granted to Thomas Crooke (founder of Crookstown) and John Bayly.

Their military profession caused the Mac Sweeneys to become deeply involved in all the Elizabethan wars in Munster. When James Fitzmaurice first raised his standard in 1569, among his earliest supporters were three brothers Edmond, Eugene and Murrough Mac Sweeney, along with their brother-in-law Dermod O Sullivan of Béarra who was married to Joanna Mac Sweeney and was the father of Don Philip, the historian. On 23 May 1571 the Earl of Ormond wrote to Burghley from his camp at Rochfordstown near Cork that he would set forth on the morrow against the Mac Sweeneys 'who aid James

Fitzmaurice when he spoils the Queen's subjects'. Next day he added that 'Morrogh ne Tolly and the gallowglasses of the Mac Swineys supply the chief force of the traitors' and that he would that day march against them. In a further letter of the 21st June he related that Morrogh na Tolly and twenty-six rebels had been slain. In September Fitzmaurice was still being maintained 'by the Mac Swineys and other loose and evil conditioned men'. The Earl of Clancare and others promised Perrott that they would maintain 200 fighting men for six months, 'and to persecute to the death such of the Mac Swynys as shall not come in before October'. The only ones who appear to have 'come in' — they were pardoned on 23 May 1572 — were Domhnall, Brian and Toirrdh-ealbhach, the sons of Owen looghy (*Eoghan an Locha*). At this period Domhnall had become chief warder of Blarney castle; the nickname *an locha* may indicate that Eoghan lived near the lake at Blarney. Domhnall had a daughter married to a son of Cormac Mac Taidhg, lord of Muskerry, and was one of the executors of Cormac's will, made in June 1583.

Not unexpectedly, members of the Mac Sweeney clan feature in 'pardons' more frequently (in relation to their numbers) than did those of any other surname in Co. Cork. Among those pardoned during the periods of the Desmond rebellions were:

1573:   Edmond Mac Swyne of Rossbrin in Carbery, Colly and Brian mac Edmond, Owen and Eryvan mac Tirlagh of Kanturk, Owen mac Tirrelaghe of Carrig(leamleary), gent., Donald ballagh of same, gent., Moylmorry mac Edmond of Castleton, yeoman, Tirlagh mergagh of same, Brian daragh of same, Moilmory and Gohorrigh mac Donogh baccagh, Murrugh ny Tully of Knockanure, gent. (Knockanure is in Ballyvourney parish; this last-named must have succeeded the Murchadh of 1571 or else Ormond was mistaken when he reported his death in that year.)

1576:   Gohyre and Rorie mac Donoughe, gallowglasses, Brian oge mac Brien of Courtbrack, gent., Owen mac Tirrelagh of Dooneen, gallowglass.

1577:   Eugene mac Edmond of Carrignamuck, gallowglass, Terelagh oge of Dooneen, gallowglass (one of Owen mac Tirrelig backagh Mac Swyny's men), Brian mac Edmond, gallowglass, Milerus or Melmory mac Donoughe baccagh; Brien mac Owen of Coolatubrid, gallowglass.

1578:   Erewane mac Morroghe of Ballyburden.

1579:   Edmond and Collne mac Edmond of Beallyhimore.

1584:   Bryn og mac Brien duff of Muskerry, gallowglass, Morrogho mac Tyrreley of Carrigleamleary, gallowglass, Edmond oge mac Edmond mac Beiry of Macroom, gallowglass, Earywan mac Morrogh of Aghamarta, gent., Conoghor mac Edmond of Macloneigh, gallowglass. (This pardon was granted to the 'Swynes galloglas'.) Brien mac Owen y loghie of Ballygarvan, gent., Donell mac Owen y loghie of Macroom, gent., Meylmorry mac Gohory of Carrignacurra, kern, Edmond and Owen mac Brien and Tirrelighe mac Edmond of Monanimy, Melemurry mac Bryan, gallowglass.

From this list we see that while the majority of Mac Sweeneys were listed as gallowglass, some achieved the status of 'gentleman' — as did the sons of Eoghan an locha whom we find in the Mac Carthy strongholds of Macroom and Ballygarvan (near Ballea). Others were prominent in the Mac Carthy castles of Carrignamuck (Dripsey), Kanturk and Dooneens as well as in the Roche strongholds of Castletownroche and Carrigleamleary. In 1582 the annals record two raids by the seneschal of Imokilly and by the Condons on Roche's country in the course of which six sons of Roche and the constables (*consabail chloinne Suibhne*) were slain. In that year also occurred the death of 'Eoghan mac Maelmuire mac Donnchaidh mac Toirrdhealbhaigh mac Suibhne, constable of Desmond, a sedate and tranquil man in the drinking-house and at the meeting, but obstinate, furious and irresistible in battle and in the field of contest'.

Even the government used Mac Sweeneys as custodians of castles — as in the case of Rossbrin, forfeited by the O Mahonys in 1562 and occupied by Perrot's men. In 1580 Pelham attempted to cess 1200 gallowglass on the lords of Munster, appointing chiefs of the Mac Sweeneys as captains over them.

It is remarkable how the Mac Sweeneys adhered to the ancestral first-names they brought from Donegal — Brian, Eoghan and Eoin, Murchadh, Toirdhealbhach, Domhnall, Éamann, Maelmhuire, Ruaidhrí, Donnchadh. A few more unusual ones appear, such as Gohory (Gothraidh or Godfrey), Colly or Collne (Colla) and Earywan (Eireamhón). A lady of the family bore the name Niamh (Niewffe) in 1601. The nicknames are the familiar ones of the period — *ballach, meirgeach, carrach, bacach, dorcha, dubh*.

After he had suppressed the first Desmond rising Sir Henry Sidney spent the Christmas of 1575 at Cork where he was attended by the nobility of the province — the Earl of Desmond, the Mac Carthys, Viscounts Barry and Roche, etc. 'Lastly,' he records, 'there came to me five brethren and the sons of two other brethren of one lineage, all captains of Gallowglas called Mac Swynes, who, although I place them last of the rest, yet are they of as much consequence as any of the rest, for of such credit and force were they grown into (though they were no lords of lands themselves) as they would make of the greatest lords in the province both in fear of them and glad of their friendship.' Yet Sidney did not quite trust them. 'I have taken pledges of all who are of any regard', he wrote, 'especially of the Mac Swynes, a brood not a little perilous to this province.'

Towards the end of 1576 Sir William Drury, President of Munster, wrote to Walsingham: 'The second of October last I began the assizes at Cork where I hanged to the number of 42 . . . two gentlemen of the Mac Sweeneys hanged, drawn and quartered; one of these being captain of gallowglass half a year before my coming, took away a prey of cattle (with his banner displayed) from Cork, the which banner he had carried before him unto the place of execution, and the same I reserve for your honour.' *The Annals of the Four Masters* tell us that one was a son of Murchadh mac Maolmuire and the other a son of Domhnall mac Maolmuire. Donnell oge Mac Sweeney with two others was executed in 1577.

As the last Desmond rebellion petered out, the once powerful Earl of Desmond must have found the actions of one loyal follower a refreshing contrast to the coat-turning of his erstwhile adherents, now rapidly abandoning him. This was Gofraidh carrach Mac Suibhne, son of Donnchadh bacach and nephew of Eoghan, the 'constable of Desmond' who died in 1582. After the slaying of his brother, Sir John Fitzgerald, and of Maelmhuire Mac Suibhne, a captain, the Earl of Desmond, (according to O Sullivan Bear's account), reduced to extremities and the greatest poverty, was gradually deserted by all but maintained by Gofraidh or Gory Mac Sweeney, his captain of the guard, who hid him in caves and woods. When Gory was arrested and questioned by the Earl of Ormond, he denied all knowledge of Earl Gerald until eye-witnesses forced him to admit it. He then confessed to having been with Gerald and promised to surrender him to Ormond if suitably recompensed. Gory was accordingly freed in order to perform this highly meritorious service but instead of bringing in the Earl as prisoner, he transferred him to other lonely places where he maintained him by hunting and by plundering until, while seeking food he was intercepted and killed. The *Annals of the Four Masters* tell us that he was slain by the kernes of Inis Caoin — apparently Enniskeane. On November 15th, 1583, Ormond wrote to the Privy Council that he had just got news 'of the killing of the traitor Gorehe Mac Swiney (Capten of Gallowglass) the onely man that relived thErle of Desmond in his extreme misery' and also news of the killing of the Earl himself. In 1584 Rory Carragh, uncle of Gory, was executed at Cork. Some years later, Florence Mac Carthy 'Mór' claimed that it was a company of his men who killed Gory Mac Swiney.

Florence himself came under suspicion ten years later, and one of his followers named by the Lord Deputy 'to be examined' was Kyrone (? Eireamhón) mac Moragho Mac Swynie. Florence had actually been fostered with a Mac Sweeney who was chief commander of Mac Carthy Riabhach's footmen. In later years he informed Cecil that he could get his foster-brother, Murchadh na Mart, 'who without exception is the most exercised commander, and of greatest skill, experience and reputation, for that country's wars, of any mere Irishman' to make an attempt on the life of Hugh O'Neill. Murchadh had, in fact, helped

Turlogh O Neill to defeat Hugh O Neill at Carricklea in 1588. Afterwards he and his two hundred Munstermen were hired by O Rourke of Breffni in whose service Murchadh lost his left eye. His remaining eye was dazzled by the beauty of O Rourke's niece, and after an abduction scandal he deserted O Rourke and returned to Munster where he joined the forces of O Sullivan Bear.

Two other followers of Donal Cam O Sullivan were Manus and Daniel Mac Sweeney. They accompanied O Sullivan to Kinalmeaky to meet Hugh O Neill prior to the battle of Kinsale. In O Neill's army representatives of the three great Ulster families of Mac Sweeneys were among his most trusted leaders. Members of the Ulster and Munster branches must have spent some enjoyable hours tracing family relationships before the rout at Kinsale separated them once more. Afterwards came the fall of Dunboy involving several of the Mac Sweeneys. Colly mac Edmond Mac Sweeney who sailed for Spain from Ardea with Connor O Driscoll had a son hanged at Dunboy. On the other hand Moylemurry mac Edmond Boy gave information to Carew regarding the landing at Kilmackillogue of Bishop Owen Mac Egan, while Owen Ologh (*an locha*) Mac Swiney, with his cousin, Mac Carthy of Drishane, led Bagenal's forces by night to Tyrell's camp where 80 men were killed.

It is obvious that the nature of their profession prevented the Mac Sweeneys from acting as a tightly-knit clan so that each group could and did function independently of the others. Back in Muskerry Owen Mac Swyny of Mocrumpy, gent., paid £100 recognizances for having pardon in July 1603, on condition that he should continue dutiful. Perhaps it was the same Owen, 'a youth in years but in courage more than manly' who, according to Philip O Sullivan, in the previous year effected the daring escape of Cormac Mac Carthy, lord of Muskerry, from Cork gaol.

There was an Owen Mac Swynie (of Desmond) who was a pensioner in the Spanish service in 1605 but this was probably Eoghan an Locha, captain of Gallowglass to the lord of Muskerry, whom Lord Danvers, President of Munster, proposed using in 1608 to infiltrate the Irish in Spain. Eoghan, 'a fellow now famous in Munster', had sisters who were married in Rome to Captains Mac Carthy and O Driscoll. He simulated enthusiasm for the plot but once he got to Spain no intelligence from him ever reached Danvers. Much later, in 1624, the Lord Deputy received from another source tidings of an impending Spanish invasion, one of its instigators being Owen Eloghie Mac Swiney, who could both speak and write in Spanish.

At home, the Mac Sweeneys of the early 17th century, with little outlet for their martial tendencies, took their place among the landed gentry of Co. Cork and intermarried with them. Domhnall of Mashanaglass' daughter, Ellen, married Conchubhar, son of Sir Fínghin O Driscoll. She appears to have been previously married to Donnchadh

Mac Carthy, son of Cormac Mac Teige and founder of the Máistir na Móna branch. Edmond and Brian óg, two sons of Brian Mac Sweeney of Kilnarovanagh (par. Macloneigh), married two daughters of Donogh O Leary of Dromcarra. In Kilbrittain Brian Ballagh Mac Swini, gent., in 1604 got an order for the restitution of 18 cows, forcibly taken from Kilkerran by Dominic Terry, under-sheriff of Co. Cork. In Duhallow, Brian, son of Eoghan an Locha, was involved in the taking of O Callaghan's castle of Dromaneen, and the Mac Sweeneys appear to have gained a foothold in Kilmeen parish, principally at Derrygalun and Derrynatubbrid.

The only outlawed member was Dowdarragh Mac Swynye, one of a band of rebels in the Muskerry-Duhallow area in 1619 with a price of £50 on his head. Only five were outlawed as a result of the 1641 rising — Owen Oge Iloghy and Donnel Oge Iloghy of Mashanaglass, Mullmurry Mac Edmond and Edmond Mac Mullmurry of Mahallagh, and Mullmurry Mac Swyny of Artaghrugh (? Ardacrow, par. Rathclarin). Edmond Mac Sweeney (of Mashanaglass) was among those who received the gratitude of Charles II in 1660.

Several survived as 'tituladoes' according to the 1659 census — Teige Sweeney of Ballymurphy (par. Knockavilla), Moylemurry Mac Sweeney of Tullyglass (par. Murragh) and Donogh Sweeney of Kilcaskan parish (Bear). But Muskerry barony is not in the census so Mac Sweeney is not given as a 'principal Irish name' in any barony except in the City and Liberties of Cork.

Ellen, widow of Edmond Mac Sweeney, of Kilbarry in Macloneigh parish, made a will in 1648 leaving her property to her son and heir, Brian, and requesting burial in Kilcrea. There is a will of Terence alias Terlagh Swynye, late of Cork, made in July 1650, bequeathing his property to his father, John O Swynye, and his brothers, who were living at Lismore. This appears to be the first occasion where Toirrdhealbhach was anglicized as 'Terence', a form which gained world-wide renown in 1920 when Terence Mac Swiney, Lord Mayor of Cork, died on hunger strike. (His father came from near Crookstown.)

Two Terence Mac Swynys were attainted by the Williamites in 1690 — one of Ballyvourney and the other of Mahallagh (par. Cannaway). The latter was probably the Major Terence Mac Swyny of 'Ballalough' who was admitted to the articles of Limerick in 1699. He was son and heir of Morrogh mac Edmond Swiny, gent., who held a lease of lands in Inchigeelagh parish. (A Murrogh mac Erevan Sweeny was with the outlaws in the mountains in 1694.) Also in the military tradition were Captains Donough and Peter and Lieutenant Peter Mac Sweeney, officers of Boisseleau's Infantry in King James' army.

The form Ó Suibhne, noticed in 1650, was sometimes used by poets of the 18th century, though Mac Suibhne continued to be the normal form. Names such as Brian, Donnchadh and Toirrdhealbhach were still in evidence; one poet was styled 'Rúghruídhe mac Eamuin mic Eogain an locha mheic Suibhne ó Mhagh Seanaghlais'.

During the 1798 period, one of the noted United Irishmen in Cork city was John Swiney. Arrested in 1798 and deported in 1802, he returned a year later for Emmet's rising, after which he escaped in a fishing boat from Crosshaven to Normandy in France where his descendants still live. Thomas William Sweeney, leader of the Fenian raid into Canada in 1866, was also born in Co. Cork.

The old family seat was brought to mind in 1896 when Patrick Valentine Mac Swiney who was born in Paris, a grandson of Dr. Valentine Mac Swiney of Macroom and a member of the Papal Household, was created a hereditary Roman marquess with the title Marquess Mac Swiney of Mashanaglass. He later settled in Dublin, joined the Irish Volunteers and was arrested after the rising of Easter, 1916.

Ó SÚILLEABHÁIN

(O) SULLIVAN

The rare personal name Súildubán (dark-eyed) was, according to early genealogies, used once by the Lagin (of Leinster) and once by Eóganacht Caisil. This latter Súildubán was chief of a branch of the Eóganacht in the 10th century. His father's name was Máel-ugrai, and he appears as eighth in descent from Fíngen mac Áeda, a king of Munster who died in 619. The kingship, however, had afterwards been assumed by Fíngen's brother, Fáilbhe, and later by his descendants (among whom were numbered the Mac Carthys) leaving the branch to which Súildubán belonged in comparative obscurity for some centuries. (Nevertheless, as late as 1598 it was noted that a new Mac Carthy Mór was not generally recognized until formally presented with the white rod of office by O Sullivan Mór.)

Súildubán's son and heir was Lorcán who was succeeded by Buadhach, described as of Áth Cró — probably the place of his death. After him came Áed and then Cathal — perhaps the O Sullivan who in company with other Munster chiefs (O Mahony, O Keeffe, O Moriarty and O Phelan) deposed Tadhg Mac Carthaigh from the kingship of Munster in 1123. Next in line was another Buadhach whose son, Mac Raith Ó Súilleabháin, was one of the nobles slain in 1176 while defending Diarmaid Mac Carthaigh, king of Munster, against his son, Cormac Liathánach, who took him (Diarmaid) prisoner. Later in the same year Cormac was slain by the nobles of Desmond, who included the Uí Shúilleabháin, and so Diarmaid was restored.

Ó Súilleabháin's ancestral lands, according to Ó Huidhrín and others, lay around Cnoc Rafann (Knockgraffon in Co. Tipperary) but it would appear that by the end of the 12th century — probably as a result of Norman and O'Brien pressure — the family group had moved into west Desmond, where they afterwards flourished. In 1196 the Gaill or foreigners of Munster and Cork ravaged Férdruim (apparently in west Cork) and killed several noblemen of the Desmumu, including the son of Buadhach Ó Súilleabháin (probably Gilla Pádraig). In the same year Gilla na Flann Ó Súilleabháin and Gerr Uille died, and an Ó Súilleabháin with the unusual name of Anad (third son of Buadhach) died in 1201. (The personal name Gilla na Flann is derived from the two Flanns, joint patrons of Doire na bhFlann — in the ancestral lands of Eóganacht Caisil — where an Ardagh-type chalice was unearthed in 1980.)

The first half of the thirteenth century witnessed a severe rift

300

between the O Sullivans and their onetime allies, the Mac Carthys. It began in 1209 with a dispute concerning the division of spoils at Leac Lachtáin (Lislaughtin, Co. Kerry) when the son of Gerr Uille (Ó Súilleabháin) slew Fínghin Mac Carthaigh with a blow of an axe on the head. Two years later the Uí Shúilleabháin handed over Cormac Ciarraigheach (son of Cormac Liathánach Mac Carthy) to the sheriff of Cork who had him blinded. At this time the chief of the O Sullivans was Domhnall Mór, son of Mac Raith. His designation was 'of Carraig Fionnmhuighe,' now the townland of Carrig in the parishes of Kilmaloda and Templequinlan, west of Timoleague. In 1214 Diarmaid (of Dún Droighneáin) MacCarthy treacherously killed the whole family of Domhnall Mór Ó Súilleabháin — except for Dúnlang and Giolla na Flann — at Ráithín na nGarraithe in Barrett's territory (? Raheen, par. Whitechurch) 'on the advice of many, if not the greater part, of the people of Desmond.'

That is the account of the massacre as found in the Book of Mac Carthaigh but there is a more detailed version in an 18th century family history believed to have been compiled by a Friar O Sullivan of Muckross. It goes as follows: '. . . Daniel More Carrigifienavy. The place from which he had that title was in Carrebry, where he had first fixed. He had ten strong active courageous sons, who had each of them a party of effective armed men to wait on him, and at all occasions under his command, so that they were greatly envy'd and dreaded, and thereupon invited, as so pretended, to a great entertainment to a place near Cork, called Lishlifionaguil, which was so well prepared for them that the said Donal More with eight of his said sons were there murdered. The two that escaped . . . were called Giollmaiuodah and Giollanavaane' (Giolla Mochuda and Giolla na Flann).

This second account seems more correct in naming Giolla Mochuda rather than Dúnlang as a survivor since there is no Dúnlang among the twelve sons of Domhnall Mór as listed in the *Leabhar Muimhneach*. There was, however, a Dúnlang son of Giolla Mochuda, ancestor of Ó Súilleabháin Mór. The other survivor of the massacre, Giolla na Flann, was progenitor of Ó Súilleabháin Béarra and of Ó Súilleabháin Maol (Mac Fínghin Duibh).

But when in 1280 the Mac Carthys united against the Normans, the son of Gilla Mochuda Ó Súilleabháin (presumably Dúnlang) once more joined them, 'and great forays were made by them.' Another Giolla Mochuda (son of An Dubhshúileach Ó Súilleabháin) receives mention in 1283 for having slain Giolla Riabhach Ó Donnabháin, his own death being recorded in 1308. The name Giolla Mochuda indicates a cult of the patron saint of Lismore which is underlined by the fact that Laurentius (Lorcán) Ó Súilleabháin, bishop of Cloyne, died in 1205 at Lismore while Friar Alanus or Alinn (? Anadh) Ó Súilleabháin tranferred from the see of Cloyne and died as bishop of Lismore in 1253. During an internecine Mac Carthy conflict in 1305, one party was led by Domhnall son of Crimthann Ó Súilleabháin. Six years later Diarmaid Mac Carthy was slain by Anadh ('na Leacan') son of Philip son of Gilla na Flann.

In 1317 the O Sullivans instigated the rebellion of Diarmaid Ruadh Mac Carthy against Mac Carthy Mór. Their chief is designated 'M' in the annals – probably Muircheartach Mór, son and successor of Dúnlang. The whole of the Uí Shúilleabháin, with the exception of Clann Gilla Mochuda and Clann Gilla na Flann, rebelled against Mac Carthy and deprived him of the sovereignty, in so far as they were able.

Clann Gilla Mochuda may have been the family of Gilla Mochuda Caoch, brother of Muircheartach Mór. In the 16th century these changed their name completely from O Sullivan to the well-known Kerry surname of Mac Gillycuddy.

Clann Gilla na Flann at this stage were represented by Anadh na Leacan, described in an English pedigree as the first lord of Bear and Bantry. One of his sons was ancestor of Ó Súilleabháin Maol (Mac Fínghin Duibh) while from another son, Amhlaoibh, descended Ó Súilleabháin Béarra. There was also a branch of the O Sullivans at Cappanacushy, more closely related to O Sullivan Mór – in fact, one genealogy states that their ancestor, Mac Raith, great-great-grandson of Muircheartach Mór, was senior to his brother, Rudhraighe, ancestor of O Sullivan Mór. Another branch, Clann Labhráis, was derived from Labhrás, son of Giolla na Flann.

It is clear that by then the O Sullivans had separated into their various groupings, with the main stem in Co. Kerry, leaving in Co. Cork the Uí Shúilleabháin Bhéarra, whose fortunes were must now follow. At what stage they displaced the O Driscolls from the lordship of Béarra is not recorded but it could have been early in the 14th century. In 1350 the Justiciar received payment for the expenses of military expeditions to suppress, among others, the 'MacDormodis, Osshowlanes, Mertorsis' of Co. Cork. Part of the lands of Clann Labhráis and of Mac Fínghin Duibh also lay in Co. Cork, on the north side of the Béarra peninsula, and part lay in the barony of Glanarought, Co. Kerry.

The various branches united against the Mac Carthys of Carbery in 1398 but suffered a severe defeat. Ó Súilleabháin Maol was killed, as were Eoghan and Conchobhar, the sons of Ó Súilleabháin Mór, and a son of Ó Súilleabháin Buidhe. This last may have been an early name for Ó Súilleabháin Béarra. Again, in 1404, the *Annals of Connacht* tells us: 'War broke out between Mac Carthaigh and Ó Súilleabháin Buidhe and the sons of Diarmaid Mac Carthaigh. Toirrdelbhach the stout Mac Mathghmahna was Mac Carthaigh's sea-captain at that time, and he came up with Ó Súilleabháin at sea, and with the sons of Diarmaid as well; Ó Súilleabháin was drowned and he captured Donnchad son of Diarmaid and Domhnall son of Eoghan (Mac Carthaigh).'

But at least one O Sullivan-Mac Carthy encounter proved to be marital rather than martial. In 1475 a lady named Murrind Inythule-bayn (Muireann Ní Shúilleabháin) was granted a papal dispensation enabling her to marry her cousin, Donald Mac Carthy.

In 1485 the annals first give the title of Ó Súilleabháin Béarra — to Domhnall who died in that year. It may have been he who erected the Franciscan friary of Bantry, believed to have been founded *c.* 1460. This was afterwards the family's burial ground.

In 1498 Thomas Fitzgerald of Desmond joined Cormac Mac Carthy in an attack on Eoghan Mac Carthy, whom they killed along with Ó Súilleabháin Béarra (Philip son of Diarmaid), his son, Tadhg an Chaennaigh, and many others. Diarmaid, son of Domhnall is the next chief of Béarra mentioned — 'a man who paid bardic bands and pilgrims, learned and ollamhs of Ireland,' according to the *Annals of Ulster* which state that he died in 1533. But he may be the same man whose obit appears in the *Annals of the Four Masters* under the year 1549 — 'Diarmaid O Sullivan, a kind and friendly man, and fierce and inimical to his enemies, was burned by gunpowder in his castle, and his brother, Amhlaoibh, took his place, and he also was killed soon afterwards.'

This was the *Diarmaid an Phúdair* of the genealogies, and his castle was apparently at Dunboy, though there was also a Castle Dermot (referred to in *Pacata Hibernia*) which gave its name to Castletown (Bear). Diarmaid's grandson, Philip the historian, relates how in 1531 an English ship captured a Spanish fishing vessel near the Durseys, whereupon Diarmaid fitted out a small squadron of ships and brought in both the English and Spanish vessels to Bearhaven. The English captain he hanged but the Spaniard he set at liberty.

In 1548 the Mayor of Cork informed the Lord Deputy that Richard Stevens, constable of Dungarvan, had been killed by O Sullivan Bear with a 'skeyne'; also that John Tomson and other captains had been put at large by O Sullivan Bear for a great sum of gold. However he wrote again later stating that both 'Tomsin and Richard Stevenson, constable of Dungarvan' had arrived in Cork harbour on Christmas Day. O Sullivan's naval power was again evident in 1564 when Sir Peter Carew, acting on behalf of Queen Elizabeth, sent three ships to Bearhaven to attack a pirate fleet headed by Haydon, Lysyngham and Corbett, who had their headquarters there. Haydon was, in fact, married to O Sullivan's sister and the castle of Dunboy was committed to his custody. The pirates mustered a force of 500 gallowglass and kerns along with over 100 of their own, so that after an exchange of gunfire, Carew's ships sailed away with their mission unaccomplished.

In 1563 O Sullivan Bear (Domhnall son of Diarmaid son of Domhnall son of Domhnall son of Diarmaid Balbh) 'was slain by a bad man, i.e. Mac Gillycuddy, and if his father, Dermot, was a man of great renown, this Domhnall was a worthy heir of him.' His brother Eoghan assumed the chieftaincy and, a year or two later, copied his overlord, the Earl of Clancarty, in submitting to the crown. Following a visit to England in 1565 he was knighted, and as Sir Owen O Sullivan received letters patent from Queen Elizabeth in respect of the sept lands. But when Domhnall's son (Domhnall Cam) came of age he appealed to the government for the lordship of Bear and Bantry, as held by his father. Both parties submitted a great deal of evidence to buttress their respective claims. One such document provides a detailed account of the whole lordship. It states that 15 quarters of land were set apart for the ruling sept of O Sullivan Bear, half of these being held by the reigning chief, along with the castles of Dunboy, Foyd and Carriganass. (Foyd is obviously Whiddy which had a castle at Reenavanny, the ruins of which were blown down during a storm in 1920. Carriganass castle was erected by Sir Owen's father.) The tanist held six ploughlands with the castle of Ardea (Co. Kerry). The next in importance (in this case Domhnall Cam) held six ploughlands while the remaining 10½ ploughlands were divided up among other near relatives of the chief. A further 20 quarters (60 ploughlands) were held by the sub-septs of the O Sullivans – Sliocht Fínghin Duibh, Clann Labhráis, Sliocht Dúnlaing, Mac mic Buadhaigh, Mac Domhnaill and Mac Taidhg, all of whom had to pay rents and cesses to O Sullivan Bear. The total fixed rent from the country was only £40. per annum, but this does not include revenue from shipping, fishing, etc., estimated at £500. per annum. O Sullivan Bear himself was liable for quite a number of yearly rights and duties in respect of his overlord, Mac Carthy Mór. In the 16th century these rents were granted by Mac Carthy to the Earl of Desmond as part of a dowry on the occasion of the Earl's marriage to Ellen Mac Carthy.

The commissioners appointed to adjudicate in the dispute recommended in 1594 a partition of the lordship. Domhnall was recognized as the senior lineal descendant of Diarmaid Balbh and was awarded the lands of Bear with the castle of Dunboy, as well as the rents from the minor septs named above, from Dermot O Sullivan of Ballaghboy, and from the O Donegans, O Linchigans, O Holighans etc. Also named was Sliocht Swleagwll (? *Súil Gaill),* an unusual name found also in a Fiant of 1585, a pardon granted to Sir Owen's tenants who included Donogh and Diermod Mac Sowlegoyll, and in another of May 1601 when Donell oge mac Sulliguille of Cloghfune was pardoned in company with Domhnall Cam.

Sir Owen got the Bantry section, with the castles of Whiddy and Carriganass, and rents from Sliocht M'Quick, Sliocht Owen Pygh, the O Sullivans of Rooska, O Sullivan Maol, the freeholders of Whiddy and part of Clann Labhráis. (It was really young Owen who was involved here, as his father, Sir Owen, was in retirement by 1594 and died later in the same year.) Sir Owen's brother, Philip the Tanist, was assigned the castle of Ardea with 1¼ quarters, free of rent. Meanwhile, both factions of the O Sullivans had become implicated in the

Elizabethan wars. After the first Desmond rebellion a pardon was granted to 'Owen O Swyllyvan of Byary Knt., alias O Swyllyvan Byary' who with his father-in-law, James Lord Barrymore, had given early support to the Earl of Desmond. Another pardon was to 'Philip O Sowlyvan, gentleman,' presumably Philip the Tanist.

In December 1570, during the second outbreak Pelham informed the council of state that Sir Humphrey Gilbert had plundered a Portuguese ship in Bearhaven 'whom he suspected to bring over some of James FitzMorris' train,' thus provoking a dispute with Sir Owen O Sullivan Bear, under whose protection the ship lay. Pelham complained that Sir Owen, whom he suspected of 'foreign practice' never came near Sir William Drury or himself 'albeit his father-in-law, the Lord Barrie, has much urged his coming.' Sir Owen eventually travelled to Limerick at Pelham's bidding and surrendered his castle (of Dunboy) to the English but not before his wife had conveyed all the ordnance and supplies out of it. So 'because he was a dangerous man and had a priest who was a principal conspirator,' Sir Owen was imprisoned in the castle of Limerick and a ward was placed in his castle. But his brother-in-law, David Barry, together with Philip O Sullivan and a group of young 'Robin Hoods', after defeating Captain Apsley's band in Carbery, drew out and slaughtered the garrisons of both Bearhaven and Bantry. Two years later Capt. Zouch set out from Cork and sent some of the Mac Sweeneys and O Donovans from Carbery to plunder Domhnall O Sullivan. But Domhnall counter-attacked and with a small force of about fifty men slew nearly three hundred of the plundering party. On 25 January 1585, after the rebellion had ended, a pardon was extended to the following: Owen O Swlevan, Knight, Diermod O Swlevan, Donell mac Fynnin Duffe, Donogho, Donell and Teig mac Donell, Dermot Oge, Conoghor, Donell, Donogh, Gillecrist and Teig mac Diermod Oge. Shane Oge mac Shane mac Keone; Donell, Owen and Donogho mac Diermod mac Teig, Shane mac Donell mac Teig, Donell mac Conoghor mac Donell Oge, Fynen Oge and Owen mac Keone mac Donogho, all in Co. Cork. These appear to have been the chief men of the name. Four following Fiants grant pardons to Sir Owen O Sullivan's tenants, 79 in all, including many O Houlihans, O Hungerdills, etc.

In 1588, just after the news of Florence MacCarthy's secret marriage to the Earl of Clancarty's only daughter and heiress had startled the establishment, Lord Burghley was informed that Sir Owen O Sullivan Bear, because of his dislike for Florence (who, it was believed, had promised to wed Sir Owen's daughter) and because he wished to acquire support for his dispute with his nephew, Domhnall, had engineered a counter-alliance. He married one daughter to Domhnall, illegitimate son of the Earl of Clancarty and a strong claimant for the title of Mac Carthy Mór, and another to the (Geraldine) Knight of Kerry's son, 'hopinge, no doubt, that they two should drawe untoe them all

SIEGE OF DUNBOY 1602 *(Pacata Hibernia)*

the evill disposed of Kerrie and Desmonde.' A third daughter later married Sir Nicholas Browne (ancestor of the Earls of Kenmare), the rejected suitor for the hand of the Earl of Clancarty's daughter. Sir Owen was also brother-in-law to David, Lord Barrymore, who was not enamoured of one of his newly-acquired nephews-in-law. He wrote to Sir John Popham in 1593 complaining of the misdeeds of Domhnall Mac Carthy who had, he asserted, twice attempted to kill Sir Owen's eldest son. Sir Owen himself died in 1594, the year in which the partition of Bear and Bantry was accomplished. Although five years previously Sir Owen had been one of the most suspected men in Ireland, thereafter it was his rival, Domhnall Cam, who became 'the arrantest and maliciousest traitor that ever this Kingdom bred,' while Sir Owen's son, Owen, remainded steadfastly loyal to the crown in the face of severe pressure from Florence Mac Carthy and Hugh O Neill.

Domhnall O Sullivan Bear was one of the few among the Munster chiefs to support O Neill to whose aid he brought 200 men before the battle of Kinsale. But when de Aguila, having surrendered Kinsale, also surrendered the castles of Baltimore, Castlehaven and Dunboy which were garrisoned by Spaniards, O Sullivan was enraged and evicted the Spanish forces from Dunboy stating that he would hold it himself for the king of Spain. On the 20th February 1602 he wrote (in Irish) to King Philip complaining bitterly that the castle of Dunboy which he had handed over to Generals de Zubiaur and de Soto when they landed at Castlehaven had been given into the hands of cruel, malignant and heretical enemies by de Aguila. He informed Philip that he proposed holding that castle for him until he should receive his instructions and had sent his five-year-old son and heir as a pledge of his loyalty. King Philip reciprocated Domhnall's friendship. He did not send a force to relieve Dunboy but did send money which O Sullivan used to equip an army of mercenaries under Richard Tyrell to ravage West Muskerry and Duhallow (while an English army ravaged all of west Cork). Domhnall also made overtures to his cousin, Owen, but Owen informed the English, and with his brother attacked and harassed Tyrell's forces on several occasions. Later they captured the castle of Dunmanus.

In March 1602 the Earl of Thomond led a large contingent of government troops as far as Bantry where Mountjoy, on learning (from Owen and others) that Tyrell was preparing to dispute the mountainous passage from Bantry to Bearhaven, decided to move his troops by sea to Bear Island from whence they could invest Dunboy. From the 6th to the 18th of June the castle with its garrison of 143 men under the command of Richard Mac Geoghegan was besieged by an army 2,000 strong with two batteries of artillery. The English first captured the island of Dursey, slaughtering not only its garrison but all the inhabitants as well. 'In this way perished about 300 Catholics, the greater part of whom were retainers of my father, Dermot', says Philip O Sullivan, the historian. (His father, Dermot, appears to have been an illegitimate son of Dermot the grandfather of Domhnall Cam.)

An attempt by Tyrell to stage a diversionary attack proved ineffectual, and the artillery barrage continued until the castle became a mass of rubble when its tenacious defenders were slaughtered or executed to the last man. As *Pacata Hibernia* put it, 'So obstinate and resolved a defence hath not been seen within this Kingdom.'

The prospect of another expedition to be sent by King Philip kept O Sullivan and Tyrell still active in Munster even after the fall of Dunboy. It was at this period that O Sullivan, aided by Cormac Mac Carthy of Blarney (who had escaped from Cork jail), assaulted and captured the Mac Carthy castle of Carrigaphooka. But Tyrell, after his force was routed, decided to return to his native Westmeath and William Burke, commander of O Sullivan's troops, prepared to pull out also. Domhnall Cam, having failed to obtain a pardon, elected to head north with Burke. So commenced the epic retreat of O Sullivan Bear. He left Glengarriff on 31st December, 1602, with about 1,000 followers (of whom only 400 were fighting men), engaging in constant rearguard actions against ubiquitous enemies along the way. Two weeks later the survivors — 35 in all — straggled into the safety of O Rourke's castle in Leitrim.

Following on Domhnall's exodus, three English regiments under Sir Charles Wilmot ravaged all the snow-covered Béarra peninsula, 'destroying all that they could find meet for the relief of men' even on the offshore islands. The castles of Ardea and Carriganass were also surrendered to them. The Lord President and Council of Munster offered a reward of £300 (alive) or £200 (dead) for 'that wicked and unnatural traitor, Donell O Swyllvane, als O Swllyvane Beare.' Having failed in an appeal to James I for the restoration of his lordship, Domhnall managed to escape to Spain where he was received with great honour, 'being more esteemed than any man whatsoever.' Although attainted at home by act of Parliament, he was created Conde de Birhaven by King Philip, much to the chagrin of the English. (*Iarla Dúna Baoi* he was entitled by the mid-17th century poet, Seán Ó Conaill.) Domhnall died of a wound received when he intervened in a brawl among some of his followers in 1618. He had at least two sons. Daniel. the elder, became a knight of Santiago in 1607 at the age of eleven but died two years later. Dermot, the younger, also a knight of Santiago, succeeded to his father's title. He died in 1659 leaving an only daughter, then aged ten. Antonia, Condesa de Biraven, was twice married, but died in 1718 without issue. The title was later revived for a relative, Colonel Daniel O Sullivan Bear, who was in the Spanish service in 1720. Colonel Tadeo O Sullivan was the bearer of the title in 1796. It was revived yet again in modern times in favour of a Spanish nobleman of Irish descent, el Conde de San Estaban de Cañongo.

Meanwhile, back in Bear and Bantry, Owen O Sullivan reaped the rewards of his loyalty to the crown and not only retained his father's lands but was given the lordship of Bear as well, including about 66 ploughlands in demesne, with chief rents from the rest of Bear. One of his sons was a page with King James; two of his brothers, Gullasne and Connoghor, were sergeants in the service of King Philip of Spain (one at least having been planted there by Lord Danvers in order to spy on his cousin, Domhnall Cam). Owen was described as of Carriganass in 1604 but subsequently seems to have taken up residence at or near Dunboy. In 1611 he got a grant of Wednesday markets at Bearhaven and Drom-leane as well as a fair at Ballyhiggovane (now part of Bantry town). He died in 1616, being described as 'Owen O Swlyvane de Downaboy als Beerhaven.' His other lands included Dromdoneen, Shandrum, Garry-duff et Ballaghlinyliggye (? Ballylickey), Whiddy, Glengarriff, and the harbours and creeks of Bear and Bantry. His son and heir was Diarmaid who was married to Joanna Fitzgerald. But Diarmaid died the follow-ing year and was succeeded by his brother, Domhnall Crón, who is referred to in a letter from the Lord President regarding precautions against piracy, written in 1632, the year after the sack of Baltimore: 'Mr. Daniel O Sullivan has a house of reasonable strength at Berehaven and takes upon him to defend it and Ballygobbin; he promises to erect five beacons – one upon the Dorseys and four upon the Great Island. I have directed O Sullivan More (who lives in the river of Kenmare) to take warning from the beacon erected on the promontory over the Dorseys.'

But Domhnall was not so amenable six years later when Robert Smyth went down to Bantry to investigate the wreck of an English ship, lost with all hands. 'I found that Daniel O Sullivan Beare, the Lord of the Manor, claimed the goods from the wreck. He is a person of great power in those parts.'

Another Domhnall, son of Philip the Tanist who was allotted the castle of Ardea under the 1594 settlement, sought a copy of that agree-ment in 1613 because, he said, he was being impleaded by Owen O Sullivan for the castle and its lands. Almost two centuries later, this very copy was still in existence. It was in 1802 that an English genealogist named Beltz was directed to a cottage in the Béarra mountains where dwelt, he was told, the last representative of the O Sullivans of Ardea. This man did not receive Beltz in his humble abode but met him by appointment standing amid the ruins of Ardea Castle, surrounded by his family and holding in his arms a bundle of mouldering parchments (one of which was the copy of the deed of settlement) while proudly reciting his descent through six generations from Philip of Ardea.

Other branches also held on to their lands in the early 17th century. An inquisition was held in 1624 into the lands of Laurencius mac Fynin O Sullivan (of Clann Labhráis) who held lands at Glengarriff, Croha, Ardagh and Breeny.

Another inquisition into his lands was held in 1626, when he was described as of Carrowfadda. Donnell, his son and heir, was then 15 years old and married. In the same year inquisitions were held into the lands of Owen mac Donnell O Sullivan of Leitrim, and those of Dermod Bwy, Donnell Bwy and Donnell Lynne O Sullivan, all of Carrowfadda (? Curragh, par. Kilcaskan). Two more were held in 1639 into the lands of David Boy mac Murtagh O Sullivan at Leitrim and Glengarriff, and those of Daniel mac Teige O Sullivan of Ardgroom.

The 1641 uprising saw the O Sullivan clan united once more against the English planter interest whose property O Sullivan Bear (Domhnall Crón) helped to pillage in Bantry, Clonakilty and other west Cork towns. His brother, Philip, was a prominent figure in the siege of Rathbarry Castle in 1642. As one might expect, wholesale outlawries followed: Domhnall Crón (described as Donnell O Sullivane Beare of Beerhaven, Esqr.) was blacklisted, as were eight other gentlemen of the name – Connor and Philip of Loughane, Donnell mac Owen of Dromgarvan, Gillicody of Trafrask, John mac Dermody of Derreeny, Owen of Dromduvane (? par. Drimoleague), Owen of Inchiclogh and Owen Reagh of Dromagowlane.

Daniel O Sullivan Bear was among the last to offer resistance to the Cromwellians. Even after Lord Muskerry had capitulated at Ross castle in 1652 O Sullivan fought on in west Cork and Kerry aided by Colonel O Driscoll and Murtough O Brien. In March 1653 with a force of 1,500 men they wiped out a party of Cromwellian soldiers and fortified the island of Dursey until it was no longer possible to hold out. They then escaped to France to carry on the struggle. An English intelligence agent wrote from Paris in 1653 that 'O Sullivan Beara begins to despayre of any succours for Ireland, and soe is much displeased as well he may since he fyndes noe bodie cares.' Later in the year a letter of Daniel's from Paris (intercepted by the Cromwellians) outlined plans for an invasion force of 9,000 exiles which 'we intend with God's help to lande about Beare or Bantry.'

At home their ancestral lands in Bear and Bantry were all confiscated from the O Sullivans who as a landowning sept were now eradicated. But the surname continued to increase and multiply. By 1659, according to the census, O Sullivans were flourishing over most of Co. Cork – in Cork City, Kinalea, Kerrycurrihy, Ibane and Barryroe, Courceys, East and West Carbery, Barretts, Barrymore, Orrery and Kilmore. But in Bear and Bantry itself only nine families were recorded, a puzzling feature until we notice that most of the other families bore such names as Mac Dermod and Dermod Oge, Mac Teige and Teige Oge, Mac Owen and Owen Oge, Mac Shane, Mac Daniel and Daniell Oge – all obviously O Sullivans. Some were specifically named as 'tituladoes' or persons of note – Owen mac Daniell of Ballylickey, Roger mac Daniell of Ardnagashel, Dun. oge Sullivan of Brenny, Teige oge Lader of Cousane, Owen mac Teige Sullivane and Owen oge Sullivane of Cahermuckee, Dermod Sullivane, Dan. his son, Ellen and Ellene, his daughters, of West Rooska,

Dan. mac Owen bwy, Dan, his son and Honor, his daughter, of Carrow-fadda (par. Kilcaskan).

But these were not landowners. The *Book of Survey and Distribution* shows that as a result of the Cromwellian plantations and settlements, the O Sullivans who in 1641 had owned practically the whole barony of Bear and Bantry (apart from a portion of Kilmocomogue parish which had come into the possession of the Brownes) now owned not a single acre there. It had all been granted to the Earl of Anglesey. The Mac Fínghin Duibh lands on the Kerry side had passed to Sir William Petty. After the Restoration Colonel Daniel O Sullivan Bear petitioned the king for the restoration of his estates. He and his nephew, Daniel, as well as Daniel O Sullivan of Dunkerron were given leave to put in claims under the Acts of Settlement, but failed to dislodge Petty who seems to have obtained the Earl of Anglesey's interest. Later Sir Thomas White acquired much of the Bantry area and was the founder of the White family of Bantry House.

When hostilities resumed in 1689, the O Sullivans, who were solidly Jacobite, suffered further outlawries — Daniel of Rossmackowen (an ensign in King James' army), Daniel of Brenish (? Breeny), Cnogher mac Dermott and Cornelius of Sheskin, Owen mac Murtagh of Bear-haven, John mac Murtagh of Lantonheme (?), Thady of Kealagowlane and Matthew of Walterstown (? Great I.). Yet destitute and landless though many may now have been, the O Sullivans still clung to their native soil. Bishop Dive Downes, travelling through Béarra in June 1700, wrote in his journal: 'Dood O' Huologhan, als. Hungry Hill . . . O Sul-levane Beere lives in a cabin at the foot of the hill'. This was probably Col. Daniel's nephew, Domhnall (son of Philip son of Owen son of Sir Owen) who was alive at the time his pedigree was compiled in 1703. Daniell O Sullivan Bear was suspected of befriending tories in the Coomhola area in 1694.

A son of one of the Owen O Sullivans outlawed in 1643, Philip, became a major in King James' army, and after the war in Ireland had ended went with Sarsfield to France where he was killed in a duel with a French officer. His sister-in-law married the eldest son of O Sullivan Mór of Dunkerron and their son, Colonel O Sullivan, was Prince Charles' chief adviser during the Scottish campaign and at the battle of Culloden.

One branch which did maintain some social standing during the Penal times was that descended from Fínghin Dubh, a younger son of Anadh na Leacan. The chief was known in the 14th-15th centuries as Ó Súil-leabháin Maol but after that became Mac Fínghin Duibh. In the late 16th century Sliocht Fínghin Duibh held 10 quarters scattered through-out Bear and Bantry. They paid the customary services to O Sullivan Bear and were regarded as foremost among his kinsmen and followers. One source states that Mac Fínghin Duibh was Domhnall Cam's closest adviser and confederate during the struggle of 1602-3. The bulk of their lands lay around the harbours of Ardgroom and Kilmakillogue, partly in Co. Cork, and partly in Co. Kerry. Their principal seat was at Dereen at the head of Kilmakillogue harbour. After the Cromwellian confiscations Sir William Petty imported large numbers of English and Welsh planters into the area while Mac Fínghin Duibh became a tenant (under Petty) of Dereen and five ploughlands nearby. In 1696 Richard Orpen, who had been Petty's agent, became the new landlord. Mac Fínghin Duibh obtained a lease of his lands and the family retained Dereen until the death of Sylvester the last Mac Fínghin Duibh, in 1809.

They had lost Ardgroom before the end of the 17th century, but a junior branch settled at Rossmackowen where they remained until the mid-19th century. Both branches were noted for their hospitality, and Dereen in particular seems to have been a focal point for gatherings of Irish poets and musicians from all over Munster. The death of the last Mac Fínghin Duibh in 1809 was lamented by many a Gaelic poet, and even more so by the local people, as recorded in her diary by Lady Louise Lansdowne who in October, 1809, came by boat into Kilmackillogue harbour where: '. . . at the bottom of a conical hill was McFinninduff's house. . . . The moment our boat reached the land, all the inhabitants of the bay, who had assembled themselves on some high ground near the shore, began to howl and lament Mc Finnin and continued to bewail him the whole time we stayed and till our boat was well out of sight. The howl is a most wild and melancholy sound and impresses one with the idea of real sorrow in the people . . .'

Even the harsh Penal laws did not lessen the high regard in which the O Sullivan name was held in the Béarra peninsula. In the eyes of the government, however, several of the name were outlaws. In 1711 'robbery warrants' were issued in respect of Owen and Teige Sullivan of Dromsullivan, 'notorious tories, robbers, and rapparees in arms on their keeping, of the Popish religion.'

In the following year £40 was paid out to their captors, while £20 was paid for the head of Owen Moyle Sullivan. But the most celebrated of the 18th century O Sullivan outlaws was Murty Óg of Eyeries who as early as 1738 was charged with harbouring tories, robbers and rapparees. We are told that he served in the Austrian army of Maria Therese, fought at Fontenoy, was with Prince Charles at Culloden in 1746 and was the handsomest man in the French army. After settling again in Béarra he carried on an extensive and profitable smuggling trade as well as recruiting for the 'Wild Geese', much to the chagrin of the authorities, represented by John Puxley who had acquired the ancestral seat of O Sullivan Bear at Dunboy. The bitter enmity between the two culminated in the shooting of Puxley by Murty Óg who then escaped to France but contrived from time to time to pay visits to his home and family. On one of these visits, in 1754, his presence was betrayed and a party of soldiers surrounded the house which they set on fire. Disdaining surrender, Murty Óg emerged holding a pair of pistols, and was shot dead. His body was brought to Cork tied to the stern of a vessel and his head spiked over Cork jail.

Richard Pococke, who travelled through Béarra in 1758, wrote that '... Gentlemen of good families, chiefly the Sullivans, have a way of portioning their daughters, by what they call Coleprits; they go round all their relations and friends, who give each family a Head of black cattle, they call it lending.... These Gentlemen have about 300 acres each, most of it let out, and the Tenants are entirely at their command, and are heads of these little clans, which have been of late reduc'd to great poverty.' He refers to Murty Óg, 'the Principal of them,' whose killing 'broke the combination and they have since been kept under by the excessive high rents they are oblig'd to pay.'

Several poetic laments in Irish were composed in honour of the dead hero. His only son, John of Inches, continued to live on his father's property. He left three daughters and a son, Murty, said to have been killed in a duel with his uncle, Mark O Sullivan, at the age of 23.

Still, not every O Sullivan was disloyal to the crown. In 1814 was recorded the death of Daniel O Sullivan Esq., of Cametringane, Berehaven, Captain of the Berehaven Loyal Infantry and the first Roman Catholic appointed to the commission of the peace in Co. Cork since the reign of Queen Anne. In 1796 when the French fleet anchored in Bantry Bay, he assembled 2,000 of the peasantry — principally his own tenants, and watched the coastline for eleven nights, driving inland all the livestock. When a boat containing a French lieutenant and crew landed, he had them arrested and conveyed to Bantry. For these services he was presented with the freedom of the Corporation of Cork.

No poetic lament appears to have been composed for this man but there was one for a later justice of the peace, Muircheartach O Sullivan of Coulagh (a relative of the last Mac Fínghin Duibh and also of Daniel O Connell), who died in 1827. In that year T.D. Sullivan was born in Bantry, and three years later his brother A.M. Sullivan. Both were noted M.P.s and literary men in the latter half of the 19th century. In the previous century two of the best known Munster poets were of the Uí Shúilleabháin — Eoghan Rua and Tadhg Gaelach — but neither was connected with the district of Bear and Bantry. By that period O Sullivans had begun to proliferate in many areas outside their original habitat, so much so that at the present day O Sullivan is the most numerous of all surnames in Co. Cork.

Ó TUAMA

TWOMEY   TOOMEY

Mathghamhain, the brother of Brian Boru, was, according to the *Leabhar Muimhneach*, the progenitor of the Uí Thuama and of six other families. While there is no way of verifying this statement, it is not easy to put forward an alternative derivation. The only one to bear the unusual personal name Tuaim in the early genealogies was Tuaim Snáma, an 8th century king of Osraigi.

Furthermore, although Co. Cork now holds about 60% of the Uí Thuama there is no record of their activities in that county before the late 15th century. If they were of the Dál Cais, it is reasonable to assume that in common with other Dalcassian families they moved south during the troubled years of the 12th-13th centuries.

The earliest mention of the name in Co. Cork occurs in 1477 when Carolus alias Cenfaelayotuma (also spelt Keanfela Otuoma — *Cennfaelad Ó Tuama*), a priest of Ardfert diocese, was vicar of the parish of Matehy. This unusual family connection between a Co. Kerry diocese and a parish in East Muskerry is evident again in 1489 when Dermot Othuama was perpetual vicar of Dromod (d. Ardfert) in succession to Maurice Othuama, while in the following year a papal mandate assigned to Donald Othuama (d. Cloyne) the vicarage of Matehy parish.

In 1478 Cornelius O Twome sold some property in Kinsale to Richard Ronan, merchant. In Cromwellian times, there was a shipwright named Thomas Toomey living in Kinsale. Although he had taken an active part in the defence of the town against the 'rebels' he was refused permission to stay in Kinsale after the war and had to give up the house which he had leased in 1635.

Nearer to Cork, in a document drawn up in 1547 we find the name of 'Kathren twomoo, widdewe', of the barony of Kerrycurrihy. It is interesting that the spelling 'Twomey' is today almost exclusively associated with Co. Cork; elsewhere it is written 'Toomey'. (Knockadooma townland in the parish of Templemartin was written *Cnoc Ó dTuamadh* by a local scribe in the early 19th century.)

Cork city itself seems to have attracted quite a number of this name from an early period. Dermicius Otuoma, a cleric, was witness to a document in Cork city in 1514, while the first recorded Twomey pardon in the Fiants was granted in 1562 to 'Dermot O Thomo, late of Cork, weaver'. Morrishe Twomy held property in Cork city from John Roche in 1614 and at the time of the survey and valuation of Cork city in 1653/4, in the north liberties, Teige Thomy had half a ploughland in Lowatibegge (Lotabeg) while Dermod Twomey, in partnership with Teige O Rierdan, held a ploughland at Ballynaheyny (Ballynahina). John Toomy of Carrigrohane was among the jurors appointed to review and correct the civil survey of the south liberties of Cork in 1655. So it is not surprising that the census of 1659 gives O Twomy as one of the principal Irish names (12 families) in the city and suburbs of Cork. Even after the Cromwellian expulsions they were still in evidence. Among those outlawed in 1690-1 for their support of King James were John Tomy, merchant, Mortagh Tromy, yeoman, and John Boy Tomy, yeoman, all of Cork city. Thomas Twomy, gent., of Cork, conformed in 1730.

The O Twomeys were most numerous, however, in East Muskerry and in the adjoining barony of Barretts, probably under the aegis of the Mac Carthys. In 1573 a pardon was granted to Teig mac Donill mac Kartie of Diserte, Co. Cork, gent., John mac Teig Y Howme (*Uí Thuama*) of same, and Teig mac Conogher Thwome. The townland in question, judging from the position of others in the same Fiant, seems to have been Deeshart in the parish of Magourney (Coachford area). An influential family of O Twomeys must have remained there as landholders up to the time of the Cromwellian confiscations. Among the Co. Cork notabilities declared outlaws in 1643 was William O Tomy of Disert, gent. At the same time Dermod O Tomy of Birne, gent., was outlawed. Birne is now Berrings. Both Berrings and Deeshart are today in East Muskerry but in the 17th century they were part of Barrett's barony.

The wife of William Brenagh (or Walsh) of Berrings was pardoned in 1600. Her name was Sylly gane ny Thomye (*Síle ghann Ní Thuama*). In the same year, in the neighbouring townland of Kilblaffer, Thomas roe mac Donell O Thomye was pardoned along with Thady roo O Thomye, both yeomen. Another Thomas O Twomy received a pardon in the following year; he was of Kilcullen in the parish of Donaghmore. Gyrane where Donogh O Twomy was pardoned at the same time could be Garraun in the same parish, but Rath where Malaghlen duff O Tomo (*Maoilsheachlainn dubh Ó Tuama*) was pardoned in 1577 is not easy to place. Other pardons in 1601 were those of Teige O Twomy of Whuidy (i.e. Whiddy Island) and Dermod and Donell mac Shane O Twomegh in Kanturk area.

Still in Barrett's country, there is a record of an agreement 'signed, sealed, etc. and truly and faithfully declared unto the within obliged in the Irish tongue', dated 27th May 1606, whereby Owen Carty, Rory Swyny, Dermod O Twomey and John O Seair agreed to pay rent to Barrett of Ballincollig for four ploughlands of Clannidonnell (*Clann Mhic Dhomhnaill*). In 1659 O Twomy was among the principal Irish names in the barony of Barretts, where with 31 families it was one of the most numerous surnames. Apart from Barretts and Cork city the name is not recorded in any other barony in that census; there are no returns for Muskerry where the name is prominent today. Daniel and William Toomy were among the Earl of Clancarty's tenants in Macroom in 1702.

During the 18th century the O Twomeys, like so many of their kind, existed in obscurity, so that only very occasionally do we get even a glimpse of their activities. During the Penal days one of the priests registered in 1704 was 'Donough Twony (i.e. Twomy), residing at Scarteen, aged 61 years; parish priest of Donnaghmore and Grenagh; ordained in 1667, at Dublin, by Bishop Plunkett (i.e. St. Oliver Plunkett). Sureties — Garret Fitzgerald, Cork, £50, and Dermot Twony of Glaneglogh, £50'. Scarteen is in the parish of Donaghmore while Glenaglogh is in the neighbouring parish of Aghabullogue. Fr. Twomy died in May 1711 and is buried at Donoughmore Cross.

The most widely-known of the name in that century was Seán Ó Tuama *an Ghrinn* (of the merriment) who was born in Co. Limerick in 1706 and died there in 1775. Part schoolmaster, part innkeeper, his tavern at Croom became a meeting-place for all the stray poets and musicians of the countryside. Needless to mention, Seán's love of poetry and of the Irish language brought little financial reward and he was forced to leave his beloved tavern.

In the present century the Ó Tuama name has been very much to the fore in the Irish language revival movement in Cork city.

WALSH

WALSHE   WELSH   BREATNACH   BREATHNACH

The most widespread of our non-Gaelic surnames and the fourth most numerous in Ireland was, in the early Norman era, written 'le Waleys' (the Welshman). The appellation could be — and was — applied to newcomers from Wales of whom there were many in various parts of Ireland in the 13th century. In 1296 for example, John of Chester was commander of six Welshmen — survivors of fourteen who came from Wales into Ireland with Stephen de Fulbourne (formerly archbishop of Tuam) to guard the peace — and of nine other Welshmen sent as replacements (at 2d per day each). In Cos. Mayo and Kilkenny Walshes were particularly numerous and formed definite family groups but there was also a concentration of the name in east Cork.

The first occurrence of the surname in the Cork area is in Giraldus Cambrensis' account of Raymond le Gros' naval battle in 1173, which seems to have been fought near Youghal, against the Ostmen of Cork whose leader, Gilbert mac Turger, was slain by a sturdy youth named Philip of Wales (*Philippus Gualensis*; similarly a half-brother of Robert Fitzstephen was named *Willelmus Wallensis* or *le Waleis*).

By 1260 there were quite a few of the name in Co. Cork, judging by the Plea Rolls which mention Galfridus and Griffin le Waleis in Bally-downis (par. Templetrine), Lewelin Walens at Magnagar in Ross diocese, David le Waleis at Aghada, Erdodenil widow of Galfridus le Waleys in dispute with Seysel le Waleys over her marriage portion in Ahalisky (par. Kilmaloda), Isolda widow of Robert le Waleys likewise at Mourne Abbey and Howel le Waleys in dispute with John le Waleys at Corbally.

Gilbert was a personal name in frequent use among them at that time. Gilbertus Walensis was one of the Co. Cork knights who were jurors at an inquisition held in Cork *c*. 1230.

It may have been the de Clare family, all-powerful as they were in south Wales, who brought the Welsh blood — and surname — into east Cork. In 1278 William le Waleys was bailiff of Gilbert de Clare in Somerset while the lands of Gilbert le Waleys at Rostellan in Co. Cork were held from the same Gilbert de Clare by the service of three knights. Gilbert (le Waleys) seems to have prospered at Rostellan; in 1281 he supplied cows to the army of Desmond for which he received payment of £55-13-4. In 1288 he was paid a fine for trespass by Jordan de Caunteton from nearby Corkbeg. Shortly afterwards, he was knighted and as Sir Gilbert le Waleis (*c*. 1290) in company with Sir William de Barry complained to the king that after they had prosecuted and outlawed

317

Donal óg Mac Carthy, Donal was afterwards granted the king's peace. In 1301 Gilbert and William le Waleys were among those requested by King Edward I to send military aid against the Scots. Sir Gilbert was named several times on juries in Co. Cork, the last reference to him being in 1313. John Walens of Trabolgan served as a juror in 1301.

Another free tenant on the de Clare estate (Manor of Inchiquin) in 1288 was Corgene le Waleys of Glenterlethain (now Ballycurraginny in Killeagh parish, probably named after Corgene). His unusual personal name seems to be Welsh; quite a number of those surnamed le Waleys in the Justiciary Rolls relating to Co. Cork between 1295 and 1300 bore such names as Lawelach, David, Gronow and Howel, indicating that they really were of the (Celtic) Welsh nation rather than Cambro-Normans. In 1301 a felon named Kenewrek le Waleys fled for refuge to the church of Kilnagleary near Carrigaline.

As early as 1295 also we find a Gaelicized form of the name in Co. Cork, namely John Brathnath (*Breatnach*). In Co. Limerick in 1306 several of the Bretnaghs abducted the daughter of the archdeacon of Limerick; a place called Bretnaghstrath in the same county is mentioned in 1345.

Sometimes the trend was in the other direction. When Philip le Waleys and Roesea his wife were charged with the murder of Symon le Waleys in Co. Cork in 1313, they were acquitted on the grounds that Simon was a *hibernicus* belonging to Philip and so his slaying could not be considered a felony. In other words, Simon was a native Irishman who had taken his master's surname.

A list dated 1301 names William le Waleys in Olethan (Barrymore), Eyvon le Waleys and Cogan le Waleys in Muskerry, and John, William and Milo le Waleys in the cantred of Fermoy. The last-mentioned was probably the Milo who held land at Ballynahalisk (near Kildorrery) in 1295; there was also a le Waleys family with lands at Garran (Garranecole, par. Clenor) and one at Castletownroche in 1367. In 1311 when a pardon was granted to the Roches who had been in rebellion against the king, the list of their followers included Milo the Welshman and Lewelin the Welshman. In 1313 John le Waleys was master of the ship *Michael* from Cork which was part of a fleet transporting men and supplies from Dublin to Barrow-in-Furness to aid an expedition against Robert Bruce.

On several occasions between 1321 and 1328 Thomas son of Gilbert le Waleys (perhaps Gilbert of Rostellan) took part in raids and rebellious practices of the first Earl of Desmond. On one of these raids, Thomas and Philip le Waleys aided the Earl in attacking the lands of William de Barry.

In 1344 Nicholas son of Ser' le Waleys and Philip son of Thomas le Waleys of Olethan joined a faction of the Barrys who went to attack Nicholas Barry of Castlelyons. Three years earlier Philip and Patrick sons of Gilbert le Waleys, with Milo Camboun, and their followers, raided Henry Cod of Cloyne — killing, incidentally, one Robert le Walshe — and afterwards Gregory le Waleys travelled to Newcastle West to obtain pardon for their felonies from the Earl of Desmond. This Gregory must have been regarded as chief of his nation and probably lived at Rostellan; there is a record of a Gregory Walsh there in an inquisition of 1386. The conflict was also referred to in the Pipe Roll of Cloyne where it was stated that as a result of war having broken out between the Walenses and the Codmen, Philip son of John Codd was forced to flee the land from fear of the Walenses.

It would appear then that the Walshes formed a strong and warlike family group in east Cork in the 14th century. It is probably from this period that we get such townland-names as Walshtown (Beg and More) in the parishes of Templenacarriga and Ballyspillane (bar. Barrymore) and Walshestown in the parish of Churchtown (bar. Orrery and Kilmore). The latter was the site of a castle, held by the Barrys in Elizabethan times, but possibly erected originally by the Walshes. Nearby was another Barry castle at Annagh. Gregory Walshe of Anath was in 1356 the assessor of a subsidy off the county of Cork. In an inquisition dated 1626 Walshestown appears as 'Wailshisland alias Ballinvallishe'; the Irish form, *Baile an Bhailisigh*, indicates that *Breatnach* was not the only Irish version used in the area. There was also Kilevallynvallishig near Ballyhea in 1608. However, Walshtown in Barrymore appears in the Fiants (1583) as Ballynybrihnagh and Ballynybreghnagh (*Baile na mBreatnach*). There is still a Ballynabrannagh near Leamlara and a Ballybranagh in Cloyne parish.

Bilingual forms of the name were in evidence among the burgesses of Cloyne in 1402 with William Bretnagh, David oge Bretnagh and Thomas mac David Walsh. Dominus Johannes Walsh was vicar of Kilmaclenine in the same year. Both forms were sometimes used by the same individual; the Richard Walche who was a canon of Cork in 1469 may have been the Ricardus Brinach who was prebendary of Inishcarra in 1493. Incidentally, the name Brayghnock — as in the case of Richard Brayghnock, abbot of Tracton in 1350 — may be a different surname, namely, 'of Brecknock', which of course could be easily confused with the various forms of *Breatnach*.

In 1382 John Walsh of Youghal, mariner, received a royal pardon for having lost a seal used in connection with customs, and from then on the name recurs in the town with increasing frequency. In the 16th century the Walshes were among the principal families in Youghal. William Walsh was elected mayor in 1527, and several times thereafter, as was John Welsh in 1565, Peter Brennott in 1583-4, and David Walsh in 1631. David was one of the Catholic forfeiting proprietors in Youghal after 1641.

Peter Walshe had been warden of the College of Youghal in 1525 and after the dissolution of the religious houses (*c.* 1540) conformed to the new regime, so retaining possession of the college and its privileges. At the inquiry into the possession of the suppressed Franciscan House of Youghal three of the jurors were Patrick Walsshe, Christopher Walsshe and Dermot Walsshe. In the same era, William Walshe, late prior of Ballindrohid Augustinian priory (Bridgetown between Mallow and Fermoy) was found to be in possession of 300 acres of the former monastic lands as well as of land at Castlemartyr and part of the former Dominican House of Youghal. The Walsh connection with Bridgetown can be traced back a century earlier. In 1426 Johannes Walsche, a canon of Ballyhay, nominated Bartholomew Walsche for the priory of Villepontis, vacant through the death of Thomas Walsche. After the Reformation Johannes Brethnagh was vicar of Schull in 1581 and of Kilbonane the following year, but Edmundus Brennaughe was deprived of the vicarage of Kilnaglory.

It need hardly be said that the name Walsh established itself in Cork city. In the year 1311 Stephen le Waleys wounded John Bederne in the city of Cork by striking him on the head with an axe, and then fled for sanctuary to the church of Holy Cross del Nard where he remained for three weeks before making his escape. During the years 1322-1325 Jordan le Waleys (also Walensis) was a bailiff of Cork. Thomas Walsh (Thomas Brenaghe in the Landgable Roll) held the same post in 1405 as did William Walsh four years later. In 1450 Patrick Galwey of Kinsale conveyed a 'messuage' in Cork to John Bratnaghe. A John Walshe was dean of Cork in 1514. In 1560 Richard Walshe of Cork, merchant, was appointed gauger and searcher in the ports of Cork and Kinsale — perhaps the Richard fitz John Walshe who in his will, dated 1583, requested that he be buried in St. Peter's church. He named his son John as heir to his property at Kilbarry and Dungarvan (Cork). This John (or his son) may be the John Welsh, named as a 'titulado' in Shandon parish in 1659. In 1594 an indenture was drawn up between Thomas Skiddy of Cork and John Brenagh fitz Morrish of same, shearman. It mentioned 'John the Baptist's church land in the tenure of Rykerd Brenagh'. There was an Edward Walsh of Cork city outlawed in 1690 for supporting King James II.

In regard to Cork county, the Elizabethan Fiants give us an idea of the distribution of the name and the forms used in the late 16th century. In the Kanturk area, for instance, in 1573, dwelt a very hibernicized Dermod mac Shane Brenagh, harper. In the townland of Coolatanavally (par. Carrigrohane Beg) there was a group of five in 1577, namely, Edmond mac Morish mac Nicholas Bernagh, Richard mac Morish mac Nicholas Branagh, Oliver mac Thomas Brenagh, Walter mac Shane Branagh and Richard mac Thomas Brenagh, kerns. Though Irish-speaking kerns were well down on the social scale it is remarkable that this group used only Norman-type personal names.

A large group pardoned at Ballincollig in September 1600 were classed as 'yeomen' or substantial farmers, but the name-pattern remains the same — Walter and William Brenagh fitz John, James fitz Redmond

Brenagh, Maurice Brenagh fitz Richard, Richard Brenagh fitz Edmund, Rickard fitz William Brenagh, John fitz David Brenagh. (There is another Walshestown near Ovens.) In Berrings, not far distant, was a further large group of yeomen – Edmund mac Robert Brenagh, William mac Robert Brenagh and his wife Sylly gane ny Thomye, Rickard mac Robert Brenagh, James mac Shane Brenagh, Redmund mac Edmund Brenagh.

The following year a pardon was granted to another group in the service of Edmund Fitzgibbon, the White Knight. Many of these were surnamed 'Brennagh mac Shearon' (i.e. *Mac Seathrúin*, son of Geoffrey).

Inishcarra which, like Ballincollig, was formerly in Barrett's barony, was the dwelling-place of Richard mac Thomas Brunnaghe and Richard mac Morish Brennaghe, pardoned in 1576. Descendants of these, perhaps, were Edmond and James Brennagh of Faghy (Faha in Inishcarra parish) who were outlawed in 1643.

In east Cork, also in the Cromwellian period, among the Catholic landowners liable to forfeiture was Morrish Bronagh of Cloyne – no doubt the Muiris Breanach who was superintendent of John fitz Edmond's house at Cloyne and whose name is inscribed on the Fitzgerald harp, dated 1621.

The surname also spread into west Cork. Farran in Kilmaloda parish was formerly known as Farrenemrenagh (*Fearann na mBreatnach*). In 1641 a Thomas Walsh owned all the parish of Abbeymahon in Ibane.

According to the census of 1659, the Walshes were among the 'principal Irish families' in all the baronies in the eastern half of Co. Cork, 'Walsh' and 'Brennagh' being listed as separate families as follows: Cork City and Liberties: Brennagh 15, Walsh 8; Youghal: Brennagh 10; Barretts: Brennagh 20, Welsh 8; Kinnatalloone: Brennagh 18; Barrymore: Brennagh 10, Welsh and Walsh 29; Orrery and Kilmore: Brennagh 10, Walsh 14.

Richard Walsh, D.D., an 18th century bishop of Cork, on his death in 1751 was lamented by the poet Seán Clárach Mac Domhnaill. Later in the century we find one of the name – Roibeard Breatnach – among the poets of Carraig na bhFear. Mícheál óg Ó Longáin calls his family 'Walshes of the boat':

> *Breatnaigh an bháid dob fhearr le sleasaibh na Laoi,*
> *Na fearaibh nár stán dá námhaid i gcaismirt na gclaíomh.*

In the 19th century another of the name, Edward Walsh (1805-1849), son of a Millstreet man, gained fame as a romantic poet who translated many of the old Irish songs into English.

In the political sphere J.J. Walsh (1880-1948), of Raharoon near Bandon, was one of the early Sinn Féin nationalists in Cork and later became first postmaster-general of the Irish Free State.

APPENDIX

(This short and by no means exhaustive bibliography includes only such books and articles as I found profitable. Furthermore, it lists only specialized studies of individual families and not works of more general concern such as those of Burke, D'Alton, O Hart, MacLysaght, Woulfe, etc., each of which is helpful in its own way. Abbreviations used are *J.C.H.A.S.*, the *Journal of the Cork Historical and Archaeological Society*, and *J.R.S.A.I.*, the *Journal of the Royal Society of Antiquaries of Ireland*.)

Mac Auliffe: A publication entitled 'Clan Mac Auliffe' by J.J. Mac A. (1941) contains several inquisitions and other material relating to the Mac Auliffes. A fuller account together with the history of that part of Duhallow, will be found in *A History of Newmarket* (1973) by Bro. D.H. Allen.

Barry: Two books in French on the history of this family have been published, also one in English on *The Last Earls of Barrymore* (G.J. Robinson, 1894). The most detailed local account is in a series of articles entitled 'Barrymore' by Rev. E. Barry in *J.C.H.A.S.*, 1899-1902.

O Keeffe: Many references to this family may be found in Grove-White's 'Historical and Topographical Notes', first published as an appendix to *J.C.H.A.S.*, 1905-1931.

Mac Carthy: Numerous books and articles on various branches of the Mac Carthys have been compiled. Some have been referred to in the text. Among the others are *A Historical Pedigree of the Mac Carthys* by D. Mac Carthy (1880), *The Mac Carthys of Munster* by S.T. Mac Carthy (1922), and a series of articles on 'Some Mac Carthys of Blarney and Ballea' by John T. Collins in *J.C.H.A.S.*, 1954-5. One of the most useful general studies is W.F.T. Butler's *Gleanings from Irish History* (1925).

O Callaghan: There is an article by H.W. Gillman on 'The Chieftains of Pobul-I-Callaghan' in *J.C.H.A.S.*, 1897. The poem *Caithréim Donnchaidh*, edited by Éamonn de hÓir, is published in *North Munster Studies* (1967), ed. E. Rynne.

Cogan: This is an abridgement of a thesis 'Borradh agus Meath Cogánach Corcaí, 1177-1655', presented by me at University College, Cork, in 1957.

Condon: An early article on 'The Condons of Cloghleigh', by P. Raymond, was published in *J.C.H.A.S.*, 1896. Details of the origins of the family will be found in St. John Brooks, *Knights' Fees, in Counties Wexford, Carlow and Kilkenny* (1950).

O Crowley: Of the three accounts of this family in *J.C.H.A.S.*, 'The O Crowleys of Coill tSealbhaigh' by John T. Collins (1951-3) is the most comprehensive.

O Daly: The O Dalys of Muintiravara form the subject of one book and part-subject of another, but neither adds much to the account given by John O Donovan in his introduction to *The Tribes of Ireland* (1852).

O Donovan: R.F. Cronelly's *History of the Clan Eoghan* (1864) has a section on this family, but a more detailed account will be found in an appendix to John O Donovan's edition of *The Annals of the Four Masters*, pp. 2430-2483.

Fitzgerald: It would be difficult to list all the articles – in *J.C.H.A.S.*, *J.R.S.A.I.*, and other journals – relating to the Fitzgeralds. For Imokilly, the most interesting is 'Uniackes and Fitzgeralds of Imokilly' by R.G. Fitzgerald-Uniacke (*J.C.H.A.S.*, 1894). There are also several books on the Earls of Desmond; the earliest was written by Fr. Dominic O Daly and was published in 1655.

O Hea: The only previously-published work is that by John T. Collins, 'The O Heas of South-West Cork', *J.C.H.A.S.*, 1946.

O Healy: See J.T. Collins, 'The Healys of Donoughmore', *J.C.H.A.S.*, 1943.

O Driscoll: The main source for O Driscoll history is the text of and notes to John O Donovan's edition of 'The Genealogy of Corca Laidhe', published in *Miscellany of the Celtic Society* (1849).

Kingston: A brief account of this family, first published in 1893, is referred to in the text. Dr. Richard Kingston, of Ulster Polytechnic, Newtownabbey, Belfast, has written a more reliable and more detailed survey of the origins of the west Cork Kingstons, *J.C.H.A.S.*, 1981.

O Lyne: As mentioned in the text, the Lynes of Bearhaven are the only branch to have been studied in detail.

Long: See J.T. Collins, 'The Longs of Muskerry and Kinalea', *J.C.H.A.S.*, 1946.

O Mahony: Material on its various branches has been published by the O Mahony clan in *The O Mahony Journals*, 1971-. The pioneer work is Canon O Mahony's 'History of the O Mahony Septs of Kinelmeaky and Ivagha', *J.C.H.A.S.*, 1906-1910.

Hurley: Rev. P. Hurley's 'Some account of the family of Hurley' (*J.C.H.A.S.*, 1905-6), is the only previously-published article.

Murphy: This is a slightly-condensed version of my own article 'The Uí Mhurchadha or Murphys of Muskerry, Co. Cork', *J.C.H.A.S.*, 1969.

Nagle: Four branches of this family are fully treated by Basil O Connell in the *Irish Genealogist* – 'The Nagles of Annakissy' and 'The Nagles of Mount Nagle', (Vol. II), 'The Nagles of Garnavilla' and 'The Nagles of Ballygriffin', (Vol. III).

Cotter: There are two short accounts of the Cotters of Bearforest in *J.C.H.A.S.*, one by James Coleman (1908) and the other by G. de P. Cotter (1983.)

O Regan: See J.T. Collins, 'The O Regans of Carbery', *J.C.H.A.S.*, 1958.

Roche: There is a useful treatise on 'The Roches, Lords of Fermoy' by E. Donnelly, in *J.C.H.A.S.*, 1933-1937.

Mac Sweeney: A well-documented account of the early history of this family may be found in the introduction to *Leabhar Chlainne Suibhne,* edited by Rev. Paul Walsh (1920.)

O Sullivan: Philip O Sullivan Bear's *History of Catholic Ireland*, first published in 1621, contains some first-hand information. An interesting 18th century account by 'Friar O Sullivan of Muckross' was published in *J.C.H.A.S.*, 1898-1900. Jeremiah King's *O Sullivan Family History* is somewhat outdated but still useful. An excellent study of one branch (Mac Fínghin Duibh) by Gerard J. Lyne was published in the *Journal of the Kerry Archaeological and Historical Society* (1976.)

INDEX OF PLACES

(Mainly baronies, parishes, castle sites, town and villages; townland names are not included. Abbreviations used: b. = barony; p. = parish (civil); c. = castle.)

326

Carrigrohane (p., c.), 15, 16, 18, 53, 57, 78, 80, 93, 176, 220, 249, 277, 314
Carrigrohanebeg (p.), 15, 17, 320
Carrigtwohill, 23, 28, 31, 39, 94, 118-120, 157, 206, 263, 265
Cashel, 1, 2, 40, 49-50, 66, 89, 186, 270, 278, 287, 300
Castle Cooke (Dún Galláin), 98, 102-3
Castlederry, 56
Castle Dod, 151
Castle Donovan, 109, 126-130, 182, 187
Castlefreke (see Rathbarry)
Castlehaven (p., c.), 14, 125, 128-131, 133, 178-181, 184-5, 268, 307
Castle Hyde (Carriganeady), 100-102
Castle Inch, 16, 18, 59, 61, 73, 203
Castleishen, 147, 150-1, 168, 197-8
Castle Island, 232
Castle Ivor, 125
Castlekevin, 163-4, 278-9
Castlelack, 237
Castlelyons, 25-31, 87, 102, 169, 203, 215, 264, 289, 318
Castlemacauliffe, 7-11
Castlemagner (p.), 42, 63, 67, 133, 287
Castlemahon, 234, 237-241
Castlemartyr, 145-149, 320
Castle Mehigan, 232
Castlemore (Dundrinan), 33, 51, 59, 78, 173, 291-3, 301
Castlemore (Mourne Abbey), 18-22, 69, 78, 292
Castlenard, 178, 183
Castleredmond, 147
Castlerichard, 145, 147-8
Castletown Bearhaven, 194-5, 218, 303, 305, 311, 313
Castletownroche, 92, 164-5, 167, 203, 206, 215-7, 259, 276, 278-82, 294-5, 318
Castletownshend (see Castlehaven)
Castleventry (p.), 112
Charleville (see Rathgoggan)
Churchtown (Bruhenny) (p.), 8,

27-8, 30, 43, 65, 104, 319
Clann Amhlaoibh (Clanawley), 7-12, 288
Cléire (Clear I.), 178, 180, 182-5, 252
Clenor (p.), 98, 258-9, 276-8, 318
Clodagh (c.), 172, 227, 272, 291-3
Cloghane (c.), 56, 182
Cloghleigh (c.), 28, 98
Cloghmacullig (c.), 18
Cloghphilip (c.), 16, 58, 216
Cloghroe (c.), 9, 16, 59, 61, 248
Clonakilty, 57, 87-8, 104, 111, 124, 132, 154, 156, 159-61, 221, 255, 310
Clondrohid (p.), 39, 93, 138, 189, 214, 224, 272-4
Clondullane (p.), 96-99, 102
Clonfert (p.), 7, 10, 31, 63, 65, 71-2, 83, 93, 134, 287
Clonmeen (p., c.), 9, 10, 39, 46, 62, 67-72, 83, 93, 154
Clonmel (p.), 87
Clonmult (p.), 134
Clonpriest (p.), 31, 140, 145
Clontead (p.), 36, 154, 255
Cloyne, 92, 99, 121, 141, 145, 147-9, 168, 170, 172-3, 188, 216, 262, 265, 287, 301, 319, 321
Coachford, 315
Cóbh (see Great I.)
Coill tSealbhaigh (Kiltallow), 107-13, 252
Condons and Clangibbons (b.), 89, 96-103, 279
Conna (c.), 26, 134, 151, 167
Coolmain (c.), 54, 56
Coolmore (c.), 80, 81
Coomhola, 194, 311
Corbally (p.), 20
Cork (city), 3, 5, 21-3, 26, 38-9, 47-8, 51-3, 58, 60, 62, 66, 68, 76-81, 87, 90, 94, 98, 100, 105-6, 119, 122, 125, 128, 130, 147, 155, 160, 165-6, 168, 172-3, 187, 199-200, 203-5, 207, 213, 216, 220,

Farahy (p.), 276, 278
Fermoy, 1, 2, 38, 41, 96-8, 105, 133, 155, 162, 168, 193, 197, 206, 216, 220, 263, 265, 275-86, 318, 320
Foaty, 29
Fontenoy (battle of), 165, 174, 187, 312
Fountainstown, 283, 286

Garranekinnefeake (Rathbarry) (p.), 29, 31
Garrycloyne (p.), 73
Garryvoe (p.), 289
Gill Abbey, Cork, 52, 58, 73, 154
Glandore, 13, 34, 126, 128-9, 189, 206
Glanmire, 49, 262, 284
Glanworth (p., c.), 14, 40-2, 95-8, 134, 162-3, 167, 216-7, 258, 276, 280-2
Gleann an Chroim, 56, 84-5, 125, 187
Glengarriff, 222, 308-10
Glenville, 46-8, 246
Glounthane, 91
Goleen (see Kilmoe)
Gortnaclogh (c.), 56, 158
Gortroe (p.), 25, 31, 133, 203, 205
Gougane Barra, 31, 209-211
Great Island (Cóbh), 29-31, 87, 91, 206, 262-4, 311
Grenagh (p.), 14, 20-1, 316

Ibane and Barryroe (b.), 27-33, 87, 112, 131, 147, 154, 156-61, 211, 265, 269, 310
Ightermurragh (p.), 284
Imokilly (b.), 20, 27, 51, 81-2, 89-93, 100, 104, 138, 140-1, 145-50, 154, 261, 284, 295
Imphrick (p.), 216
Inchigeelagh (p.), 13, 94, 104, 206-13, 288, 298
Inchiquin (c.), 31, 140, 145, 318
Inchydoney, 104, 159, 254
Inishcarra (p.), 9, 15-21, 44, 61, 92, 127, 196, 204, 235, 240, 319, 321
Inishkenny (p.), 20, 154, 188,

204, 271, 283-4, 287, 291
Innishannon, 34-6, 51, 76, 122, 134, 138, 231, 245, 252, 283, 286-7

Johnstown (c.), 281

Kanturk, 39, 42, 45, 62-4, 93, 248-9, 294-5, 315, 320
Kerrycurrihy (b.), 58, 78-81, 94, 119, 143, 166, 204, 215, 218, 288, 310, 314
Kilbolane (p., c.), 134, 150, 154, 168, 198-9
Kilbonane (p.), 154, 225, 320
Kilbrin (p.), 26, 63, 70-1, 135, 281
Kilbrittain (p., c.), 54-7, 75-6, 87, 104, 109, 112-3, 119, 131, 160, 211, 238, 252-4, 266, 269, 278, 298
Kilbrogan (p.), 240
Kilcaskan (p.), 193, 221, 298, 310-1
Kilcatherine (p.), 221
Kilcoe (p., c.), 56, 138, 180, 187, 235-6
Kilcolman (c.), 151-2, 258
Kilcorney (p.), 289
Kilcrea, 48, 51, 58-61, 70, 122, 139, 189, 213, 218, 245, 247-8, 272, 292, 298
Kilcredan (p.), 92, 141, 205, 287
Kilcrohane (p.), 117-19, 187, 236
Kilcrumper (p.), 95-7, 100, 162-3, 223
Kilcully (p.), 105, 199
Kildorrery, 89, 96, 265, 276-7, 318
Kilfaughnabeg (p.), 126, 268
Kilgarriff (p.), 112, 159, 283
Kilgobbin (c.), 54, 57
Kilgullane (p., c.), 41, 99, 102, 281
Kilkerranmore (p.), 158, 160
Killaconenagh (p.), 222
Killanully (Killingley) (p.), 119, 204, 215, 223
Killaspugmullane (p.), 31, 188, 224
Killathy (p.), 105

ADDENDA AND CORRIGENDA

This reprinting of *Family Names of County Cork* provides an opportunity to make reference to new material published since 1985, supplementing the short Appendix on pp. 322-4. It also enables me to remedy some errors and omissions arising from the 1985 edition. For many of these corrections I am indebted to my correspondents, among them Reverend James Coombes, Timoleague (O Driscoll, Harrington), Mr Henry M. Coughlan, Hornchurch, Essex (Coughlan), Mr Charles W. Kingston, Duncan, British Colombia (Kingston), Mr James H. Bath, Paddington, New South Wales (O Keeffe), M. Jean Swiney, Caen, France (Mac Sweeney) and in particular, Mr Paul McCotter, Ballincollig; who provided new information on the origins of the Fitzgeralds and other early families of Norman descent, much of it from the forthcoming edition of *The Pipe Roll of Cloyne* which he and Mr K.W. Nicholls of UCC are preparing.

I am grateful also to The Collins Press for undertaking this reprint, and to their editor, Ms Maria O'Donovan, for her valued supervision.

Barrett: (p. 14, l.3) Castelgeych (Caisleán na Gaoithe) was not near Ballyhea; it is now known as Castleventry (near Clonakilty).

(p. 14, para. 7) As early as 1301 Milo and John Barret were among the jurors in the barony of Muskerry.

(p. 15, para. 1) Garrycloyne parish near Blarney was another Barrett stronghold in Muskerry. Thomas Barret fitz John sought an advowson there in 1327, while John fitz John Barret held it in 1353 and it remained with the Barretts down to the seventeenth century. (For these and other details of early Barretts see K.W. Nicholls, 'The development of lordship in Co. Cork 1300-1600', in P. O'Flanagan and C.G. Buttimer, eds., *Cork: History and Society* (Dublin 1993) 169-172).

(p. 19, para. 1) The Barrett connection was earlier than this; Moreton (i.e. Barrett's castle near Mourne Abbey) along with Carrigrohane and Doundrynan, was granted to Richard Baret in 1369. (*Cal. Ormond Deeds* ii, no. 147).

Barry: (p. 26, l.30) For 'Philip' (1402) read 'John' (i.e. Seán Ciotach).

(p. 32, para. 3) William Maol held Coyltescastle (Clonakilty) and the surrounding district, Toughnakilly, at the time of his death, but this was later lost to Mac Carthy Riabhach. Laurence may have been a son, rather than a brother, of William Ruadh. (See K.W. Nicholls, loc. cit., 176-181).

(p. 34, l.23) Hilary de Cogan's daughter (Amabilia) married a Philip de Barry, and their son was named Odo.

(p. 34, para. 4) Sir Thomas Barry Óg was a brother (rather than son) of Philip, and Henry (p. 36, l.17) his cousin (rather than nephew). (K.W. Nicholls, loc. cit., 184-5).

O Keeffe: (p. 45, l.26) Cathaoir (son of Conchubhar) was not the Cahir O Keeffe who leased Derragh. On 24 February 1738 (n.s. 1739) the pedigree supplied to the College of Arms by Arthur O Keeffe of Piccadilly (see p. 47, para. 4; Arthur was of the Ballymacquirk branch, not of Dunbulloge, as stated) was examined and certified at Ballyhoolahan by O Keeffe, i.e. Charles (Cathaoir) of Athone (? Athnowen), Co. Cork, along with Charles (Cathaoir) of Derragh, Owen, Arthur of Cullen, Manus of Ballyhoolahan, and Timothy of Ballymeggy (? Ballymichael) – as well as by Mac Carthy More, etc. (Extract from the Records of the College of Arms, London, dated 31 March 1830).

(p. 46, l.22) Fr Eoghan Ó Caoimh was a widower when ordained in 1717. He had been married to Eleanor Nagle in 1681, and was father of Art, Eoghan, Seosamh, Caomh, Onóra, Siobhán and Máire. (See Breandán Ó Conchúir, *Scríobhaithe Chorcaí 1700-1850* (B.Á.C. 1982).

Mac Carthy: (p. 54, paras 2,3) In 1467 Donnchadh's son Cormac, with the assistance of the Earl of Desmond's son, took the castles of Kilgobbin, Monteen and Coolmain, replacing his uncle, Diarmaid an Dúna, as lord of Carbery. But Diarmaid's son, Fínghin, recovered the lordship from Cormac around 1478, an event celebrated in a poem by Mathghamhain Ó Dálaigh. (See Brian Ó Cuív, 'A fragment of Irish annals', *Celtica* 14 (1981) 83-104 (93), and 'A poem for Fínghin Mac Carthaigh Riabhach', *Celtica* 15 (1983) 96-110.

(p. 57, para. 6) For Clann Taidhg Ruaidh na Scairte (and of Durrus) see my article in *JCHAS* 1994, 32-46. For further details on the Carbery Mac Carthys' involvement with the sub-infeudation and descent of the Fitzstephen/Carew moiety of Desmond, see Paul McCotter, *JCHAS* 1996, 64-80.

(p. 58, l.17) Inis Aille is not Inchirahilly but Incheally, now Knocknagoul, par. Aglish.

(p. 58, Muskerry, para. 2) In 1467 Cormac Láidir, with the help of An Barrach Mór, captured the castle of Carrigrohane, and was permitted by James Fitzgerald to retain it. (Ó Cúiv, *Celtica* 14, p. 94).

(p. 62, Duhallow, para. 3) Donnchadh óg (son of Donnchadh mac Cormaic) was lord of Ealla in 1467 when he assisted Barry Mór in a Geraldine dispute (ibid.).

O Callaghan: (p. 70) An article on the O Callaghans of Kilcranathan (par. Ballyclogh), based on an Irish manuscript in the Royal Irish Academy, has been published by Joseph F. O'Callaghan in *JCHAS* 1987, 106-112. A second article of his (*JCHAS* 1990, 30-40) deals with the O Callaghans and the rebellion of 1641.

Coughlan: (p. 76, para. 1) Timothy Coghlane of Crookhaven married Susanna, daughter of Pearce Arnop, through whom he inherited a leasehold of the 4 ploughlands and the 3 half ploughlands of Crookhaven. In a dispute over these lands he was supported by Jeremy and Richard Coghlan (Chancery Bill, 26 June 1712).

The careers of Captain Jeremiah Coghlan (RN) of Crookhaven (b. 1777, d. in the Isle of Wight 1844), and of his son, General Sir William M. Coghlan (1804-1885), are recounted by C.J.F. MacCarthy in *Seanchas Chairbre* 2, pp. 5-24.

Collins: (p. 82, para. 3) As early as 1397 a Nicholas O Cullen held a messuage in Youghal.

(p. 87, para. 6) For details of Seán Ó Coileáin's career see B. Ó Conchúir, op. cit., 41-6.

Coleman: (p. 90, para. 3) A Kinsale ship, *Mighell*, on a trading voyage to Bristol in 1537 had a master named Colman.

Crowley: (p.108) In 1493 a papal mandate was issued in favour of the noble man Aulanus Yernolage (Amhlaoibh Ó Cruadhlaoich), lord of Cayllcalbaygh (Coill tSealbhaigh), and Cornelius Yornolage, a cleric of Cork diocese. Amhlaoibh had previously erected a new church at Kilnagross, dividing the old parish of Cruary into Kilnagross (his section) and Templeomalus, and this arrangement now received ecclesiastical approval. In the following year David Ocrolay was assigned the rectory of Ryllmyd (i.e. Kyllmyd or Ballymartle. (*Cal. Papal Letters* xvi, nos. 110, 350).

O Donovan: (p. 126, para. 3) Clann Chonghalaigh: a lament for Conchubhar Mac Conghalaigh, harper to Domhnall Ó Donnabháin (chief of Clann Chathail 1584-1639), composed by Tadhg Olltach Ó'n Cháinte, was published by Seán Ó Súilleabháin and Seán Donnelly, 'Music has ended', *Celtica* 22 (1991) 164-175.

Fitzgerald: (p. 145) The Fitzgeralds, Knights of Kerry, were involved in Imokilly affairs from the mid-fourteenth century.

(p. 147, l.7) John was a grand-nephew (not cousin) of Gerald.

(p. 148, l.20) Thomas Gankagh, son of James: this James was not the Dean, but James, son of Dean Edmond.

(p. 148, para. 3) The Culogorie Fitzgeralds were tenants of Sir John fitz Edmond, Dean of Cloyne, and were not those who held

Glenane from the early seventeenth century. James fitz William of Glenane is mentioned in a deed of 1638. His son, William, was a lieutenant in Ormonde's regiment in 1648-9, later MP for Lismore and knighted for his services. His son, James, was outlawed for supporting King James, but pardoned in 1699, and it was his son, William (not Sir William), who was involved in the Barry incident. The last of the Ballymartin Fitzgeralds, William Edmond, died unmarried in Australia in the early 1900s.

(p. 149, ll.8, 13) Richard and Garrett fitz Edmond were not brothers of Sir John of Cloyne. The former was known as Colonel Richard of Castlemartyr and Glennageare; his residence at Rostellan occurred through his marriage to the widow of James fitz Thomas of that place. (Paul McCotter, pers. comm.).

O Flynn: (p. 155, para. 2) It was from Flann's brother, Airmedach, that the tribal segment of Uí Bláthmaic were descended, and from a later Flann (mac Flannchada) of this group the Uí Fhlainn took their surname. (See Pádraig Ó Riain, 'Achadh Bolg', *Cork: History and Society* 45-61 (48)).

(p. 155, para. 3) For further details on Donnchadh (Bán) Ó Floinn, see B. Ó Conchúir, op. cit., 69-77.

O Hea: (p. 161, para. 3) A religious census of Rathbarry parish, taken in 1766, shows that Hea (Hay/O Hay) was the most numerous of the Catholic surnames in the parish – with 13 households out of a total of 131. (See C.J.F. MacCarthy, 'The people of Rathbarry in 1766', *Seanchas Chairbre* 3, 44-52).

Hennessy: (pp. 164-5) Further details of the Ballymacmoy Hennessys have been published in L.M. Cullen, 'Blackwater Catholics', *Cork: History and Society* 540-551.

For an account of Fr John Hennessy, a controversial parish priest of Doneraile from 1726, see article by Ceall Hyland, *Mallow Field Club Journal* 6 (1988) 109-111.

Ahern: (p. 168, para. 3) Aherns at Ballymaloe: John Oge O Haghery of Ballymaloe, yeoman, was a trustee for Sir John fitz Edmond in 1608. His son, Maurice, obtained leases of Glenane (1612) and Shanavagoon (1621), and was father of John fitz Morrish (para. 3) and Owen fitz Morrish (para. 4).

O Driscoll: (p. 183, para. 5) O Driscoll Óg's main residence was more likely the castle of Rincolisky (Whitehall, par. Aghadown). Ballinard (Castlenard) was in Collymore, and those named in connection with it would have belonged to the O Driscolls Mór.

Harrington: (p. 195, l.3) Donogh (Dionissio Hingurdil) later sought a pension from the king of Spain, as did his brother, who was O Hingurdíl, chief of his house. The latter 'had vassals, lands and possessions and, apart from his own soldiers, he maintained at his own cost forty soldiers brought in from other parts. Under the leadership of the lord of Biraven he distinguished himself above all others ... when the lord of Biraven was surrounded and hard pressed by the enemy, he made boats from the hides of his own horses, after the custom of the country, and crossed a great river with him ... Among the subjects of the lord of Biraven he is the one who suffered most losses and rendered greatest service'. (See Micheline K. Walsh, O'Sullivan Beare in Spain', *Archivium Hibernicum* 45 (1990) 52).

Noonan: (p. 197, l.14) The correct date for Richard Ohenwonham's carucate at Tullylease was in the early 1340s.

(p. 199) Dónall Ó Núnáin was an early nineteenth-century Irish scribe in Aughrim, par. Shandrum, as was Mícheál Ó Núnáin, also in north Cork. (B. Ó Conchúir, op. cit., 173).

Kingston: (p. 201, l.3) For 'Col. James Kingston' read 'Col. Samuel Kingston' of Skeaf (p.200, l.34) – whose great-grandson, James, was the mayor of Cork in 1785 (p. 200, l.11).

Leahy: (p. 203, l.26) Dermod O Leaghie of Garranjames was probably the Darby O Leighy who in 1620 leased land around Glenane from the Earl of Cork.

O Leary: Mannen was probably an early name for the settlement that later became the village of Inchigeelagh, just west of the old church site. A more detailed survey of the O Leary lands and lords may be found in my article ' Gaelic land tenure in Co. Cork', *Cork: History and Society* 213-248).

Long: (p. 228) In 1989 the Chief Herald of Ireland authorised the use of the title 'O Long of Garranelongy', by patent granted to Denis Long of Glenville House, Farnanes, who traces his descent from John Long of 1643 and Darby Long, MP, 1689. (See *Iris Oifigiúil* 18 Feb. 1994).

Nagle: (p. 256, l.25) David son of Alan de Naungle (1309) was a grandson of Richard de Naungle of Monanimy, who must have been settled there by the mid-thirteenth century.

(p. 259) For further details of the Nagles of Monanimy, Annakissy, etc., see L.M. Cullen, loc. cit., 551-560.

Cotter: (p. 262, l.4) For 'Carrige Cotter' read 'Carrig Cota' (now Castlemary near Cloyne, which had no connection with the Cotters).

(p. 262, para. 4) The Cotter presence in Farrancotter and Great Island probably dates from the sixteenth century.

O Regan: (p. 265, para. 2) Thomas O Regan was a chaplain in Imokilly barony in 1301.

O Riordan: (p. 270, l.32) Thomas Orewordan of 1341 was named on a jury (at Buttevant) in a case involving Lackeen, and not as a tenant there,

(p. 271, para. 1) In 1497 another cleric, Matthew O Riordan, detained the vicarage of Kilbrin. (*Cal. Papal Letters* xvi, no. 750).

Roche: (p. 275, last para.) Alexander's father married Synolda, daughter and heiress of Alexander fitz Hugh, so David was heir to western Fermoy even before his Caunteton marriage.

Mac Sweeney: (p. 299, l.6) It was to Brittany that John Swiney made his escape; his descendants reside at Caen in Normandy.

Twomey: (p. 314, par. 3) Aulanus Otumna (Amhlaoibh Ó Tuama) was also a priest of Ardfert diocese in 1493. (*Cal. Papal Letters* xvi, p. 626).

Walsh: (p. 317, para. 5) The Walshs were in Rostellan by 1220, before the de Clares. The Mac Sliney family who sold their Rostellan property in 1565 to John fitz Edmond were probably descended from a Stephen le Waleys.